M000035092

# Hands of Honor

# Hands of Honor

Artisans and Their World
in Dijon, 1550–1650

JAMES R. FARR

Cornell University Press

*Ithaca and London*

Copyright © 1988 by Cornell University

All rights reserved. Except for brief quotations in a review, this book, or parts thereof, must not be reproduced in any form without permission in writing from the publisher. For information, address Cornell University Press, 124 Roberts Place, Ithaca, New York 14850.

First published 1988 by Cornell University Press.

International Standard Book Number 0-8014-2172-1
Library of Congress Catalog Card Number 88-47724

Printed in the United States of America

Librarians: Library of Congress cataloging information
appears on the last page of the book.

The paper in this book is acid-free and meets the guidelines for
permanence and durability of the Committee on Production Guidelines
for Book Longevity of the Council on Library Resources.

TO JOANNE

# Contents

# Illustrations

# Acknowledgments

Along its arduous journey to publication, helpful and good-natured criticism, comment, and suggestion from many directions significantly transformed this book. The greatest debt of gratitude I owe to E. William Monter, who generously offered that most precious of commodities—time. As an advisor, perhaps he ultimately had to see more of this piece than he had bargained for. Philip Benedict read an early version of the manuscript, and I thank him for his extraordinarily helpful and incisive criticism on how to make a book of it; he has closely followed its transformation to this final form. For reading all or parts of the manuscript and offering helpful criticism, I also thank James Amelang, B. J. T. Dobbs, Carol Lansing, Michael McDonald, John Martin, Sarah Maza, Guido Ruggiero, and Bruce Wheeler. Dialogues on methodology with John Bohstedt, Cathy Matson, and again Guido Ruggiero and monologues with myself on those miles of walks with my German shepherd, Biz, helped me to clarify my own positions. James Dunigan of the University of Tennessee Computing Center patiently guided me through the arcane world of computer-assisted statistical analysis.

Funding for the various research trips was provided by Northwestern University (Dissertation Year Fellowship), the University of Tennessee (the Amon Carter Evans Research Award), and the Institut

Français (the Gilbert Chinard Scholarship for French Studies), and the Newberry Library supported a summer of irreplaceable paleographical training expertly taught by Professor Bernard Barbiche of the Ecole des Chartes. In Dijon no scholar could hope for a warmer reception than that offered by the *conservateur* of the Archives Municipales de Dijon, Marie-Hélène Degroise, and her able and extremely pleasant assistants, Margaret Jacquette, Pierre Berthier, Michel Emery, and Michel Benoît. My lengthy stays in Dijon were made all the more pleasant and productive by their winsome ways and efficient help. I have a special debt of gratitude to them. I also thank the helpful staffs at the Archives Départementales de la Côte-d'Or and the Bibliothèque Municipale de Dijon.

Special thanks go to John Ackerman, editor-in-chief at Cornell University Press, for his staunch support for the manuscript from the outset, and to Judith Bailey, for her prompt, complete, and extremely able editing.

Part of Chapter 6 appeared in different form in *French Historical Studies* 14:2 (1985): 192–214. I thank the editors for permission to reprint.

As a recently arrived student ill-prepared to deal with the Burgundian accent, I had the great good luck to encounter Professor Michel Baridon at the Université de Dijon. Not only did his superb English smooth the transition to life abroad, but our scholarly interests were the same, and what began as a chance meeting has developed into a lasting friendship. He and his wife, Gisèle, and their children, Claudine and Laurent, have enriched our stays in Dijon beyond measure; nothing I can say here can express how deeply thankful my wife and I are for what they have done.

Finally, I thank my wife, Joanne Lax-Farr, not for typing the manuscript, which she did not do, but, more important, for believing in me.

JAMES R. FARR

*Knoxville, Tennessee*

# Abbreviations Used in the Notes and Bibliography

AMD            Archives Municipales de Dijon.
ADCO          Archives Départementales de la Côte-d'Or.
BMD           Bibliothèque Municipale de Dijon.
*Annales: ESC*    *Annales: Economies, Sociétés, Civilisations.*
*MSHD*         *Mémoires de la Société pour l'Histoire du Droit et des Institutions du Pays de Bourgogne, Comtois, et Romands.*

# Hands of Honor

# Introduction

In 1619 many guilds joined to file a collective grievance with the king against the town council of Dijon, protesting the city fathers' attempt to expand admission to mastership. For decades the master craftsmen had been trying to accomplish precisely the opposite, and they had been largely successful. Though this "class-action suit" is written in the corporate idiom (separate guilds are listed as the plaintiffs) it reveals a master artisanat united in defense of an interest that transcends guild boundaries. This one dense example illustrates the problematic of this book: alongside the corporate persona that master artisans had to assume in their dealings with the authorities (the corporate idiom was the legal language of the day), there existed a cultural identity shared by masters of different guilds. Whatever their differences, the masters recognized that they shared similar interests and occupied a similar place in the shifting constellation of economic, social, and power relations characteristic of early modern France.

This book focuses on the permanent resident master craftsmen of sixteenth- and seventeenth-century Dijon. These visible and important citizens of Dijon, though not a monolithic bloc, are identifiable as a group. They performed similar social and economic functions and self-consciously distinguished themselves from other social groups. They pursued strategies that reinforced this cohesiveness

(seen most clearly, but certainly not exclusively, in marriage relations and regulation of guild membership). Generally speaking, from
1550 to 1650 and beyond Dijon's master artisans became increasingly
intramural, prosperous, and artisanally (rather than corporately) and
geographically endogamous. Moreover, many of their actions give
evidence of shared attitudes. As we shall see, a single code of honor
mediated their relations (from commercial to marital) with one another, and their daily lives expressed a strong, shared desire for order
and stability.

In deemphasizing corporate, or guild, autonomy, this book departs
from most institutional and political histories, which have stressed
the autonomy of guilds and the conflicts between them. True, master
artisans did identify with their guilds, and they formed bonds with
fellow guildsmen, but the central argument of this book is that this
identity was only one of many overlapping and reinforcing lines of
solidarity in their lives. Furthermore, most of these lines transcended
guild boundaries yet remained within the artisanat. Master craftsmen
defended traditional guild privileges not because they were reaction-
aries who opposed social and economic change but because they recognized that their own interests, from maximizing prosperity to
maintaining journeyman subordination, could be served before the
law only by advancing them within the corporate framework.[1]

Legal prescription, however, need not determine either practice or
thought, and the experience of Dijon's master artisans drives this
point home. My major aim is to delineate the boundaries of the cul-

1. Alexis de Tocqueville's portrait of eighteenth-century France as fractured into
autonomous corporate cells, each dependent on the monarchy for survival, is attractive
and has been very influential among recent historians, most notably William Sewell,
*Work and Revolution in France: The Language of Labor from the Old Regime to 1848*
(Cambridge, 1980), but perhaps the corporate idiom has been overstressed. Michael
Sonenscher, "The *Sans Culottes* of the Year II: Rethinking the Language of Labor in
Revolutionary France," *Social History* 9 (Oct. 1984): 301–28, rightly points out that
behind the publicly employed corporate idiom the realities of artisanal production and
relations between masters and journeymen may have been very different indeed. As he
puts it (313–14), the corporate idiom was "the language used by master artisans when
they met, paid their taxes, engaged in litigation, enforced the statutes of their trades or
participated in the formal collectivity of public life. It was the *persona* adopted by
master artisans in their relationship to the royal government and the courts, and its
connection with the everyday transactions of the *boutique* was not without its ambiguities and limitations. . . . The language of labor of the eighteenth-century master
artisan, at least in its public mode, was redolent of [the seventeenth-century jurist]
Loiseau."

tural consensus masters displayed, which, I believe, approximates that of a nascent class not at odds with corporatism. But I do not wish to suggest that the craft world was conflict free. Artisans competed among themselves over commodities, market share, skilled labor, and even marriage. Naturally, this competition generated discord, but even such conflict was in many respects an inadvertent product of concerted artisanal strategy, and the antagonists were playing by rules and assumptions they shared with their fellows.

Since the late Middle Ages, Dijon had been among the most important towns in east central France. During the early modern centuries it ceased to be a manufacturing center of national importance and became instead the judicial, administrative, fiscal, and commercial hub of an increasingly integrated Burgundy. In the transformation of this regional capital many of its inhabitants prospered.

The Treaty of Senlis (1479) had split the two Burgundies, the duchy (which included Dijon) reverting to France, the county remaining part of the Holy Roman Empire. Until 1678 when Lorraine and the county (the Franche-Comté) were added to France, the former Duchy of Burgundy was a frontier, and Dijon a strategic and vulnerable outpost. Under the constant threat of foreign invasion—for the imperial Habsburgs and the French Valois and later the Bourbons were frequently at war during this period—the Dijonnais, and the artisans no less than the others, developed an intense concern for security. The 1550s saw extensive fortification building, interrupted by the Wars of Religion but resumed in the seventeenth century. To make room for bastions and gun placements, most of Dijon's suburbs were demolished and their inhabitants packed inside the walls. In fact, between 1550 and 1650 the streets of Dijon became much more crowded; the population of the town increased from fewer than fifteen thousand inhabitants to more than twenty-one thousand.

Dijon's streets bustled with merchants, vendors, vignerons, and artisans, but the men of the law had the greatest increase in population. Dijon was the seat of one of France's eight parlements and derived considerable prestige from that royal court. In addition, Dijon was host to the venerable Chambres des Comptes (established in the fourteenth century), the Table de Marbre (1557), the Bureau des Finances (1577), a bailliage, and chancelleries at the bailliage and at the Parlement. It was an occasional residence of the royal governor (a military rather than judicial or administrative officer), and the seat of the provincial estates (charged with negotiating the provincial tax burden with the king and then allocating it among the taxpayers). It is understandable, then, that so many men of the robe, both noble and common, resided here. Moreover, venality of office contributed mightily to this burgeoning population, for to accommodate the new officials additional "chambers" were created in the various courts— such as the Chambre des Requêtes and the Chambre des Enquêtes at the Parlement. The judicial, fiscal, and administrative institutions gave work to an army of lawyers, notaries, secretaries, scribes, and government functionaries. Dijon also possessed a powerful, affluent, and growing clergy, though it won a bishopric only in 1731.

With so many different judicial, fiscal, and administrative bodies at work, it should hardly be surprising that conflicts over jurisdiction were continual. The crucial battle, for Dijon's artisans, at any rate, was waged not between royal courts, but between the royal courts and the municipal authorities. Like so many other French towns in the Middle Ages, the commune of Dijon had gained extensive privileges from the dukes of Burgundy, which guaranteed relative freedom from ducal and, later, royal interference. Dijon's municipal authorities jealously guarded these privileges and tried to force the French kings of the sixteenth and seventeenth centuries to respect them. Of course, the king's interests or those of his officials did not always coincide with those of Dijon's town council. The mayor, elected annually by the citizens, selected the procureur syndic and six incumbent lay aldermen (*échevins*). These eight men annually selected fourteen new lay and five clerical aldermen. It was a system of co-optation that created an entrenched oligarchy comprising mainly merchants in the sixteenth century and lawyers in the seventeenth. In addition, the mayor was master of a militia of one to two thousand men, and he held the keys to the city's gates and to the arsenal. As a permanent commissioner of the *élus* of the provincial estates (judges of tax matters), he wielded considerable influence over regional finances and, if he was shrewd, knew the strategic importance of Dijon as a frontier town. Mayors were forces to be reckoned with and, especially during the Wars of Religion and later during the Thirty Years' War, walked the fine line between treason and loyalty to advance, or at least preserve, traditional municipal autonomy against encroachment by various royal institutions and even the king himself.

The transformation of Dijon's population which attended its political alterations assured an affluence with far-reaching ramifications. In the fifteenth century Dijon had lived from its textile industry, and Burgundian cloth made from hemp maintained a high reputation. But the prosperity and prominence were not to last. Throughout France the Wars of Religion devastated the cloth industry, and only the strongest towns rebounded afterward. Dijon was not among them. Its textile industry shifted to the countryside, where protoindustry took hold.[2] The drastic decline in the number of Dijonnais artisans working in this industry (carders, fullers, cloth cutters, dyers, and others) testifies to the collapse. Even in the period after the religious wars, so prosperous for many of Dijon's craftsmen, the industry did not revive. In 1634 the municipal authorities took over the manufacture of *drap*, seeking to provide employment for the poor and orphans and to resuscitate a moribund industry.[3] Not even state control could save it; cloth production went elsewhere, leaving Dijon as a distribution center.

Indeed, there was very little manufacture concentrated in Dijon during the early modern period, but the town prospered nonetheless. As its industrial importance declined, its economic significance as a hub of commerce and place of passage increased. Traffic from Paris and the north of France floated down the Seine and trundled by *grande voie* from Troyes to Dijon. From there, goods and people traversed major roads to Auxonne or Saint-Jean-de-Losne from which they moved down the Saône toward Lyons or points farther south.

Dijon had long been a commercial center, regularly attracting merchants and merchandise from Flanders, Lorraine, Paris, Lyons, Auvergne, Langres, and Normandy.[4] In the sixteenth century it was one of the most important domestic markets in France and, along with Troyes, Orleans, and Paris, one of the most important centers for redistribution of Languedoc wool.[5] Its fairs had attracted goods

2. James R. Farr, "Dijon, 1450–1750: The Changing Social and Economic Structure of an Administrative Capital and Commercial Hub," in *Urban Society in Ancien Regime France*, ed. Philip Benedict (London, forthcoming).

3. AMD, B272, fol. 68v, 18 July 1634.

4. AMD, B202, fol. 41v, 2 Aug. 1565, contains a reference to merchandise from these and other places. AMD, B278, fol. 110v, 19 Oct. 1640, reveals close relations between Dijon's tanners and leather merchants in "Lion," Auvergne, and Langres. ADCO, BII 360/60, 14 May 1644, contains a reference to a merchant "tailor from the country of Normandy" who "ordinarily" trafficked in Dijon.

5. Richard Gascon, *Le grand commerce et la vie urbaine au 16e siècle*, 2 vols. (Paris, 1971), pp. 66, 138.

and merchants from Reims, Amiens, Rouen, and many other places throughout France in the fifteenth century, and during the second half of the sixteenth century they reached their apogee. In 1562 Charles IX thought the fairs of Dijon so prosperous that he considered moving the declining fairs of Lyons there. In 1588 Henri III granted Dijon three fairs per year, each to last one month (a privilege he revoked when the town went over to the Holy League shortly thereafter). Their end came abruptly in 1618 when Louis XIII suppressed Dijon's fairs as part of a general decline in fairs throughout seventeenth-century France.[6]

Yet Dijon's prosperity did not diminish when its fairs were abolished. Its wealth stemmed from other sources. Certainly the growth of the administrative, judicial, and fiscal classes pulled wealth in from the surrounding countryside in the form of court costs, legal fees, tax farms, and the like, and the "bourgeois conquest of the land," whereby Dijon's prosperous inhabitants bought up the land in the surrounding countryside from an increasingly indebted peasantry, channeled ground rents inside the walls. In addition there were commercial sources.[7] Wine and grain commerce thrived in Dijon, though there are not enough surviving records to quantify trade activity during the early modern period. In the sixteenth century Burgundy was Lyons' breadbasket, and so great was the demand in that burgeoning town that Burgundian merchants became integrated into a regional network that enriched traders from Auxonne, Pontarlier, Gray, Chalon-sur-Saône, and Langres—as well as Dijon.[8]

Wine consumption increased in France after 1500, and since Burgundian wines maintained a good reputation, its fine vintages found a ready market both up the Seine at Paris and down the Saône at Lyons. This expanding wine trade triggered a demand in Dijon for wine casks and the labor of the *tonneliers*, or coopers, who made them. Not surprisingly, the cooper population in Dijon grew substantially during our period, as did the number of master cooper *jurés*, guild officials appointed by the municipal authorities to regulate the wine

6. Emile Collette, *Les foires et marchés à Dijon* (Dijon, 1905), pp. 51, 53–55. See also Prosper Boissonnade, *Le socialisme d'état* (Paris, 1927), p. 88.

7. On the "bourgeois conquest of the land," see Gaston Roupnel, *La ville et la campagne au XVIIe siècle: Etude sur les populations du pays dijonnais* (Paris, 1955), pt. 3, chap. 1.

8. Gascon, *Le grand commerce*, p. 786.

market on Saint Jean Square. The numbers of jurés grew from two in 1550 to five in 1597, and to eight by 1637.[9]

The rest of Dijon's artisans were an independent lot, producing not for export but for the local economy, which, in any case, was booming as the consuming classes mushroomed in Dijon and wealth trickled down to many master craftsmen. Significantly, unlike many of their fellows in other European towns, they remained free of merchant exploitation in the form of the putting-out system, primarily because merchants were busy capitalizing on the transit trade in grain and wine. Dijon's artisans had greater control of their economic destiny, since no merchants were manipulating craft production to conform to the demand of a distant market.

Dijon's master craftsmen, as producers for a thriving local market, showed no great capital accumulation; they had relatively small inventories and small workshops. Seldom do we encounter an artisan with tools and stock worth more than two or three hundred livres.[10] Small inventories do not suggest production for large, distant markets; rather, Dijon's artisans procured their own raw materials, frequently going to nearby fairs or villages to do so.[11] Then they fashioned the product alongside their journeymen in small workshops and had their wives sell it to other Dijonnais and customers from the nearby countryside.

The lack of interest in expanding the market displays a mentality that was still not capitalist. Master artisans thought in terms of lim-

---

9. For 1550, see AMD, B188, fol. 17r; for 1597, AMD, B235, fol. 36v; and for 1637, AMD, B275, fol. 28r. The cooper jurés were also entrusted with the not unpleasant task of tasting wine for quality control—that is, until they "abused" this privilege. More jurés could reflect increased municipal surveillance, but the need for such surveillance may be further testimony that the volume of trade was substantial.

10. ADCO, BII 356/7–20 (postmortem inventories). We have only indirect evidence on the size of workshops, but they could not have been large. We know that Hugues Sambin, a master cabinetmaker, architect, and sculptor of national visibility, retained eight journeymen, but Sambin was an unusually busy and important man. Few of Sambin's artworks survive. He carved the door to the Palais de Justice in Dijon; the original is in the Musée de Beaux Arts in Dijon, and a handsome reproduction hangs in its place at the palais. For the most recent study of Sambin, see Henri Giroux, "Essai sur la vie et l'oeuvre dijonnais d'Hugues Sambin," *Mémoires de la Commission des Antiquités du Département de la Côte-d'Or* 32 (1980–81): 361–413. See also H. David, *De Sluter à Sambin: Essai critique sur la sculpture et le décor monumental en Bourgogne au 15e et 16e siècles,* 2 vols. (Paris, 1932).

11. See, for example, AMD, B216, fol. 78v, 16 Dec. 1578, for butchers buying beef on the hoof at a local fair; and ADCO, BII 360/47, 4 April 1565.

ited wealth; they sought to improve their economic position not by
making the pie bigger through expanded production but by cutting
bigger pieces from the local pie and distributing them to fewer craftsmen.[12] In addition to regulating production by curtailing the number
of masters producing, they also exploited the labor under them,
chiefly by denying journeymen access to mastership. Such policies
put the masters on a collision course with the municipal authorities
as well as the journeymen. As they pursued their interests and encountered resistance, the masters coalesced more and more into a
cohesive culture in which most relations were mediated by a code of
honor. This culture, though not capitalistic, nonetheless took on the
contours of a nascent class.

To place artisans within Dijonnais society as a whole it is necessary first to achieve a working definition of *artisan*. For us no less
than for men and women of the sixteenth and seventeenth centuries
the term connotes skilled labor, usually performed by males. Unfortunately, the sources keep journeymen, wives, widows, and single
females in the shadows, and only occasionally have I been able to
coax them into the light. Nevertheless, it is certain that a sexual
division of labor obtained in early modern Dijon. Probably the largest
cluster of skilled women artisans (not including the widows of masters, who were allowed to keep their husbands' shops open) worked in
some branch of the clothing industry, as seamstresses, *lingères*, or
tapestry weavers—far from lucrative employment.[13] If most single
females were consigned, like Claudine Gauthier, to such menial
tasks as making *"coiffes* and other little things,"* many wives of mas-

12. Even the wealthiest craftsmen had limited inventories, evidence of small-scale
production for only a local market. Damien Mariette, for example, a master shoemaker
among the wealthiest taxpayers in town, had only one hundred pairs of shoes in his
shop when he died. Hugues Bourrie, another master shoemaker of average wealth, had
an inventory of two pairs of boots, three pairs of flat-heeled shoes (*escarpins*), four pairs
of children's and eleven pairs of adult shoes. True, postmortem lists may reflect a
dissipated or exhausted inventory of an elderly man, but Bourrie was carried off by the
plague, so he was presumably still active in his trade when he died. Jean Constantin
was also a master shoemaker of average wealth with an inventory of four dozen shoes,
while Bénigne Fay, a master pinmaker, had total assets of 180 livres, including a shop
inventory worth 87. These are isolated examples, but these artisans were by no means
poor relative to the rest of the population. For inventories, see ADCO, BII 356/7–20.

13. For seamstresses, see, for example, ADCO, BII 360/58, May–Sept. 1642, 360/60,
5 Oct. 1643; on *lingères*, see the tax rolls, AMD, L170; on tapestry weavers, see ADCO,
BII 360/48, 20 Sept. 1568.

ters probably complemented their husbands' activities in family-run workshops.[14] In the typical small workshop wives probably handled much of the retail side of the business. The wives of butchers certainly did, tending the *bancs* while their husbands slaughtered the beasts and prepared the meat, often (illicitly) in the back of the house.[15] Other wives, especially those of poorer craftsmen (many, no doubt, journeymen), worked at such unrelated jobs as hawking vegetables, eggs, cheese, and other foodstuffs.[16]

Since the sources do not always clearly distinguish between master and journeyman, we must rely upon inference from context or the correlation of different sources to make this important distinction. It is relatively easy to define labor and productive relations but much more difficult to discern differences in the realm of attitudes. Distinctions in the latter may be misleading anyway, since many, perhaps most, journeymen held on to the hope (generally illusory) that they would one day be admitted to mastership. In material relations, however, distinctions were clear-cut. Both masters and journeymen manufactured (or, in the case of some masters, actively directed such activity), but only masters were legally permitted to sell the products. Thus, the artisanat included artisan-workers and merchant–master artisans, but manual labor was common to both. In theory, journeymen were trained to produce a whole product, for the production of a masterpiece was a criterion for admission to mastership. During the seventeenth century, however, there are signs that some, perhaps

14. ADCO, BII 360/53, 12 Feb. 1591. There is a growing bibliography on women and work, but for the most recent treatment, see Barbara A. Hanawalt, ed., *Women and Work in Preindustrial Europe* (Bloomington, Ind., 1986); Natalie Z. Davis, "Women in the Crafts in Sixteenth-Century Lyon," ibid., points out that most female work was "hidden from the streets," and Martha C. Howell, "Women, the Family Economy, and the Structures of Market Production in Cities of Northern Europe during the Late Middle Ages," also ibid., argues that the family-based economy slowly eroded during the early modern period to 1700 as the market economy expanded. Before the eighteenth century in Dijon few women besides widows appear on Dijon's tax rolls as heads of households, suggesting a still vital family economy. For a discussion of the demographic and economic changes experienced by women from 1450 to 1750 see my "Dijon, 1450–1750."

15. AMD, B216, fol. 80v, 30 Dec. 1578.

16. Examples abound of artisans' wives, out of "necessity," selling diverse items. See, for instance, AMD, B212, fol. 73v, 3 Sept. 1574, where the wife of the cobbler Claude Millot was fined sixty-five sous for "having kept a *banc* in *plaine rue*, where [she] . . . sold [without permission] all sorts of foodstuffs." See also ADCO, BII 360/47, 1565, where a wife of a baker becomes a hawker.

many, journeymen specialized in only one task and could no longer produce completely finished products.[17]

We should not classify an artisan as a merchant simply because he operated a *boutique* in addition to a workshop (*atelier*), for it was a legal privilege of masters to open a *boutique* and engage in commercial activity. The crucial element for early modern contemporaries was the master's connection to production; a craftsman became a merchant only when he abandoned manual labor and devoted his energies entirely to commerce.

In my working definition, then, an artisan was a skilled worker (man, woman, master, or journeyman) who may have operated a shop but who, because of his or her involvement in production, must be distinguished from a merchant.

In every early modern French town artisans were a numerous and economically and often politically important group, but especially before the eighteenth century, they have yet to receive the close attention of historians employing interdisciplinary methodology so important to the writing of "microhistory." This book seeks to begin to fill that gap. Methodologically, it borrows from cultural anthropology, which has helped me to probe meaning in the artisan's world, and from social theory, which has enabled me to balance the active agency of individuals (the conscious pursuit of interest) against the coercive nature of inherited structures. I hope this book will prove of interest and use to historians of early modern Europe and to readers interested in the more general problem of the relationship between purposive action and restrictive structure.

A historian of early modern France is in for a pleasant surprise when he or she encounters Dijon's archives. The uniqueness of these repositories stems from the impressive range of kinds of sources, each extraordinarily rich. The resulting combination presents an unusual, indeed perhaps a singular, amount of detail about city life in general and artisan experience in particular. Four kinds of sources form the

---

17. For example, the master hatter Jean Courtoysie testified that Jean Petit, a candidate for mastership, made hats that only "journeymen are accustomed to make." In the same document a journeyman hatter specified that Petit lacked expertise in dyeing hats, a task reserved for the masters of the trade. AMD, G89, Feb. 1640. A master baker testified that Symphorien Jobelin, a journeyman baker, made only *"pain molet,"* and could not verify that Jobelin was capable of making other kinds of bread, a prerequisite for mastership. ADCO, BII 360/58, 23 March 1640.

armature of this study. First, the tax rolls (bound registers in the Archives Municipales de Dijon, Series L) of 1556 and 1643 roughly punctuate its chronological boundaries. Most towns of France were exempt from the taille *personnelle*, and so the many rolls of this "progressive" tax to be found in Dijon are rare indeed. On the rolls from 1556 and 1643 the household heads of all seven parishes are listed by street, occupation, and tax assessment or exemption.

Second, the deliberations of Dijon's town council (Archives Municipales, Series B) exist in an unbroken series of bound registers beginning long before 1550 and extending long after 1650. Few other towns of France can boast such a complete series of these transcriptions from original minutes (even some of the originals survive), which contain important indicators, from the elite perspective, of relationships between artisans and the civil authorities.

Third are the notary contracts, an ocean of documents housed in the Archives Départementales de la Côte-d'Or. For the dates 1550–1650 there exist over six hundred *cotes* of sixty-six different notaries, each bundle containing several hundred transactions. I sampled about 150 *cotes* from forty different notaries, recording data from marriage contracts (a sample of 983) and real estate transactions (524) involving artisans. From the marriage contracts I have charted marital patterns as well as changing levels of wealth expressed in dowry and *apports*. From the real estate transactions I have sought patterns of capital investment, along with the value system that guided it.

The fourth and most interesting pool of documents comprises the criminal dossiers from the mayor's court at the bailliage (housed in the Archives Départementales). One of the privileges the commune of Dijon gained from the dukes of Burgundy was criminal jurisdiction of first instance over the town and *banlieue*, for which the municipal authorities insisted on ratification from each succeeding duke and French king. These trial records, also quite rare for the sixteenth century, are dominated by artisans and winegrowers, and contain plaintiff petitions, witness depositions and confrontations, interrogations of the accused, and occasionally sentences. They are extraordinarily numerous but seldom complete, so a systematic study of artisan criminality has not been undertaken. Nonetheless, I was able to read over a thousand accounts of artisans' direct observations about daily life, buried higgledy-piggledy in these invaluable and entertaining bundles. These are not transcriptions. The scribes faithfully recorded the earthy and informal language of the street voiced in depositions, in sharp contrast to the "proper" discourse of the elite interrogators. In these original documents I have explored the murky waters of artisan mentality. Through the richness of artisan discourse in its social context, I have tried to assemble the pieces of a mentality, the values, aspirations, hopes, and fears shared by Dijon's artisans during the "iron century."

# 1 The Artisan's World of Work

## The Ideology of Work

In old regime France the meaning of work—for those who did it as well as for those who did not—was ambiguous. Work functioned as a means of social classification and social control and so carried a moral value, but it was also, according to traditional Christian teaching, Adam's curse. For magistrate and master artisan alike work was a central part of a system of human relations, and it bore social and political as well as economic connotations. The artisan was more than a toiling cog in the machine of production.

The Middle Ages bequeathed to the early modern era a society organized by corporation, in which collective bodies, such as universities or craft guilds, were considered legal persons. By the thirteenth century, corporatism in the towns of Burgundy was already becoming a lay and urban phenomenon and was beginning to dominate economic, social, and juridical life. By the fifteenth century, corporatism was established as the legal armature of the kingdom. It would continue as the dominant idiom until the French Revolution.[1]

1. François Olivier-Martin, *L'organisation corporative de la France d'ancien régime* (Paris, 1938), pp. 83, 67, 105, 138; Emile Coornaert, *Les corporations en France avant 1789*, 2d ed. (Paris, 1968), p. 66.

At bottom the corporation was a device designed to organize and order society. As William Sewell has pointed out, the idea of order is embedded in the very word *corps*. Like the physical, organic *corps*, or "body," the corporation was a single entity, its members subsumed in a common substance and presumed to possess a united interest.[2] As the human body had a rational and order-giving soul, so the social "body" had its esprit de corps.[3]

Corporatism entailed a view of work as a collective social responsibility[4] and thus as public in character. The ruling classes of the old regime, unlike Marx, did not consider work the "natural and free exercise of the activity of man" but rather a concession of the public authority.[5] Both royal and municipal authorities found it in their interest and believed it their duty to administer and control the artisan's world of work for the welfare of *la chose publique*.[6] By law and custom, artisans were to be faithful producers of items for public use, and for this reason craftsmen were required to work in their shops *à fenêtre*, or visible to public scrutiny. Those who wished to open a shop and "work publicly" had to apply to the town council for mastership. The corporate guilds to which masters belonged were public bodies whose raison d'être was to provide the essential needs of the social whole. They were integrally linked to the crown, since it was the king's duty to ensure the public good,[7] and by the fourteenth century they were referred to as *choses du roi*. Royal letters patent

2. William Sewell, "Visions of Labor: Illustrations of the Mechanical Arts before, in and after Diderot's *Encyclopédie*," in *Work in France: Representations, Meaning, Organization, and Practice*, ed. Steven L. Kaplan and Cynthia J. Koepp (Ithaca, 1986), pp. 258–86, suggests that in sixteenth- and seventeenth-century etchings each mechanical art is presented to the viewer as a harmonious, unified whole. These, of course, are portrayals of the public personas of the guilds and, hence, the corporate ideal.

3. William Sewell, "*Etats, Corps*, and *Ordre*: Some Notes on the Social Vocabulary of the French Old Regime," in *Sozialgeschichte Heute: Festschrift für Hans Rosenberg*, ed. Hans-Ulrich Wehler (Göttingen, 1974), p. 55.

4. Keith Thomas, "Work and Leisure in Pre-industrial Society," *Past and Present* 29 (1964): 58.

5. Henri Hauser, "Les pouvoirs publics et l'organisation du travail dans l'ancienne France," in *Travailleurs et marchands dans l'ancienne France*, ed. Hauser (Paris, 1920), p. 133.

6. Boissonnade, *Le socialisme d'etat*, p. 7.

7. Olivier-Martin, pp. 480, 85, and on the public character of corporations, especially chap. 8. See also AMD, G85, 29 Dec. 1617.

provided craft guilds with immunities and privileges (most notably monopoly over the sale of their product) in exchange for their service to the public. Thus artisan corporations were considered judicial persons.[8] Corporately organized crafts had come to serve an order-giving moral function, and their members were seen as imbued with a collective mentality defined corporately.

Clearly, order was a primary concern of the authorities who regulated work. Early modern magistrates were obsessed with the *désordre* that plagued their times. If little could be done about the cosmic disorder of a Christendom sundered by the Protestant Reformation, perhaps closer regulation of work could alleviate the more mundane disorder created by the huge increase in the number of beggars to be seen in the streets of French cities after the mid–sixteenth century. Beggary and idleness (*oisivitez*) more and more were identified as signs of moral disorder, and the magistrates, not surprisingly, sought to remedy these ills by governing work more closely. To facilitate this more stringent control the authorities could work through a public institution that was already in place, the guild.

The guild members, the master artisans, largely shared this ideology of work. The corporate idiom was the legal language of the kingdom, and in order to defend guild privileges granted by the crown, master artisans had to speak this language in the public arena. Furthermore, though each guild was, according to the corporate idiom, an internally unified body, they were legally separate from one another. According to Sewell, "Gens de métiers [as a whole] did not constitute a solidary unit. . . . The old regime's idiom of art emphasized their differences. Each art had its own distinct qualities and its own rules that distinguished it from every other art. Thus each métier formed a particular community devoted to the perfection of a particular art, and these communities of artisans had no bonds uniting them with one another."[9]

The corporate idiom, then, traditionally defined the network of relationships not just between masters and magistrates, but also among the guildsmen themselves. It also defined masters' relationships with their journeymen, and for masters bent on worker subor-

8. Coornaert, chap. 3. Craft corporations possessed seals, common funds, coats of arms, and sometimes property. See Olivier-Martin, p. 146.
9. Sewell, *Work and Revolution in France*, p. 28.

dination, no less than for magistrates, control was at the heart of the system.[10] The specter of disorder that haunted them took the shape of *compagnonnages*—worker organizations aimed at wresting control of the labor market from the masters.

Despite this vested interest in the guild structure, however, it would be a mistake to conclude that the masters' social identity was completely determined by the corporate idiom. True, the inherited organizing framework of the guild retained its usefulness to masters, but it is important to remember that the corporate idiom was the legal language, the medium that masters were required to use in their dealings with the public authorities. It was only through the institution of the guild that masters could legally defend their privileges before any public power, from the town council to the king. Despite the legal concept, artisans were individuals and their culture was not static. As we will see, alongside the inherited traditional framework of corporatism new forces were at work, forces that would transcend the guild and would knit the masters together in a relatively solidary community.[11]

## The Corporate Framework

Three modes of work organization obtained in early modern France: *en jurande*, *libre*, and *privilègié*.[12] The last, pertaining to work directly licensed by the crown, apparently did not exist in Dijon during the late sixteenth and early seventeenth centuries; the other two forms contested for dominance during this period. Despite its name, work organized in "free trades" (*métiers libres*) was not pursued under the principles of laissez-faire. The concept of unregulated work was foreign to medieval and early modern mentalities; so the difference between "sworn trades" (*jurandes*) and free trades concerned not the degree of regulation but who did most of the regulating. In theory,

10. See the seminal study on corporatism in the eighteenth century, especially concerning subordination, by Steven L. Kaplan, "Réflexions sur la police du monde du travail, 1700–1815," *Revue Historique* 261 (1979): 17–77.

11. Sonenscher, "The *Sans Culottes* of the Year II," passim, makes the important distinction between the corporate persona and others in artisan life.

12. Henri Hauser, "Des divers modes d'organisation du travail dans l'ancienne France," *Revue d'Histoire Moderne et Contemporaine* 7 (1906): 357–87.

craft guilds in the *villes jurées* (towns of sworn trades) were self-regulating, while the municipal authorities had a monopoly of regulation in the *villes libres*.[13] In practice these pure types did not exist. In Dijon, a ville jurée, the municipal authorities ruled in conjunction with appointed officials from the guilds themselves.[14]

One of the major characteristics of villes jurées was the requirement of an oath from all members of corporations, in a sense a collective contract, in which they bound themselves to observe the statutes of the guild.[15] In Dijon, every craft corporation had its statutes stipulating the customary bylaws of the guild. In most jurandes, but by no means all (the juridical variations between guilds could be considerable), no candidate could be admitted to mastership without first completing his apprenticeship, producing a masterpiece, and paying a fee. All members of jurandes had to receive visitations and inspections of their shops by *jurés*, guild representatives appointed by the civil authorities, and by aldermen from the town council and had to accept the administration of the guild's internal affairs by its assembly of masters. The most important benefit garnered in exchange for these concessions was the guild's monopoly of the product it manufactured or the service it rendered.[16]

Masters, journeymen, and apprentices were all required to obey the statutes of the guild, but only masters swore to uphold the regulations of the guild (the oath was part of the ritual of admission to mastership), and only masters, and perhaps not all of them, participated in its internal administration. Only the masters had the right to sell the products manufactured in their workshops; only they could be proprietors of workshops. Journeymen and apprentices could sell their labor only to masters and had no control over the products they made, though journeymen frequently did own their tools.

13. Henri Hauser, "L'organisation du travail à Dijon et en Bourgogne au XVIe et dans la première moitié du XVIIe siècle," in *Les débuts du capitalisme*, ed. Hauser (Paris, 1927), p. 126.

14. *Villes de commune* like Dijon were known for their privileges, gained in the Middle Ages, of which intramural police autonomy (and thus craft regulation) was one of the most prized. Henri Hauser, *Ouvriers du temps passé* (Paris, 1899), chap. 7. The typical *ville libre* was Lyons. Crafts in such towns had no guild statutes—for example, no limits on the number of journeymen and apprentices allowed each master. They were policed by the municipality for quality control and price manipulation, as well as other economic practices.

15. Hauser, "Des divers modes," p. 365.

16. Ibid., p. 360.

Even though the craft guilds constantly appear in the archival records of early modern Dijon, there is almost total silence about their
internal administration. How did they govern themselves? In the
Middle Ages, according to the legal historian François Olivier-Martin,
craft guilds elected, "more or less freely, the members who administered the common affairs. . . . [They] represented the craft in its
relations with other crafts and with the superior [i.e., municipal] authority; they administered its common treasury and the goods that it
might possess."[17] The labor historian Emile Coornaert adds that the
basic organ of administration was the assembly, usually an annual
affair held in a guildhall, a monastery, or even in the hôtel de ville.[18]

Certainly Dijon's crafts maintained the broad outlines of this form
of internal administration. They had their treasuries (usually connected to the craft's confraternity) and paid annual dues, and they had
their assemblies. An element of the medieval tradition of communal
democracy seems to have continued at these assemblies in Dijon, at
least among the master shoemakers. They submitted a written request to the town council for approval of an ordinance concerning
their craft, drafted "by common consent given by all the said shoemakers in their assemblies."[19] On the other hand, hierarchical elements were unquestionably embraced as well. Probably hierarchy
and democracy coexisted, for as we will see, paradox was no stranger
to craft culture.[20]

In Dijon it was during the fifteenth century that statutes were
promulgated for most crafts and bound in the "green book" kept in
the hôtel de ville.[21] These bylaws were probably invoked until the
eighteenth century when new statutes were drawn up.[22] As the crafts
became more specialized and new crafts appeared in the sixteenth

17. Olivier-Martin, p. 93. Unless otherwise noted, all translations are my own.
18. Coornaert, p. 217.
19. AMD, B262, fol. 229v–230r, 7 June 1625.
20. In Besançon the craft assemblies were organized hierarchically based on seniority. Frédéric Grosrenaud, *La corporation ouvrière à Besançon (16e–17e siècles)*
(Dijon, 1907), p. 103. See also Maurice Garden, "The Urban Trades: Social Analysis and
Representation," in Kaplan and Koepp, p. 291. Daniel Roche, "Work, Fellowship, and
Some Economic Realities of Eighteenth-Century France," in Kaplan and Koepp, p. 59,
notes how in the eighteenth century the corporate system maintained a delicate balance between equality and inequality within the guilds.
21. AMD, G3.
22. A. Chapuis, *Les anciennes corporations dijonnaises: Règlements, statuts, ordonnances* (Dijon, 1906), p. 24.

and seventeenth centuries, additional statutes were composed and existing ones were amended. The blacksmiths were organized into a jurande only in 1602, the vinegar and mustard makers in 1634.[23]

Guild statutes gained authority from their venerable age but also from another quarter. Letters patent from the king were required for a craft to become a jurande.[24] In other words, all statutes required royal approval, and this approbation gave them the force of law. Thus, the authority of the statutes rested on both custom and law—each with its own form of police power.

Guild statutes had three primary functions: to ensure quality production, to protect the guild monopoly on the sale of the items produced, and to regulate admission to mastership. The shop visit was the chief method used for quality control and to safeguard the monopoly. Visits were made at regular intervals—weekly for some crafts, monthly for others. The visiting jurés and aldermen would ask the craftsman whose shop was being inspected to declare under oath whether he had any illicit goods. They would then proceed to inspect the premises.[25] If poor workmanship or faulty raw materials were found, penalties were assessed. For example, a tinsmith (potier d'étain) could be fined forty sous for using pewter of poor quality in a piece constructed with poor workmanship. For poor workmanship alone no fine was assessed, but in either case the offending object was destroyed.[26]

To protect the monopoly jurés had authority to inspect shops of those craftsmen most likely to become illegal competitors. For example, the locksmith jurés had the right to visit goldsmiths, founders, pinmakers, blacksmiths and toolmakers, and shoemaker jurés were permitted to inspect cobbler shops to make sure the latter were not

23. AMD, G49, 22 March 1596, where the blacksmiths contended that it was fitting for Dijon, as "capital" of the province, to follow the example of Paris. On the vinegar and mustard makers, see Chapuis, Les anciennes corporations, p. 123. The vinegar and mustard makers asked to have statutes drawn up in 1608, citing the examples of Troyes and Paris, but were denied by the town council. AMD, B246, fol. 141v, 21 Nov. 1608.

24. Olivier-Martin, p. 206.

25. AMD, B217, fol. 74r, 8 March 1580, pertains to weekly visits of cobbler shops. The statutes imply that some trades left the frequency of visitations up to the jurés' discretion. See Chapuis, Les anciennes corporations, pp. 178 (on cloth cutters), 204 (on weavers), 211 (on hatters). On monthly visits, see AMD, B197, fol. 34v, 3 July 1559, B200, fol. 19v, 2 July 1563.

26. Chapuis, Les anciennes corporations, p. 378.

making and selling new shoes.[27] Maintenance of boundaries was a central concern in the statutes. Encroachment from similar trades was rigorously precluded, and competition from foreigners strictly regulated. The bakers' statutes stipulate that "pastrycooks will not be able to mix in or undertake to make anything of the bakery trade to sell publicly . . . in any way whatsoever, nor, similarly, the bakers, anything that touches the pastry trade."[28] The statutes of the hatters, hosiers, glovers, and many others, allowed the sale of their products by foreign merchants only if the goods had first been inspected by the jurés and aldermen. Even then, they could be sold only from the central marketplace.[29]

The bylaws of several crafts stipulate the status of widows within the guild, giving them relatively independent positions compared to other women of their day. The bakers, for example, allowed the widow of a master to keep his shop open if she did not remarry and if she could prove that she had "good and sufficient workers" in her service. If she remarried a son of a master baker, her new husband had only to give a dinner to the jurés and aldermen in order to be admitted to mastership. If she remarried outside the craft, however, she could not keep her shop open under any circumstances. Pastrycooks, butchers, hatters, and many others had similar provisions.[30] It is likely that such regulations contributed to the considerably higher rates of corporate endogamy among widows than among first brides.

Some guilds required candidates for mastership to serve an apprenticeship in Dijon. The toolmakers specified two years, furriers and hosiers three, and goldsmiths six.[31] Even in those trades that had no requirement of apprenticeship in their statutes, moreover, the letters of mastership often mention such service by candidates. Perhaps this criterion became common only during the sixteenth and seventeenth centuries, long after the statutes were drawn up. We know, for example, that by 1600 the bakers and shoemakers were requiring appren-

---

27. Ibid., pp. 342 (locksmiths), 294 (shoemakers). It was not necessarily a two-way street, either. For instance, before 1650 the cobbler jurés had no visitation rights to shoemaker shops, according to Chapuis. Only after the shoemakers won the right to sell used shoes did the cobbler jurés gain the right of reciprocal visitation. Chapuis, *Les anciennes corporations*, pp. 291, 294.

28. Quoted in Chapuis, *Les anciennes corporations*, p. 43.

29. Ibid., pp. 211, 223, 245.

30. Ibid., pp. 42, 58, 77, 213.

31. Ibid., pp. 354, 308, 280, 227.

ticeships of three years, but none had been required in the statutes of the fifteenth century.[32]

Several crafts required applicants for mastership to give a dinner for the jurés and aldermen and to pay fees to the town council, the aldermen and jurés, and frequently to the confraternity of the craft. The amount of the fee paid the magistrates varied widely. The butchers paid five livres to the town council, five to the jurés and aldermen, and five to the mayor. Shoemakers paid forty sous to the town council, twenty to the jurés and aldermen, and twenty to the confraternity. The amounts do not seem to have corresponded to the collective wealth of a craft. The relatively poor trade of cloth cutting set fees at eight livres, whereas goldsmiths (wealthy craftsmen) paid only sixty sous.[33] In addition, the town council exacted a fee of citizenship (*droit d'habitantage*) from new masters and was quite insistent upon collecting it. No craftsman could receive his mastership letters from the council until it was paid.[34] Nearly all the guilds required an applicant to make a masterpiece—usually at his own expense[35]—in the presence of a juré and an alderman. Many statutes described precisely what was to be made. The hatters demanded three hats, and they stipulated the kind of cloth to be used, color, and other specifications. Their statutes also declared that the work was to be done *chez juré*. The hosiers required two pairs of hose *de couleur* worth at least eighteen gros. If the hose were *souffissants*, the applicant had only to give a dinner for the masters; if not, he had to pay the masters ten sous for their trouble.[36]

When the candidate for mastership was the son of a master of the craft, many of these requirements were waived. Frequently a master's son had only to demonstrate that he was "able and sufficient" (*ydoine et souffisans*) in the craft. No masterpiece or fees were required, though the candidate might still be expected to give a dinner for the jurés and aldermen. There were some exceptions. In addition to a

32. AMD, B237, fol. 155v, 156r, 12 May 1600.

33. Chapuis, *Les anciennes corporations*, pp. 76, 450, 286, 177, 308–9.

34. Collecting this fee was a constant concern. See, for example, AMD, B192, fol. 207v, 13 Nov. 1554, where the town council asserted, no *droits* paid, no mastership letters. Repeated in AMD, B262, fol. 102v, 11 Oct. 1624, and G294, G89, 1642.

35. For example, Chapuis, *Les anciennes corporations*, pp. 230, 209. The goldsmiths' statutes did not require masterpieces until sometime in the sixteenth century. Joseph Garnier, *Les anciens orfèvres de Dijon* (Dijon, 1889), p. 14.

36. Chapuis, *Les anciennes corporations*, pp. 209–10, 223, and see 451.

dinner, sons of master hatters had to give the mayor a "handsome and good" hat, and sons of master tinsmiths had to give the jurés and aldermen a *septier* of wine.[37]

These official requirements made it easy for sons to pursue their fathers' trade but more difficult for outsiders to enter. As we will see, during the sixteenth and seventeenth centuries a number of unofficial accretions also enabled masters to block the route to mastership for many journeymen, increasing the masters' control and reducing the social mobility of their employees.

In addition to exacting fees, the civil authorities investigated the "life and morals" (*vie et moeurs*) of every master candidate. The chief criteria, as in the early modern German "home towns," were familiarity and community acceptance.[38] Religious orthodoxy was also important, and it seems to have been preferable, perhaps mandatory, to be married.[39] The primary preoccupation in these investigations was how well the applicant was known in the community. Applicants often declared how long they had been in Dijon, emphasizing their roots there if possible. In depositions taken by the town council, the vast majority of responding artisans told how long and how well they had known the applicant, frequently adding that as neighbors they were very familiar with him, that he was a peaceable man, not a troublemaker, and so on. Naturally, the immigrant was at a disadvantage. In one case, for example, the master tailors petitioned the town council to block the admission of a journeyman to mastership because he was "unknown and foreign" (*incongneu et etranger*).[40]

Knowing who somebody was meant knowing his family, so these investigations explored the candidate's family background. Legitimacy of birth was a major concern; depositions usually mention both the social status of the parents and their marital state when the

37. On these regulations and waivers see ibid., pp. 77, 212, 287, 42, 58, 212, 379. On the bakers, see AMD, B235, fol. 150r–v, 5 Dec. 1597. The Edict of Orleans demanded masterpieces from sons of masters but remained a dead letter in Dijon. See AMD, G302, 1584, G186, 1588. See also AMD, B209, fol. 32v, 17 July 1571.

38. Mack Walker, *German Home Towns: Community, State and General Estate, 1648–1871* (Ithaca, 1971), esp. chap. 3.

39. Many petitions for mastership declare how long the applicant had been married, and the number of recent marriages implies that they were undertaken as a precondition to mastership. François Laurent, a journeyman hatter, stated explicitly that he contracted marriage "in order to attain mastership." AMD, G89, Jan. 1639, and see G86, April 1618 (a shoemaker), and May 1618 (a tailor).

40. AMD, B215, fol. 202v, 6 Nov. 1579.

applicant was born.[41] Once again, the emphasis upon familiarity favored the local boys, especially the masters' sons. Because their background was common knowledge, it made perfectly good sense to lessen their requirements for mastership. The immigrant, on the other hand, had to prove his worthy background, sometimes by notarized document.[42] Failure to satisfy these rigorous requirements kept many journeymen out of the charmed circle of mastership.

Nearly every deposition in the records declares the applicant to be a "good Catholic," and often they mention his church attendance, recent pious acts, and so on. Vicars and priests often testified about their parishioners, recalling, for example, the marriage of a candidate or his communion the previous Easter.[43] The Edict of Nantes formally suppressed investigations of the religious orthodoxy of applicants for mastership, but in staunchly Catholic Dijon the authorities continued to attempt to verify religious orthodoxy even after 1600.[44]

Relations between masters and journeymen were another topic of guild statutes, which, along with labor contracts, provided the legal muscle behind social control and institutionalized the subordination of journeymen. Few written labor contracts from the sixteenth and seventeenth centuries survive in Dijon, but they were not uncommon there in the late Middle Ages. In Paris, certainly, they were rigorously upheld in the Châtelet.[45] In a study of fifteenth-century labor contracts in Dijon, Philippe Didier has found a pronounced emphasis upon the *fidélité personnelle* owed by the *valet*, or journeyman, to his master. In return for this moral obedience, the master was responsible for the actions of his valet as if he were the man's father.[46] This vertical paternalistic bond, as we will see, survived into the sixteenth century but was undermined by growing horizontal ties among journeymen defined in opposition to masters.

Journeymen and laborers were usually hired by masters either for a

---

41. On the respectability of parents, see, for example, AMD, G83, May 1586.

42. The town council occasionally sent for notarized documents as part of its investigation into the applicant's background. See for example, AMD, B215, fol. 202v, 6 Nov. 1579.

43. For example, AMD, G83, Feb. 1593.

44. See, for example, AMD, G86, July 1618, G88, Jan. 1621, G89, Nov. 1638, July 1640, Dec. 1643.

45. On Dijon, see Philippe Didier, "Le critère de la distinction entre louage de services et entreprise," *MSHD* 29 (1968–69): 197–214. On Paris, see Bronislaw Geremek, *Le salariat dans l'artisanat Parisien aux 14e–15e siècles* (Paris, 1968), p. 58.

46. Didier, "Le critère," pp. 207, 211.

fixed time or for a particular task.[47] If a journeyman was hired *à la tâche* (by the job or the piece), only masters in his craft could employ him, and the journeyman remained legally bound to his employer until the task was completed. Journeymen chafed under this unwelcome yoke. The incidents in which they encroached on the privileges of the masters by independently undertaking work commissioned by other citizens are legion, as are the occasions when journeymen slipped away from master employ seeking better working conditions or better pay. If apprehended, and many were, the malefactors were inevitably admonished by the town council to work only for their original masters, *à la journée*.[48]

Workers hired *à la journée* were paid a "daily" wage but in fact were usually employed by the week. Apparently, this kind of employment was the norm in the Middle Ages, reflecting a situation in which some workers were highly mobile.[49] Other journeymen, probably a minority, remained in the employ of one master for long periods, occasionally up to ten years. Such stability is astonishing. Perhaps, as the journeymen's chances of admission to mastership declined between 1550 and 1650, these workers remained with the same master in the hope of earning his good graces and a favorable reference. It was crucial to have a master vouch for the applicant, and familiarity and trust might be powerful and beneficial sentiments. On average the sixty-nine journeymen fortunate enough to rise to the rank of master between 1590 and 1642 had spent almost three years in the service of their last employer.[50]

Masters themselves gained work by their exclusive privilege to contract directly with other citizens to perform a task or make a product. Master craftsmen, unlike journeymen, were bound to their employer by a contract of "enterprise," not by a labor agreement. In such arrangements the details of the job were spelled out meticulously. Dimensions of the object to be made, who provided the raw materials, who paid transportation costs were all articulated in a

47. Ibid., p. 198.
48. See, for example, AMD, B253, fol. 108v, 4 Sept. 1615, where a journeyman roofer, hired by a widow to repair her roof, was haled before the town council for undertaking "ouvrage en gros," which was reserved for masters of the craft, and B210, fol. 100v, 19 Dec. 1572, for admonishment of journeymen.
49. Geremek, *Le salariat*, p. 60.
50. AMD, G83–89. In 1618 three weavers had each spent ten years with one master before gaining mastership themselves. AMD, G86.

notarized document. Many of these contracts have survived, and there seems to be little change in their terms from the fifteenth to the seventeenth century. Usually the master craftsman, not the client, secured the raw materials and supplied any necessary means of transport.[51] Cabinetmakers and carpenters provided the wood, masons and roofers the stone and tile, and goldsmiths even the gold.[52] Usually the client made a down payment, which provided the artisan with enough capital to obtain the raw materials, and then paid the balance in installments or when the work was completed. If gold were the raw material, down payments could be substantial. In 1632, for example, one Jean Ampain was advanced two thousand livres to make a golden platter.[53] Contracts always stipulated a completion date and occasionally required that the artisan work continuously on the project.[54] Satisfaction was usually guaranteed, and if the client was not pleased, the craftsman received no payment.[55]

Confident of their ability and proud of their skill, craftsmen, for their part, expected these contracts to be honored. Jean DuThu, a master locksmith, had done work for a certain M. LePicardet, the procureur général at the Parlement, but was not paid. When LePicardet asked him to do some more work, DuThu refused, telling the procureur général to get his "regular locksmith" to do it. DuThu no doubt believed his work deserved payment, but the dominant classes took another view of his "audacious" behavior. The town council reprimanded him for his "insolence" and informed him that "the artisans are held and obliged when they are requested and invited to work . . . to do it."[56]

---

51. For example, ADCO, *Notaires* #1699, 30 March 1618, where the master mason Prudent Gueryot was required to provide the horses and wagon used in the remodeling of the home of the lawyer Pierre DeVillers. For the fifteenth century, see Didier, "Le critère," pp. 198, 205. The textile trade was an exception, since the putting-out system obtained there. See ADCO, *Notaires* #1225, 28 April 1625, for a contract between a merchant and two master dyers which articulates the cost per piece for the work to be performed and gives great detail about the specifications.

52. See, for example, ADCO, BII 360/53, 14 Jan. 1592, *Notaires* #384, 10 May 1626, #36, 4 April 1647, #384, 23 Sept. 1625.

53. AMD, B270, fol. 59v, 23 July 1632. For the fifteenth century, see Didier, "Le critère," p. 203.

54. For example, ADCO, *Notaires* #36, 4 April 1647, where the mason Esme Patarron is required by the contract to "work immediately without stopping."

55. ADCO, *Notaires* #1699, 30 March 1618, is typical.

56. AMD, B246, fol. 251r, 29 May 1609.

The most coveted employer, especially in the seventeenth century, must have been the city itself. Public works projects increased tremendously after 1600, and artisans were the major beneficiaries. Whether by intention or not, municipal authorities distributed a portion of tax wealth to several master artisans. The account books of the municipal receiver show that from June 1556 to June 1557, municipal expenditures to artisans on public works amounted to just over 27 livres. In 1577–1578 just over 310 livres were spent on such work, but in 1609–1610 the town council paid artisans nearly 5,000 livres.[57] With the end of the Wars of Religion came prosperity and the means to make much-needed repairs. Street paving and church, bridge, and fortification repair became high priorities for the town and a major source of income for some master artisans during the first half of the seventeenth century; in 1642–1643, masters were still being paid over four thousand livres annually for public works.[58] Though the public sector did not generate wealth, it did channel some tax money into the hands of master artisans (tax exemptions of the privileged were frequently waived in assessments for public repairs).

Work was allocated by competitive public bid. In 1610, for example, bids were taken for the repair of the clock and tower of Notre Dame Church. One carpenter initially bid 340 livres, but the competition was so keen—nine other master carpenters entered the lists—that the contract was finally awarded for 195 livres, with the bidder supplying his own materials.[59] This intense competition was often acrimonious and detrimental to corporate solidarity. Moreover, the cutthroat bidding probably had an adverse effect on the quality of workmanship, as masters were tempted to regain the margin they had lost to the bidding process by shaving corners. Woe to the artisan who got caught "stealing" from the public in this manner, however. Esme

57. The account books are in series M of the municipal archives. I consulted M94, M115, M146, and M210 for the years 1556–57, 1577–78, 1609–10, and 1642–43, respectively. Craftsmen in my sample employed by the public authorities included locksmiths, masons, carpenters, plasterers, roofers/tilers, earth masons, cabinetmakers, chandlers and torchmakers, tinsmiths, engravers, pastrycooks, cordwainers, painters, pavers, coopers, bakers, butchers, tapestry weavers, and embroiderers.

58. AMD, M210. The register of the deliberations of the town council for 1610, AMD, B248, is especially representative of the extent of public building. On fortification repair, see also AMD, H136, and on the sixteenth century, for example, H136, 27 June 1565.

59. AMD, B248, fol. 951-v, 31 Aug. 1610. For other examples, see AMD, B248, fol. 168v, 17 Dec. 1610, B256, fol. 142r, 2 Oct. 1618.

Pinguet, a mason convicted in 1579 as *fraudateur des ouvrages publicqs*, was flogged until bloody and then banished from the town.[60]

Although large public works contracts were made only after competitive bidding, many small commissions appear to have been awarded without it, perhaps as an attempt by the authorities to still the waters they themselves had churned in bid projects. The account books of Dijon's municipal receiver are quite detailed about the type of work performed and on occasion specify if such work followed a prearranged contract, even a verbal one.[61]

The system left the door wide open for patronage. Sometimes the patronage was earned by a craftsman's expertise, as with master mason Jean DeBringué. He was reputed to be a *grandement bon ouvrier*, especially in works of fortification, so good that the town council of Dijon decided to set him up with a workshop and contracted with him "to work on repairs of the town walls."[62] But most patronage of this sort was probably intended by the magistrates to secure the loyalty of the masters.

Patronage and loyalty paid off. Most artisans receiving public commissions were well above average in wealth (see Table 1.1). Some, such as the mason Nicolas Camus, may have worked for no one else. Camus contracted a great deal of work with the civil authorities and was paid handsomely. No doubt public works employment contributed much to the sharp rise in his wealth, reflected on the tax rolls of 1579, when Camus was in the 46.5 percentile of tax distribution, and 1610, when he was in the 91.7 percentile.

Such were the enviable positions of some master artisans, but the civil authorities also needed unskilled laborers for public works projects. The common practice, at least in the sixteenth century, seems to have been that any *ouvriers et ouvrières* who had not found work by eight o'clock in the morning could be put to work in public employ for two sous and a pound of bread per day. The aim was to secure

60. ADCO, BII 360/51, 25 July–6 Oct. 1579. See also ADCO, BII 360/53, 24 July 1591. Such competition may have had something to do with the trial of Esme Pinguet, a mason who was flogged and banished for cheating on a public works project. The key witness for the prosecution was Nicolas Camus, another mason who sought public works commissions (and got them thenceforth). AMD, B215, fol. 290v, 8 July 1580.

61. On verbal contracting, see AMD, M115, fol. 159v, where two earth masons did work at the *collège* "according to the contract made verbally." On written contracts, see for example, AMD, M146, fol. 420r.

62. AMD, B256, fol. 319r, 14 June 1619.

**Table 1.1**
Wealth of artisans receiving public works commissions

| Artisan | Percentile ranking among taxpayers (year) | | Earnings from public works[a] (period)[b] | |
|---|---|---|---|---|
| *Masons* | | | | |
| Antoine Villot | 63.3 | (1556) | 40L | (1556–57) |
| Nicolas Camus | 46.5 | (1579) | 3,184L | (1580–82) |
| | 91.7 | (1610) | 1,146L | (1609–10) |
| Estienne Jacoillot | 46.5 | (1579) | 210L | (1580–82) |
| Jacques Louet | 74.6 | (1579) | 97L | (1580–82) |
| Hilaire Magnien | 92.3 | (1643) | 12L,10s | (1642–43) |
| Nicolas Coquart | 25.2 | (1643) | 1L,10s | (1642–43) |
| *Carpenters* | | | | |
| Michel Perrenet | 87.7 | (1579) | 15L | (1577–78) |
| | | | 144L | (1580–82) |
| Lazare Laurenceot | 46.5 | (1579) | 7L | (1577–78) |
| | — | | 54L | (1609–10) |
| Germain Chambrette | 65.6 | (1579) | 11L | (1577–78) |
| | | | 7L | (1580–82) |
| Nicolas Chausset | 79.1 | (1643) | 6L | (1642–43) |
| *Roofers/tilers* | | | | |
| Mongin Bergier | 46.5 | (1579) | 52L,17s | (1577–78) |
| | | | 21L | (1580–82) |
| Estienne Pierrot | 56.7 | (1579) | 282L | (1580–82) |
| Charles DeVaux | 56.3 | (1643) | 6L | (1642–43) |
| *Locksmiths* | | | | |
| Jean Mausan | 92.1 | (1579) | 3L,14s | (1577–78) |
| | | | 5L,12s | (1580–82) |
| Jacques Mausan | 81.7 | (1579) | 2L | (1577–78) |
| | | | 1L,17s | (1580–82) |
| Pierre Mausan | 92.1 | (1579) | 5L | (1580–82) |
| Toussaint Sebilotte | 65.6 | (1579) | 79L,10s | (1580–82) |
| Pierre Chardenon | 82.9 | (1643) | 161L,3s | (1642–43) |
| *Cabinetmakers* | | | | |
| Jacques DesVarennes | 73.3 | (1556) | 1L | (1556–57) |
| Claude Motot | 96.6 | (1579) | 25L | (1577–78) |
| | | | 66L,9s | (1580–82) |
| Jacques Charmot | 31.6 | (1579) | 6L,10s | (1580–82) |
| Bénigne Collot | 92.3 | (1643) | 100L | (1642–43) |

Sources: AMD, H137, M94, fo. 179v, 180r, M115, fol. 156r, 158r, v, M146, fol. 346v, 354r, 424r, 437r, 438v, M210, fol. 161r, 216r–v.

[a]Given in livres and sous.

[b]In each case the period is one year, dated from Saint John the Baptist Day (23 June), except 1580–82, which represents the period 1 July 1580 to 9 Feb. 1582.

cheap labor, of course, but also to prevent beggary. By employing such workers, the town council was attacking what was considered a source of moral and physical disorder—idleness.[63]

The crafts were represented before the public authorities by their jurés, who, with two exceptions, were appointed from the ranks of the guilds by the town council. Only the goldsmith guild and eventually the pastrycook guild maintained the right to elect jurés from their corporation and submit them for approval to the municipal authorities. (As we will see, this became a major point of contention between the magistrates and the pastrycooks.) The jurés represented the corporation in its collective relationship with the authorities, with other crafts, and, in police matters, within their own guild. Legally, jurés had to be accompanied by aldermen during their visitations of shops to police their guild. As the deliberations of the town council make clear, however, jurés preferred to make their visits alone. Injunctions continually flowed from the council admonishing jurés to make visits only with an alderman in attendance, for the magistrates wished to associate government power with the jurés and thereby to reinforce control over the guilds.[64]

Naturally, individuals invested with these offices could become quite powerful. In addition to the control they had over their colleagues, they were paid for their duties. They received a portion of the aforementioned fees paid by new masters,[65] but a far larger source of income was their share of the fines they imposed upon artisans for inadequate materials or workmanship. One could hardly devise a system more suited to encourage abuse, and indeed, the visitations were frequently occasions of disagreement, sometimes leading to violence.[66] There are many instances in the records when jurés used their authority to harass craftsmen with whom they had previously quarreled.[67] Further, some jurés were open to bribes. If they found

63. AMD, B235, fol. 47r, 4 July 1597, repeated on fol. 209v, 6 March 1598.
64. AMD, B197, fol. 81r, 20 Oct. 1559, B210, fol. 42v, 29 July 1572, B215, fol. 298r, 29 July 1580.
65. For example, Chapuis, *Les anciennes corporations*, p. 286.
66. See AMD, B191, fol. 150r, B188, fol. 191v–192v, 21 April 1551, where a saddler refused to open his shop door to the jurés and aldermen and was fined 160 sous, B215, fol. 321r, 11 Oct. 1580, where bakers threatened jurés during a shop visit; ADCO, BII 360/51, 15 Jan. 1588, where the town council prohibited craftsmen from threatening, slandering, or outraging jurés on visitations. See also, AMD, B190, fol. 69v–70r, 30 Aug. 1552, and B191, fol. 166v, 6 March 1554.
67. For example, ADCO, BII 360/51, 15 Jan. 1588, where the master cabinetmaker

items of inferior quality, they might be persuaded to look the other way, for a fee. In 1617 the shoemaker jurés were caught affixing the "good mark of the town" to two pieces of leather which were of unacceptable quality. In its deliberations, the town council made it clear that bribery was at issue.[68]

Being a juré virtually ensured affluence. At least one juré, the gold-smith Guillaume DesVarennes, was exempted from taxes; others were among the richest taxpayers in town. Of twenty-four jurés whose names were listed on both the juré rolls for 1555–1556 and 1556–1557 and the tax rolls of 1556, nine (or 37.5 percent) were in the wealthiest 10 percent of taxpayers.[69] Percentages were similar in the other years I sampled. In 1579, twelve of thirty-seven (32.4 percent), in 1610, four of thirteen (30.8 percent), and in 1643, nine of twenty-nine (31.3 percent) were in the wealthiest 10 percent. Jurés loyal to the town council could expect rewards in the form of public works commissions. Claude Motot, juré for the cabinetmakers from 1561 to 1564 and again in 1567, 1569, 1579, and 1587, received many such commissions (see Table 1.1).[70] Others who won public works con-tracts were the carpenters Germain Chambrette (juré in 1566 and 1586) and Nicolas Chausset (1640–1642), the roofer Mongin Bergier (1559–1561, 1565–1568, 1572, 1578), the mason Jacques Louet (1578, 1586, 1593, 1606), the locksmith Jean Mausan (1561, 1563–1564, 1566, 1568–1569, 1572, 1579, 1589), and the cabinetmaker Bénigne Collot (juré in 1636, 1637, 1642). Some jurés were not rich when they came into office, but the emoluments of office, especially public works contracts, would soon enhance their prosperity. The rise of Nicolas Camus, who repeatedly served as juré, was a case in point.[71]

Municipal authorities, viewing the jurés as instruments of govern-mental control over the crafts, jealously guarded the right to appoint them, no doubt in the interest of naming loyal and "safe" men. Once

---

Regne DuBois complained to the authorities that the juré Jean Guillaumet was biased in his visitation because of the quarrels and bad words they had exchanged prior to the visit.

68. AMD, B254, fol. 173r, 19 Jan. 1617.

69. The juré rolls are located at the beginning of each register of the town council deliberations (AMD, B).

70. AMD, B198, fol. 15v, B199, fol. 17v, B200, fol. 10v, B203, fol. 20v, B205, fol. 17r, B216, fol. 15r, B224, fol. 26r.

71. Camus served, for example, in 1579 (AMD, B217, fol. 13r), 1593 (B231, fol. 43v), and 1597 (B235, fol. 36r).

the magistrates found someone like Motot, whom they could trust and work with, they kept him or members of his family in the post, frequently for years. Bénigne Ramaille was juré of the hosiers continuously from 1559 to 1567.[72] The roofer Claude Perrot was juré in 1594, 1598, 1600, 1607, 1609, 1611, and 1616.[73] So eager were the magistrates to put their men in these posts that they occasionally tried to appoint men who had not even been admitted to mastership, prompting howls of protest from the guildsmen, who bristled at the prospect of having their work judged by "incompetents." In such cases, the town council was forced to yield on this issue.[74]

Since the Middle Ages the goldsmiths had held the privilege to elect one of their two jurés (the other being appointed by the town council), but their choice had to be approved by the town council and the guild had to obtain permission before holding an election. In 1563, for example, the council annulled an election held without prior approval and fined the guild twenty livres.[75] The goldsmiths were the only craftsmen with this privilege, limited as it was, until around 1600, when the pastrycooks of Dijon decided to elect their own jurés as well.

This bold venture challenged municipal power at a time when the city magistrates were trying to extend and solidify it. That the king, Parlement, and royal bailliage would also enter the fray suggests the serious implications of the dispute for political authority in general. The resolution of the conflict reflects the complexity of the exercise of authority in early modern France. There could be no simple imposition of royal will on recalcitrant subjects, for the France of 1600 was a tangled skein of interests and jurisdictions.

Some historians of absolutism now emphasize the paradoxes of state building and centralization. As William Beik notes, the state is a creation of social processes, not some transcendent entity operating above society. The early modern French state was the product of a system of clientage and venality of office, and royal authority was a

72. AMD, B197, fol. 20r, B198, fol. 16r, B199, fol. 18r, B200, fol. 11r, B201, fol. 15r, B202, fol. 14r, and B203, fol. 21r.

73. AMD, B231, fol. 44r, B235, fol. 36r, B237, fol. 44v, B244, fol. 42v, B246, fol. 53v, B248, fol. 61v, and B253, fol. 33r.

74. For example, AMD, B195, fol. 34v, 42v–43v, 7–13 July 1557 (sword polishers), B199, fol. 62r, 19 Sept. 1561 (drapers), G27, July 1577 (roofers), G64, 6 Sept. 1585 (painters), G69, 1586 (toolmakers), B262, fol. 53r, 23 July 1624 (shoemakers).

75. AMD, B200, fol. 51r–v, 25 Aug. 1563.

prisoner of its historical roots. Ownership of bureaucratic office and
personal ties and loyalties could prove formidable obstacles to the
imposition of royal will, even if that will was clearly articulated (and
it often was not).[76] Royal authority, as Beik puts it, "had been constructed out of, and in reaction to, seigneurial power. . . . [It] reproduced the shared degrees of jurisdiction . . . which characterized
the seigneurial landscape, and in its differentiation into layer upon
layer of rival agencies and its unequal treatment of each town [and]
. . . corps . . . it reflected the historical conditions under which the
monarchy had gradually taken over a pre-existing system of frag-
mented and diversified jurisdictions. Inequality . . . was built into the
system, along with considerable 'autonomy' on every level, deriving
from the fact that privileges were 'owned' as well as 'conferred.'"[77]
Centralization had not progressed far. It is not surprising, therefore,
that confusion reigned over the pastrycook affair and over guild regulation in general (a topic to which we will have occasion to return).

The dispute emerged from the Wars of Religion. The pastrycooks
had remained loyal to Henri of Navarre, who rewarded them in 1595
with a revised set of statutes modeled after those of their Parisian
counterparts, including the privilege to elect their own jurés.[78] For
the next twenty-eight years the pastrycooks, the town council, the
Parlement of Dijon, the royal court at the bailliage, and the king
would be embroiled in a conflict over jurisdiction. The town council
saw the case as a threat to its hold over the guilds. To lose the right to
appoint jurés would be to lose police authority and with it the sizable
income from fines. The craftsmen, of course, hoped to extend their
independence from government regulation.

On 28 June 1595 the bailliage received the controversial letters
patent from Henri IV, and on 29 May 1596 the Parlement registered
them. On 7 December 1601 the pastrycooks brought suit in the Parlement against the town council for denying them their electoral privilege. The following year, on 3 April, they won an arret from the
Parlement, which ordered the city magistrates to allow the master

76. William Beik, *Absolutism and Society in Seventeenth-Century France: State
Power and Provincial Aristocracy in Languedoc* (Cambridge, 1985), pp. 12–15. See also
Sharon Kettering, *Patrons, Brokers, and Clients in Seventeenth-Century France* (New
York, 1986).

77. Beik, *Absolutism*, p. 336.

78. Chapuis, *Les anciennes corporations*, p. 64. AMD, G61 contains the entire
affair.

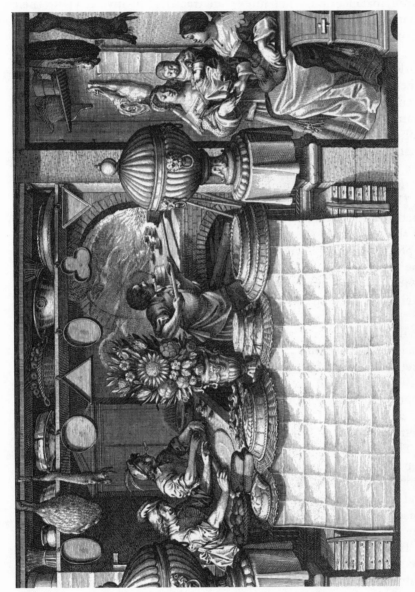

A seventeenth-century pastrycook's shop; photo Bibliothèque Nationale, Paris

pastrycooks to elect their jurés. On 13 July 1602, two weeks after the municipal election, when jurés were traditionally invested with their charge, the pastrycooks were back in court complaining to the Parlement that the town council had refused to accept the oath from their elected jurés and would not invest them with their office. Again the Parlement issued an arret requiring the city magistrates to comply. Then, almost exactly one year later, on 15 July 1603, the same events recurred. On 1 May 1604 the town council petitioned the Parlement, claiming that since "time immemorial" it had had the privilege of policing the crafts, including the authority to name jurés. On 7 August 1606 it submitted a "civil request" to the Parlement asking for the abrogation of the previous arrets (there had been three), but the Parlement denied the request.

There was a lull in the conflict until 1613, when the town council made a direct remonstrance to Louis XIII, protesting his confirmation of the statutes of the pastrycooks the previous year.[79] Receiving no reply, the municipal authorities gave in for a while, but on 6 July 1622 the pastrycooks sent a *suplis* to Parlement. They asserted that since 1613 the town council had not tried to prevent them from electing their own jurés, but now the council was refusing to accept the oaths of the guild's nominees. The town council defended itself with the claim that the pastrycooks had been permitting many abuses in their trade, that they had such *grande intelligence* among themselves that their jurés were not enforcing quality control. One week later the Parlement upheld the pastrycooks' position; again the magistrates submitted a civil request to annul the arrets supporting the pastrycooks, and in December 1622 the pastrycooks challenged the validity of that civil request in Parlement.

The whole affair finally came to an anticlimactic end on 5 September 1623, when the pastrycooks and the town council struck a compromise. Thenceforth, one juré was to be elected by the pastrycooks and one was to be named by the municipal authorities. This compromise flouted royal, or at least parlementary, authority, for it ignored the arrets, but peace reigned at last.

The protracted battle well illustrates the interdependencies of public authority. It is likely that the king wished to reduce municipal autonomy, but to do so he was forced into the position of supporting

79. Chapuis, *Les anciennes corporations*, p. 65.

the traditional autonomy and privilege of a corps, the pastrycook guild. He met considerable resistance, and in the end the disputants each took a share of authority, ignoring the commands of the king and Parlement.

This was not to be the only jurisdictional battle fought over regulation of the craft guilds, and the question of interest did not pertain only to the ruling classes. Dijon's master pastrycooks were far from pawns in a distant power struggle. In this instance they worked as a guild in the hope of advancing their own interests. As we will see, guildsmen could transcend corporate boundaries in similar jurisdictional disputes.

## Government Regulation of Guilds

When Burgundy was united with France in 1479 Louis XI granted the town council of Dijon far-reaching police powers over the crafts. He allowed "the right of authority . . . [and] power . . . to make statutes and ordinances in and on all and each mechanical trade and art in the said town, suburbs and surrounding region, . . . [the authority] being on the erection, institution, police, order and regulation of the above said trades as well as on the reformation of them, all and as many times as they [the magistrates] deem expedient . . . for the public welfare of the said town."[80] So jealous of its powers was the town council that it insisted upon their renewal with each new reign. The council deliberations are continually preoccupied with the many aspects of policing the crafts, one of the most important functions of municipal government in early modern Dijon.

In theory, as the grant of powers stated, the object of craft regulation was to benefit the public welfare by regulating both production and distribution. In practice, however, the motivations of the magistrates were not all impartial benevolence. It was in their interest (that is, the interest of the dominant classes) to maintain order and thereby preserve their superior position in society. No doubt, the council pursued this objective throughout its history, but there is convincing evidence in its deliberations that after 1550 the magistrates tried

80. Quoted in Paul Labal, "Le monde des métiers dans le cadre urbain: Aspects de la vie des métiers à Dijon de 1430 à 1560" (Dijon, 1950; unpublished Mémoire de diplôme d'études supérieures in the Bibliothèque de l'Université de Dijon), p. 54.

harder than ever before to make theoretical control a reality. In the last half of the sixteenth century hardly a council meeting passed without some discussion of enforcing police powers over the guilds and the authority to collect fines from them, topics that had come up relatively infrequently in the preceding decades.[81]

The municipal regulatory privilege was all-encompassing. Prices were established through municipal tariffs, quality control by regular workshop visits, and even work time was regulated. Many festivals were mandatory holidays, and the time during which one could buy foodstuffs at the markets was strictly controlled. For example, bakers could not enter the grain marketplace until two hours after the citizens had entered and met their needs, lest the bakers' demand inordinately stimulate prices.[82]

To the magisterial mind, the most effective way to control Dijon's master craftsmen was to limit the space within which they operated. By confining commercial activity to specified places, the council hoped to make it easier to regulate. Thus, markets, especially for bulk items, were centralized in Dijon. Though there were several food and grain markets in the town, the Halles de Champeaux, built in the fifteenth century, was a clearinghouse for leather goods, textiles, grain, meat, and many other commodities. All "foreign" merchants were required to bring their goods there directly for inspection and registration.[83]

Spatial regulation had a hygienic purpose, too. Slaughtering and tanning by butchers, tripers, curriers, and tanners were of major concern to the civil authorities, who worried a good deal about the diseases that might be spread by this bloody work. They frequently issued ordinances requiring masters to work outside the town walls or in the municipal slaughterhouse. These craftsmen, it seems, pre-

81. It is difficult to know whether fines were always collected, but we do know that on occasion sergeants of the mayor were dispatched to collect them and that they confiscated household objects if payment was refused. On other occasions the town council reduced fines following suitable contrition or explanation on the part of the miscreant. See, for example, AMD, B193, fol. 79v, 17 Sept. 1555. I found no evidence of a debtor's prison.

82. See, for example, BMD, ms 1496, "Arrêt du Parlement de Dijon," 19 March 1572, concerning the "police of grains," and AMD, B194, fol. 219v, 19 March 1556.

83. A. Chapuis, *Les foires et marchés de Dijon* (Dijon, n.d.), p. 21. On regulation of the *draperie* trade at the halles, see, for example, AMD, B188, fol. 194v, 24 April 1551, on shoes, G24, 12 Feb. 1643.

ferred to do their tasks in their houses and then jettison the wastes into the streets.[84]

As the many ordinances aimed at the tradesmen indicate, control was far from absolute. Enactment of regulations does not necessarily produce compliance, and enforcement is not always successful. After 1550, municipal deliberations often dwelled on the difficulties of policing the apparently perpetual violations of trade ordinances. In a town of fifteen to twenty thousand inhabitants, a police force of twenty sergeants and twenty aldermen could do little to prevent illicit activities. Though malefactors were constantly being arrested and fined for avoiding the halles and buying or selling unregistered commodities, spatial regulations were largely ignored, and the black market boomed. Peddlers, hawkers, and even merchants, determined to avoid the taxes on transactions at the halles or other regulated markets, furtively wandered the streets, selling their wares. Many Dijonnais master artisans and merchants went into the suburbs and nearby villages, beyond municipal scrutiny, to buy large quantities of produce and then returned to town to sell it at a propitious moment with a substantial markup. The magistrates regarded such speculation as hoarding, and it troubled them greatly since it affected the flow of foodstuffs to Dijon.

Indeed, no area attracted more regulatory attention than food production and distribution, since dislocation in this sector had the most immediate repercussions. The *peuple* got restive when food became scarce.[85] Consequently, the bakers and butchers were regulated more closely than any other artisans in Dijon—and bucked most violently under this unwelcome yoke.

As we will see in the next chapter, population growth, inflation, and increased poverty in the sixteenth-century Dijon gave the distribution of grain and the pricing of bread paramount importance for the authorities. Since the Middle Ages the chief objective of, and justification for, regulating the grain trade was to ensure an adequate supply of bread. Maintaining a regular flow of grain into the mar-

---

84. AMD, B195, fol. 178r, 7 May 1558. On ordinances to slaughter outside the town walls, see, for example, AMD, B200, fol. 60r, 17 Sept. 1563, B201, fol. 70v, 24 Nov. 1564. On slaughtering only in the public slaughterhouse, see AMD, B235, fol. 86v, 28 Aug. 1597.

85. See, for example, AMD, B206, fol. 48r, 23 Aug. 1569, B210, fol. 97r, 16 Dec. 1572, B254, fol. 41r, 5 July 1616.

ketplace was deemed the best way to keep bread prices down and thus to pacify the populace. The magistrates knew that the volatile grain market was a time bomb that could explode into riot. And the bakers knew it too.

Traditionally, the price of bread was established by the assize, whereby the magistrates periodically purchased several measures of variable-quality wheat and went through the production process, noting the costs along the way, including the margin of *prouffit* to the baker. Out of this fixed margin, the baker had to meet such "incidental" expenses as wood, wages, and rents, which the magistrates excluded from their calculations of cost. Clearly, this system could squeeze the baker in times of general inflation, and from the 1530s, it seems, prices were rising all across the board. Consequently, between the early 1530s and the mid-1560s, the regulatory picture began to be cluttered with baker "abuses"—selling underweight bread or mixing inferior flour into it, fraudulent balances, overcharging. Bakers clamored for more frequent assizes, and magisterial roundups and fines for cheating increased.[86] In the 1560s the tone of regulation and baker complaints became more shrill. Though Dijon lacks any systematic price lists before 1568, it appears that inflation accelerated in the mid-1560s; 1565 and 1566 saw serious dearth in the town, and bakers complained vociferously about increased production costs beyond grain price inflation.[87] They probably had a case; between 1564 and 1568 the cost of a *moule* of wood for fuel increased by nearly 30 percent in Dijon.[88]

To regain control of what was rapidly becoming a chaotic situation, Parlement abandoned the assize. In 1573 it issued an arret that pegged the retail price of bread to the free-market price of wholesale wheat. Other provisions of this arret stipulated that white bread be marketed at a standard weight of one livre (one pound of sixteen ounces) and brown bread (*pain bis*) at twice that weight, that bakers display their balances in their shop windows, and that they sell only fresh bread.[89]

---

86. See, for example, AMD, G293, 3 June 1547, B191, fol. 163r, 2 March 1553, B192, fol. 133v–134v, Aug. 1554, B197, fol. 44v, 30 July 1559, B198, fol. 91v–92v, 17 Jan. 1561.

87. See AMD, G300, 12 Oct. 1565, B202, fol. 178r, 7 June 1566, G300, 26 Aug., 2 Sept. 1567.

88. AMD, B200, fol. 137v, 14 Jan. 1564, B204, fol. 147r, 17 Feb. 1568.

89. BMD, ms 1496, "Arrêt du Parlement," 14 March 1573.

The new pricing method did not silence the bakers; they continued to complain of being squeezed, and with some cause. The arret assumed (mistakenly) that the other production costs for bread would remain directly proportional to the wheat price. In fact, the bakers experienced disproportionate rises in the cost of wood for their ovens, wages for their workers, rent for their shops, and mill taxes and subsidies. In 1638 the town council at last relented, testimony that the bakers wielded some power.[90] Subsequently, however, the authorities became much less inclined to let those caught cheating off with a warning, as had been common in the sixteenth century; they began to impose fines without appeal.[91]

Nevertheless, both before and after 1638, bakers cheated. They had no scruples about hoarding grain to drive up prices, even during times of dearth.[92] Overcharging was rampant.[93] So was producing bread of poor quality, especially during times when the lesser grains used to make brown bread were expensive relative to wheat. Since the price of brown bread was based on that of white bread, which was pegged to wheat, a rise in the price of other grains reduced the profit on brown bread. The bakers would respond by cutting the quality of the brown bread, victimizing the poor, who were its primary consumers, and bringing another crackdown from the magistrates.[94]

The most common form of cheating was selling underweight bread. In the ovens of that era, of course, evaporation during baking could not be precisely regulated, and it was difficult to calculate cooked weight from raw dough. Mistakes of an ounce or two were to be

90. AMD, B275, fol. 180r–181r, 12 Jan. 1638. For an earlier example of this type of complaint, see AMD, B224, fol. 33v, 1 July 1586.

91. See especially 1641 (AMD, B278).

92. AMD, B202, fol. 178r–v, 7 June 1566, B231, fol. 157r, April 1594.

93. For example, AMD, B203, fol. 35v, 12 July 1566, B278, fol. 216v, 16 April 1641, B281, fol. 125v, 18 Aug. 1643. Master shoemakers, and probably other craftsmen, also felt pinched between production costs and fixed retail prices. See, for example, AMD, B217, fol. 81r, 12 April 1580, when Jehan Mesnageot was fined for overcharging and protested that he could not sell at the established price "without total ruin in serving the public."

94. For an example of production of bread of poor quality, see AMD, B223, fol. 30v, 19 July 1585. Stale bread was also fobbed off on the poor. The town council demanded that enough bread be baked to feed the town, frequently justifying this regulation by citing the protection and provisioning of the poor. See, for example, AMD, B195, fol. 24r, 26 June 1557, B202, fol. 166v, 6 May 1566, B227, fol. 295r, 18 May 1590. No doubt the council acted to avoid "la grande clameur du peuple" (AMD, B202, fol. 88r–v, 12 Oct. 1565).

expected, but the bakers also knew that skimming a couple of ounces, and frequently more, was much harder to detect than overcharging. Only an alderman on visitation was likely to catch the short weight. Even though such visits were frequent (judging from the huge numbers of cheaters hauled in and fined), they did little to deter the practice. Throughout the period it seems that nearly every master baker in town (or his widow) was caught cheating at some time or other. On 22 August 1550 no fewer than twenty-nine bakers were arrested for selling light bread; in August 1554, twenty were arrested, even though the tax rolls of 1556 list only thirty-seven bakers in all of Dijon. Similarly, on two lists of malefactors (one from 1638 and the other from 1643) forty-five different master bakers appear, and only fifty-nine bakers appear on the tax rolls of 1643. Frequently the same names recur. Nicolas Roze was caught in August 1550, June and October 1551, August 1554, and May and July 1557, and no doubt at other times.[95] Nor does poverty seem to have been the only motivation to cheat. As a group the bakers were not poor, and several of the repeaters were quite wealthy. Roze was well off; Antoine Leschenet, among the richest taxpayers in town in 1643, was caught selling light bread on several occasions.[96] No doubt the rewards far outweighed the fine one would be assessed if caught. It is tempting to surmise a connection, however circumstantial, between the massive cheating by the bakers and their relative wealth.

Such activities were commonplace, but the real power of the bakers was in their threat to withhold production. Choking off the supply of bread was the loudest form of protest the bakers could make, sure to get the attention of the magistrates. The bakers employed the collective recourse in 1581, 1586, 1640, and perhaps at other times.[97] In

95. AMD, B188, fol. 66r–67v, 22 Aug. 1550, B192, fol. 133v–134v, B281, fol. 124r–125r, B188, fol. 67r, B189, fol. 42r, fol. 124v, B192, fol. 133v, B194, fol. 253v, B195, fol. 38v.

96. On Leschenet, see AMD, B275, fol. 240r, 19 March 1638, B281, fol. 124r, 18 Aug. 1643, fol. 249r, 1 Feb. 1644. For earlier examples of cheating, see AMD, B188, fol. 67v, 22 Aug. 1550, B192, fol. 133v, Aug. 1554, where Nicolas Masson, who was in the 80th percentile of taxpayers in 1556, was caught cheating; Paule Henry, often before the magistrates from 1550 to 1566 for cheating, was in the 70th percentile in 1556.

97. AMD, B219, fol. 22v, 57v–58v, 1581, B223, fol. 201v, 1 June 1586, B278, fol. 47v, 3 July 1640. Labal, "Le monde des metiers," pp. 66–67, finds evidence of strikes before 1560. The bakers were not the only craftsmen to strike. The oil makers did on 24 July 1640 (AMD, B278, fol. 61v). The painters tried to strike for higher wages for public employ in Jan. 1629, but the town council clapped them in jail instead (AMD, B266, fol. 199r–v, 17 Jan. 1629).

1640 the authorities received complaints from "a great number of inhabitants about the disobedience of the bakers, who by a spirit of malice and in contempt of the deliberations of the town council" had not baked enough bread to supply the citizenry. Whereas in the sixteenth century a striking baker might get off with a fifteen-sou fine, during the shutdown of 1640 the town council ordered the bakers to furnish the inhabitants with bread or face fines of five hundred livres and suffer demolition of their ovens.[98] The strike ended in compromise; the bakers went back to work and in a new tariff granted by the authorities the profit margin between bread prices and wheat prices was widened.[99]

The bakers were not the only food purveyors to give the magistrates trouble. The conflict between the butchers and the municipal authorities was most pronounced in the sixteenth century, coming to a climax in 1579, but there is evidence that the butchers continued to flout municipal regulations in the seventeenth century, if less blatantly. The regulations followed the same form throughout the period: the butchers were enjoined to market fresh meat daily, to display it publicly on their *bancs*, not to sell unsalted pork, to keep their scales in public view, and most important, to sell *à la livre*, by weight and not by the piece.[100]

As with the bakers, the magistrates established the relationship between retail and wholesale prices by performing an assize, during which they bought several animals on the hoof, appointed a butcher to slaughter them, and determined from the yield what price per pound was requisite to cover the costs of wholesale production and still allow a "fair" margin of profit to the butcher.[101] The sources are silent on which butchers were appointed for such tasks, though we

98. AMD, B278, fol. 47v, 3 July 1640. See AMD, B219, fol. 57v, 14 July 1581, where Jean Millen and Alexandre LeGrand protested the low price of white bread and were fined fifteen sous.

99. The margin between the price of bread and the cost of wheat was fluid because the authorities established retail bread prices based on the wholesale cost of wheat but revised the tariff only periodically, whereas the wheat prices fluctuated, sometimes dramatically, from one market day to the next.

100. For example, AMD, B224, fol. 155v–156r, 18 Nov. 1586, B284, fol. 162r, 14 Dec. 1646. Stiff penalties were meted out for marketing diseased or rotten meat. See, for example, AMD, B203, fol. 13v, 23 June 1566, B241, fol. 96r, 31 July 1603. On selling unsalted pork, see, for example, AMD, B191, fol. 124r–v, 9 Feb. 1553, B201, fol. 64v, 3 Nov. 1564.

101. For a detailed description of a municipal assize in the sixteenth century, see Joseph Garnier, *Histoire du quartier du Bourg* (Dijon, 1853), p. 32.

know the magistrates were suspicious of collusion among masters in other trades which could affect the impartiality of the assize. For example, they brought in a master shoemaker from Cîteaux and Saint-Jean-de-Losne to perform a shoemaking assize.[102]

Like the bakers, the butchers felt squeezed by the inflexible relationship between floating wholesale and fixed retail prices. Their collective recourse ranged from price fixing above the municipal tariff, to intimidating wholesale sellers, to refusal to sell by weight, and ultimately, to shutting down production.[103] The most resisted regulation was selling meat by weight. The butchers preferred to cut a piece of meat, put it on the banc, and sell it whole for a set price. This practice was especially prejudicial to the poor, who could not afford large cuts, and so the magistrates ordered the butchers to sell the meat by weight in whatever size was desired by the consumer. The butchers were not eager to comply, for it was easier to exceed the established price per pound on the larger pieces without being detected. This ruse was constantly employed, and the magistrates continually dragged the butchers in for fines.

The conflict came to a head in 1578–1579. In September 1578 word reached the town council that the butchers were selling meat at double the tariff and not by the pound.[104] Three months later the servant girl of a royal official's widow came to the magistrates, saying that no one in the *bourg*, where the butchers were concentrated, would sell her meat by the pound. The syndic marched over to the bourg with her and had her identify the culprits; she did and they were fined.[105] The butchers complained in January 1579 that no other butchers in the region "nor in Troyes" were constrained to sell by the pound, and if the magistrates did not rescind this regulation they would stop

102. AMD, B215, fol. 196v, 23 Oct. 1579, B215, fol. 199v, 31 Oct. 1579. For a detailed account of the assize of the latter, see AMD, G24, 31 Oct. 1579.

103. References to butchers sharing *intelligences* and engaging in *monopolles* (price fixing) are legion. See for example, AMD, B188, fol. 128r, 5 Dec. 1550, and G305, 8 Oct. 1620, where complaints reached the town council that the butchers engaged in *monopolles et intelligences* in the purchase of animals. One butcher would bid a price, then disappear, and successive butchers would each bid a lower price. Meanwhile, the butchers dealt surreptitious blows to the unfortunate beast so that the seller could not take his injured commodity to another market. AMD, B189, fol. 135v, 6 Nov. 1551, and fol. 164v–168r, 31 Dec. 1551, which contains an informative interrogation of a servant girl about her master's marketing practices.

104. AMD, B215, fol. 40v, 30 Sept. 1578.

105. AMD, B216, fol. 80v, 31 Dec. 1578.

butchering. The town council turned a deaf ear but did concede the butchers' request for a new assize, following which they reiterated the former regulations under pain of a hundred-livre fine.[106] The butchers responded with a production slowdown. On 30 January, nine butchers were arrested for not producing enough meat for the "nécessité du peuple."[107]

The power struggle continued. In March a butcher juré was bold enough to tell the magistrates to their faces that the butchers did not wish to go to the fairs that month to buy the beef to provision the town. He was clapped in jail, and the regulations were proclaimed again.[108] By September the butchers were back at it, claiming that the people did not want to buy by the pound and, besides, that it was customary to sell by the piece.[109] One butcher's audacious remarks to the aldermen who caught him violating the regulation—"The thieves who made the tariff can go to the devil!"—won him a flogging at both ends of the bourg for his arrogance. He was forced to beg forgiveness of "God, king and justice" on his knees before the mayor.[110]

Such harsh measures may have tempered the butchers' direct challenge to municipal authority; we hear no more of work stoppages and slowdowns. The town council, however, continued to rail against the butchers in the seventeenth century, though perhaps not as frequently as before.[111] As late as 1647 the butchers complained that the price of beef on the hoof had risen so much as to make the existing tariff obsolete; the town council refused to raise the tariff, and one month later complaints reached the magistrates that the butchers were not selling by the pound, to the detriment of "artisans and vignerons in particular."[112] *Plus ça change . . .*

So the civil authorities struggled to make their theoretical control over the guilds real. They fought the battle through daily regulation

106. AMD, B215, fol. 79v–83r, 9, 13 Jan. 1579.

107. AMD, B215, fol. 88r, 30 Jan. 1579.

108. Ibid., fol. 113r, 27 March 1579.

109. Ibid., fol. 187r–v, 22 Sept. 1579. On the assertion of customary practice, see AMD, B215, fol. 110v, 24 March 1579.

110. AMD, B217, fol. 57r–58r, 20 Nov. 1579.

111. See, for example, AMD, G304, 12 July 1581, which is an arret ordering the butchers to sell meat "by the pound." AMD, B224, fol. 79r, 10 Nov. 1587, B231, fol. 77v, 19 Aug. 1593, B246, fol. 229r–v, 10 April 1609; BMD, ms 1500, fol. 65, 17 Feb. 1624, which is an arret from the Parlement prohibiting *monopolles* by the butchers.

112. AMD, B284, fol. 211v, 24 Jan. 1647, fol. 215r, 1 Feb. 1647, fol. 220r, 8 Feb. 1647.

of production and distribution not just of the butchers and bakers but of all the guilds. They also wrestled for control of access to the charmed circle—mastership. Between 1550 and 1650 the guild masters strove to close off the avenues to mastership, while the municipal authorities were continually trying to open them up.

Though masters appear to have shared a common culture, it would be inaccurate to suggest that they constituted a monolithic bloc either within or between guilds, all sharing identical interests in all aspects of their lives. Similarly, since we know little of how guilds governed themselves, we cannot know if guild interests always coincided with the interests of all masters or simply those who directed the guilds. Nevertheless, masters of every guild stood to benefit from a policy that curtailed admissions to their ranks, and so it is likely that most of them supported it. The evidence points to a collective strategy that transcended corporate boundaries and united masters within guilds.

As we will see, the population of Dijon grew considerably faster than that of the artisanat. As a result, the wealth of many master craftsmen increased, and masters from nearly all the guilds became aware that limiting access to mastership could mean greater wealth for established masters. Thus, they did their best to reduce the number of newcomers.

The town council, alarmed by this attempt at self-regulation, which threatened municipal authority, tried its best to keep the routes to mastership open. The magistrates were concerned that reducing the supply of men qualified to contract to produce goods and services would raise prices and lead to scarcity. It was in their interest to keep prices down and consumers placated. Moreover, they feared disorder among the mass of workers denied access to mastership. In their view, allowing reasonable numbers of journeymen to advance would help prevent frustration from building and thus would foster public tranquility.

The masters who hoped that restricting their numbers would increase their wealth also wanted to keep the wealth within their own families. Masterships could not be passed down from father to son, but master artisans found many ways to ease the accession for their sons, and not just the eldest. There are many examples of masters whose brothers were also masters, either in the same guild or in others.[113] Indeed, the vast majority of masters' sons remained craftsmen. Between 1551 and 1600, according to the marriage contracts in which the guilds of both father and son are listed, only 5 sons of 78 native master artisans left the artisanat, while 59 of them worked in the same trade as their fathers. Upward social mobility by profession was even rarer in the first half of the seventeenth century, when only 2 of 116 left the artisanat, and 89 took up their fathers' trades, presumably to gain mastership one day.[114] A substantial minority of sons of master guildsmen (14 of 78 in the last half of the sixteenth century and 25 of 116 in the first half of the seventeenth) became masters in craft guilds other than their fathers', forging bonds that transcended guild boundaries. Corporate bonds, though strong and important, certainly did not preclude the formation of many such links among master craftsmen, as we will see, for the masters, though they plied different trades, had much in common.

Masters used many stratagems to regulate the number of new masters. The prospective master had to have access to some capital, since costs of admission to mastership were high and getting higher in the seventeenth century. The fees to the confraternity, to the jurés and aldermen, and to the town council, plus the expense of a masterpiece paid for by the applicant, could be prohibitive. For instance, the masterpiece of locksmith Guillaume Girard cost a hundred livres, more than the highest-paid journeyman could earn in Dijon in a year.[115] Add to this the illegal expenses levied by the masters (the most notorious and expensive was the banquet the candidate had to give them), and mastership was priced beyond the means of most journeymen. Nor were these the only costs involved in assuming a mastership. Outfitting a shop with raw materials and tools could run to several hundred livres, as the shoemaker Bénigne Rebourg could attest. It

113. For example, ADCO, *Notaires* #1283, 16 July 1569, #772, 21 Sept. 1572, #374, 15 June 1596, #375, 12 Oct. 1597, #1716, 14 Feb. 1604, #1941, 19 Dec. 1627, #1938, 20 Feb. 1636, #1948, 17 August 1639, #1929, 19 Dec. 1647.

114. Mastership letters, though fewer, show a similar high percentage (thirteen of twenty between 1562 and 1576 and seven of eight between 1638 and 1643), suggesting that mastership would come to most of these sons one day.

115. ADCO, *Notaires* #1771, 17 Jan. 1649. Of all journeymen, carpenters earned the highest daily wage, six sous, for work at the Carthusian monastery in Dijon. At 270 working days per year (a maximum, given Sundays and religious holidays when work was prohibited), they would have made only eighty-one livres a year.

cost him three hundred livres to buy materials and tools to *dresser la boutique* in 1632.[116]

Obviously, such expenses were beyond the means of the average journeyman, unless he could find a lender or a bride with a substantial dowry. The marriage contract of master shoemaker Jean Lucotte announced that he had "heretofore passed master at his own expense . . . [and] he is at present burdened with some debts for this."[117] A preferable alternative to indebtedness, of course, was to find a benefactor. Often parents or in-laws directly subsidized the candidates, increasingly so in the seventeenth century. From 1551 to 1600, among 429 artisans or their sons married in Dijon, only 8 parents, future in-laws, or relatives (2 percent) explicitly offered to pay the groom's expenses to pass mastership. But from 1601 to 1650 this incidence increased to 15 percent (66 of 440).[118] Apparently the total costs of mastership increased in the seventeenth century, necessitating more aid from the family. Furthermore, between 1601 and 1650, all but five of these financial patrons were Dijonnais, and forty-eight of them local masters. A significant minority (eleven) of these forty-eight pursued a different trade from that of the beneficiary. The parochialism that was increasing in so many areas of artisan life is manifested in this desire of native masters to smooth the route to mastership (even in another guild) for their sons, sons-in-law, or nephews.

The other side of this policy was the exclusion of those who were not in the family. Traditionally, journeymen could anticipate promotion to mastership after apprenticeship and several years in the service of a master. As costs rose and the masters tightened their control, however, more and more journeymen were forced to remain

116. ADCO, *Notaires* #1952, 3 March 1632. Frequently, shop tools alone could cost fifty to one hundred livres. On the coppersmiths, see ADCO, *Notaires* #1941, 19 Dec. 1627, where tools of the trade are said to cost a hundred livres. Even the widow of a vinegar maker had tools worth forty livres. ADCO, BII 356/20, 3 Aug. 1645.

117. ADCO, *Notaires* #1948, 9 Feb. 1640. See also, for example, #1952, 30 March 1633, where parents agreed to pay the debts, including those "sustained in passing mastership."

118. See, for example, ADCO, *Notaires* #1683, 20 April 1625, where the mother of a cabinetmaker gives her son forty-five livres for "expenses of masterpiece," #1941, 21 Jan. 1627, where a father gives his son, a furrier, forty livres to "pass mastership," #36, 13 Dec. 1648, where parents of a chandler promise to pay his "mastership expenses," and #1944, 12 May 1650, where an uncle offers, as a wedding gift, to pay the expense of mastership for his nephew, a locksmith.

highly skilled wage laborers for years, even decades. Master shoemaker Louis Maillard, for example, had a forty-year-old journeyman from Lorraine in his service in 1643.[119] To men like Jean Barrot and Guillaume Mugnier it must have seemed as though mastership would never be attained. Barrot, a journeyman plasterer in 1556, was still not a master in 1573; the tailor Mugnier had been a journeyman for sixteen years in Dijon before he finally got his chance at mastership when the town council temporarily abolished the jurandes in 1617.[120] Between 1618 and 1622, among applications that tell us how long a candidate had worked in his trade (seventy-two cases involving sixteen trades), the average was over 10 years.[121] Weavers and shoemakers averaged 13.6 and 12.5 years respectively, perhaps because their guilds were more successful at restricting membership. Not surprisingly, many longtime journeymen were immigrants. Only one-seventh of the extant mastership letters granted before 1617 went to immigrants (53 of 357), but from 1618 to 1643, close to half (74 of 165) of them did.

These new masters had the town council to thank for their success. In 1617 the magistrates, backed by the crown, abolished the system of jurandes, replacing them with *métiers libres*. With this action, the council wrested control from the masters, albeit temporarily. It was, in one respect, an expression of exasperation on the part of the municipal authorities in the face of a blockade of admission to mastership. But it was also part of the broader issue of political jurisdiction, which concerned not only the town council of Dijon but the crown as well.

For a number of reasons the king favored a system of jurandes modeled on that of Paris for the entire kingdom. Several royal edicts in the sixteenth century explicitly display this intention, while revealing the abuses that most disturbed the crown. Villers-Cotterets in 1539 forbade the requirement of "dinners and banquets" used by masters to keep poorer journeymen out of their ranks.[122] More sweeping was the edict of 1581, by which Henri III sought to establish jurandes in every French town where they did not already exist. His intention was

---

119. ADCO, BII 360/60, 31 Dec. 1643.
120. AMD, B210, fol. 100v, 1573, G86, April 1618.
121. AMD, G83, 86, 87, 88, and 89 (mastership letters).
122. Quoted by Olivier-Martin, pp. 220–21.

to give order . . . against excessive expenses that the poor artisans of
the sworn towns are ordinarily constrained to make in order to
obtain the degree of mastership, against the tenor of the old ordinances, being sometimes a year and more to make a masterpiece
such that it pleases the jurés, which finally is found bad, and broken
by them if there is not a remedy by the said artisans, with infinite
presents and banquets. That drives many of them away from reaching the degree [of mastership] and constrains them to leave the
masters' [service] to labor *en chambres*: in which being found and
tormented by the said jurés, they are constrained once again to
work for the said masters, quite often less capable than they, only
being received to mastership by the said jurés those who have more
money and the means to give them gifts.

To prevent such abuses, "all artisans . . . working in . . . [the trades] at
the time of this publication will be required to take the oath of mastership before the ordinary judge of the place, either royal or subaltern."[123] Despite its forceful language, however, the edict remained
a dead letter, for the crown was preoccupied with the Wars of Religion and too weak to enforce its commands.

Henri III was addressing problems common to all French towns,
including Dijon. Venality and corruption repeatedly appear in the
Dijon documents. Masters continued to require applicants to supply
lavish banquets, whose onerous costs served as such an effective
obstacle to mastership. In 1606, for example, a cobbler complained to
the town council about the *festins et banquetz* demanded by the
masters of those "wishing to pass mastership," against the prohibitions of Parlement and the town council, not to mention royal
edicts.[124] The corruption of Dijon's jurés in the judgment of masterpieces, moreover, might have served the king as a model of this abuse.
Jurés loyal to their fellow masters wanted liberty to admit to mastership only the chosen few, and the assessment of masterpieces provided good opportunity to discriminate against undesirables. Thus
control over appointment of jurés was crucial both to masters intent
on closing ranks and to municipal magistrates intent on opening
them. No wonder the town council searched for loyal jurés and stayed
with them when they found them!

123. Quoted by Coornaert, p. 131.
124. AMD, B244, fol. 75r, 4 Aug. 1606. See also, AMD, G24, 8 Jan. 1584, where the
syndic petitions in the interest of nonmaster shoemakers and tailors protesting the
excessive cost of masterpieces and banquets and harassment by the masters, which is
contrary to the ordinances of the town council and the arrets of the Parlement of Dijon.

The statutes of all guilds stipulated that an alderman must be present at the judging of a masterpiece, no doubt as a precaution against prejudicial assessment, but jurés did their best to evade this regulation. In 1555 the locksmiths judged a masterpiece without calling an alderman, and forty years later the syndic of Dijon could still complain that many jurés were judging masterpieces without aldermen present and that they even had the "audacity and boldness" to admit individuals to mastership without notifying the municipal authorities.[125] The syndic renewed the command that an alderman witness the judging, but like previous ordinances, this one went unheeded. In 1606 the pastrycooks admitted Chrétien Guillen (the son of a master) to mastership without the permission of the town council.[126] By 1611 the syndic was complaining that a majority of the jurés of all the trades were judging masterpieces without aldermen present. His protest that such an "abuse is not reasonable to tolerate or suffer" was in vain.[127]

Another ploy was to demand more and more costly or difficult masterpieces of the applicants. To keep down expenses, the town council on several occasions ordered the masters to provide the raw materials for a candidate.[128] But the masters proved wily and dedicated foes, quite resourceful about their discrimination against unwelcome newcomers. One journeyman hatter protested to the town council that the masters were requiring him to make a masterpiece that was fifty years out of style—so obsolete that no master could even instruct him in how to make it! The masters responded that the statutes called for such a piece, that they could not just change the regulations on whim—and besides, the style might return. The magistrates ordered the applicant to do a simpler masterpiece in the house of a "nonsuspect" master and added to the statutes the qualification that masterpieces conform to current styles.[129]

Under the system of jurandes, the guilds, or perhaps more accurately the masters who politically dominated the guilds (we cannot assume that these were democratic institutions in an increasingly oligarchic age), had the authority to admit candidates to mastership;

125. AMD, B192, fol. 271v, 19 March 1555, B232, fol. 238v–239r, 7 April 1595.
126. AMD, B244, fol. 62v, 14 July 1606.
127. AMD, B248, fol. 247v, 11 May 1611.
128. For example, AMD, B215, fol. 219r, 7 Dec. 1579, B224, fol. 93r–v, 20 Sept. 1586, fol. 178v, 10 Jan. 1587.
129. AMD, B216, fol. 104r–v, 5 May 1579.

the town council had only the right of final approval. So rampant were the abuses, however, that the municipal magistrates became convinced that the only effective way to reform the selection of new masters was to abolish the jurandes. They envisioned a guild system in which application for mastership and proof of capability would go directly through the town council. The new system would wrest control of the flow of new masters from those who had a vested interest in stemming that flow and would give the council a larger hand in guild governance.

It was not a new idea. As early as 1529 the mayor of Dijon had tried to abolish the jurandes, but without success.[130] Since that time, the power and independence of the guilds had increased so much that by 1600 the municipal authorities were truly alarmed. When the Estates General of 1614 recommended doing away with jurandes throughout the realm, Dijon's mayor capitalized on the opportunity; he asked the king, futilely it turned out, to do so for Dijon.[131] By then the Dijon authorities felt that the masters' stranglehold on admission to mastership was, among other things, creating a shortage of skilled workers. Ambitious and capable journeymen were not inclined to remain in a town where access to mastership appeared a remote possibility; they preferred to migrate to more open towns like Lyons or other *villes libres*.[132]

The problems were not localized in Dijon. Other "sworn towns" in Burgundy felt the same pressure, and one by one, they began to abolish the jurandes. Autun acted in 1615, and as a ville libre it became a magnet for journeymen in Burgundian "sworn towns." These towns soon felt the loss of workers, and so Chalon-sur-Saône followed suit in 1616, and Beaune in 1617.[133] Suffering the loss of skilled labor to neighboring villes libres, Dijon soon abolished its jurandes too.

Abolition required royal approval, and the crown found itself in an awkward position. The system of jurandes was in the royal interest, but the crown was on record against the abuses of that system. In the case of Dijon, moreover, there were other considerations. Louis XIII was not completely convinced of the loyalty of the frontier town. Scarcely twenty years before, Dijon had staunchly supported the duc

130. Hauser, "L'organisation du travail," p. 128.
131. Chapuis, *Les anciennes corporations*, p. 13.
132. Hauser, "L'organisation du travail," p. 142.
133. Ibid., pp. 134 (Autun), 136 (Chalon), 140 (Beaune).

de Mayenne against the Bourbons during the Wars of Religion, and
the memory was still painfully fresh. The young king opted for mol-
lification. On 22 August 1617 when the municipal request for the
abolition of the jurandes in Dijon reached him, he approved it. Letters
patent revoking the statutes were issued in September and registered
at the Parlement of Dijon on 17 November:

> Louis . . . having recognized the great abuses and monopolies that
> are committed by means of masterships . . . under the pretext of
> masterpiece, that are rendered so expensive by the master jurés
> because of the superfluous and useless expenses that they constrain
> those who wish to pass mastership to make, which has rebuffed a
> quantity of good workers who wished to live in the said town, in
> which the worst are received for money and by corruption; it has
> been deliberated by us . . . to have . . . the suppression and abolition
> of the said masterships. . . . Having more of an occasion to gratify
> our said town of Dijon than any other of our province of Burgundy,
> for being the most capable of it and the most recommendable, the
> petitioners [Dijon's magistrates] having always demonstrated to our
> predecessor the King and to our service a great loyalty and affection
> . . . we, by revoking and suppressing the said . . . jurandes, say and
> declare . . . that in the future it be permitted to all artisans to labor
> in their trades . . . and to open a shop . . . [in Dijon], without being
> subject to make any masterpiece.[134]

The new system retained jurés but left primary regulation of the
corporations to the town council and did away with all the requirements the masters had used so effectively to block accession.

The howl of protest from the masters was immediate. The master
pastrycooks appealed directly to the king, contesting the legality of
the revocation of their statutes. Much to the consternation of Dijon's
magistrates, Louis responded with letters patent exempting the pastrycooks from the general suppression, citing the precedent of his
father's letters patent, which had extended their autonomy, and his
own confirmation of them in 1613.[135] Spying the chink in municipal
armor, other guilds rushed to follow the pastrycooks' example. They
filed what was in effect a class-action suit with the king, contesting
the abolition of the jurande system in Dijon. The registers of the
Conseil Privé du Roy in December 1619 recorded the results:

134. Louis quoted ibid., p. 146.
135. AMD, G61, 22 May 1619.

Between the Master Painters, Glassmakers, Embroiderers, Tailors, Tinsmiths, Roofers/Tilers, Carpenters, Cabinetmakers, Shoemakers, Glovers, and other residents of the Town of Dijon, Plaintiffs in Request of the 16th day of May 1619 on the one hand; and Master Barthélemy Morreau, Procureur-Syndic of the said Town of Dijon, Defendant, on the other. SEEN by the King in his Council the said request . . . THE KING IN HIS COUNCIL . . . ORDERED AND ORDERS that no one will hereafter be admitted to open a shop, and exercise *Art* or *Mestier* in the Town of Dijon, without having made the masterpiece . . . which . . . will be done without expenses, banquets or festivities: And the said masterpieces will be made in the presence of an Alderman of the Town [and] . . . two Masters of the Trade. . . . And to this end will be addressed Letters Patent to the . . . Parlement of Dijon.[136]

Essentially, it was a restatement of Henri III's stillborn edict of 1581. The royal turnabout, tantamount to a resurrection of the jurande system, muted the recent victory of a now sorely embarrassed town council. It returned the council and the guilds to the bitter status quo ante, the masters trying to curtail admission to mastership and the magistrates trying to open it.

Judging from the numbers of mastership letters granted by the town council immediately after the abolition, for a time the council had the upper hand. Even before the king came to their rescue in late 1619, however, the guilds had tried to keep to their old ways. The syndic reported to the town council in August 1618 that all the guildsmen, by common agreement among themselves, were continuing to require masterpieces of candidates for mastership.[137] Disturbed by a solidarity that crossed guild lines, he added that "shoemakers, cobblers, butchers, blacksmiths, and others" were manifesting serious discontent, gathering in vociferous assemblies to protest the abolition of the jurandes and to demand their reestablishment. To the magistrates, such collective behavior smacked of sedition; a *proclamat* was issued prohibiting "all artisans of whatever condition . . . to assemble or *faire conventiculles* either in houses, in the streets, or elsewhere" in groups of more than two or three "under pain of being hanged and strangled."[138] The threat of rebellion was in the air.

---

136. AMD, G77, 30 Dec. 1619, a file containing a small bound volume: *Arrest du conseil privé du roy* (Dijon, 1674).

137. AMD, B256, fol. 104r, 21 Aug. 1618.

138. Ibid., fol. 178r–179r, 7 Dec. 1618.

Municipal proclamations and even the royal edict notwithstanding, in 1620 a journeyman chandler complained to the authorities that the masters of his trade had conspired in "illegal assemblies" to keep him from mastership. In 1624 another journeyman protested to the town council that the master cabinetmakers were preventing him from finishing his masterpiece and were requiring him to give banquets and festivities for the masters. Evidently the council had accepted the king's abrogation of the abolition of the jurandes, for they ordered this man to finish the masterpiece.[139]

For the next decade or so the sources are frustratingly silent on this issue. Until 1636 the town council said nothing about admission to mastership in its deliberations, and from 1622 to 1638 few mastership letters exist (whether they have been lost or were never issued is unknown). We do know, however, that in 1646 Dijon's magistrates once again challenged the requirements of masterpieces, festivities, and "payment of immense sums" by those seeking mastership. This time they chose a new tack, invoking the authority of the royal letters patent that had suppressed the jurande system and disregarding its subsequent reestablishment.[140] Perhaps not coincidentally, letters of mastership begin to turn up in the municipal archives again after a hiatus of nearly fifteen years.[141]

The same litany of complaints that filled the petitions for admission to mastership in 1617 reappear in the petitions after 1638. A weaver claimed that his masterpiece was rejected by the jurés "in hatred"; a hatter accused the masters of not allowing him to finish his masterpiece; a journeyman currier begged the council to release him from his "oppression," claiming that the masters had "conceived a mortal hatred against him, and [were] resolved not to admit him to mastership," or at least to make it cost more than he could afford.[142] The masters meant business, and their tactics could sometimes get violent. François Millière, for example, alleged that the master carpenters had a "conspiracy" against the journeymen and had even dealt blows to intimidate them from seeking mastership.[143]

139. AMD, G88, Dec. 1620, B262, fol. 66r, 9 Aug. 1624.
140. AMD, B284, fol. 113r, 1646.
141. The flood of letters after the abolition of the jurandes lasted into 1621, but only one letter from 1622, one from 1629, and one from 1630 appear in the archives. Then, in 1638 seven appeared. AMD, G88, 89.
142. AMD, G89, Nov. 1638, Jan. 1639, Feb. 1642.
143. Ibid., May 1642.

Dedicated to regulating their numbers and thereby increasing their wealth, the masters proved a recalcitrant foe. When the town council struck again in 1646, this time abolishing the jurande system by municipal decree, enforcement proved difficult. The magistrates considered the "absolute power" of the masters over admission to mastership an affront to magisterial authority. Moreover, the high costs of mastership made it necessary for those who did get in to charge high prices for their products in order to recoup their entry expenses. Consumers, the magistrates noted, had to bear the brunt of expensive masterships. The council was also afraid that journeymen would not remain in a town where access to mastership was but a remote possibility and that Dijon would therefore lose its skilled work force. This time, the town council took every precaution, authorizing massive fines of five hundred livres for any violation.[144]

Henri Hauser tells us that the city magistrates succeeded and that 1646 marks the end of Dijon's jurande system.[145] In fact, however, the gap between complete municipal control over the guilds desired by the council and the reality of substantial guild autonomy still yawned. There is evidence that the masters persisted in their old tricks and even tried some new ones. Again they spanned guild boundaries; masters of different guilds gathered in secret assemblies and agreed not to give depositions regarding an applicant's *vie et moeurs* or his capability—requisite preconditions for mastership according to the new municipal decree.[146] The masters were even suspected of trying to incite "popular sedition" against the magistrates (just how is unclear).[147] Galvanized by economic interest and girded by a solidarity that transcended guilds, the masters continued to try to enforce the old way. In February 1647, for example, one master tinsmith threatened a candidate for mastership with a beating if he did not do a masterpiece (no longer legally required), and in May of that year the master hatters tried to make Jean Petitjean pay thirty-four livres for a banquet for them before admitting him.[148] In light of these incidents, it seems likely that the jurande system of work or-

144. AMD, B284, fol. 1131–1151, 12 Oct. 1646.
145. Hauser, "L'organisation du travail," pp. 158–60. Hauser seems to have been unaware of Louis's abrogation of the letters that abolished the jurandes in Dijon and so had some difficulty explaining the resurgence of the jurandes between 1618 and 1646.
146. AMD, B284, fol. 179r–v, 20 Dec. 1646.
147. Ibid.
148. Ibid., fol. 235v, 6 Feb. 1647, fol. 291r, 27 May 1647.

ganization did not suddenly die in 1646 when the council abolished it. Instead, master and magistrate continued at loggerheads at least until the middle of the seventeenth century.

The struggle between the guilds and the municipality has much to say about the distribution of power within Dijon and also throughout the kingdom. Clearly, the master artisans understood that the king would look kindly upon any effort that might undermine municipal authority. They exploited the king's desire to subject the cities to royal authority and assumed an important role in the contest over the bounds of royal and municipal jurisdiction. As more and more studies are showing, the *mainmise royale*, though at times evident in early modern France, was hardly a smooth or uninterrupted process. Venality of office and systems of clientage rendered ostensibly royal institutions semi-independent, and overlapping jurisdictions virtually assured competition between them.

For example, especially in the seventeenth century, the royal officials at the bailliage assertively confronted municipal authority over the *police des métiers*. If part of the royal plan was to reduce municipal autonomy, these officials seem to have been loyal to the king's will. Baillis were loosely defined as *juges de police* so they could justify their jurisdiction over questions of work. They had actively intervened in the life of the craft guilds since the late Middle Ages in other parts of France.[149] Thus there was ample precedent to draw upon when the bailliage court in Dijon turned its attention to the guilds. Master artisans, perhaps aware of the conflict between royal and municipal jurisdiction, often played the town council against the bailliage by appealing municipal decisions to this royal court. It was a well-chosen tactic, since the records show that there was a good chance that the bailliage would rule against the municipal position, occasionally without explanation. For example, in 1625 the master coopers appealed to the bailliage to overturn a municipal decision to raise the number of its jurés from six to eight because of the large wine harvest that year. The bailliage ruled in the coopers' favor but supplied no reasons for its position.[150] In the majority of the documents I have located the bailliage reversed the decision of the town

---

149. Hauser, "Les pouvoirs publics," p. 192. Coornaert, pp. 96–97, states that a "regular procedure was established in the courts of the bailliage for the constitution of guilds, the making of regulations, the election of *jurés*, [and] the reception of masters."
150. AMD, G72, June–July 1625.

council.[151] Usually the council appealed to the royal Parlement, where it apparently received a more favorable hearing. There is no clear evidence, at least, of bias against the council.[152]

Another royal institution that challenged municipal authority was the Cours des Monnaies, which tried to seize control of trades using precious metals, especially goldsmithing. Again the issue centered on that all-important office of juré. Since the Middle Ages the town council had had the right to appoint one goldsmith juré and approve the election of the other. Sometime in the second half of the sixteenth century, apparently, the officials at the Cours des Monnaies attempted to assume these functions, for in 1587 the council petitioned Parlement to enjoin them from receiving and investing the goldsmith jurés with their office.[153] It is unclear how these royal officials justified this new jurisdictional claim, but the assault continued in 1604, when the town council again protested the encroachment of the officials of the Monnaies. In their petition to Parlement the magistrates asserted that "the jurisdiction of the town of Dijon has been founded since time immemorial upon a grant from the dukes of Burgundy, predecessors of our kings who have conceded the said jurisdiction." They added that these exclusive prerogatives of the town council included regulation of the goldsmiths—specifically the privilege of shop visitation to detect "faults and abuses," to judge masterpieces, to invest the jurés with their office, and perhaps most important of all, to assess fines. Contrary to what the général des monnaies claimed, the city magistrates asserted, the officials of the Monnaies had never had this authority, and even though some goldsmiths had let these royal officials visit their shops, this usurpation was illegal and was not authorized by the crown.[154]

151. See, for example, AMD, G32, concerning a cloth cutter admitted to mastership by the bailliage against municipal opinion, G9, July 1553, in which the bailliage overturns a municipal decision on workmanship quality, G293, 13 April 1566, G62, June 1609–5 Feb. 1611, and G30, 1629. The bailliage issued letters of mastership sold by the crown for ceremonial celebrations (for example, ADCO, E3453, 3 Dec. 1583), but this prerogative was challenged by the town council (AMD, G29, July–Aug. 1588).

152. Appeals were possible only if fines exceeded sixty-five sous or there was a question of bodily mutilation or death. C. Bertucat, "La jurisdiction municipale de Dijon: Son étendue," *Revue Bourguignonne* 21 (1911): 172. The general contours of a conflict over centralization between crown and town are clear enough, though a thorough study of royal patronage as well as recruitment to the royal courts would be useful in clarifying the dynamics of this jurisdictional conflict.

153. AMD, G60, 11 July 1589.

154. Ibid., 7 May 1604.

Even though the council pointed to royal justification in this juris-dictional conflict, by 1637 it had lost the battle for control of the wealthy goldsmith guild. Thenceforth, regulation of the goldsmiths, with the concomitant revenue, was the exclusive prerogative of the Cours des Monnaies.[155] I could find no evidence that the officials of the Monnaies were acting on explicit instructions from the central administration, but it does appear that royal officials were con-tinually gaining the upper hand over municipal magistrates. In that year, for example, a journeyman goldsmith received his letters of mastership not from the town council but from the général des mon-naies of Burgundy and Bresse.[156]

The beleaguered town council also found itself in conflict with *juges-consuls*, or judges of merchant courts, which were established by royal decree in November 1563 upon request from the merchants of Paris and quickly extended throughout the realm.[157] On 10 April 1565 a court of juges-consuls was established in Dijon by letters pat-ent "for the judgment of causes and affairs concerning the fact of merchandise."[158] This vague jurisdictional specification left the door open for conflict among judicial bodies. A parlementary arret, follow-ing a request from the town council, prohibited the juges-consuls from hearing cases involving artisans (undoubtedly meaning masters since they were by law the only artisans permitted to engage in com-merce). The arret repeated that their jurisdiction was limited to cases between merchants and forbade artisans to take cases to the mer-chant's court under pain of a three-hundred-livre fine.[159]

Apparently, the arret was not rigorously observed, for twenty years later Parlement found it necessary to issue a nearly identical arret, and in 1612 the town council again complained to the Parlement that juges-consuls were encroaching on the magistrates' jurisdiction over cases involving artisans.[160] The crown further muddied the waters when the king's Conseil d'Etat, responding to a request from the juges-consuls of Dijon, issued an arret of its own, granting the mer-chant's court jurisdiction to hear "cases of merchants *and artisans* for

155. Garnier, *Les anciens orfèvres*, pp. 15–16. See also Boissonnade, p. 100.
156. AMD, G60, 6 July 1637.
157. Emile de Levasseur, *Histoire des classes ouvrières en France depuis la con-quête de Jules César jusqu'à la révolution*, 2 vols. (Paris, 1859), 2:45.
158. Bertucat, p. 174.
159. AMD, G231, 10 Feb. 1589.
160. Ibid., 8 Aug. 1609, 16 May 1612.

the fact of merchandise" and permitting them "to impose and raise
from . . . [the merchants and artisans] the sum of fifteen hundred
livres, in order to establish a 'council chamber' for the exercise of
their said jurisdiction in the . . . marketplace of the said Dijon." The
town council protested, fearing a loss of jurisdiction over the commercial activity of the increasingly prosperous master artisanat.[161]

In 1622 the juges-consuls attempted to tax merchants and master
artisans. Again the town council protested to the Parlement, claiming
that the impost included many "simple artisans" who by no stretch of
the imagination could qualify as merchants. The Parlement asked the
juges-consuls for a list of those to be taxed; on this roll were a number
of artisans and even vignerons, and 76 of the 183 on the list were
craftsmen with no designation of merchant at all.[162] Much of the
confusion stemmed from differing interpretations of the word *merchant*; so in 1625 Parlement stipulated that artisans who did not
"make traffic and negotiation of merchandise wholesale" were exempt from the jurisdiction of the merchant's court.[163] Legislating
was one thing, however, and enforcing quite another. Despite the
arret, the battle continued at least to 1641, when another parlementary arret, again issued at the request of the municipal magistrates,
repeated that artisans were not under the jurisdiction of the juges-
consuls and prohibited artisans from taking the title of merchant.[164]

The juges-consuls, like the royal judicial officers, simply could not
resist the temptation to draw the artisans into their jurisdictional net.
It is likely that the growing economic resources of the craftsmen
provided as much stimulus as any abstract notion of the royal will.
Opportunity opened for the juges-consuls because master artisans
were engaged in mercantile activity—quite likely many pursued both
retail and small-scale wholesale trade—and found it reasonable to
take their cases to the merchants' court (they doubtless preferred it
to the town council in any case). Economic realities seldom conform
to neat juridical boundaries.

At any rate, and this is the important point, master artisans were

161. Quoted by Bertucat, pp. 174–5, my italics. See also, AMD, B250, fol. 173r.
162. Since many of the occupational descriptions are in a different ink, they may
have been added later, perhaps by the Parlement after it was determined who was an
artisan. AMD, G232, 16, 22 March 1622.
163. AMD, G231, 9 Dec. 1625.
164. Bertucat, p. 175; BMD, ms 1496, arret, 15 April 1641.

important actors in the jurisdictional conflicts that pertained directly
to the effectiveness of royal power in the provinces. Master artisans
exploited these conflicts to advance their own interests, and at least
until 1650 it was the municipal authority that appeared the greatest
threat to the autonomy they desired.

## Conflicts and Solidarities at Work

Master artisans unquestionably possessed a solidarity that transcended guild boundaries. Certainly there was conflict between craft
guilds, but corporatism did not necessarily set masters of one trade
against those of others. Curiously enough, corporate monopolies
could enhance master solidarity, for if they were respected, monopolies prevented competition outside the craft and hence eliminated
discord among artisans in different trades. Corporatism, if properly
enforced, encouraged peaceful relations among master craftsmen and
tended to produce consensus. In fact, of course, harmony did not
always prevail, and complaints of encroachment and interloping between trades are by no means rare. We know that the privilege of
monopoly was jealously guarded and, judging from the number of
complaints reaching the authorities, that it was increasingly violated.

There was seldom any dispute about the legal boundaries between
trades. Specialization of technique was carefully delineated in the
guild statutes, especially for related trades, where the opportunity to
encroach upon the monopoly of another lay ready to hand. It was easy
for a tailor of men's clothing to make women's.[165] A baker could omit
the leavening and thereby bake items reserved to the pastrycooks.[166]
A saddler could easily make a harness,[167] or a cobbler a new pair of

165. The division of labor among tailors advanced to the specialization of makers of
men's and women's clothing in the sixteenth century. Chapuis, *Les anciennes corporations*, p. 228. This distinction was institutionalized before 1577, when a tailor was
accused by the jurés of working on men's clothing though his masterpiece was done in
women's. AMD, B208, fol. 148v, 12 Feb. 1577. For a similar dispute, see AMD, B244,
fol. 73r, 31 July 1606.

166. For example, on 20 July 1625 the town council declared that it was a violation
of the pastrycooks' monopoly for anyone else to make "unleavened cakes or *gallettes
de pâtes.*" AMD, B263, fol. 54r. For an earlier example of bakers encroaching on the
pastrycooks by making "flans, tarts and cakes," see AMD, B208, fol. 183r-v, 30 April
1577.

167. For example, AMD, B212, fol. 168r, 22 April 1575.

shoes. But these were considered serious violations, occasionally even reaching the Parlement for adjudication, and were punished with severity.[168]

Nevertheless such poaching increased, and the masters had their own policy to blame. They had done their best to control their numbers in the interest of improving their economic standing, and they had generally succeeded. While the artisan population was held in check, the general population of Dijon grew, stimulating demand for local products and increasing the wealth of the masters. But the masters were unwilling to accept all the consequences. Chandlers could not abide it when butchers illicitly sold candles (easily produced from the by-products of the butchers' trade), nor would hosiers stand for it when tailors made and sold stockings.[169]

Most monopoly infringement was probably not done by masters, however. Though it is often difficult to determine the status of the offender against the monopoly, it is certain that a major motivation to encroach upon another's trade was poverty. Since most masters were not poor, it seems likely that most of the interlopers were journeymen or other nonmasters, as was the case in illegal competition within a trade. Those caught frequently claimed that they had no other way to earn their living.[170] Even more telling, in 1596 the blacksmiths requested guild statutes for the first time from the town council because "many abuses are committed in the exercise of their art, because a great number of vagabonds are drawn into this town and are practicing the blacksmith trade."[171] Similarly, peddlers and hawkers sold meat on the black market in remote alleyways to avoid the butchers' visitation.[172] Because examples of encroachment are so

168. For example, in 1639 the shoemakers appealed all the way to the Parlement, arguing that the cobblers had been making new shoes, a prerogative reserved for the shoemakers. ADCO, E3388. On a conflict between the cabinetmakers and carpenters, see AMD, G186, 9 June 1607. Carpenters were allowed to work only "with white wood like fir in making boards." AMD, B217, fol. 27v, 31 July 1579.

169. For example, AMD, G7, n.d.

170. There are many examples throughout the period, but they are most frequent in the sixteenth century. See, for example, AMD, G67, 29 July 1561, B204, fol. 60r–v, 12 Aug. 1567 (where sixteen men and women were accused of selling candles and oil and all claimed they did it to make ends meet), B205, fol. 55v–56r, Aug. 1568, B237, fol. 52v–53r, 12 Nov. 1599.

171. AMD, G49, 22 March 1596.

172. AMD, B200, fol. 90r, 26 Oct. 1563.

frequent in the archival records, it is impossible not to conclude that demand for consumer items surpassed the productive capacity of Dijon's master artisans and tempted many nonmasters into clandestine production to fill the vacuum.[173] Of course, this kind of monopoly infringement would draw masters together.

In some respects masters also formed a solid and cohesive bloc within the guild. Beyond the mutual interest of curtailment of admission to mastership, there was the economic advantage of the legal monopoly to unify them. Nonetheless, discord there was. Because of the nature of the sources, conflict reaches the eyes of the historian much more readily and frequently than peaceful consensus, but the numerous incidents of conflict among masters and between masters and journeymen in the same trade suggest that legal corporatism did not ensure complete solidarity within crafts. There were many instances of illicit, clandestine competition from journeymen. Tempted by growing demand, vast numbers of them were contracting with clients or producing and selling items, activities reserved exclusively for masters. The problem of "room-workers" (*chambrellans*), entered the deliberations of the authorities with extraordinary frequency, and they found themselves in an ambiguous position with regard to this abuse. They recognized that such production helped fill demand. Still, totally unregulated production and sale were anathema to both magistrate and master, though for different reasons. As long as chambrellans escaped municipal regulation, the town council, always worried about social control, could neither protect consumers by safeguarding quality and controlling prices nor collect fines for violations. The masters, of course, felt the competition in their pocketbooks. At their urgings, the town council periodically rounded up dozens of chambrellans from different trades and hauled them in. The culprits were then fined and ordered to work only for masters, or if the council was actively trying to increase the number of masters, they were commanded to make their masterpieces.[174]

173. Besides poverty, social pressure could drive a craftsman to violate a monopoly. To cite perhaps a typical example, a tailor was apprehended by the hosier jurés for making stockings. Under questioning the culprit revealed that he had been asked by a "gentleman" to make them and had been given the cloth to do so. AMD, B192, fol. 95r, 20 July 1554. An identical instance occurred in 1580. AMD, B217, fol. 68v, 29 Jan. 1580. It was certainly not in a master craftsman's interest to decline such requests, especially if he, like many masters, was entwined in his superior's clientage network.

174. For example, AMD, B190, fol. 142v, 2 Dec. 1552 (plasterers), B202, fol. 12r, 14

Masters disputed with each other for many different reasons. They accused the jurés of prejudicial visitations or incompetence.[175] They argued over debts.[176] By far the greatest source of conflict among masters in the same guild, however, was the division of the market and especially the labor supply. We have already seen how competitive the bidding for public works contracts could be. There are other examples of competition for the expanding market of Dijon. In 1608 a chandler told the magistrates that the jurés had unjustly accused him of making poor-quality candles; he alleged that the visitation was prompted by animosity on the part of the other master chandlers because he was selling at a lower price. Perhaps the other masters were justified in their suspicions, since the confiscated candles were underweight and had inadequate wicks. No wonder he could sell for less![177] Two weeks earlier two master pastrycooks had apprehended another master's apprentice selling *oublies* in the street. Resenting such competition in front of their shop, they upset his box and spilled his crackers onto the pavement.[178]

Jealousy over market share is probably the reason most masters objected to admitting "masters of letters" to the guild. Journeymen with sufficient funds could sometimes circumvent the requirement of making a masterpiece by purchasing letters of mastership from the crown. One of many royal fiscal expedients, these letters were ostensibly issued to celebrate the births of dauphins. The masters of letters were harassed by the established masters, who often referred to these unwelcome newcomers as "mortal enemies."[179] The masters were far from eager to share the market and the labor supply.

Masters in the same corporation also had to compete for the supply of skilled labor, which, because of their own exclusionary policies,

---

March 1553 (painters), B199, fol. 40v–41r, 29 July 1561 (chandlers), B200, fol. 116r, 3 Dec. 1563 (locksmiths), B203, fol. 77v, 3 Sept. 1556 (many trades), B217, fol. 44r, 18 Sept. 1579 (tailors), B203, fol. 147v, 21 Jan. 1567 (parchment makers), B210, fol. 78v–79r, 31 Oct. 1572 (roofers), B217, fol. 20r, 3 July 1579 (coppersmiths), fol. 79r, 22 March 1580 (many trades), B235, fol. 82r, 22 Aug. 1597 (carpenters), B248, fol. 134r, 26 Oct. 1610, B275, fol. 144v, 1 Dec. 1637 (cabinetmakers), B273, fol. 245v–246r, 27 April 1635 (masons).

175. For example, AMD, G24, 17 May 1571.

176. For example, ADCO, BII 360/60, 6 Oct. 1643.

177. AMD, G7, 1 Dec. 1608.

178. ADCO, BII 360/57, 19 Nov. 1608. On competition for raw materials, see AMD, B217, fol. 19r, 30 June 1579.

179. For example, AMD, B188, fol. 219r–220r, 5 June 1551, B191, fol. 172r, 16 March 1554, B203, fol. 42v, 17 July 1566.

remained limited. Unemployment or underemployment of skilled journeymen and apprentices seems not to have existed in Dijon for most of the period. The general population growth and expanding wealth buoyed demand for artisan services and products. In the sixteenth century the Wars of Religion drained off journeymen into the armies, creating a labor shortage that masters decried.[180] Meanwhile, the masters' exclusivism discouraged many journeymen from remaining in a city where they had little hope of becoming masters themselves. The resultant scarcity of skilled labor put masters in conflict with each other, and it was the catalyst for two significant developments: proletarianization of some poorer masters and the growth of journeymen brotherhoods called *compagnonnages*.

Poor masters worked as salaried laborers for other masters in Paris as early as the thirteenth century, and this practice was still in evidence in Lille at the end of the seventeenth.[181] In Dijon it appeared sometime after the Wars of Religion,[182] evidence of a dearth of skilled labor in the face of heavy demand, which pushed into the wage-earning ranks those impoverished masters (certainly a small minority as my economic discussion in Chapter 2 will show) who, for one reason or another, could not compete with the other masters. Not accidentally, this phenomenon coincided with the firm institutionalization of compagnonnages as autonomous forces in the battle for control over the labor market.

The masters tried to suppress competition in their own ranks by regulating the distribution of labor in Dijon. The statutes of several guilds stipulate how many workers a master may retain, and significantly, some trades added such requirements during the late sixteenth or early seventeenth centuries.[183] This portioning-out of workers suggests that the issue had become a source of friction among masters. Certainly, such regulations would have had little

180. A master complained to the magistrates that all the good workers were in the army and those available were undisciplined ne'er-do-wells. See AMD, B223, fol. 131r–v, 10 Jan. 1586.

181. On Paris, see Geremek, *Le salariat*, p. 67; on Lille, Alain Lottin, *Chavatte, ouvrier Lillois: Un contemporain de Louis XIV* (Paris, 1979), p. 98.

182. Some marriage contracts state that master craftsman grooms receive *avis* from their masters, sometimes adding that they reside with them. I have found examples of shoemakers, bakers, cobblers, cabinetmakers, blacksmiths, turners, and toolmakers. See for example, ADCO, *Notaires* #730, 14 June 1583, #202, 24 Nov. 1602, #1951, 31 Jan. 1637, #1949, 6 July 1642, #1944, 20 Jan. 1649 and 22 May 1650.

183. For example, Chapuis, *Les anciennes corporations*, pp. 178 (cloth cutters), and 288 (shoemakers).

purpose had there been a glut of skilled workers. Moreover, the same pressure that generated the bylaws produced many violations.[184] The most frequent offenders in the seventeenth century were masters who enticed workers away from other masters. Shoemakers, cabinet-makers, tailors, locksmiths, weavers, and no doubt others accused their colleagues of luring their journeymen away.[185]

The most important threat to the master's attempt to control the labor supply, however, came from the compagnonnages, one of the earliest forms of worker solidarity, formed in the crucible of conflict with the master. These brotherhoods of journeymen were essentially but not exclusively economic institutions designed to help workers control the labor market and, indirectly, the wages paid.[186] They developed within craft corporations; in the sixteenth and seventeenth centuries there was no worker solidarity across corporate boundaries nor were there competitive brotherhoods in the same trades. But unmistakably, in some trades some journeymen were squaring off against their masters.

The situation was by no means a monodimensional confrontation between well-defined classes. Relations between masters and jour-neymen were complex and ambiguous. Antagonism over job place-ment, for example, could often be muted by traditions of *fidélité personnelle*, particularly if a journeyman felt his prospects for admis-sion to mastership were reasonably bright (to avoid demographic sui-cide the masters had to admit some journeymen to mastership). On the other hand, the exclusionary policy created a pool of workers who, seeing that their chances at mastership were slim, concluded

184. For example, AMD, B193, fol. 34r, 16 July 1555, B194, fol. 65v, 4 Aug. 1556, B213, fol. 167v, 5 June 1576. There are other indicators of labor shortage. The cabinet-maker jurés denied a turner the service of a journeyman cabinetmaker, because the master cabinetmakers demanded that the journeymen work only for them. AMD, G9, 14 Aug. 1584. The tailor jurés ordered a widow who had been secretly keeping three tailor journeymen in her service to release them to go to work for the masters in the trade. AMD, B219, fol. 119v, 9 March 1582.

185. Examples are frequent, as are the town council's pronouncements against *ser-viteurs et servantes* who left their masters without prior permission. See, for example, AMD, B237, fol. 184v, 20 June 1600, B256, fol. 132r–v, 25 Sept. 1618, B272, fol. 192v, 12 Jan. 1635, G186, 16 Dec. 1644.

186. Henri Hauser, *Les compagnonnages d'arts et métiers à Dijon aux XVIIe et XVIIIe siècles* (Paris, 1907), p. 1. See also Cynthia M. Truant, "Independent and Inso-lent: Journeymen and Their 'Rites' in the Old Regime Workplace," in Kaplan and Koepp, pp. 131–75.

that control of the labor market could at least improve their conditions as lifelong workers.

The compagnonnage was not just an economic institution; it was also a social one, though again it was defined in the face of the intense parochialism of the antagonistic native Dijonnais masters. Since most journeymen came from outside Dijon, they were not easily integrated into a society that prized familiarity and close social relations and therefore was suspicious of transients and immigrants. Outsiders, for their part, tended to seek out their fellows and remain segregated from the natives. Nonetheless, the institutional development of the compagnonnage, which accelerated in the sixteenth century, cannot be attributed to the need for socializing. Transients and immigrants had been seeking out their own kind since the Middle Ages, but only under the new economic conditions did the position of many journeymen crystallize in opposition to that of the masters.

The basic characteristics of the compagnonnages were much the same throughout France. Their roots, perhaps, were in the migrations of artisans during the Middle Ages. In some places by the fourteenth century it was already difficult for journeymen to become masters, and some migrated to seek a better opportunity to rise. But the important factor was the varying demand for workers. By the second half of the sixteenth century it had become customary for journeymen to seek favorable situations, moving if work was unavailable and being drawn to areas where workers were in short supply, but now these workers were becoming better organized, no doubt because labor scarcity was increasingly acute.[187] By 1650, common attributes were largely defined. One of the most important was the *tour de France*, first mentioned in written sources in 1469 and likely an outgrowth of the migrations of journeymen. By the early modern period the tour was undertaken by journeymen from many trades and many regions of France.[188] Young artisans embarked on the tour for different reasons. Many petitions for admission to mastership proudly state that the applicant went on the tour to gain experience with a wide variety of masters and techniques and also, quite a few add, "to see the country."[189] The tour might end at any time, perhaps when a journey-

187. Bronislaw Geremek, "Les migrations des compagnons au bas moyen âge," *Studia Historiae Oeconomicae* 5 (1970): 67, 78.

188. Luc Benoist, *Le compagnonnage et les métiers*, 4th ed. (Paris, 1980), p. 25.

189. Albert Colombet, *L'artisanat en Bourgogne* (Strasbourg, 1976), p. 20. See for

man fortuitously found a town where the route to mastership looked promising. But since many, no doubt, were lured to the open road by the promise of adventure, untimely ends were all too common. Journeymen were aware of the danger of traveling early modern roads, and some made out their wills before embarking.[190]

Dijon was one of the most important stops on the tour, though no prescribed route was set out until the nineteenth century.[191] A shoemaker might go from Dijon down the Saône to Chalon, Tournus, Mâcon, Lyons, and Vienne, while a glover might visit Paris, Lyons, Avignon, Marseilles, and other towns including Dijon. One remarkable cabinetmaker not only stopped in Lyons, Provins, and Grenoble before coming to Dijon but had wandered down into Italy as well.[192] Journeymen from all over France—Gascony, Toulouse, Rouen, Brittany, Picardy, Lorraine, and elsewhere—appear in Dijon's records.

When a compagnon arrived in a town he went to the house of the *mère*, usually an inn or a tavern, where he received lodging until he either found employment or left. There was a network of these way stations and clearinghouses throughout the realm.[193] After being received by representatives of the compagnons already situated in the town, the journeyman paid a fee called the *bienvenue*, had his name inscribed on a roll, and frequently had to pay for some form of festivities or libations. In Dijon the cutlers were assessing newcomers a bienvenue as early as 1464.[194] The fees went into a common treasury, the *boîte*, which was used by the compagnonnage for religious services, to care for sick members, or for other forms of mutual aid.[195] Occasionally the newcomer was required to demonstrate his abilities

---

example, AMD, G86, 11 Oct. 1630. I found tanners (AMD, G86, Feb. 1618), bakers (G86, March 1618), tailors (G88, July 1619), cobblers (G88, Jan. 1621), plasterers (G89, March 1642), shoemakers (G86, March and May 1618 and Oct. 1630), cabinetmakers (G88, Nov. 1618 and June 1619), and glovers (G87, Feb. 1619, and G88, Oct. 1621)—all engaged in the tour.

190. See, for example, ADCO, *Notaires* #965, 2 April 1643, #1223, 1 Sept. 1648.

191. Agricol Perdiguier, the nineteenth-century journeyman, articulated a set route in his *Mémoires d'un compagnon* (Paris, 1964; orig. pub. 1854).

192. AMD, G86, March 1618, G87, Feb. 1619, G86, Nov. 1618.

193. Hauser, *Les compagnonnages*, p. 18.

194. Labal, "Le monde des métiers," p. 87. Labal has also found reference to a *mère* in Dijon in 1540.

195. Coornaert, p. 204; Boissonnade, p. 306 (on the *boîte*). See also, Hauser, *Les compagnonnages*, p. 14.

in the craft. In some parts of France the authorities viewed the rites of the compagnonnages as sacrilegious parodies of church ritual. The Sorbonne condemned the brotherhoods in 1655 for that very reason.[196] But in Dijon the authorities never referred to any mysterious ceremonies and made no direct reference to the Sorbonne's pronouncement.[197]

Isolated examples hint that these brotherhoods were becoming institutionalized before 1550. In a sentence of the Châtelet in Paris in 1505, for example, journeymen tailors were forbidden to elect a "king" of their company.[198] Similarly, the company of *Griffarins* formed by the journeymen printers in Lyons had elements of early "trade unionism."[199] Not until the second half of the sixteenth century, however, do the records bear any substantial evidence that the compagnonnages of some trades had been institutionalized as a national network. Demand for skilled labor was growing throughout France, but in Dijon the labor shortage occasioned by war, population growth, and the exclusionary policy of the masters was particularly acute.[200] It is not surprising, therefore, that the earliest known written references to the institution of compagnonnage are to be found in the records of Dijon. Here the journeymen first challenged the traditional relationship with the masters cast in the mold of paternal authority and filial obedience; here they began to substitute for it an economic relationship in which the journeyman commanded considerable power. Aware that their labor could be sold like a commodity to the masters and that this commodity was in great demand, they forged from the informal social group an economic institution. Over the next century the brotherhoods would spread rapidly to embrace many crafts.

The threat to "public tranquility" posed by organized efforts to defend the collective interests of the journeymen against the masters of a craft was not missed by royal authorities. In 1539 the edict of

196. On rites of initiation, see Benoist, p. 66. On demonstration of competence, see Sewell, *Work and Revolution*, p. 49. For the text of the Sorbonne's condemnation, see René de Lespinasse, ed., *Les métiers et corporations de la ville de Paris* (Paris, 1879).

197. Neither Hauser, *Les compagnonnages*, p. 29, nor I found reference to sacrilege.

198. Labal, "Le monde des métiers," p. 87.

199. Natalie Z. Davis, "A Trade Union in Sixteenth-Century France," *Economic History Review* 19 (1966): 48–69.

200. See Boissonade, p. 131 (though he does not mention population growth, which occurred throughout France).

Villers-Cotterets prohibited "any alliance or *intelligence* between . . . [journeymen], any assembly on their part for whatever cause, in short, any coalition directed against the masters."[201] The edict made explicit connections between confraternal organizations and the dangerous brotherhoods by abolishing "all confraternities of . . . artisans" and forbidding journeymen "of any trade to make any congregations or assemblies great or small and for whatever cause or occasion." They were not to "make any *monopole* and be united or hold any intelligences among themselves." Subsequent codes, including those of Orleans (1560), Moulins (1566), and Blois (1576), restated these prohibitions.[202]

On this issue the interests of Dijon's masters and its magistrates coincided. The municipal authorities were greatly concerned about the development of the brotherhoods. Perhaps they had heard about the strikes by journeymen at Lyons in the 1530s. Certainly they worried about disorder from raucous assemblies, and they feared manipulation of prices by concerted wage demands.[203] In short, they were troubled by the threat to public order.

The threat came early in Dijon. Compagnonnage was definitely in full bloom among the cabinetmakers by 1579 and probably among the locksmiths, tailors, and shoemakers before 1600 and among blacksmiths after that.[204] On 17 December 1579 the syndic brought ominous news to the magistrates that the journeymen cabinetmakers had drawn up "laws and statutes" for themselves and had elected a captain, a lieutenant, a receiver, and a sergeant as officers. The magistrates were so alarmed that they called a special meeting to proceed against these journeymen. They banished the newly elected captain, Jean Champignon of Rennes, as well as "Little John" from Bordeaux, the brother in charge of the boîte, and they confiscated the rollbook and the contents of the boîte, ten and a half sous, which were distributed to the poor. In conclusion, the council prohibited *all* journeymen of whatever trade from assembling, electing officers, collecting dues, or making among themselves "any deliberations or resolutions" to establish prices for their products, to set wages, "or to prevent

201. Quoted in Hauser, *Les compagnonnages*, p. 23.

202. E. Martin Saint-Léon, *Le compagnonnage: Son histoire, ses coûtumes, ses règlements, et ses rites* (Paris, 1901), pp. 34, 39.

203. Hauser, *Les compagnonnages*, p. 52.

204. Hauser incorrectly believed that the first compagnonnage was that of the shoemakers, first mentioned in 1608. Hauser, *Les compagnonnages*, p. 1.

journeymen of their trade from seeking and finding masters [to work for] that seem good to them," under penalty of corporal punishment and arbitrary fine.[205] Clearly, there was at least one institution in Dijon with bylaws, officers, and a treasury, functioning as a compulsory placement service dedicated to raising wages for its members. There would be others.

Because they filled a need, the compagnonnages were irrepressible, and prohibitions against them were futile. In 1585 the authorities arrested ten journeymen cabinetmakers who had gathered to watch a newcomer display his competence—a ritual typical of compagnonnage.[206] In 1605 the town council again prohibited assemblies of more than three journeymen and forbade journeymen to draw up *articles et rolles* listing names and surnames of journeymen. They were not to prevent newcomers from seeking and finding work wherever they wished, nor were they to take newcomers to taverns to eat and drink and later to "roam the streets" at night. In 1619 these prohibitions were repeated in response to violations, again by the journeymen cabinetmakers.[207] Their compagnonnage had endured.

Shoemakers seem to have formed a compagnonnage almost as early as the cabinetmakers. The public authorities certainly thought so. In 1581 they prohibited all journeymen shoemakers, cabinetmakers, and locksmiths from assembling in numbers greater than three. The following year, responding to a request from the master shoemakers and cobblers, the magistrates prohibited their journeymen from naming provosts, captains, or chiefs of their "companies" or collecting dues from their fellows.[208] Sometime in the next forty years the shoemaker compagnonnage became a worker placement service, for in 1621 the masters added to their statutes a clause making it illegal for journeymen to practice *embauchage* (labor placement) and to collect dues from newcomers to be spent on "games, banquets, and other debauches." According to the masters, the compagnons were the principal causes of the "disorder" that reigned in their craft.[209]

205. AMD, B215, fol. 223v, 18 Dec., and 226v, 26 Dec. 1579, B217, fol. 64r, 29 Dec. 1579.

206. AMD, B223, fol. 28r–v, 16 July 1585. Journeymen from Provence, Paris, Picardy, and Normandy were all present.

207. AMD, B256, fol. 224r–v, March 1619, in which the proclamation of 14 Jan. 1605 was repeated.

208. AMD, B219, fol. 23r, 14 July 1581, fol. 142v–145v, 29 May, 8 June 1582.

209. AMD, G3, fol. 259v, 30 July 1621.

*The Shoemakers*, Abraham Bosse; National Gallery of Art, Washington; Rosenwald Collection

The locksmith journeymen also seem to have been collectively organized in the sixteenth century. In 1563 ten of them accompanied one of their fellows to the shop of a master for whom he had worked and who he claimed owed him wages. No doubt eleven journeymen could speak with greater effect than one.[210] Evidently the locksmiths saw the wisdom of organizing, for as we have seen, the magistrates named the locksmiths along with the shoemakers and cabinetmakers when they banned assemblies in 1581. By 1635 the institution of compagnonnage was definitely in place in this craft. In that year the town council again addressed the journeymen locksmiths, prohibiting them from "making any journeymen arriving in this town pay for any festivities . . . under the pretext of bienvenue and *ambauchage* [sic]."[211]

Among the tailors there was a national network by 1588. In that year Jean Philippe, innkeeper of the Fatted Capon, was arrested for lodging guests without reporting their names to the magistrates. An alderman raided the place and discovered eight journeymen tailors in a room upstairs playing cards, making stockings, and just lying about. Interrogation of Philippe and the journeymen revealed that tailors on the tour de France knew that the Fatted Capon was their way station in Dijon. The travelers could stay there until they found regular work with a master who would allow them to move in with him or until they moved on again. Apparently the magistrates found no evidence of rolls, officers, or dues, but the direction of their questioning indicates their suspicion that they had uncovered a compagnonnage.[212]

Their suspicion was well founded. In 1599 the master tailors complained to the authorities that Philippe was "accustomed to receive and retain in his house the journeymen [tailors]. . . . Indeed, at present he has six there in his house, which is the reason why they [the masters] are badly served." The town council ordered Philippe to evict his guests and forbade him to lodge journeymen for more than one night.[213] We hear no more of Philippe, but in 1603 the master tailors amended their statutes to require newly arrived journeymen to present themselves directly to the masters of the trade; innkeepers were specifically forbidden to receive them first.[214] In 1612 the mas-

---

210. ADCO, BII 360/46, 20 Feb. 1563.
211. AMD, B272, fol. 208r, 9 Feb. 1635.
212. ADCO, BII 360/51, 17–22 Aug. 1588.
213. AMD, B237, fol. 74r, 20 Dec. 1599.
214. AMD, G3, 20 July 1603.

ters complained that this clause was being violated.[215] Without a doubt, the journeymen tailors had institutionalized a labor placement service, too.

An extraordinary document from 1643 gives a detailed account of the reception of a newcomer among the journeymen blacksmiths.[216] Nicolas Maillefert arrived in Dijon and met another journeyman, called the Gascon, who told him he knew of a shop where Maillefert could work. First, however, the Gascon took the newcomer to another shop to have him prove his capability in the trade. After that, along with three other journeymen blacksmiths already working in Dijon, they went to the inn of their mère, where Maillefert was to eat, drink, and sleep. Calling Maillefert comrade and the innkeeper mère, the Gascon ordered food and drink worth nearly three livres. What happened next is unclear, but ultimately Maillefert went to the authorities claiming that the Gascon and his friends had tried to pick a fight with him for no reason and, after roughing him up and stealing his doublet and cash, had left him. He implicated the mère, alleging that she refused to call for help even after she heard his cries (some mères were women, some men). The mère said that she thought it was customary among the journeymen blacksmiths to act this way, for every week or so a newcomer was brought to her inn. She understood that if the newcomer proved capable in his test of skill, the local journeymen would pay the bill for the food and drink, but if he proved incapable then the newcomer had to pay. Under interrogation, the four journeymen declared that Maillefert had violated their customs, that it was up to him to pay for the meal. When he would not, they took his doublet and money. According to one witness, when Maillefert refused to pay the *escot*, or entrance fee, the Gascon had "invited him to go pray to God in a closet that was nearby," which, the witness added, was a manner of speaking among the journeymen. He defended the taking of Maillefert's clothes by saying that among the journeymen it was customary for a newcomer to surrender his new clothes and don old ones, the new ones going to the journeyman with the greatest seniority in town. Maillefert either was unaware of the customary rite of passage of the blacksmith compagnon-

215. AMD, B250, fol. 110r–v, 30 Oct. 1612.
216. ADCO, BII 360/60, 6 Oct. 1643. The sentence that restored Maillefert's property was issued on 13 Oct. 1643 and also appears in AMD, B281, fol. 175v–176v.

nage or unwilling to abide by its rules. In either case, he was brought to heel, and only through the authorities could he retrieve his property. As far as we know, the authorities took no action against the compagnonnage, an indication, perhaps, that by 1643 they no longer troubled to fight a fait accompli.

As the compagnonnages developed their distinctive institutional trappings between 1570 and 1650, the masters were slow to react. It was the city magistrates who moved first to crush the brotherhoods. In this case the master artisans made no attempt to block municipal intervention in craft matters. When it became clear that the town council had failed to halt the institutionalization of the compagnonnage, however, the masters decided to meet the threat with their own program of worker placement.

In 1624 the master cabinetmakers created the elective office of *clerc embaucheur*, or labor placement officer. All journeymen cabinetmakers coming into town were to report immediately to this clerc, who would then place them with a master in need of labor.[217] When the master shoemakers followed suit in 1633,[218] the clerc embaucheur was on his way to becoming an essential personage in the struggle for control of the labor market.

Unfortunately for the masters, this counteroffensive was blunted by division within their own ranks. In 1637 fourteen master cabinetmakers filed suit with the town council against eight recalcitrant colleagues who had refused to accept the institution of the clerc embaucheur. The eight defendants had refused to sign a document that validated the election of Pierre DelaPoulière as clerc for the guild. They claimed he was "un homme misérable et defamé," who would never send any new journeymen to their shops. The magistrates commanded all the masters to obey the statutes but also instructed them to elect another clerc.[219] This compromise failed to heal the rift between the masters. Two months later the magistrates had to issue another ordinance arrogating the appointment of this officer to the town council. In an attempt to preclude favoritism, the council also ordered the clerc to assign journeymen to masters according to their seniority and need. Journeymen who were related to a master could

217. AMD, B275, fol. 160v, 1624.
218. AMD, B284, fol. 116v, 1633.
219. AMD, B275, fol. 160r–162r, 15 Dec. 1637, fol. 182r–183v, 12 Jan. 1638.

work for him, bypassing the clerc, but all others, including those who wanted to change shops, had to apply to him for placement. The council made it plain, however, that the clerc was to have no authority over apprentices.[220]

The relations among the master shoemakers were no more amicable than those of the cabinetmakers, and they too had difficulty establishing the new placement system. In 1643 Claude Gondard, a master shoemaker, got into a fistfight with his guild's clerc, Claude Rouy. Gondard asserted that Rouy was denying him journeymen, that the clerc had told a third party he had no intention of supplying Gondard with labor because Gondard was a "robber." Rouy, for his part, protested that he had not given Gondard any journeymen because he had none to give, but Gondard insisted that Rouy had placed four in other shops in the two days preceding their fight.[221] Rouy was not above suspicion. Three years later another master shoemaker, Philibert LeJeune, accused the clerc of violating the amended statutes of 1633, which required the placement officer to distribute journeymen to those with the greatest need. Rouy, he charged, had placed three journeymen together in one shop while denying LeJeune altogether.[222]

This sort of wrangling is evidence of how badly masters needed skilled workers. Unfortunately, we know next to nothing about how long a journeyman was likely to stay once he entered a master's service or about why, how, or how often journeymen were dismissed by their masters. There is some documentation of the length of time spent in the service of masters by journeymen who became masters themselves, but there is no way to gauge whether the many lifelong journeymen had more or less stable working patterns than those who achieved mastership. The dynamics of worker placement, however, are clear. As demand for their services increased, journeymen did their best to take control of the market. Effective organization entailed establishing the authority of the organization over all journeymen. Surely those few who felt their chances at mastership were reasonably bright were the most difficult to persuade, but solidarity was vital. Every journeyman arriving in Dijon had to be brought un-

---

220. AMD, B275, fol. 230v–231r, 12 March 1638.
221. ADCO, BII 360/60, 31 Dec. 1643.
222. AMD, B284, fol. 116v–117v, 12 Oct. 1646.

der the purview of his peers, who would decide if he would be placed or ordered to "move on" (*passer outre*).[223] The countermeasures of the masters testify to the effectiveness of compagnonnage. It is not yet possible to discern a working class, but a form of worker solidarity was unquestionably being forged in the crucible of the early modern labor market.

223. Hauser, *Les compagnonnages*, p. 43.

# 2 Population, Wealth, and the Conditions of Life

## Demography

Demographic analysis of sixteenth-century urban French society is bedeviled by one major lacuna—the extreme paucity of parish registers.[1] This lack, however, is compensated in Dijon by an extraordinarily rich collection of another index useful for population and wealth analysis—tax rolls. To discover the long-term demographic contours of early modern Dijon, I have used the tax rolls from non-crisis years near the beginning and end of the period of this study—the taillon from 1556 and the taille from 1643.[2]

Like most of northern France, Dijon's population was assessed taxes on "personal wealth." The tax rolls give us the name of the head of household, but they only occasionally (and perhaps not consistently) reveal extended family arrangements and never list dependents in the conjugal family. The social groups most likely to elude such lists in sixteenth- or seventeenth-century France were ecclesiastics, the hospitalized sick, and those who did not run a household—

1. A notable exception is Nantes. See Alain Croix, *Nantes et le pays nantais au XVIe siècle* (Paris, 1974).
2. AMD, L170, L234.

servants, most journeymen, apprentices, and of course, children. Dijon's rolls do list many of the tax-exempt laity and some of the floating poor, who played out their wretched existence crowded into inns and tenements, squatting in cellars, or camping in gardens—and paying taxes.

The population of Dijon began to expand in 1425, the year of the lowest recorded number of households, 1,500. By 1464 there were 2,371 households in the town,[3] and growth leveled off, to resume in the 1550s. The total population of Dijon in 1556 likely approached at least 14,500, burgeoning to perhaps more than 21,000 by 1643 (see Appendix). From 1556 to 1580 the number of recorded households grew from 2,822 to 3,591, many of the newcomers probably refugees from a war-torn countryside. The next two decades saw a decrease to 3,029, but with peace the population swelled again, so that by 1626 Dijon's rolls listed 3,984 hearths, and 4,081 by 1643.[4] Thus between 1556 and 1643 Dijon grew by almost half.

The tax rolls list the *qualité*, or "condition" (usually an occupation but occasionally a description like *bourgeois* or *monsieur*), of most household heads, but not, unfortunately, such honorific descriptions as *maître* or *honorable homme*, which would permit us to distinguish between masters and journeymen. These rolls record that artisans, 70 to 80 percent of whom must have been masters (see Appendix), were more numerous than any other occupational group, surpassing the population of winegrowers as well as that of merchants and men of law, including barristers, solicitors, and notaries (see Table 2.1).

As Dijon developed into a judicial and administrative center and a commercial crossroads, the ranks of the legal profession and the tax-exempt laity (most of whom were *officiers* at one of the many royal courts) swelled, as, on a more modest scale, did those of the merchants. The number of vignerons remained constant, presumably because the agricultural technology of the day did not permit intensification of cultivation and the extent of viable vineyard land was finite.

---

3. AMD, L159.
4. Roupnel, *La ville et la campagne*, p. 109. In 1698 there were 4,331 households in Dijon, and 6,075 at the outbreak of the Revolution. Pierre Gras, ed., *Histoire de Dijon* (Toulouse, 1980), p. 144.

**Table 2.1**
Occupational groups, male household heads on tax
rolls, 1556 and 1643

| Occupational group | 1556 | 1643 | Percentage change |
|---|---|---|---|
| Men of law | 69 | 222 | 222.0 |
| Merchants | 42 | 74 | 76.2 |
| Winegrowers | 370 | 373 | 0.8 |
| Artisans | 910 | 877 | −3.6 |
| Tax-exempt laity | 148 | 426 | 187.8 |

Source: AMD, L170, L234

For a fairly substantial number of heads of households, (22.5 percent in 1556 and 27.2 percent in 1643), the tax rolls list no condition. No doubt many, perhaps most, of these were the abject poor, who drifted in and out of town, maintaining a miserable existence by day labor, beggary, or crime.[5] Many others, as in most French towns, must have worked in the construction industry. Building was active in Dijon during the period, and since this industry required a large work force of unskilled laborers, it seems probable that many day laborers worked at Dijon's construction sites but were not listed by any occupation on the tax rolls. Significantly, no one described as *journalier* and extremely few *manouvriers* appear on these rolls; yet we know from other studies of cities and towns in early modern France that urban populations included large masses of these unskilled workers, who belonged to no guild. Unlike masters or even journeymen, such people would probably not identify themselves with any particular occupation; nor would the tax collector perceive them as pursuing any vocation.

Dijon's tax collectors did not confuse merchants with artisans or occupations within the artisanat.[6] Although most of the individuals

5. AMD, B25, fol. 215r. See also Bronislaw Geremek, *Inutiles au monde: Truands et misérables* (Paris, 1980).

6. Using the method described in the Appendix, I have cross-referenced 235 artisans from 1550 to 1563 with the tax roll of 1556, and 411 artisans from 1638 to 1650 with the roll of 1643. Only 8 of the 235 individuals (3.4 percent) who were described as artisans in outside sources appeared on the tax rolls from 1556 without any occupational designation, and 56 (13.6 percent) of the 411 on the rolls of 1643. Thus, the tax rolls of 1556 appear quite accurate in occupational designation, though those from 1643 bear some discussion. The cross-referenced names of artisans from 1638 to 1650

for whom no occupation was listed were not artisans, enough were to warrant an estimate that the artisan population was underrepresented on the tax rolls of 1556 by about 3 percent and on those of 1643 by slightly over 13 percent. It is quite possible that by 1643 there had been more growth in the journeymen's ranks than in the masters', especially if we consider it unlikely an honor-conscious master would let a tax collector omit his condition from a legal document. In any case, there can be no doubt that the growth of the artisan population, even adjusted for possible error in the tax rolls, did not come close to keeping pace with that of the overall population.[7] Indeed, on the tax rolls there is a decline in the number of artisan heads of household, from 950 in 1556 to 910 in 1643. By adjusting for an error of 3.4 percent in the first listing and 13.6 percent in the second, the figures can be modified to show a modest increase from 982 in 1556 to 1,034 in 1643, but even these numbers reflect a proportionate decline. Whereas, by either calculation, artisans constituted over a third of the population in 1556, by 1643 they made up only a fourth of it.

The sixteenth-century figures for Dijon are similar to those of other French towns of the period, but the decline is not typical.[8] Certainly,

---

appearing without occupation on the rolls of 1643 show an occupational and economic profile similar to that of those designated as artisans on the tax rolls. The food, leather, and construction trades were the most populous in both, and the median tax assessment of the cross-referenced names put them only one category below the artisans articulated on the tax rolls (the 52d percentile vs. the 57th). Using the same method of cross-referencing, it appears that artisans were only very rarely confused with merchants in the eyes of the tax collector (only one of seventeen individuals labeled merchant on the tax rolls of 1556 appeared as an artisan in another source, and in 1643 only four of fifty-eight. Even more convincing, none of the names on a complete list of the sixty-three master tailors in Dijon in 1611 (AMD, B248) matched the names of merchants from the 1610 tax rolls. Similarly, none of the names on the rolls of master goldsmiths from 1566 and 1640 appeared among the merchants on the tax rolls of 1579 and 1643. ADCO, E3432, fol. 14v, 22r–23r. And finally, only once does the tax collector appear to confuse crafts. In 1643 a Bénigne Rebourg appeared as a cordwainer on the tax rolls but as a shoemaker in his marriage contract, though perhaps there were two men with this not uncommon name.

7. For artisans to keep pace with population growth for the whole town (44.6 percent), their number would have had to increase by 423 in 1643 over 1556 levels. The names with no occupation listed grew by only 476 in those years, so nearly every new unknown would have had to have been an artisan, an extreme implausibility.

8. For example, in the late Middle Ages, Geremek, *Le salariat*, p. 13; Marcel Couturier, *Recherches sur les structures sociales à Châteaudun, 1525–1789* (Paris, 1969), p. 117.

since most of the artisans listed on the tax rolls were masters, the efforts of the guilds to limit the number of new masters had their effect. Varying demand for artisan products also affected the equation, as did competition from rural protoindustry.

Most craft groups lost members, some more than others. Textile crafts were the biggest loser, victims of the ravages of war and a growing rural protoindustry.[9] Their numbers in Dijon contracted by over 40 percent. Fullers and carders, for example, totally disappeared from Dijon by 1643 (there were nine and eleven, respectively, in 1556), and cloth cutters declined from twenty-two to three. It was the culmination of a trend that had begun late in the fifteenth century. Metals and weapons crafts suffered the second largest decline (the numbers of blacksmiths fell from nineteen to eight).

A few craft groups grew during the period, suggesting a growing demand for their services or perhaps an inability to regulate their numbers. The most remarkable growth was among the wine-related trades, which mushroomed by over 50 percent. The number of coopers alone grew from twenty-nine to forty-six. Dijon during this time became an increasingly important regional wine distribution center, and there was an explosion in the number of taverns, signaling increased local consumption. Both factors stimulated the demand for barrels and casks—and for the coopers who made them.[10] The leather crafts posted the other great increase (by over a third), led by the cobblers (from thirty-five to eighty-five).

Broadly speaking, from 1550 to 1650 a shift from industrial to service crafts is visible (see Table 2.2). Textiles, the largest protoindustry in the general European economy, essentially disappeared from Dijon, leaving the field primarily to such service crafts as shoemaking, tailoring, baking, and the like. Dijon was becoming less and less an industrial center and more and more an administrative and judicial center, which required a substantial population of workers in service-oriented crafts geared for local production and sustained by a burgeoning class of elite consumers.

The residence patterns of the city reflect these changes. Like most other cities of early modern Europe, Dijon was organized by parish,

---

9. On the emergence of a textile protoindustry in Burgundy in the late sixteenth century, see my "Dijon, 1450–1750."

10. On changing wine consumption and its impact, see ibid.

**Table 2.2**

Households by craft group, as percentage of all artisans, 1556 and 1643

| Craft group | Male hearths | | Female hearths | | Total | | Percentage of artisanat | | Percentage change |
|---|---|---|---|---|---|---|---|---|---|
| | 1556 | 1643 | 1556 | 1643 | 1556 | 1643 | 1556 | 1643 | |
| Food | 148 | 127 | 2 | 3 | 150 | 130 | 15.8 | 14.3 | −13.3 |
| Construction | 140 | 136 | 5 | 4 | 145 | 140 | 15.3 | 15.4 | −3.4 |
| Leather | 138 | 189 | 5 | 4 | 143 | 193 | 15.1 | 21.2 | +35.0 |
| Clothing | 119 | 98 | 6 | 11 | 125 | 109 | 13.2 | 12.0 | −12.8 |
| Textiles | 106 | 66 | 6 | 1 | 112 | 67 | 11.8 | 7.4 | −40.2 |
| Metals and weapons | 81 | 62 | 8 | 1 | 89 | 63 | 9.4 | 6.9 | −29.2 |
| Woodworking | 53 | 53 | 3 | 3 | 56 | 56 | 5.9 | 6.2 | 0.0 |
| Luxury | 50 | 47 | 4 | 2 | 54 | 49 | 5.7 | 5.4 | −9.3 |
| Wine-related | 38 | 58 | 1 | 2 | 39 | 60 | 4.1 | 6.6 | +53.3 |
| Miscellaneous | 37 | 41 | 0 | 2 | 37 | 43 | 3.9 | 4.7 | +10.8 |
| Total | 910 | 877 | 40 | 33 | 950 | 910 | | | −4.2 |

Source: AMD, L170, L234.

Note: These are the exact figures from the tax rolls. I have not compensated for possible omissions from the rolls because the samples for particular craft groups are too small for statistical projection without distortion. Nevertheless, the orders of magnitude can be trusted, since the cross section of the cross-referenced sample from other sources matches the occupational distribution in this table.

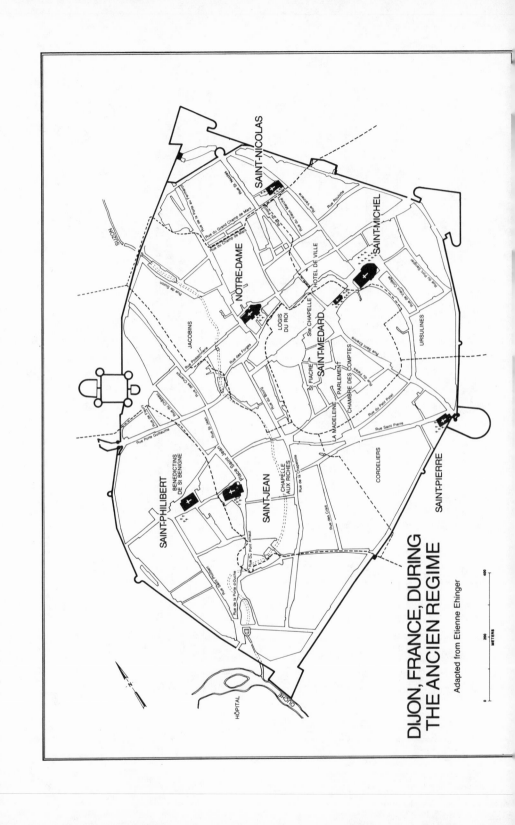

# DIJON, FRANCE, DURING THE ANCIEN REGIME

Adapted from Etienne Ehinger

SAINT-NICOLAS

SAINT-MICHEL

NOTRE-DAME

SAINT-MEDARD

LOGIS DU ROI

Ste CHAPELLE

HOTEL DE VILLE

URSULINES

JACOBINS

St FIACRE

PARLEMENT

LA MADELEINE

CHAMBRE DES COMPTES

SAINT-PHILIBERT

BENEDICTINS DE St BENIGNE

SAINT-JEAN

CHAPELLE AUX RICHES

CORDELIERS

SAINT-PIERRE

HÔPITAL

OUCHE

SUZON

Rue de Suzon

Rue du Grand Champ de Mars

Rue de Bois et de la Rue

Rue de Norge

Rue du Champ de Mars

Rue Buffon

Rue Rouleau

Rue des Forges

Rue Posséchatelle

Rue des Champs

Rue des Champs

Rue Porte Guillaume

Rue St Jean

Rue Saint Jean

Rue de la Chapelle

Rue des Crais

Rue du Pont Arbat

Rue de la Porte d'Ouche

Rue Saint Etienne

Rue du Parc Nogent

Rue de la Rue Burgun

Rue Saint Pierre

Rue du Petit Potet

N

0        200        400

METERS

Table 2.3
Artisan households by parish, 1556 and 1643

| Parish | Artisan households | | Percentage change | Percentage of parish | | Percentage of artisanat | |
|---|---|---|---|---|---|---|---|
| | *1556* | *1643* | | *1556* | *1643* | *1556* | *1643* |
| St. Jean | 260 | 297 | +14.2 | 41.7 | 32.1 | 27.4 | 32.6 |
| Notre Dame | 253 | 195 | −22.9 | 47.3 | 26.2 | 26.6 | 21.4 |
| St. Michel | 171 | 156 | −8.8 | 27.9 | 20.1 | 18.0 | 17.1 |
| St. Philibert | 118 | 34 | −71.2 | 32.2 | 4.7 | 12.4 | 3.7 |
| St. Nicolas | 68 | 116 | +70.6 | 20.5 | 25.1 | 7.2 | 12.7 |
| St. Pierre | 40 | 49 | +22.5 | 23.3 | 25.0 | 4.2 | 5.3 |
| St. Médard | 40 | 63 | +57.5 | 22.0 | 24.9 | 4.2 | 6.9 |
| Totals | 950 | 910 | −4.2 | | | | |

Source: AMD, L170, L234.

and each of its seven parishes had separate and distinct characteristics. Notre Dame was the home of most merchants and a locus of commercial activity. Within its boundaries was the *bourg*, a bustling hub of butchers, shoemakers, fowlers, grocers, and a multitude of other vendors and producers. The butchers had been concentrated in this parish since the thirteenth century, adding the blood from their slaughtering to the household wastes that clogged the streets. Despite the resultant stench and the smoke from the taverns and the shops of the *rôtisseurs*, Notre Dame parish thrived.[11] Rich officials and others who had purchased tax exemptions clustered there, and only one parish surpassed Notre Dame in number of artisans despite a sharp decline during the period. In 1556 artisans represented nearly half of the parish population, and over one-fourth of Dijon's artisans lived there; by 1643 their numbers had dwindled considerably, while the population of Notre Dame as a whole grew by almost 40 percent (see Table 2.3).

The hemorrhage was caused by the collapse of the textile industry (in 1556 there had been thirty-five households headed by textiles craftspeople, but by 1643 only eight remained). Artisans practicing service-oriented trades, such as butchers, tailors, and shoemakers, remained the mainstays of its artisan population.

St. Jean was Dijon's largest and most populous parish (see Table 2.4). The grand houses of rich parlementaires rimmed St. Jean Square,

11. Garnier, *Histoire du quartier du Bourg*, pp. 4, 16.

**Table 2.4**
Parish population, 1556 and 1643

| Parish | 1556 | 1643 | Percent growth |
|--------|------|------|----------------|
| St. Jean | 624 | 926 | 48.4 |
| St. Michel | 612 | 775 | 26.6 |
| Notre Dame | 535 | 743 | 38.9 |
| St. Philibert | 366 | 725 | 98.1 |
| St. Nicolas | 331 | 463 | 39.9 |
| St. Médard | 182 | 253 | 39.0 |
| St. Pierre | 172 | 196 | 14.0 |

Source: AMD, L170, L234.

the site of the most important public festivals, and the bell of the parish church rang the curfew for the town. More artisans lived in St. Jean than in any other parish—between one-fourth and one-third of them. Nearly every trade was represented; the tailors, bakers, shoemakers, and cabinetmakers predominated in 1556. By 1643 the cobblers had increased their number from nine to twenty-five, and the coopers, probably attracted by the market and distribution center for Dijon's expanding wine trade, St. Jean Square, more than doubled, from seven to seventeen. Many metals and weapons craftsmen continued to inhabit this parish as well. Of eighty-one such artisans in Dijon in 1556, thirty-two lived in St. Jean, and thirty of sixty-two in 1643.

In St. Michel there was an overall decline in artisan population which masks the increasing density of construction artisans there. In both 1556 and 1643 the majority of carpenters called this parish home (eighteen of thirty-five and thirteen of twenty-one, respectively). Only ten of fifty-three Dijonnais masons lived in the parish in 1556, but by 1643 almost half of them (twenty-seven of fifty-six) were residing in St. Michel. The roofers/tilers showed a similar increase, from two of seventeen to thirteen of twenty-six. By 1643 the construction craftsmen formed the dominant artisan group in St. Michel. The vigneron population also increased substantially, and by 1643 more winegrowers lived in this parish than in any other.

In St. Nicolas every fifth inhabitant was an artisan in 1556, one in four in 1643. By the mid–seventeenth century this parish had joined St. Philibert as Dijon's poorest. Bakers, tailors, and wheelwrights consistently favored St. Nicolas, and by 1643, twelve cobblers had moved in as well. All shared space with a burgeoning population of vignerons.

St. Philibert nearly doubled its population during the period, increasing from 366 to 725 households. Very few of these households were headed by the tax-exempt wealthy or by craftsmen. The tax rolls depict a dramatic artisan exodus from St. Philibert, but this picture may be slightly illusory. Of the artisans identified in outside sources dated 1638–1650 whose names matched those of individuals of unknown occupation on the tax rolls of 1643, more were from St. Philibert than from any other parish (see Appendix). Apparently, the tax collector was not very careful in noting the occupations of these parishioners.[12] Even so, St. Philibert unquestionably lost a large number of artisans, probably more than any other parish. As St. Philibert was growing poorer, the artisans, as a group, were becoming more prosperous by catering to the expanding number of consumers attracted to Dijon. No doubt the artisans were persuaded to seek more affluent neighborhoods nearer their clientele. The tanners offer a dramatic illustration. Throughout the period Dijon's tanneries were located on the River Ouche in St. Philibert parish. In 1556 nearly all the tanners (thirteen of fifteen) lived near their workshops, but by 1643 none did. Most of these wealthy craftsmen (fourteen of sixteen) now dwelled in Notre Dame or St. Jean. Having become increasingly preoccupied with the commercial aspect of their trade, they moved to the mercantile districts of town.

At the other end of the scale from poor St. Philibert stood St. Médard, the administrative nucleus of Dijon, site of the extensive court system. This small parish was filled with solicitors, barristers, and high officials. In 1556 over 20 percent of its households were tax exempt, 30 percent by 1643. During the period the artisan population jumped by over half, considerably outstripping its overall growth. Although absolute numbers remained small, prosperous artisans were moving into this affluent neighborhood as their wealth increased. Pastrycooks and goldsmiths, for example, were generally

12. From 1638 to 1650, of the fifty-six artisans identified in sources other than the tax rolls but who appear without occupational designation on the tax rolls of 1643, twenty-four hailed from St. Philibert parish, thirteen from St. Michel, twelve from Notre Dame, five from St. Jean, and one each from St. Pierre and St. Nicolas. On the tax rolls of 1643, 537 individuals had no occupational designation.

quite wealthy in 1643, and craftsmen from these trades settled more densely in St. Médard (and St. Jean) than they had in 1556.

Another relatively affluent parish was the ecclesiastical center, St. Pierre, which grew by 14 percent during the period. Perhaps artisans were attracted by proximity to wealthy customers; certainly their number swelled by 22.5 percent. No particular craft predominated, but most were represented.

The habitation patterns displayed by the artisans between 1556 and 1643 hint at two significant developments. First, there is a relationship between geography and work identity. Several crafts and craft groups evidently sought geographic propinquity with their colleagues. Construction craftsmen congregated more and more in St. Michel parish; butchers clustered in Notre Dame; pastrycooks and goldsmiths favored St. Médard and St. Jean. Second, settlement patterns roughly correlate with relative affluence. Many artisans moved away from St. Philibert parish, which suffered impoverishment during the period, while more artisans moved near Dijon's wealthy elite.

## Artisan Wealth

### Wealth and Taxes

Burgundy, like most of northern France, was subject to the taille *personnelle*, a relatively "progressive" tax, whose records provide a rough index of total individual wealth. From 1479 to the Revolution it was assessed in much the same way. Once a total amount was agreed upon by the Estates of Burgundy and the king, the tax burden was divided among the inhabitants according to the principle that "the strong carry the weak." The tax was based, at least in theory, on individual ability to pay. Assessors were to take into account both mobile and immobile forms of wealth, including resources from commerce or manufacturing. The clergy and the nobility were exempt. The taillon, a supplementary tax begun in the sixteenth century, was assessed in the same way.

The *élus* of the Estates apportioned the burden by *généralité* and left it to the town council of Dijon to apportion the total by parish and household. An assessor and collector (taxpayers elected by the general assembly of inhabitants and subject to fine and imprisonment if they failed to do their job properly) figured the appropriate tax by conducting a *cherche des feux*. They enlisted the help of neighbors to determine liability, and since each parish was collectively responsible for a predetermined amount, this practice encouraged equitable distribution of the burden. Neighbors, who knew better than anyone else what their neighbors possessed, would find it in their interest to make sure that all declared their full liability.

The taille *personnelle* was more or less progressive in the sense that the more affluent the taxpayer, the higher the tax rate. We cannot assume, however, that someone who paid, say, twice the tax of another was twice as wealthy. The tax burden on artisans and vignerons, for example, was relatively heavier in 1643 than it had been in 1556, compared to the burden on merchants and men of the law, but the latter remained at the top end of the tax distribution scale. This change in the pattern of assessment suggests that wealth was becoming increasingly polarized, with the richest pulling away. Nevertheless, the *relative* distribution of tax assessment does correlate to the relative distribution of wealth. Percentiles correspond to the numbers of taxpayers rather than to the total tax collected. They have the advantage of rendering comparison between years possible. For example, in 1556 there were seventy-one tax rates. Of 2,651 taxpayers, 142 paid less than one sou, thus constituting the 5th percentile. In 1643 there were sixty-six rates, and 213 of 3,641 taxpayers paid less than ten sous. These taxpayers thus constituted the 6th percentile, comparable on the scale of wealth to those 142 in 1556.

Historians have come to accept the reliability of the taille *personnelle* as an index of relative wealth.[13] As Pierre Goubert has pointed out, "The fiscal hierarchy of taxpayers reflects broadly, but with a certain fidelity, the hierarchy of fortunes. . . . With one reservation: we must take care to place the tax exempt . . . generally at the top of the scale."[14] There is no way to determine absolute distribution of wealth from this source, but polarization of wealth in early modern

13. See Françoise Humbert, *Les finances de Dijon du milieu du XIVe siècle à 1477* (Paris, 1961), chap. 4; Martin Wolfe, *The Fiscal System of Renaissance France* (New Haven, 1972), app. G; Roger Doucet, *Les institutions de la France au XVIe siècle*, vol. 2 (Paris, 1948), 2:562–77; Marcel Marion, *Les impôts directs sous l'ancien régime* (Geneva, 1974), pp. 4–32.

14. Pierre Goubert, *Beauvais et le beauvaisis de 1600 à 1730: Contribution à l'histoire sociale de la France du XVII siècle*, 2 vols. (Paris, 1960), 1:260.

France was extreme. We can be sure that the exempt and even the taxpayers at the top end of the wealth distribution scale were probably economic worlds away from those toward the bottom of the scale. Ultimately, it is impossible to say how far up the scale the threshold of poverty could creep, though there are hints that at least the bottom third of taxpayers were perilously close.

Poverty certainly worsened from the 1550s until the end of the Wars of Religion. During this period Burgundy, and France in general, lost the economic prosperity of the previous century. With peace, prosperity returned to Burgundy, but from 1625 to 1640 the region suffered an economic crisis. Fortunately, the tax rolls I have primarily relied on are from 1556 and 1643. Neither was a year of crisis or of unusual prosperity.

In both 1556 and 1643 wealth was geographically polarized (see Tables 2.5, 2.6). In 1556 the richest clustered in St. Médard and Notre Dame, the poorest in St. Nicolas. By 1643 St. Médard became an exclusive haven reserved for the very rich, while Dijon's poorest inhabitants crowded into the slums of St. Philibert and St. Nicolas. A close look at Edouard Bredin's map of Dijon in 1574 shows how the types of dwellings varied across the town. The tenements of the poorer sectors give way to the *hôtels* of the more affluent neighborhoods. Between the rich and the poor were those of moderate means, who clustered in St. Jean and St. Michel. Among them were fully half of the artisans in Dijon.

Those who were exempt from the taille were probably the wealthiest inhabitants of Dijon. The clergy held far-reaching domains from which they received "goods, tithes and rents," as well as numerous mortgages on houses in Dijon.[15] Many royal and some municipal officials, as nobles, were also exempt and the number of public officials nearly tripled during the period. By 1643 every tenth lay household was exempt, whereas only one in twenty had been exempt in 1556. In the Parlement alone there were nine presidents and seventy royal councillors in 1636, compared to two presidents and sixteen councillors in 1511.[16] The financial courts and subaltern offices experienced a similar expansion, part of the burgeoning of the administrative class in Dijon.[17] If their wealth grew at least as much as that of

15. Roupnel, pp. 198–99.
16. Gras, p. 120.
17. Philip Benedict, *Rouen during the Wars of Religion* (Cambridge, 1981), p. 12,

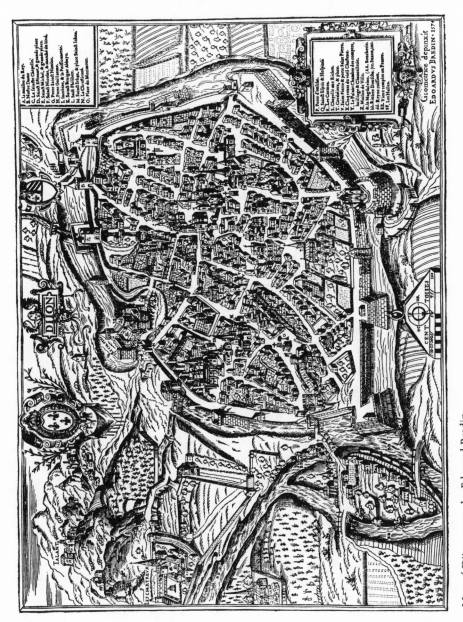

Map of Dijon, 1574, by Edouard Bredin

**Table 2.5**

Economic rank of parishes by average tax paid (in sous), 1556 and 1643

| Parish | All taxpayers[a] | | Artisans | | Vignerons | | Merchants | | Men of the law | |
|---|---|---|---|---|---|---|---|---|---|---|
| | 1556 | 1643 | 1556 | 1643 | 1556 | 1643 | 1556 | 1643 | 1556 | 1643 |
| St. Médard | 19.0 | 131.6 | 11.9 | 88.1 | 6.0 | — | — | 117.5 | 37.4 | 186.3 |
| Notre Dame | 16.7 | 72.7 | 10.7 | 56.2 | 4.0 | 28.0 | 65.8 | 135.1 | 26.7 | 166.0 |
| St. Pierre | 9.8 | 76.9 | 7.5 | 62.4 | 8.7 | 20.6 | — | — | 38.2 | 133.2 |
| St. Philibert | 8.2 | 33.8 | 11.7 | 41.3 | 4.2 | 19.5 | — | 35.0 | 15.0 | 100.0 |
| St. Jean | 7.0 | 48.5 | 6.6 | 48.1 | 5.2 | 26.5 | 18.0 | 92.3 | 24.6 | 121.1 |
| St. Michel | 6.5 | 56.0 | 5.3 | 38.7 | 4.8 | 29.2 | 37.5 | 126.7 | 17.4 | 146.9 |
| St. Nicolas | 5.6 | 35.8 | 4.3 | 40.3 | 2.5 | 36.5 | 22.5 | 126.7 | 8.0 | 62.5 |
| Overall average | 9.5 | 55.0 | 8.3 | 50.5 | 4.8 | 30.7 | 58.6 | 121.9 | 30.4 | 148.5 |

Source: AMD, L170, L234.

[a]This category includes both male and female taxpayers, but all other categories include only male heads of household, since it is unclear if widows appearing on the rolls with their husband's name and occupation after theirs are still active in the business. The average tax for all male taxpayers in 1556 was 9.7 sous, and 56.1 sous in 1643.

**Table 2.6**
Economic rank of parishes by tax exemptions, 1556 and
1643

| Parish | Number of households exempt | | Exemptions as percentage of parish population | |
|---|---|---|---|---|
| | *1556* | *1643* | *1556* | *1643* |
| St. Médard | 39 | 75 | 21.4 | 29.6 |
| St. Pierre | 12 | 49 | 7.0 | 25.0 |
| Notre Dame | 35 | 93 | 6.5 | 12.5 |
| St. Jean | 34 | 86 | 5.4 | 9.3 |
| St. Michel | 19 | 82 | 3.1 | 10.6 |
| St. Nicolas | 5 | 17 | 1.5 | 3.7 |
| St. Philibert | 4 | 24 | 1.1 | 3.3 |
| Totals | 148 | 426 | | |

Source: AMD, L170, L234.

the taxable legal establishment, which is likely, their increasing
numbers did not diminish their affluence. The average tax of a member
of the legal establishment was considerably below that of the
average merchant in 1556 but well beyond it by 1643 (see Table 2.5).
Yet most merchants were high on Dijon's wealth distribution scale
(see Table 2.7).

If the clergy, public officials, and those in commercial and liberal
professions were the richest in Dijon, the poorest were primarily
widows, *gens sans aveu*, and some artisans and vignerons. In 1556, of
142 individuals assessed less than one sou and therefore among the
poorest 5 percent of taxpayers, only 31 were male artisans and 16
were winegrowers, but 48 were widows (at least 2 of them widows
of artisans), and the remainder were individuals (mostly men) without
vocation. In 1643 an assessment of less than ten sous placed the
taxpayer in the bottom 6 percent. Of the 213 wretches in this category,
28 were male artisans and 7 were winegrowers, but 94 were widows
(at least 3 being widows of artisans), and 67 had no listed vocation.

Economically speaking, the artisans were increasingly a middling
sort.[18] In terms of average assessment by occupational group, artisans

---

notes that the law court personnel in Rouen, a Parlement town like Dijon, mushroomed after 1550.

18. Goubert, 1:264, found similar circumstances in a city of comparable size.

**Table 2.7**
Distribution of wealth by occupational group (in percentage), 1556 and 1643

|  | 0–40th percentile | | 40–80th percentile | | Above 80th percentile | |
|---|---|---|---|---|---|---|
|  | *1556* | *1643* | *1556* | *1643* | *1556* | *1643* |
| Artisans | 35.1 | 28.2 | 47.2 | 53.3 | 17.8 | 18.9 |
| Vignerons | 47.6 | 51.5 | 43.3 | 44.3 | 9.1 | 4.3 |
| Merchants | 2.4 | 0.0 | 4.8 | 30.6 | 92.8 | 69.4 |
| Men of law | 0.0 | 2.8 | 12.3 | 21.7 | 87.7 | 75.5 |

Source: AMD, L170, L234.

fell between the winegrowers, another large and stable group on the lower side and the mercantile and legal establishment on the upper side. It is true that there were artisans dispersed across the wealth distribution scale, but between 1550 and 1650 proportionately more artisans were coalescing into the middling economic ranks. As Table 2.7 illustrates, in 1556 less than half of all craftsmen fell between roughly the 40th and 80th percentile of all taxpayers, arranged by distribution of tax assessment.[19] By 1643 that percentage had climbed to 53.3 for the comparable range. Moreover, the figures indicate that artisans were escaping the ranks of the poor rather than dropping from the heights of the rich. The percentage of artisans in the bottom 40 percent declined considerably, while the percentage of those in the top 20 percent remained nearly constant.

The metals and weapons crafts and the construction trades exemplify this development. Whereas in 1556, 55 percent of the former (44 of 80) could be found in that upper middle 40 percent of taxpayers, by 1643 almost two-thirds (41 of 62) were there. As for the construction craftsmen, during this period the percentage in the upper middle rank increased from 45 percent (63 of 140) to 58.9 percent (80 of 136). Only the food and clothing trades failed to increase their representation in this middle rank, the former because of dramatically increasing affluence. From just over a quarter to nearly half the artisans in the food trades moved into the top 20 percent of taxpayers between

19. To render a general picture the many rates were best bracketed by percentile. I have focused on the range between 40 and 80 percent because artisans disproportionately clustered there between 1556 and 1643. Of course, the taxes they paid may reflect fiscal bleeding by the authorities, but that in itself might suggest a perception by the authorities of enhanced ability to pay.

1556 and 1643. The clothing trades slid in the other direction. Whereas barely one in three (34.2 percent) of these artisans were in the bottom 40 percent of the wealth scale in 1556, by 1643 nearly two in five (38.8 percent) were.

It would be tedious and not especially enlightening to sketch the status changes of every craft, but a few trades deserve mention. The shoemakers were among the fortunate artisans who improved their condition. In 1556, 44.1 percent of them were in the upper middle rank; by 1643 that percentage had increased to 64.4. Moreover, the percentage falling into the bottom rank declined from 35.5 (twelve of thirty-four shoemakers) to 24.4 (eleven of forty-five). This drift to the middle was evident among the most affluent 20 percent as well. Seven of the thirty-four shoemakers (20.6 percent) fell into this rank in 1556, but in 1643 there were only seven of forty-five (15.6 percent) of them among the most affluent. Likewise, the percentage of carpenters in the upper middle rank increased in the same period from 57.1 (twenty of thirty-five) to 66.6 (fourteen of twenty-one). Again, the newcomers came from the ranks of poorer colleagues, which declined from twelve of thirty-five to five of twenty-one.

At the top end of the scale, no artisans made a more startling improvement in their economic well-being than the pastrycooks. Spread, like other guilds, across the scale in 1556 (with eight of thirty-six in the top 20 percent, nineteen in the upper middle 40 percent, and nine in the bottom 40 percent), they accomplished a radical shift by the next century. By 1643 fully twenty of twenty-four were in the top 20 percent, and eleven of those were in the top 10 percent. All the others were in the upper middle rank. In fact, in 1643 no *pâtissier* fell below the 71st percentile!

The fortune of the pastrycooks was counterbalanced by the misfortune of the tailors and cobblers. Over half of Dijon's tailors (thirty-eight of seventy) clung to the upper middle rank in 1556, but by 1643 several had lost their grip and fallen into the bottom 40 percent. Only thirty-five of seventy-one were still in the upper middle, and the bottom had swelled from 31.4 percent to 38.6 percent (twenty-two to twenty-seven). The top rank remained essentially unchanged. The fate of the cobblers was even more dismal. Relatively poor in 1556 (over 60 percent of the thirty-three cobblers were at the bottom, 27.3 percent were in the middle, and 12.1 percent at the top), the cobblers lost ground in the ensuing century. By 1643 the bottom 40 percent, like the cobbler population as a whole, had swollen. Fifty-four of eighty-three cobblers (65.1 percent) were now at the bottom. Although the middle rank grew slightly, to almost a third (twenty-seven cobblers), it gained at the expense of the upper level, which contracted to merely two.

But upwardly or downwardly mobile crafts were exceptions to a pattern in which more and more artisans settled into the upper middle 40 percent of wealth distribution in early modern Dijon. By and large the masters succeeded in keeping their numbers low. As the population of Dijon grew, each master served a larger share of the total, and personal wealth increased.

## Masters and Journeymen

The picture is less clear for journeymen. The tax rolls provide an excellent index of the distribution of wealth in Dijon and the position of artisans (mostly masters) in that scale, but they do not permit us to differentiate the positions of masters and journeymen. To coax the journeymen out of the shadows and distinguish their wealth from that of masters, we need sources that are both more sensitive to honorific epithets and better able to indicate wealth. Notarized marriage contracts and real estate transactions allow comparison of levels of wealth for both masters and some journeymen better than the tax rolls, but even these sources have their limitations.

In marriage contracts, one key clause is the declaration of financial contributions to the marriage, that is, the *apports*, including inheritances, credits, real estate owned, and other financial assets. Another important specification is the *douaire* for the bride, in the customary law of Burgundy the amount brought by her to the marriage, which, in the event of her husband's death, would revert to her before the estate was settled.[20] Also to go to her *avant partage* if her husband

20. Abel Ridard, *Essai sur le douaire en Bourgogne* (Dijon, 1906). On the use of apports as indicators of wealth, see Maurice Garden, *Lyon et les lyonnais au XVIIIe siècle* (Paris, 1975), pp. 195–205. Payment of apports was frequently deferred or made in installments over a number of years. See, for example, ADCO, *Notaires* #371, 8 March 1592, #3770, 6 Feb. 1594. What percentage of the artisanat used marriage contracts is difficult to know for sure. Given the patrimonial stakes, it is likely that most master artisans did. Many poor people also used marriage contracts, however, though it is likely that some did not. Underrepresentation of poor journeymen in Dijon might skew the sample and underrepresent the numbers of journeymen who did marry

died first were the *bagues et joyeux*, the gifts of the groom to the bride. Their worth was always equivalent to the value of the groom's tools and weapons, which would go to him *avant partage* if his wife died before he did. Clearly, such information is invaluable for determining the wealth of the couple.

Yet we cannot be sure that the apports fully reflect the wealth of the father or the spouse, since it was not unusual to find assets listed with no cash value given. This kind of listing was especially common with the trousseau.[21] Moreover, in Burgundy siblings shared equally in any inheritance from their parents, but we cannot tell from the contracts how many brothers and sisters the bride or groom had. The douaire and bagues et joyeux do not conceal assets unconverted to cash value, but we cannot know if their amounts, like those of apports, were determined by the number of siblings or were altered to favor one child over another. Finally, it is important to remember that the pool, by definition, includes those who marry in Dijon; those journeymen or their daughters who did so were probably a relatively well-off minority. Still, if absolute levels of wealth elude us, marriage contracts do permit a rough comparison of the wealth of some journeymen and masters.

A sample of 491 marriage contracts dated 1551–1600, in which the groom was an artisan or the son of one or the bride was the daughter or widow of an artisan, provides much useful information. Clearly, masters who declared cash apports for their daughters gave more than twice as much as journeymen provided for their girls (see Table 2.8). The male profile is similar: 175 masters or their sons averaged 41.4 livres in bagues et joyeux, far outstripping the 215 journeymen or their sons, who averaged only 22.6 livres. Grooms were much less inclined to declare apports than bagues, but among those who did, the difference between masters and journeymen was even greater. The

---

in Dijon, but it seems unlikely that journeymen marrying into the master ranks could do so without a contract, since patrimonies were growing and the assets of the journeyman, as we will see, were his vehicle into the master circle.

21. In a sample of 491 marriage contracts between 1551 and 1600, 65 of 203 daughters of masters and journeymen brought apports in kind, of which 58 were trousseaux. During the same period, only 29 of 429 artisans or their sons brought apports in kind. In a sample of 492 between 1601 and 1650, 101 of 219 daughters of artisans brought apports in kind, of which 83 were trousseaux, while 76 of 440 artisans or their sons brought apports in kind.

**Table 2.8**
Average apports given for daughters of masters and journeymen,
1551–1650

|  | Average cash value given in contract[a] (in livres tournois) | |
| --- | --- | --- |
|  | *1551–1600* | *1601–1650*[b] |
| Daughters of masters | 142.9 (N = 91) | 357.2 (N = 157) |
| Daughters of journeymen | 70.6 (N = 36) | 136.3 (N = 22) |

Source: Based on a sample of 983 marriage contracts in ADCO,
*Notaires.*
    [a]Figures reflect only those contracts in which cash value was given;
apports that were listed in kind cannot be accurately translated into cash.
    [b]Figures adjusted to reflect purchasing power of grain; nominal whole-
sale price of wheat, as recorded annually after the harvest, increased by an
average of 12.6 percent between the two periods.

cash apports of the 38 masters or their sons who declared them averaged over 241 livres, compared to only 64 livres for the 32 journeymen.

The gulf between master and journeyman wealth was even greater
during the next half century. In the 492 marriage contracts sampled,
the cash value of bridal apports declared by masters averaged 408.7
livres (357.2 when adjusted to reflect buying power of grain). By the
first half of the seventeenth century, significantly enough, many
fewer journeymen's daughters were marrying in Dijon (only thirty-
nine appear in my sample), and the few who declared cash-value
apports (twenty-two) averaged only 156.0 livres (adjusted, 136.3).
Masters, thus, were able to give nearly three times as much as journeymen. The groom profile shows a proportional narrowing of the
gap, for reasons I will soon discuss. Nearly all the masters or their
sons (232 of 236) declared bagues et joyeux (averaging 55.3 livres), and
154 stated apports (averaging 480.0 livres—adjusted, 419.5). The
mean for the journeymen or their sons declaring bagues (203 of 204 in
the sample) was 32.1 livres, and the 100 cash apports averaged 282.4
livres (adjusted, 246.8).

These figures are significant in two ways. First, they depict the
great difference in wealth between masters and journeymen, a gulf
that would certainly be greater if we could figure in the value of
trousseaux and other noncash assets. Moreover, the journeymen ap-

pearing in the marriage contracts are presumably those who were financially secure enough to consider establishing an independent household. As we will see, many of them were the ones fortunate enough to be marrying the daughter of a master and were thus headed for mastership themselves. How much greater must have been the gap between the wealth of established masters and that of the many journeymen on the tour de France. Second, unless there was dowry inflation of 150 percent from the second half of the sixteenth century to the first half of the seventeenth, the rise in the value of dowries suggests a considerable increase in wealth. Calculated in terms of buying power of grain, the apports of daughters of masters were one and one-half times higher in the fifty years after 1600 than in the half century before. The grooms' apports also burgeoned, notably among journeymen, though this increase can probably be attributed to the premium masters with eligible daughters to marry were exacting from journeymen with financial assets. Of course, not every journeyman marrying in Dijon married a master's daughter. It is also possible that the decline in the number of journeymen marrying in Dijon and the increase in their wealth may well reflect the success of the compagnonnages.

The marriage contracts, thus, reveal what the tax rolls do not. The taxes assessed show only the relative wealth of artisans within taxpaying society as a whole, and relative to the rest of Dijon, the artisans experienced little change in their position: they simply tended to coalesce in the upper middle of the scale. Moreover, the tax rolls did not distinguish between masters and journeymen. The marriage contracts, however, and especially the bridal apports, imply that artisan wealth increased in absolute terms (see Table 2.8). This was true for masters as well as journeymen. Even so, there was a great gap between them, despite the fact that the journeymen represented were privileged individuals for their rank. If artisan, especially master, wealth was increasing while the relative position of artisans in the hierarchy of all taxpayers was changing little, Dijon as a whole must also have been growing richer. Indeed, this is a conclusion one would draw from the general economic and administrative picture of the city at this time. The artisans of Burgundy's capital were a cork on a rising tide.

There are other indications of increasing prosperity among artisans to add to these. The abundant notarial records of real estate transactions are especially illustrative. Since many artisans, both masters and journeymen (at least for a time), were parties to these transactions, this source can show economic status (which artisans bought and sold and when) and values (where artisans invested their capital and why).

The system of mortmain in medieval Burgundy made opportunities to buy land rare indeed. By the beginning of the sixteenth century, however, much peasant land had become enfranchised and thus alienable.[22] During the early sixteenth century there were a great many small proprietors in the countryside surrounding Dijon.[23] At the same time, Dijon had a growing upper class with capital. The wars and inflation of the second half of the century impoverished the Burgundian countryside, driving the peasant proprietors or their children (many of them journeymen) to sell their land to urban investors who aspired to hold a rural domain as an investment, a status symbol, or collateral for credit.[24] By the middle of the seventeenth century nearly all the bailliage around Dijon belonged to the city's inhabitants.[25] The respected Burgundian historian Gaston Roupnel suggested that Dijon's richest artisans joined the local merchants and legal elite in this acquisition of rural properties, and the available evidence bears out his contention—to some extent.

Tables 2.9 and 2.10 tell us several things. Between 1550 and 1650, master artisans participated frequently in the real estate market both within and outside Dijon, but they increasingly concentrated the bulk of their capital in urban properties, the vast majority of them dwellings. This tendency was especially evident during the first quarter of the seventeenth century, while the surge in apports was being

---

22. Roupnel, p. 221.

23. Henri Drouot, *Mayenne et la Bourgogne: Etude sur la Ligue, 1587–1596*, 2 vols. (Paris, 1937), 1:55.

24. Ibid., 1:43. See also Roupnel, p. 187.

25. Roupnel, p. 197. Roupnel found that 57 of 107 villages had no peasant proprietor at all in the first half of the seventeenth century. This exploitation by urban capital is corroborated by Jean-Pierre Gutton, who says that, in 1665–66, 53 of 104 communities in the Burgundian bailliage of Arnay-le-Duc had been wholly or partially alienated since the end of the sixteenth century, most during the Wars of Religion and the war against Spain, 1635–59. He suggests that the situation was similar in Lorraine, 1575–1600. See Gutton, *La sociabilité villageoise* (Paris, 1979), pp. 116–17. Benedict, *Rouen during the Wars of Religion*, p. 275, suggests that the extension of bourgeois capital over the surrounding countryside was a national trend in the sixteenth century.

**Table 2.9**
Real estate transactions of masters, 1550–1650

| | Urban Property (Dijon) | | | | Rural Property | | | | Total |
| | Bought | | Sold | | Bought | | Sold | | Contract |
| Period | N[a] | Mean value[b] | N | Mean value | N | Mean value | N | Mean value | Sample[c] |
|---|---|---|---|---|---|---|---|---|---|
| 1550–1584 | 28 | 192.5 | 22 | 185.8 | 57 | 45.5 | 29 | 54.2 | 207 |
| 1585–1595 | 12 | 263.3 | 11 | 304.1 | 21 | 33.6 | 13 | 82.6 | 54 |
| 1596–1624 | 30 | 909.6 | 19 | 842.4 | 59 | 57.6 | 35 | 161.6 | 151 |
| 1625–1636 | 19 | 831.0 | 21 | 976.7 | 11 | 181.8 | 18 | 192.4 | 54 |
| 1637–1650 | 12 | 1,202.0 | 10 | 1,569.9 | 26 | 106.6 | 12 | 108.6 | 58 |
| | | | | | | | | | 524 |

Source: ADCO, *Notaires*.

[a]N is number of transactions.

[b]In livres tournois, nominal value.

[c]May be higher or lower than sum of number of transactions, since total includes transactions by journeymen, and several contracts between masters.

**Table 2.10**
Urban capital invested and divested by masters, 1550–1650

| Period | Total capital (in livres tournois) | Percentage of capital in urban property | Number of transactions |
|---|---|---|---|
| 1550–1584 | | | |
| Invested | 7,984 | 67.5 | 85 |
| Divested | 5,659 | 72.2 | 51 |
| 21585– | | | |
| 1595 | | | |
| Invested | 3,865 | 81.7 | 33 |
| Divested | 4,418 | 75.7 | 24 |
| 1596–1624 | | | |
| Invested | 30,686 | 88.9 | 89 |
| Divested | 21,662 | 75.9 | 54 |
| 1625–1636 | | | |
| Invested | 17,789 | 88.8 | 30 |
| Divested | 23,974 | 85.6 | 39 |
| 1637–1650 | | | |
| Invested | 17,195 | 83.9 | 38 |
| Divested | 17,002 | 92.3 | 22 |

Source: ADCO, *Notaires.*

recorded. Apparently, masters had much greater capital to invest during this period.

Up to 1585, master artisans invested about one-third of their capital in rural property. Because of population growth in the Burgundian countryside, land was being divided among more and more heirs. The parcels inherited under the rule of equal partition rapidly became quite small—too small to farm successfully—but a peasant's son become a journeyman could convert his small inheritance into cash to be put toward the cost of a wedding, a mastership, or the purchase of tools and supplies. After 1560, with the disruption of economic life and the growing insecurity caused by war, many journeymen must have felt it prudent to unload arable land, vineyards, and orchards, and they found ready buyers in the urban master craftsmen. When war intensified in the 1580s, however, masters decided that intramural investments were safer, and they began spending their money in town. They continued this trend even after the Wars of Religion, at least to the mid-seventeenth century, trading quite heavily and mainly within Dijon (see Tables 2.9, 2.10). Between 1596 and 1650 the

value of urban investments dwarfed rural ones by over seven to one
(total urban investment by the sampled masters amounted to 57,502
livres while rural investment reached only 8,168 livres). In the second
half of the sixteenth century the ratio was under three to one, and
much smaller amounts had been involved (8,550 livres went into
urban properties, 3,299 livres into rural).

Like marriage contracts, real estate transactions made careful use
of honorific epithets, and so it is easy to distinguish between masters
and journeymen.

Table 2.11 vividly shows a pattern of divestiture by journeymen
before 1584, then a vertiginous decline in trading; after 1625, journeymen virtually ceased trading in real estate. Those few who still had
property after 1595 must have been persuaded to sell in a market of
escalating values and demand. Masters continued to buy and sell at a
more or less constant rate, but the level of capital investment grew
considerably (see Table 2.12). Journeymen, meanwhile, were priced
out of the market.

As masters increasingly came to prefer urban property, specifically
houses or parts of houses, the prices they paid also rose (see Table
2.13). Either the cost of houses in Dijon was skyrocketing, or masters
were investing their new wealth in more expensive houses. It was
probably a combination of both. The nominal value of housing stock
that masters were buying nearly quadrupled by the first half of the
seventeenth century, and nearly all masters were purchasing the entire dwelling. Furthermore—and it is hardly surprising—houses
bought by masters were far beyond the means of journeymen. Between 1550 and 1595 only eleven journeymen purchased houses. On
average 71.2 percent of the house was involved and the price was

**Table 2.11**
Real estate transactions of masters and journeymen, 1550–1650

| Period | Masters | | Journeymen | | Contracts in sample |
| | Bought | Sold | Bought | Sold | |
|---|---|---|---|---|---|
| 1550–1584 | 85 | 51 | 33 | 81 | 207 |
| 1585–1595 | 33 | 24 | 5 | 8 | 54 |
| 1596–1624 | 89 | 54 | 7 | 17 | 151 |
| 1625–1636 | 30 | 39 | 2 | 1 | 54 |
| 1637–1650 | 38 | 22 | 2 | 3 | 58 |

Source: ADCO, *Notaires*.

**Table 2.12**
Capital investment in real estate by artisans (in livres
tournois), 1550–1650

| Period | Masters | Journeymen | Total Sample |
|--------|---------|------------|--------------|
| 1550–1584 | 7,984 | 1,548 | 207 |
| 1585–1595 | 3,865 | 76 | 54 |
| 1596–1624 | 30,686 | 1,907 | 151 |
| 1625–1636 | 17,789 | 45 | 54 |
| 1637–1650 | 17,195 | 2,250 | 58 |

Source: ADCO, *Notaires.*

138.3 livres—just over half the value of the houses masters were
buying. By the seventeenth century, journeymen essentially disappear from the sample; after 1575 only six journeymen bought housing. Apparently, nearly all of them had been priced out of an inflationary
market altogether.[26] During the same period, however, particularly
after the Wars of Religion, not only were masters paying higher prices
but more of them were entering the market.[27]

That the masters chose to invest their new wealth intramuros suggests the increasingly parochial thinking taking hold in the master
artisanat (recall the proliferating requirements for local apprentice-

26. Sales of houses follow the same pattern of rising prices and percentage of property sold. From 1550 to 1595, twenty masters sold property in Dijon. The average price
for 80 percent of the property was 460 livres. During the ensuing half century, 1596–
1650, thirty-seven sellers were masters. They sold an average 87.8 percent of the
dwelling for 1,398.3 livres. Selling property need not imply poverty. Those traceable to
the tax rolls were far from poor. In 1555 Jehan Girault, a goldsmith who fell into the top
20 percent of taxpayers, sold one-fourth of a house worth 880 livres. Two years later
Claude Chaulin, a shoemaker in the top 30 percent of taxpayers, sold a house worth
260 livres. In 1562 pastrycook Claude Robert, among the richest 10 percent of taxpayers, sold a house worth 400 livres; more than eighty years later (in 1643) another
pastrycook in the top 10 percent, Estienne Barbier, sold a house worth 900 livres.
Antoine Leschenet, a baker as wealthy as these pastrycooks, was very active in the
rural land market but also sold a house worth 3,000 livres in 1643. ADCO, *Notaires*
#305, 26 Sept. 1555, #295, 6 Aug. 1557, 16 June 1562, #1950, 1 Aug., 22 June 1643.
There is a suggestion of a lively and quite plausibly speculative market.
27. Between 1550 and 1573, nine master buyers bought housing stock averaging
358.7 livres, acquiring an average of 75 percent of the property. Between 1574 and 1595,
the average climbed to 508.7 livres, but the masters (eighteen of them) acquired only
64.7 percent of the property. From 1596 to 1624, however, twenty-five masters averaged 1,041 livres and 96.5 percent. Even during the crisis period of 1625–37, thirteen
masters averaged 1,218.8 livres and 89.7 percent.

**Table 2.13**
Houses in Dijon purchased by masters, 1550–1650

| Period | N | Mean purchase price | Percentage of dwelling purchased[a] |
|---|---|---|---|
| 1550–1595 | 26 | 232.1 livres | 70.4 |
| 1596–1650 | 44 | 1,206.8 livres | 95.0 |

Source: ADCO, *Notaires*.
[a]Between 1550 and 1595 only four contracts with master purchasers did not specify the fraction, and between 1596 and 1650 only three did not. Omitted from the table, these do not affect the general trend visible here.

ship during this period). If this inward turn is apparent throughout the period, it became especially pronounced during times of insecurity or crisis. As Table 2.14 suggests, master artisans cast their acquisitive net wide, both geographically and occupationally, during times of relative stability, but during uncertain times they preferred to trade with fellow masters living within the walls of Dijon. As we will see, this closing of ranks applied to many areas of artisan life.

There is evidence that it was not only the wealthy masters who participated in the real estate market. Certainly, there is a wide range of purchase prices. For example, between 1596 and 1624, twenty-six master artisans bought houses in Dijon. The two most expensive cost 3,000 livres each, but others sold for as little as 192, 36, even 30 livres. Clearly, some houses were available to craftsmen with only moderate capital. Of course, we cannot know for sure whether rich artisans

**Table 2.14**
Real estate transactions between masters, 1550–1650

| Period | One party a Dijonnais master | Both parties Dijonnais masters | Percentage |
|---|---|---|---|
| Times of Stability | | | |
| 1550–1584 | 134 | 32 | 23.9 |
| 1596–1624 | 139 | 28 | 20.0 |
| 1637–1650 | 54 | 18 | 33.3 |
| Times of Crisis | | | |
| 1585–1595 | 51 | 18 | 35.0 |
| 1625–1636 | 68 | 34 | 50.0 |

Source: ADCO, *Notaires*.

were buying the inexpensive properties as well as the costly ones, but a correlation of the master craftsmen who bought houses in Dijon between 1633 and 1650 with the tax rolls of 1643 demonstrates that not just the richest were buying in the seventeenth century. Of eleven masters traceable to the tax rolls, seven had above average wealth. Two of them were among the richest 3 percent of taxpayers; two fell into the 91st percentile, and three into the 80th. Another three were of only average wealth, falling into the 53d percentile, and one was considerably poorer than average, in the 38th percentile. This admittedly small sample suggests that the rich master artisans were not the only ones buying houses.

Most artisans focused on urban acquisitions, but some, including many of the richest, bought rural property as well. We can assume, of course, that any buyer was at least solvent, but we know that artisans who bought *repeatedly* were rich, and masters all. For example, Jacques Gamot, a master mason in the 92d percentile of taxpayers in 1579, was a big buyer between 1562 and 1573, spending 347 livres on farm and vineyard land, much of it contiguous. Like many other craftsmen in Dijon, Gamot was evidently trying to piece together a rural domain that would provide his heirs an income from something other than manual labor and thus would raise their social status. Denis Vallée, a master roofer and one of the richest taxpayers in 1610 (95th percentile) likewise spent 783 livres between 1602 and 1625 on parcels of land near the village of St. Apollinaire, most of them contiguous. Denis Valnet displayed a similar desire for a rural domain; this master shoemaker of considerable wealth (top 8 percent in 1643) was active in buying up properties in his native village of Curtil. In over five hundred real estate contracts involving artisans between 1550 and 1650, however, no one matched the record of Antoine Leschenet, a wealthy master baker (top 8 percent in 1643), who between 1634 and 1645 invested over three thousand livres in arable land, vineyards, and houses, 30 percent of it paid in cash.[28] Artisans like these were economic worlds away from their journeymen, who by 1600 were essentially propertyless.

28. During the period 1550–1650, ten artisans in my sample were party to three or more contracts each. Of the seven who could be matched to the tax roll nearest their purchasing activity, not one fell below the 71st percentile in the wealth scale, and four were in the top 10 percent. For other examples, see ADCO, *Notaires* #371, 21 Dec. 1592, #1704, 1 Oct. 1605, #1695, 7 March 1615, #1696, 27 July 1619.

## Female Artisans

Like journeymen, widows of artisans tend to elude the records, and unmarried female artisans are practically invisible. Independent women artisans were juridically recognized only if they were widows; seamstresses and *lingères* did not belong to any guild. The few who appear on the tax rolls as heads of households certainly represent only a small portion of a substantial and important labor force, impossible to study systematically. Aside from widows, the tax rolls of 1556 list only four women artisans as household heads, and in 1643 only eight, all but one being seamstresses. Yet other documents show that many women, especially unmarried younger women, engaged in this sort of work. Widows of artisans, on the other hand, were members of their husbands' guilds as long as they did not remarry outside the guild, and occasionally they appear as heads of household on the tax rolls. In 1556, for example, thirty-six artisan widows were assessed an average 6.4 sous (compared to 8.3 for male craftsmen). By 1643 the number of artisan widows on the rolls had dropped to twenty-five, and they were assessed an average of 39.1 sous (the male artisan mean was 50.5).

Widows who were remarrying were usually disinclined to declare the value of their apports. For example, in my sample of artisan marriages between 1601 and 1650, of forty-three widows of artisans, only twenty-three declared apports (averaging 575.7 livres). A half century earlier they had been even more secretive about their assets; only fifteen of fifty-one stated apports. The mean was 593.5 livres, a misleading figure since one very rich widow distorts the sample. Without her, the average drops sharply, to 285.4 livres.

Like other widows on the tax rolls, widows of artisans ranged from very rich to very poor. As a group, however, like their male colleagues, they rose together with their class and the town as a whole.

## Material Life: Bread and Pewter

### Wages

The period 1550–1650 has been called the iron century. In many regions of northern Europe real wages, which had previously risen, declined during the second half of the sixteenth century and the first half of the seventeenth. Not until 1650 did the purchasing power of wage earners resume its rise.[29] So widespread was this trend that some historians have assumed it was universal. Yet in terms of purchasing power of wholesale grain, some Dijonnais craftsmen saw their real wages climb during this period. For example, master carpenters and wheelwrights in 1615 were earning two to three times the maximum daily wage they could have received in 1580, outstripping grain inflation over the same period.

The ruling classes of the sixteenth century believed rising wages to be the chief cause of dearth and responded to the "menace" with ordinances establishing maximum rates for wages, like the one decreed by the Parlement of Dijon and published in 1580.[30] Such ordinances were guided by the concept of a "moral economy," designed to provide the people with the necessary merchandise and food *à l'usage de l'homme* (i.e., grain, bread, wine, wood, meat, leather, and clothing).[31]

The Carthusian monks in Dijon did their part to keep wages down, too. Their account books record nominal daily wages that are lower than the maximums established in the *Règlement politique* of 1580 (see Table 2.15). Moreover, the wages paid master painters, carpenters, and wheelwrights working on public projects in 1615 are much higher than those paid by the monastery during the same period.[32] These and incidental references in other sources suggest that the monks were rather parsimonious.[33] Nevertheless, if we should be wary of generalizations based upon absolute figures, perhaps the Carthusian wages can reliably indicate trends and relationships. For example, for some crafts a distinction is made between wages paid

29. Jan de Vries, *The Economy of Europe in an Age of Crisis, 1600–1750* (Cambridge, 1976), p. 187.

30. *Règlement politique* (Dijon, 1580).

31. See Gascon, *Le grand commerce*, p. 805.

32. AMD, B253, fol. 171r, 17 Nov. 1615.

33. Other incidental references to wages show the Carthusians to be close to normal. For example, in 1565 some master masons contracting privately earned six to seven sous per day (AMD, B201, fol. 1531–155v, 12 June 1565); some roofers in 1588 earned twenty-six ecus per year, or 5.8 sous per day, at 270 workable days (ADCO, BII 360/51, Jan. 1588). By way of comparison, an interesting arret from the Parlement of Dijon on 24 Jan. 1559 posted rates (*taxes*) for legal service; solicitors (*procureurs*) were to be paid thirty sous per day for cases before the Parlement, twenty sous before the bailliage and chancellerie, and barristers (*avocats*) forty and thirty sous per day at the respective courts. BMD, ms 1496, fol. 148v–149v.

**Table 2.15**
Average nominal daily wages paid by the Carthusian monastery of Dijon (in sous and deniers), 1500–1643

| Craftsman | 1500–60 | 1561–74 | 1575–89 | 1590–1610 | 1611–43 | Percentage change 1561–1643 |
|---|---|---|---|---|---|---|
| Carpenter | | | | | | |
| master | 3s6d (fed) | 5s | 6s (fed) | 9s6d | 10s | 100.0 |
| journeyman | 3s | 3s4d | 3s4d | 3s4d | 6s | 81.8 |
| Plasterer | | | | | | |
| master | 4s | 4s | 4s | 12s (1593) | 12s | 200.0 |
| journeyman | 3s | 3s | 3s | 3s | 3s | 0.0 |
| Mason | | | | | | |
| master | 4s | 4s6d | 4s6d | 9s | 9s6d | 111.1 |
| journeyman | 2s6d | 2s6d | 2s6d | 2s6d | 5s | 100.0 |
| Cooper | | | | | | |
| master | 5s | 6s | 6s | 7s | 7s | 16.7 |
| journeyman | 2s | 3s4d | 3s4d | 4s | 4s | 20.1 |
| Cabinetmaker | 3s6d (fed) | 5s | 5s | 5s | 5s | 0.0 |
| Roofer/tiler | 3s (fed) | 5s | 6s | 6s | 10s | 66.7 |
| Coppersmith | 1s8d | 5s (1570) | 5s | 5s | 5s | 0.0 |
| Chandler | 5s | 5s | 5s | 5s | 5s | 0.0 |
| Shoemaker | 1s8d | 1s8d | 1s8d | 6s6d (1604) | 6s6d | 289.2 |
| Furrier | | | | | | |
| master | — | — | — | 20s (1610) | 20s | 0.0 |
| journeyman | 1s8d (fed) | 1s8d (fed) | 1s8d (fed) | — | — | 0.0 |
| Tailor | 4s6d | 4s6d | 4s6d | 4s6d | 4s6d | 0.0 |
| Painter | 4s3d | 4s3d | 10s (fed) (1588) | 10s (fed) | 10s (fed) | 135.3 |

Source: Cyprien Monget, *Histoire de la Chartreuse*, pp. 418–19.

master and journeyman, and the rise in journeyman wages generally lagged behind the rise in wages paid the masters. The wages of master carpenters had been rising for fifty years—since 1561—before those of the journeymen moved at all. There was a similar lag among masons. Worse yet, master plasterers tripled their wages between 1575 and 1611, while their journeymen enjoyed no increase whatsoever.

It is likely that wage trends were similar for all employers, for most craftsmen whose real wages from the Carthusians increased also improved their position in the wealth scale (based on the tax rolls) over the same period. For instance, between 1561 and 1643 real wages paid the carpenters (both masters and journeymen) rose steadily as these craftsmen grew wealthier. Between 1556 and 1643 their median tax assessment jumped from the 50th percentile to the 71st. Similarly, the shoemakers' wages climbed between 1575 and 1610, as did the median tax status of these craftsmen, which was at the 63d percentile in 1556 and the 71st in 1643. The roofers' wages rose precipitously between 1610 and 1643, too, and they also rose in the scale of relative wealth: their median tax in 1556 put them in the 40th percentile; in 1643 in the 64th.

The inverse is also true. The median tax ranking of the cabinet-makers, whose wages remained stagnant throughout the period, fell between 1556 and 1643 from the 63d percentile to the 53d. Tailors, too, suffered a decline in real wages and thus a decline in their median tax ranking, from the 63d to the 53d percentile between 1556 and 1643.

These comparisons between the Carthusian wage index and the wealth distribution scale suggest that wage increases benefited the poorer members of the trades in question. Between 1556 and 1643 as the wages paid carpenters went up considerably, the number of poor carpenters declined (four of thirty-five were in the bottom 23 percent in 1556, but only one of twenty-three was in the bottom 25 percent by 1643). The case of the shoemakers is even more telling. In 1556, eleven of thirty-six were in the bottom 23 percent of the tax scale, but by 1643, after nearly a century of rising wages, the ranks of the poorer shoemakers were considerably thinned. Only four of forty-five were in the bottom quarter. Conversely, the ranks of the poor swelled if real wages declined. In 1556 eleven of seventy tailors were in the bottom 23 percent. Wages remained unchanged in subsequent years, and by 1643, twenty of seventy-one suffered in the bottom fourth.

Certainly other factors than wages could and did influence the wealth status of various crafts, but the correlation between relative poverty within a trade and the rise or decline in real wages is both obvious and important. The poorer members of a trade, whether masters or journeymen, were more likely to be wage earners than contractors and were more affected by variations in wage rates than the more prosperous masters, who must usually have worked *à la tâche* and paid wages to workers themselves.

## Patterns of Consumption

The actual amounts of wages are meaningless, of course, unless we know their purchasing power. As we have seen, several crafts appear to have posted advances in real wages measured against wholesale grain prices, but this generalization obscures the fact that prices oscillated annually, even weekly. In his work on sixteenth-century Lyons, Richard Gascon sketched a useful family budget that could keep a working-class household above the threshold of poverty in an economically stable year.[34] Of course, not all years were stable, and so, using Gascon's model, I have tried to illustrate the difference in the buying power of wage earners between stable and catastrophic years (see Table 2.16). Municipal tariffs provide the price of brown bread, the staple food of wage earners, and in years of more than one tariff, the price is averaged. An average household of 4.5 persons would consume seven pounds of bread a day, 365 days a year. It is a simple matter, then, to figure the requisite daily wage needed to buy this much bread if the work year comprises 270 days. It is important to remember that males were not the sole breadwinners in the preindustrial family economy, but whether the family earned other income or not, these minimum wages would be required for sustenance, and they provide useful comparisons.[35] Of course, bread prices did not increase at the same rate as such other elements in the budget as rent or meat, but since bread was the necessity, it provides a good minimum on which to base the budget. If the prices of most other commodities grew faster than that of bread, as appears to have been

34. Gascon, *Le grand commerce*, p. 742.

35. Louise A. Tilly and Joan W. Scott, *Women, Work and Family* (New York, 1978), esp. chap. 3.

**Table 2.16**
Common family budget, selected years, nominal values

|                                                    | 1580 (stable year) | 1595 (crisis year) | 1636 (crisis year) | 1646 (stable year) |
| -------------------------------------------------- | ------------------ | ------------------ | ------------------ | ------------------ |
| Price of brown bread (in deniers per pound)        | 3.75               | 8.0                | 14.0               | 6.0                |
| Annual Budget (in livres tournois)                 | 78.9               | 170.4              | 299.4              | 127.8              |
| Requisite Daily Wage (in sous)                     | 5.9                | 12.6               | 22.2               | 9.5                |

Source: AMD, B218, B233, B274, B284.

the case (see Table 2.17), the family's diet and quality of life would suffer. In extreme cases, children might be forced into the streets to beg.

Earnings were always precarious. A family had to eat every day, but, since bad weather and religious festivals encroached on productivity, even during stable periods wage earners worked a maximum of 270 days. When war and plague joined in, the number of working days declined even more. To make matters worse, dearth invariably led to unemployment.[36] In the crisis year of 1595, workers would have had to earn more than twice the wages they had in 1580 just to stay above poverty level; yet few craftsmen experienced this kind of wage increase, at least at the Carthusian monastery (see Table 2.15).[37]

Of the artisans employed for wages by the Carthusian monks in 1580, master carpenters, coopers, roofers, and painters were paid enough to support the hypothetical budget, but only the painters were comfortably above it. The maximum rates decreed in the *Règlement politique* would have supported nearly all masters and their families, but the wives of all married journeymen and master shoemakers would have had to earn as much as their husbands to make ends meet. In 1595 only the master plasterers and probably the painters and furriers working for the Carthusians kept their heads above water, and just barely. In 1636 all wage earners fell below the thresh-

36. Goubert, 1:302, 303, sees an invariable grim schema: "dearth, unemployment... contagion."

37. During the same period the cost of living nearly doubled in Lyons as well. See Gascon, *Le grand commerce*, p. 936.

**Table 2.17**
Wholesale nominal prices of lowest quality commodities, St. Martin's Day
market (October 11), selected years

|                                              | 1580 (stable year) | 1595 (crisis year) | 1636 (crisis year) | 1646 (stable year) |
| -------------------------------------------- | ------------------ | ------------------ | ------------------ | ------------------ |
| Wine (in livres tournois per *queue*)        | 12                 | 18                 | 24                 | 14                 |
| Peas (in sous per *quarteranche*)            | 18                 | 40                 | 55                 | 40                 |
| Broadbeans (in sous per *quarteranche*)      | 13.4               | 30                 | 50                 | 25                 |

Source: AMD, B218, fol. 42r, B233, fol. 209r, B274, fol. 259r, B284, fol. 142v.

old of poverty, and only the stability of a year like 1646 rescued the
master plasterers, carpenters, masons, roofers and painters. By then
only the master furriers were comfortably above the budget. Wage
earners in crafts like tailoring and cabinetmaking were never able to
provide their families with all the elements of such a budget. They
survived with the help of working wives and by curtailing expenditures on such nonessentials as meat or vegetables or presumably by
sending children out as servants.

Even if Carthusian wages were below market rates and if the wives
of wage-earning artisans were contributing to the family income,
many wage-earning families clearly had a tough time making ends
meet. The wages required to maintain Gascon's living standard illustrate the devastating effect of war, plague, and harvest failure on
wage-earning craftsmen. They also show how generalizations about
rising real wages over the long term need to be interpreted to render
an accurate picture of the experience of many early modern wage
earners.

Yet however important wage rates may have been, many craftsmen—especially masters—typically worked not for wages but *à la
tâche*; that is, they were paid for the individual piece or the job.
Masons and carpenters usually followed this practice, as did many
other artisans, no doubt. Unfortunately, quantification eludes us. For
instance, a master shoemaker in the 1620s might earn three to four
sous per pair, and a journeyman half as much, but depending on his
age and agility, a shoemaker could make anywhere from three to

eight pairs of shoes per day.[38] Peak productivity could bring in a fair income for a master, and in most years could keep a journeyman and his family out of the clutches of destitution.

Another glimpse of the cost of living comes from an admittedly impressionistic but nonetheless useful document. Between 1634 and 1647 a Dijon notary kept an account book of expenses incurred by guardians (first a master shoemaker, then his widow, then a master parchmentmaker) for the support of an orphan.[39] The book gives an interesting picture of what it might cost an artisan of moderate wealth to raise a girl from childhood to marriage. To keep this child in clothing and shoes cost an average of fourteen livres, four sous, per year. Bed and board cost another thirty livres per year from 1634 to 1636 and thirty-six livres from 1637 to 1640. In 1641 and 1642 the orphan was apprenticed as a seamstress; her bed and board cost fifty livres the first year and sixty the second. After she returned to the widow's home in 1643, she paid thirty livres per year through 1647. Such expenses could not have been met by an artisan on the threshold of poverty, but these guardians were not among Dijon's wealthiest craftsmen either. This girl would not have been put out to apprenticeship had she come from a wealthy family, since her prospects of a good marriage would have made it unnecessary for her to learn a trade. According to the account book, it cost nearly fifty livres per year, or nearly four sous per day (excluding the cost of apprenticeship), to support a daughter. Sons would be that much more costly, and adults even more. It seems likely that a family of four or five of this middling status would need an income of at least twenty sous per day to provide clothes, shoes, food, and lodging. As we have seen, such an income was well beyond the daily rates of almost all wage earners.[40] Therefore, a hypothetical family of this status would enjoy a better standard of living than those wage earners on the common budget for the years 1636 and 1646. Indeed, in the catastrophic year of 1636 even craftsmen of middling wealth must have found themselves perilously close to the threshold of poverty.

38. AMD, G24, 31 Oct. 1579.
39. ADCO, *Notaires* #1934.
40. To be sure, the cost of running a household has more variables than those listed here, but the amounts in the account book were probably figured against what it cost to support the child. Even so, the hypothetical requisite wage is likely low, since consumption by other members of an "average" household (especially males) would be greater than this girl's.

If, as we have seen, most masters were of middling wealth, then most must have worked by the task and not for wages. The rates being paid simply are not sufficient to account for the surging prosperity of Dijon's master artisans. They help explain why the floor of poverty was raised among resident artisans and why journeymen rarely married in Dijon after 1600 but not why so many master craftsmen were doing so much better economically in the seventeenth century.

## Personal Possessions

Tables that show the distribution of wealth, though invaluable, cannot give a rounded picture of assets. In the possessions an artisan held dear, however, we can begin to read the contours of a value system. Marriage contracts provide an excellent starting place, for parents often gave sizable amounts of cash or other valuables to launch the new household and the new workshop. One master locksmith gave his daughter a trousseau worth three hundred livres in 1626. Even during hard times in 1633, a master plasterer found it possible to give his daughter four hundred livres' worth of "golden jewelry, linen, clothing and [household] utensils." In 1637 a master shoemaker, Damien Mariette, offered his daughter a choice between five hundred livres cash or one hundred livres cash plus a trousseau. Sons were also favored. The mother of one coppersmith, for instance, gave her son at marriage the tools of his trade, worth a hundred livres. Others had acquired their tools before marriage. In 1643 a master locksmith declared that he had tools and his masterpiece, worth a hundred livres, and five years later a master shoemaker declared to his future wife that he had assets including "a furnished shop, furniture [and] merchandise of his trade," worth two hundred livres.[41] These are examples not of fabulous wealth, of course, but of a comfortable life.

Some master artisans even possessed public offices, a sure sign of considerable affluence. One Dijonnais tanner inherited from his father a fifth part of the office entrusted with "marking" hides in the nearby village of Bellegarde, worth six hundred livres. Claude Maitron, daughter of a master shoemaker, married a man who held an

41. ADCO, *Notaires* #384, 29 Sept. 1626, #1952, 3 March 1633, #1951, 31 Jan. 1637, #1952, 3 March 1632, #1771, 17 Jan. 1649, #1934, 1 July 1648.

office from the Abbey of St. Bénigne worth eight hundred livres.[42]
Wealthy goldsmiths were prime candidates for the coveted office of
royal mintmaster in Dijon, and rich painters sought the tax-exempt
and lucrative offices of painter of the royal escutcheon or conservator
of the Salle des Peintres in the *logis du roi*.[43]

Wealthy master artisans also competed among themselves and
with merchants for municipal tax farms. In 1629 Jacques Brechillet, a
master pastrycook, could afford to bid twenty-six hundred livres per
year for three years for the tax farm in Dijon on iron imports. In 1641
the master baker Antoine Leschenet became the farmer of the municipal wine tax by paying thirty-two hundred livres per year for three
years. He was among the richest taxpayers in town. Even some tailors
were quite wealthy. Master Philippe Larmier bought Leschenet's
tax farm in 1647, paying eighteen hundred livres per year for three
years.[44]

Postmortem inventories, though not overly abundant in Dijon, give
a good idea of an artisan's standard of living, and occasionally the
deceased can also be located on an extant tax roll. The lists of possessions in conjunction with position on the scale of wealth can indicate
how people of certain economic and social strata furnished their
homes, what type of dwellings they inhabited, and indirectly, what
they valued. Frequently the same sort of items appear in inventories
of rich and poor, but the rich have more and no doubt better goods.
People of all classes owned feather beds, linen, and pewter, for example. Gold, silver, jewelry, sumptuous clothing, and income-producing
bonds (*constitutions de rentes*) were reserved for the more affluent.[45]

A journeyman on the tour de France would have a tool, a sword or
dagger, and a spare shirt in his knapsack, but nothing more.[46] A more

42. Ibid., #1950, 23 Aug. 1643, #1223, 7 Dec. 1648.

43. For goldsmiths, see AMD, B196, fol. 89v, 22 Nov..1558, B215, fol. 350r, 24 Jan.
1581. For painters, see AMD, B235, fol. 188r, 6 Feb. 1598 (in which Nicolas Drouhin
received letters from the king which exempted him from nightwatch duty, civic im-
posts, and, most important, the taille); and Chapuis, *Les anciennes corporations*, p.
393. The conservator oversaw the maintenance of statues and paintings housed in
administrative buildings in Dijon.

44. AMD, B267, fol. 130v–131r, 20 Dec. 1629, B278, fol. 259r, 24 May 1641, B284,
fol. 306r, 14 June 1647.

45. *Rentes* were loans at interest under the guise of a sales contract in which the
purchase price is the principal and annual rent is the repayment with interest figured
in. See Goubert, pp. 536–37; Bernard Schnapper, *Les rentes au seizième siècle: Histoire
d'un instrument de crédit* (Paris, 1957).

46. ADCO, BII 360/51, 17–22 Aug. 1588.

sedentary craftsman of slight means might furnish a rented room with some iron and ceramic kitchen utensils, a table, a few chairs and stools, and a bedstead—the last his most valuable possession. Jean Corderot, a tailor, was one such. His total household assets amounted to only ten livres. By comparison, Jean Gendot, a master tailor inventoried one year before Corderot, had household assets of seventy-one livres.[47] Ten years earlier Gendot had been in the 46th percentile of wealth distribution. Corderot, then, must have been among the poorest resident artisans in town.

One of the first valuable things bought by artisans, even those of modest means, was pewter—a preference they shared with Dijon's bourgeois and many gentlemen.[48] Jérome Miot, a master tailor inventoried in 1581, owned quite an array of pewter items: four bowls, four plates, two platters, a large tankard, a pitcher, a small mustard pot, a goblet, and a saltcellar. Eight years later Jean Constantin, a master shoemaker in the 46th percentile in 1579, had eighteen pewter plates and seven platters.[49] It is likely that pewter was considered an investment, for it had intrinsic value, and that value tripled from 1589 to 1645.[50] Wealthier artisans like Jean Piot, a master tailor whose inventoried household possessions were worth 731 livres in 1605, had nearly sixty-two livres' worth of pewter.[51] In 1645 Antoine Leschenet, the wealthy master baker, left possessions worth over a thousand livres, including seventy-six livres' worth of "common" and "fine" pewter.[52] Clearly, pewter was much sought after.

Like medieval Florentine patricians and seventeenth-century Dutch farmers, Dijon's artisans avidly collected linens and blankets. Cloth of any kind was valuable in early modern France, and in the cold, damp winters typical of Dijon a household could not have too many blankets. Moreover, dining with neighbors, as we will see, was an important aspect of social life. Since frequent washing was impractical, it was sensible to acquire as many napkins and tablecloths as

47. Ibid., 356/7, 10 Feb. 1590, 23 Aug. 1589.
48. Emile de Levasseur, *Histoire des classes ouvrières et de l'industrie en France avant 1789*, 2 vols. (Paris, 1900–1901), 2:19–20.
49. ADCO, BII 360/51, 5 May 1581, 356/7, 24 April 1589.
50. The value of common pewter increased from three and a third sous a pound in 1589 (ADCO, BII 356/7, 12 Sept. 1589) to ten sous a pound in 1645 (ADCO, *Notaires* #1936, 5 Oct. 1645).
51. ADCO, BII 356/16, 1 June 1605.
52. ADCO, *Notaires* #1936, 5 Oct. 1645. "Fine" pewter was appraised at sixteen sous a pound.

possible. Some of these linens came to the household in the wife's trousseau; others were bought as finances allowed. It was not unusual to find inventories of master artisans listing a dozen sheets and blankets, several dozen napkins, a half dozen tablecloths, and so on.[53] Bénigne Fay, a master pinmaker inventoried in 1605, had over 23 livres' worth of linen out of total household possessions worth 180 livres. Master cobbler Claude Quelon had nineteen *drapts de lit*, twenty-four napkins, and nine tablecloths when he died in 1645; of total possessions worth 261 livres, 10 sous, his pewter and linen collection alone surpassed 100 livres.[54] Along with pewter, linens seem to have been one of the primary acquisitions made by those who found themselves above subsistence level.

Even poorer artisans, of course, owned clothing, though the poorest had none worth inventorying.[55] Each morning most of the poorer craftsmen might choose between two or three shirts, a couple of doublets, and two pairs of hose, though they probably had but one cloak and hat. Their wives seem to have had less—a dress and a few blouses perhaps. This limited wardrobe was a far cry from that of the courtly class, which typically included twenty-five or thirty different outfits.[56] Nonetheless, to the artisan no less than the noble, appearance was important; dress was part of the style that "made" him. The inventories reveal that fine clothing could be expensive, and craftsmen, even the relatively affluent, seem to have invested in only one elegant piece of clothing, which served for all ceremonial occasions. Jean Gros, an armorer with a total household worth 125 livres in 1605, had only 15 livres' worth of clothing, but his wife's coat alone was worth six livres. No doubt it was a prize possession. Sixteen years

---

53. For example, ADCO, BII 356/20, 26 Jan. 1645, 356/16, 28 June 1605, 356/20, 3 Aug. 1645. Jan de Vries, *The Dutch Rural Economy in the Golden Age, 1500–1700* (New Haven, 1974), pp. 220–21, finds in the postmortem inventories of Dutch farmers, 1583–99, that textiles constituted over half the total value of their movable property, excluding livestock. In 1698 one widow had twenty tablecloths, sixty-one napkins, forty-eight bedsheets, and fifty-three pillowcases—in a house with only three beds. In an as yet unpublished study of thirteenth-century Florentine magnates, Carol Lansing has found extensive cataloguing of linens in testaments.

54. ADCO, BII 356/16, 28 June 1605, 356/20, 26 Jan. 1645.

55. Jean Corderot, for example, had none listed at all. See also, ADCO, BII 356/6, 31 Oct. 1554, in which a weaver's widow had no clothing inventoried at all after her death, meaning her clothing probably consisted of worthless rags.

56. Levasseur, *Histoire avant 1789*, 2:7, for an observation made by a Venetian ambassador to France.

earlier the master shoemaker Hugues Bourrie counted nearly thirty livres' worth of clothing in a total household of 131 livres. A doublet edged with gray silk, worth nine livres, and a cloak with a velvet collar, worth six, were his prizes. The clothing in master cobbler Quelon's estate consisted of two skirts, a cloak, a doublet, and a camisole of red serge, worth a total of eighteen livres. The master tailor Gendot's wife had a dress worth seven livres, representing 10 percent of the total household assets. Jean Piot boasted a new cloak valued at twenty-seven livres, the prize possession of a wardrobe worth seventy-five, and the clothing of the rich baker Leschenet and his wife was worth eighty-seven livres.[57] It appears, then, that for rich and poor alike, quality was more important than quantity. Work clothes and daily outfits were quite plain and inexpensive,[58] but the ability to appear on the public stage sporting fine feathers was of the utmost importance. It is as if public opinion reserved its judgment of clothing for special occasions.

Nearly all master craftsmen, then, invested in pewter, linen, and their "fancy dress"; the difference between rich and poor was one of degree, not kind. But the richest also shared the tastes of the bourgeois and the lawyers, buying some items that were beyond the reach of the poorer artisans. In the inventories of rich craftsmen we find gold, silver, jewelry, and rentes. For example, 20 percent of baker Leschenet's worth at his death was tied up in silver plate, including a pitcher worth fifty-four livres. Evidently Leschenet dined in style, as befitted an aspiring *rentier*. To escape the stigma attached to the practice of a trade like baking, he had become a creditor, holding several rentes with principals totaling 660 livres and collecting interest on half a dozen loans. One master carpenter owed him 328 livres.[59] Antoine Lebrun, a wealthy master tailor, left ten gold rings and assorted pieces of silver plate, amounting to nearly 10 percent of the worth of all of his household possessions. His investments also went into rentes, yielding him a hundred livres a year in interest on principals totaling over sixteen hundred livres.[60] Jean Piot, another

---

57. ADCO, BII 356/16, 21 May 1605, 356/7, 12 Sept. 1589, 356/20, 26 Jan. 1645, 356/7, 23 Aug. 1589, 356/16, 1 June 1605, *Notaires* #1936, 5 Oct. 1645.

58. Depending on quality, shirts ranged from five to twenty sous; doublets cost a minimum of fifteen sous.

59. ADCO, *Notaires* #1936, 5 Oct. 1645.

60. Ibid., BII 356/20, 2 Aug. 1645.

master tailor a generation older than Lebrun, owned a cashbox when
he died. In it were nineteen golden ecus, two Spanish quadruples, four
Spanish double pistolets and two simples, and an Italian ducat and
pistolet. Next to the cash was a cache of jewels including nine gold
rings, a lapis lazuli, a turquoise, a garnet, a diamond, and a signet.
This small fortune was rounded out by eleven gulders of silver, a
silver bar, and a small silver model gondola. In addition, Piot owned
three rentes with principals totaling over seven hundred livres, two of
them on inhabitants of Langres.[61]

Through these litanies of valuable possessions we can glimpse the aspirations and desires of poor and rich artisans alike. To be sure, the
wealth of an individual at death may not accurately represent the
standard of living that individual enjoyed in life. Perhaps meager
savings were dissipated, or prolonged old age without the capacity to
work reduced an artisan's assets. Yet if the individual case cannot be
read with certainty, the pattern is nevertheless unmistakable. The
first desire of even the poor artisan was to acquire pewter, linens, and
an expensive change of clothing (the first two partly as investments).
Most artisans achieved no more, but the rich ones, whose economic
standing was on a par with that of some merchants and professionals,
would next invest in silver, gold, jewelry, and rentes.

Like these possessions, the dwellings that housed them ranged
from the very modest to the impressive. We know more about the
living conditions of master artisans than journeymen, since they appear in the after-death inventories more frequently. A journeyman on
the tour de France would stay at an inn, at least until hired by
a master who could house him or provide him with employment
steady enough to warrant renting a room. A poorer artisan like Corderot the tailor would certainly be able to afford only a room; he and
his family, if he had one, would all cook, eat, and sleep there.[62] Most
masters had a workshop on the ground floor, facing out upon the
street, and a room on the same level in the back, which, depending
upon the craftsman's wealth, might serve as kitchen, dining room,
and perhaps bedroom as well. If he had more money, he might have a
room or two on the second floor for use as sleeping quarters. Some

61. Ibid., 356/16, 1 June 1605.
62. Ibid., 356/7, 10 Feb. 1590. Corderot's condition seems to have been typical of the
poorer artisans up to the Revolution throughout France. See Coornaert, p. 281; Couturier, p. 205.

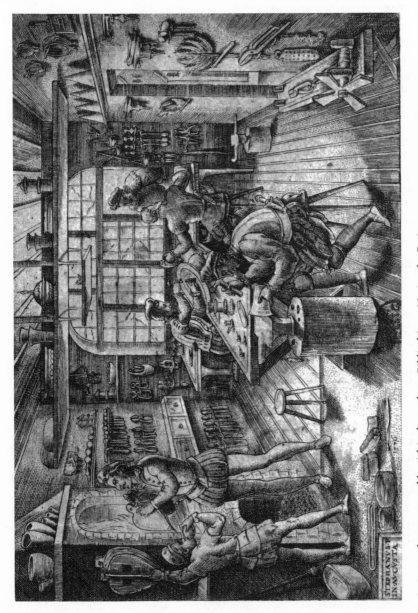

A sixteenth-century goldsmith's shop; photo Bibliothèque Nationale, Paris

**Table 2.18**
Artisan housing correlated to estate inventory, selected years

| Craftsman | Description of housing | Household assets, excluding rentes (in livres) | Date of inventory |
|---|---|---|---|
| Tailor | 1 room | 10 | 1590 |
| Master tailor | 1 room, shop below, attic above | 71 | 1589 |
| Shoemaker | shop, 2 rooms up, baptery[a] | —[b] | 1589 |
| Master armorer | 2 rooms down, 2 up | 125 | 1605 |
| Master cordwainer | 1 room down, 1 up, attic | 136 | 1645 |
| Master currier | shop, 1 room, cellar | 147 | 1645 |
| Master pinmaker | 1 room, baptery | 180 | 1605 |
| Master cobbler | shop, 1 room down, 1 up, cellar | 261 | 1645 |
| Master tailor | shop, 1 room, attic | 347 | 1645 |
| Master shoemaker | shop, 1 room down, 2 rooms up | —[c] | 1589 |
| Master tailor | shop, kitchen, 1 room down, 2 on 2d floor, 2 on 3d floor, attic, cellar | 725 | 1645 |
| Master tailor | shop, 1 room down, 2 up, 2 small bed-rooms, baptery, at-tic, cellar | 731 | 1605 |

Source: ADCO, BII 356/7–20 (postmortem inventories).
[a]Kitchen-pantry.
[b]This man was ranked in the 46th percentile of the tax scale in 1579.
[c]Ranked in the 94th percentile in 1579.

even had a third floor, where journeymen, apprentices, and servants could sleep in cramped quarters. Some dwellings also had attics and cellars. Table 2.18 describes some typical living quarters, relating them to the wealth of the artisan at death.

If the houses seem rather small, it is important to remember that buildings were packed tightly within the walls of Dijon. The city's medieval configurations were snug, the density probably being close to that of Lyons (five to six hundred persons per hectare).[63] In six-

63. Gascon, *Le grand commerce*, p. 346; Jacques Heers, *Family Clans in the Middle Ages: A Study of Political and Social Structures in Urban Areas*, trans. Barry Herbert (Amsterdam, 1977), finds similar density in medieval Genoa.

teenth- and seventeenth-century Dijon, renovations of the town's fortifications reduced the living area, and the simultaneous destruction of several suburbs by war encouraged the populace to move inside the walls.[64] Meanwhile, Dijon's population was increasing. The closely packed houses with their interior courtyards and gardens made an increasingly dense environment, which, in some respects, helped foster social solidarity and cohesion. As we will see, this crowding served as a bulwark against violence by making it easy for neighbors to communicate quickly.

64. Gras, p. 113.

# 3 Hierarchy and Solidarity

## Hierarchy

Sixteenth- and seventeenth-century France was a society stratified into a hierarchy of "orders," ranked "according to the esteem . . . [and] honor . . . that society attribute[d] to social functions."[1] Social status was also closely tied to the distribution and exercise of power, since coercion was one of the strongest means of maintaining the established hierarchy. Legally, every person belonged to a specific *état*, whose privileges and duties were codified. The état determined to whom one owed deference, what one could wear, and even how fancy a bed one could sleep in.[2] Although the members of the higher ranks were usually wealthy, wealth alone could not determine rank. Therefore, even though the wealth of some artisans approached that of some merchants and lawyers, it could not dissolve connection to a rank that placed a craftsman below a merchant or a lawyer.

Artisans found themselves in the lower middle of the status scale, beneath the merchants, surgeons, apothecaries, booksellers, and oth-

1. Roland Mousnier, *Social Hierarchies, 1450 to the Present*, trans. Peter Evans (New York, 1973), p. 23.
2. Many marriage contracts specify that the nuptial bed in the bride's trousseau is "decorated according to her rank" (*garny à son estat*).

er "professionals" but above the vignerons. At the very bottom were the unskilled day laborers, transients, and beggars, and above the merchants were the lesser members of the legal establishment (greffiers, bailiffs, solicitors, and notaries), then barristers and doctors with noble rank. Finally, in Dijon at any rate, perched at the very top was the *noblesse de robe* staffing the sovereign courts.[3]

In hierarchically stratified societies like that of old regime France, dress and comportment visually register rank. Those who wear clothing that is above their station, thus, threaten the sharp demarcation of strata. Frequently, the response is sumptuary legislation designed to maintain the system of social deference. The authorities of early modern France certainly responded in this way, promulgating copious sumptuary codes specifying the kind of clothing to be worn by each état.[4] Like everyone else, artisans were allowed to wear only specific styles of dress which clearly showed their social status. Too much silk or too wide a band of velvet on a garment was seen as an attempt to step out of one's natural position in the social hierarchy— a punishable offense. Of course, when the wealth of an artisan placed him in an economic stratum above his social rank, he had both motivation and means to try to cross the boundaries established in the sumptuary codes. In 1529 the mayor of Dijon condemned the unseemly display of some artisans. "The *gens de mestiers*, their wives and families and domestics," he said, "are superfluously and more richly dressed . . . than belongs to their rank, wearing silk cloth on their doublets . . . dresses and other [items of clothing]."[5] The mayor's complaint notwithstanding, artisan aspirations continued unabated; in 1577 the Parlement urged the mayor to punish the "excessiveness of indecent dress" among the artisans, who were, said the Parlement, adorning themselves "without discretion or measure." The ineffectiveness of this admonition can be judged from the fact that it was repeated in 1625.[6]

Enforcement was haphazard. Occasionally a miscreant was fined.

3. Roupnel, *La ville et la campagne*, pp. 154, 170, AMD, B214, fol. 192r, 31 May 1578, details the order of the procession of the Sacred Host (individuals marched in order of social prestige), which corroborates Roupnel's observations.

4. For example, AMD, I103, 8 May 1561; *Règlement politique*; AMD, I103, 19 Nov. 1610; and BMD, ms 1500, fol. 82, 27 Feb. 1625.

5. AMD, G4.

6. AMD, B214, fol. 851, 5 Nov. 1577; BMD, ms 1500, fol. 82 (article 9), 2 Feb. 1625.

In 1580, for example, master sword polisher Guyon Bonier was found wearing "three velvet bands on his stockings," and he paid a stiff fine of one ecu for his sartorial arrogance. A master counterpointer and a master carpenter were fined for wearing hats decorated with taffeta, and a master shoemaker's wife was fined one ecu for wearing a velvet band on her dress, "against the form of the ordinance that prohibited this to . . . artisans."[7] But many such offenses went unpunished, and sumptuary legislation notwithstanding, masters and their wives continued to dress beyond their rank (if not beyond their means) throughout the period, demonstrating one weakness of societies of orders.

The hierarchy in society as a whole is plain enough, but it is less clear whether there was a legal hierarchy within the artisanat. Of course, the law subordinated journeymen to masters, but stratification among guilds is difficult to establish for Dijon. In many other French towns such corporations had juridical definition and a status within the *corps de ville*.[8] The constitution of the commune of Dijon, however, was absolutely independent of the *corps de métiers*, and so no formal hierarchy of trades was enforced by the municipal government. Nevertheless, though we have no accounts of marching order in local parades (a useful indicator of status in other towns), we do have documents from 1585 and 1601 in which French kings appear to have ranked most of Dijon's guilds in order to affix a price to the mastership letters that the monarchs wanted to sell. What determined the royal categorization is impossible to say, but in these documents trades were divided among three categories: *meilleurs*, *medyocres*, and *moyens*.[9] Despite a few changes in the lists (for example, nineteen guilds were *meilleurs* in 1585, and twenty-two in 1601), there is enough consistency to show the royal perception of the proper hierarchical position of each craft. Though the king had ample interest in swelling the ranks of the *meilleurs*, there is no absolute correlation between rank and wealth. For example, carpenters, tailors, and cabinetmakers were ranked at the top, above the wealthier *medyocres* guilds of parchmentmakers and sword polishers. In fact,

---

7. AMD, B217, fol. 76v, 81v, 11 March 1580.
8. Roland Mousnier, "Les concepts d'*ordres*, d'*états*, de *fidélité*, et de *monarchie absolue* en France de la fin du 15e siècle à la fin du 18e," *Revue Historique* 247 (1972): 301–2 (applies to Paris). See also, Labal, "Le monde des métiers," p. 18–19.
9. AMD, G77.

even the *moyens* furriers were relatively richer than some craftsmen in the *meilleurs* category. But these rankings reflect the perceptions of the elites, and whether artisans subscribed to them is questionable. If, as I believe, artisans possessed a solidarity that transcended guilds, then it is likely that the sense of hierarchy among guilds was not very pronounced.

Social structures are inherently dynamic and so embody tensions and ambivalence in relations among their members. The ambiguities of social interaction are especially evident in a society of orders. In such a system the domination of the upper classes and their exercise of power are balanced against a recognition of the necessity for trust in human relations to preserve order on the one hand, and on the other the desire to sustain hierarchy.[10] In a state possessing only rudimentary police power, naked force alone was insufficient; order, so fervently cherished by nearly everyone (but not always for the same reasons), also required trust and reciprocal obligation between social ranks. To ease the tensions inherent in the interweaving of trust with the exercise of power, mechanisms of symbolic alliance, such as ritual kinship and friendship, were created to serve as mitigating mechanisms of social control which linked people from different social categories. Both were sanctioned in terms of the most important values held by the entire society—most notably through the sacraments of baptism and marriage. In the ceremony of baptism "spiritual" kinship was created between the godparents and the family of the child, and in the signing of the marriage contract ritual friendships were solemnized between the families united and the individuals "advising and consenting" to the match.

Although artisans rarely married above their rank, they seem to have been clients in a patronage network that reached the top of society. The master embroiderer Claude Robelot was a valet de chambre of the duchesse de Lorraine, exempted from municipal tax levies for his service. Martin Maupois, as master shoemaker for the duc de Mayenne, gained exemption from service in the night watch. Hugues Sambin, a member of the cabinetmaker guild but also a renowned architect and recent author of a treatise on his art, was given

---

10. S. N. Eisenstadt and Louis Roniger, *Patrons, Clients and Friends: Interpersonal Relations and the Structure of Trust in Society* (Cambridge, 1984), p. 16.

protection by the governor Chabot-Charny in the spring of 1572—a dangerous time for Protestants like Sambin, who joined the governor's entourage and found a haven at Pagny.[11]

It is worth asking how these three men and others like them sealed their ties with their superiors. John Bossy questions whether godparenthood in early modern Europe was a form of patronage, preferring to see it instead as only "a special case of friendship."[12] He bases his case on the relative rarity of godparents of higher social status than the godchild. To be sure, little is known about the status of godparents in Europe in general. Dijon, however, offers an exception to Bossy's supposition; there, it is certain that some patron-client relations were forged or ratified at baptism and also in the ritual of the signing of the marriage contract.

The two sources that reveal most about clientage involving artisans are baptismal registers listing godparents and marriage contracts listing social superiors who gave their *avis et consent* to the match. The spiritual kinship between godparents and godchildren and their parents established voluntary ties impossible to achieve through marriage because of the stigma of mésalliance. Baptism, thus, became an alternative way to institutionalize bonds of fidelity so important to a deferential society.[13] During a time when so many channels of upward social mobility were blocked, the alliances formed in this way must have seemed increasingly attractive.[14] There

11. On Robelot, see AMD, B201, fol. 34r, 18 July 1564. On Maupois and artisans in the clientage system in general, see Drouot, *Mayenne*, 1:113. On Sambin, see Giroux, 375–76.

12. John Bossy, "Godparenthood: The Fortunes of a Social Institution in Early Modern Christianity," in *Religion and Society in Early Modern Europe, 1500–1800*, ed. Kaspar von Greyerz (London, 1984), p. 197.

13. Jean-Louis Flandrin, *Families in Former Times*, trans. Richard Southern (Cambridge, 1979), p. 30. François LeBrun, *La vie conjugale sous l'ancien régime* (Paris, 1975), p. 122, notes that both the Council of Trent and popular belief placed capital importance on godparents. Frequently a godparent was present at the signing of a marriage contract, giving his or her *avis et consent*.

14. See Arlette Jouanna, *Ordre social: Mythes et hiérarchies dans la France du XVIe siècle* (Paris, 1977), p. 94. Roupnel, p. 167, writes that in the late sixteenth and seventeenth centuries the route from the "mercantile life" to the sovereign courts was closing off. Drouot, *Mayenne*, 1:53, suggests that the lawyers had their channels of social advancement choked off beginning in the 1560s. Among artisans, the tanners may have been an exception to the rule. The Requelenes were tanners in the sixteenth century, but by the seventeenth some had entered the merchants' ranks, probably

was a tacit assumption that the godparent would aid the godchild, and it was therefore important to choose a social superior if possible, someone who would be a powerful protector for the child and its family. More and more artisans established ties with the noble and common legal establishment, sealing the bond by receiving a gift from the godparent and providing a meal in return. Gift giving has been interpreted as a ritual that creates an obligation in the recipient (in our case loyalty and deference), and since the value of gifts was escalating considerably in the late sixteenth and early seventeenth centuries, we might speculate that the obligatory bonds tightened apace.[15]

When, in 1581, master locksmith Odot Arvillet asked Pierre Jachiet, a solicitor at the Parlement, to stand as godfather to his newborn son, he was part of a rising tide. Of artisan fathers listed on Dijon's baptismal registers between 1578 and 1595, about a third (66 of 181) chose godparents above them in social rank. When in 1642 master tailor François Truche persuaded noble Jacques Lucotte, a royal councillor at the Parlement, to be godfather to his son, he was among 121 artisan fathers who found socially superior godparents between 1642 and 1646, out of a total of 277 (44 percent). Indeed, throughout the period in only a handful of instances did artisan fathers select a socially inferior godparent (eight vignerons and one *manouvrier*). Naturally, the most valued godfather was a noble of some sort—preferably a royal councillor from one of the sovereign courts or some other royal official. If no noble was available, then a barrister, solicitor, merchant, notary, or bailiff would do. Among the sixty-six sixteenth-century godfathers who clearly outranked the artisan father, twenty-one were merchants, seventeen were solicitors, fifteen were government officials (commoners), eight were nobles of the robe, and five were barristers. By the 1640s Truche was one of many craftsmen brought into the clientage network of the nobles. Two of five (49 of 121) socially superior godparents were now nobles (almost all royal officials, and of the robe), while twenty-eight were merchants, twenty

---

dealing wholesale in hides and thus no longer tied to the workshops. Couturier, *Recherches*, p. 200, notes a similar situation in early modern Châteaudun. In Dijon, as the marriage contracts analyzed in this chapter show, very few sons of master craftsmen went into socially superior occupations.

15. AMD, B232, fol. 141r–v, 16 Nov. 1594, 1103, 19 Nov. 1610.

were non-noble government officials, thirteen were solicitors, and eleven were barristers.[16]

An important consideration is whether godparenthood established a new and persisting relationship with the child or reinforced a relationship with the parents. Unfortunately, the nature of the documentation precludes certainty, although there is a strong suggestion that prior bonds were being strengthened. It is likely that elite godparents were also business customers of the craftsmen—not surprising in view of the increased orientation of the artisanat toward service occupations—but even though many master shoemakers, tailors, goldsmiths, painters and others who catered to an elite clientele were tied into the clientage network, so were many weavers and cloth cutters, who presumably had no close business ties to the nobles or the legal establishment.

Though both master and journeyman fathers were able to arrange for socially superior godfathers in substantial numbers, marriage contracts suggest that Dijon's elites were increasingly involved in bringing *master* artisans into the patronage network between 1550 and 1650. The telling indicator is the clause listing those who gave their *avis et consent* to the marriage. Relatives were included and, whenever possible, individuals of superior rank, who are described as friends and, not infrequently, neighbors (evidence that neighborhood bonds were powerful forces for social solidarity).[17] In the second half of the sixteenth century only one journeyman managed to persuade a superior (a merchant) to sanction his marriage, and in the first half of the seventeenth only six won the formal approval of a superior for their own marriage or that of a daughter. Masters were receiving most of the attention.

Not only were family ties strengthening during this period (as evidenced by the large increase in the number of family members present to give their approval to a marriage), but more unrelated social

16. The data from most of the parish registers is too scanty for comprehensive analysis. The baptismal registers of this sample are from St. Jean parish (1578–79 and 1594–95, AMD, B490, 1642–43, B492), St. Michel (1581–83, B494, and 1646, B497), St. Nicolas (1588–89, B504), St. Pierre (1586–88, B506), and Notre Dame (1592–93, B482, 1643, B485). On Arvillet, see B494 (St. Michel), 31 Aug. 1581; on Truche, B492 (St. Jean), 1 Feb. 1642.

17. See, for example, ADCO, *Notaires* #1295, 26 Feb. 1576, when a daughter of a master tailor has the *avis et consent* of "Noble Master Pierre Fourneret, Royal Councillor and Auditor in the Chambre des Comptes, their friend and neighbor."

superiors were also present at the signing. In 1648 the marriage of master chandler Pierre DesBauges and Michelle Thoreau, daughter of another master chandler, was blessed by several prestigious individuals, nobles all: Jean Chrestiennot, royal councillor and receiver of the taillon at the bailliage, M. DelaPlante, master at the Chambre des Comptes, and M. Blanot, royal councillor at the Parlement and commissioner at the Chambre des Requêtes.[18] Indeed, nobles and members of the legal establishment increasingly became the predominant patrons present at the signing of the marriage contract (see Table 3.1). As more and more nobles of the robe, barristers, solicitors, bailiffs, and others affiliated with the burgeoning judicial and administrative class in Dijon became involved in this ritual, masters were intertwined in a clientage system that started at the top of society. Because this network crossed social barriers, it probably militated against social antagonism—at least between the wealthier artisans and their superiors—and reinforced the hierarchical structure of society.

Ritual kinship and ritual friendship established vertical ties of trust and functioned as mechanisms of social control. I would argue that these symbolic alliances were forms of patronage, not simply friendship. For the patron, the value of the patron-client ritual is the legitimation of the exercise of power, and so a form of domination. It was not just a question of order but also of deference, since power in this society was the product of cumulative deference. A man's power was, in the words of Jean-Louis Flandrin, "calculated on the basis of the number and fidelity of his clients."[19] Probably the greatest benefit to the patron was the loyalty of the client, sealed in the code of honor cherished by both. The loyalty of common men (not just master artisans but also journeymen and vignerons) was far from insignificant in the eyes of local elites, who sometimes seemed paranoid about the threat of disorder and the lack of coercive force to prevent it. The evidence suggests that artisans—especially, though not exclusively, masters—were deemed useful clients to some of the most powerful men in Dijon.

Master artisans were favored partly because of their increasing wealth. It is also possible that the elites hoped to diffuse the threat of

18. ADCO, *Notaires* #36, 13 Dec. 1648.
19. Flandrin, *Families in Former Times*, p. 62.

**Table 3.1**
Marriage contracts of masters or their children
sanctioned by nonrelated male social superiors,
1551–1650

|                 | *1551–1600*       | *1601–1650*       |
| --------------- | ----------------- | ----------------- |
| Merchants       | 11  (4.2%)        | 25  (7.6%)        |
| Nobles          | 12  (4.6%)        | 75  (22.7%)       |
| Solicitors      | 3  (1.2%)         | 40  (12.1%)       |
| Other notables  | 8  (3.0%)         | 37  (11.2%)       |
| Totals          | 34 (13.1%)        | 177 (53.6%)       |

Source: ADCO, *Notaires.*
Note: Male social superiors were not kin, guardians, or godparents.

horizontal solidarity among artisans by cutting through it with vertical ties.[20] Moreover, many patrons of artisans came from the *noblesse
de robe,* and we must not forget that these officials were engaged in a
war over jurisdiction. The battleground of municipal authority was
an important theater of conflict, and the nobles may have seen the
artisans' resources as spoils to the victor. They also valued the master
as an important ally. Master artisans formed a significant percentage
of the citizen electorate (and were thus able to affect mayoral elections), and they were the backbone of the local militia. Significantly,
in my entire sample only three godfathers of artisan children were
*municipal* officers of substantial rank (a greffier, a receiver, and a
former mayor).

As artisan wealth and material interests increased, master craftsmen, for their part, became interested in finding powerful protectors,
and friends in influential positions also made good customers. The
political clout of Dijon's merchants was waning. They had dominated
sixteenth-century town councils but in the seventeenth century were
overtaken by the lawyers. As Dijon became an administrative and
judicial center, the locus of power shifted toward the men in government and the men of law. It made sense, therefore, for artisans to turn
to these men for patronage.

Of course artisans themselves were socially superior to some Di-

20. Anthropological studies of patron-client relationships generally find that clients
owe patrons deference and tacit acceptance of the status quo and are obliged to bring
new clients into the patron's circle. See Verena Burkolter, *The Patronage System:
Theoretical Remarks* (Basel, 1976), p. 9.

jonnais. The most important of their inferiors, and the closest to them in rank, were the vignerons. Several historians of Dijon have contended that a deep gulf separated the craftsman from the vigneron; especially, so the argument goes, during the Wars of Religion. Artisans, it is thought, were attracted to Protestantism but winegrowers, conservative traditionalists, were staunch Catholics.[21] Certainly religious antagonism existed, but it is unwarranted to assume that it reinforced social cleavage. Factors other than occupation played a role in confessional conviction. Furthermore, poor artisans manned the barricades alongside the vignerons in the Lanturelu rebellion of 1630. Artisans and vignerons were frequently related. Many artisans were uncles, cousins, and even brothers or sons of vignerons.[22] Craftsmen, as higher-status acquaintances, frequently witnessed marriage contracts of vignerons or, like master carpenter Didier Oresme for winegrower Claude Jona, stood as godparents to their children.[23] Even marriages occasionally bound artisan and vigneron families. Far from unusual was the match between master cooper Jean DeVillemereux and Claudine Doudey, widow of a winegrower.[24] In a land of wine exportation, the coopers made little else but wine casks, and the manufacture of barrels moved at the same pace as the grape harvest. Prosperity or dearth for both coopers and vignerons was dictated by the same factor, the quantity and quality of the annual grape harvest.

The hierarchical "chains of fidelity," as Roland Mousnier calls them, which united patrons and clients from the top to the bottom of the social scale, were fashioned in the forge of paternalism.[25] This mindset, based upon the household and carried out through legal custom, permeated the society of the old regime. In Burgundy the custom promulgated in 1459 only implies the extent of paternal power, but later commentators inferred a man's right to usufruct of

---

21. Labal, "Le monde des métiers," p. 89; Henri Drouot, *Notes sur la Bourgogne et son esprit public* (Paris, 1937), p. 27.

22. For examples, see ADCO, *Notaires* #766, 1563, #374, 1596, #1715, 12 Feb. 1601, #1716, 1604, #1942, 7 Oct. 1624, #1936, 1646, #766, 1563, #1704, 15 Nov. 1605, #384, 2 Nov. 1626, #1705, 1610, #1704, 20 Feb. 1605.

23. AMD, B494 (St. Michel), 1 Oct. 1581. For examples of artisans witnessing marriages of vignerons, see ADCO, *Notaires* #766, 1562, 1565, #751, 1572, #752, 1574, #363, 1583, #358, 1590, #487, 1628.

24. ADCO, *Notaires* #1716, 24 Feb. 1604. See also #1952, 18 Oct. 1634.

25. Mousnier, "Les concepts," 303.

goods and inheritance of his children and required the father's approval before his children under the age of twenty-five could marry.[26] The latter provision was also stated in a royal edict of 1556, and local marriage contracts show that it was applied. Other archival sources I have studied suggest that paternalism was a powerful attitudinal force in artisan families. According to the Fourth Commandment, children were obliged to honor their fathers, a precept that the Council of Trent further emphasized. Marriage contracts declare that the stepfather is to support his new children and that the children are to "obey and honor" their new father as good children "ought to do." Such prescriptions seem to have permeated artisan mentality, if the master baker Clement Menestrier is any indication. He complained in court that his son-in-law, also a baker, had called him a "thief, robber, double-robber," and a "werewolf," insults violating the "honor and reverence" owed to him by his son-in-law. Such an indignity was serious enough to warrant taking even family matters before the law.[27] Similarly, Claudine Robert, the widow of master roofer Estienne Pierrot, in 1593 disinherited her son for "disobedience."[28]

Paul's epistle to the Ephesians granted a father authority over his wife, children, and servants (including journeymen and apprentices), who were exhorted to obey him as Christians obey God—that is, absolutely. Throughout France subordination of the wife to the husband was becoming increasingly pronounced by 1600.[29] One master tapestry weaver took his authority over his wife to the extreme of ordering her to kill a fellow guildsman with whom he had quarreled. A witness claimed that he had told his wife: "By the death of God! Take a knife and when you find him stab the thief . . . in the stomach! I will have you do it and I authorize you."[30]

Roger Chartier and Dominique Julia have noted that "world-turned-upside-down" imagery of sons beating their fathers was quite common in early modern France, suggesting that the principal pater-

26. Georges Pieri, "Les particularités de la puissance paternelle," *MSHD* 26 (1965): 59, 77.

27. ADCO, BII 360/53, 21 Aug. 1594, and see 360/57, 23 Sept. 1623, in which an embroiderer attempts to discredit a witness by claiming the witness does not obey his parents and speaks irreverently to his mother.

28. ADCO, *Notaires* #560, 25 Jan. 1593.

29. Flandrin, *Families in Former Times*, p. 126. On the superiority of the husband, see also LeBrun, *La vie conjugale*, p. 12.

30. ADCO, BII 360/48, 20 Sept. 1568.

nal role was physical chastisement of the family.[31] This darker side of paternal power, wife and child beating, may have been common, though perhaps not usually of the shuddering intensity displayed by one Guillaume Obrest, a master locksmith who severely beat his wife and then tried to burn her in the fireplace. A neighbor rushing to her aid found her draped over the andirons, unable to move, and her excitable husband fleeing out the back door.[32] Another craftsman, when asked by the civil authorities if he disciplined his children, responded that, yes, he beat them, adding, as if to exonerate himself, only when they deserved it.[33]

As we have seen, in theory the relationship between master artisans and journeymen was paternalistic too. In return for the fidelity and obedience of their journeymen, masters were responsible before the law for the actions of their charges. The wording and intent of the ordinance issued by the town council in 1563, for example, are typical of the entire period: masters were held responsible for the unauthorized assemblies of journeymen "in their service and under their power."[34] Such was the ideal, but the growing battle for control of the labor market drove a wedge between many masters and journeymen. The fraternal solidarity of the compagnonnages must have loosened the paternal bond between many a master and his journeyman.

## Solidarity

This kind of solidarity among the members of a given rank coexisted with the hierarchical stratification sanctioned by law. Vertical ties helped maintain the structure of society, but the horizontal bonds within ranks served quite different functions. It is important to understand not only how master artisans related to others in their society but also how they defined themselves as a distinct social group. Marriage strategies can reveal a good deal about interrelationships among masters.

During the second half of the sixteenth century almost three-

31. Roger Chartier and Dominique Julia, "Le monde à l'invers," *Arc* 65 (1976): 52.
32. ADCO, BII 360/57, 17 April 1608.
33. Ibid., 360/48, 20 Sept. 1568.
34. AMD, B200, fol. 25v, 13 July 1563, and B281, fol. 175v–176v, 13 Oct. 1643.

quarters of the daughters of artisans married artisans or their sons in their first marriages. This ratio increased to nearly four-fifths in the first half of the seventeenth century. It is implausible to think that wealthy artisans would turn their backs on the possibility of marrying a daughter up the social scale. The other side of artisan endogamy, therefore, is the closing off of the marital route of upward social mobility. Prospects for such advancement were never bright in early modern Dijon, but they appear to have grown even dimmer after 1600 (see Table 3.2). Craftsmen were somewhat more successful than their daughters in marrying into higher social ranks during the sixteenth century, but in the first half of the seventeenth their opportunities declined markedly.[35] For example, of the 429 artisans or artisans' sons married in Dijon between 1551 and 1600, one in ten (44, or 10.3 percent) married a merchant's daughter, whereas only one in sixteen (29 of 440, or 6.6 percent) was able to wed such a bride between 1601 and 1650.

It is also clear that daughters of masters were marrying those of equal status within the artisanat more frequently in the early seventeenth century (see Table 3.3). The incidence of marriage between daughters of masters and masters increased from 36.4 to 47.8 percent. These percentages would be even higher if we added the twenty-seven journeymen who were actually sons of masters.[36] The number of daughters of masters marrying in Dijon went up in the second half of the period, while the number of journeymen's daughters was plummeting. Throughout the period most journeymen who married in Dijon married masters' daughters. It is likely that marriage continued

35. This pattern is contrary to that of Châteaudun, where hypergamy was a feminine phenomenon. Couturier, p. 129. In Paris in the first third of the seventeenth century 15 percent of the master craftsmen married the daughters of merchants, and 5 percent the daughters of bourgeois (probably modest *rentiers*). Roland Mousnier, *The Institutions of France under the Absolute Monarchy, 1598–1789: Society and the State*, trans. Brian Pierce (Chicago, 1979), p. 256. Other routes of social mobility were not very promising either. Though some artisans purchased offices and others rentes, they were a distinct minority, as were the sons who entered the bar by way of education.

36. Mousnier, *Institutions . . . Society*, pp. 256–57, asserts that in Paris in the first third of the seventeenth century 40 percent of the master craftsmen married daughters of master craftsmen and 31 percent married daughters of craftsmen of unspecified status or servants; 30 percent of the sons of journeymen or laborers married daughters of master craftsmen, while 48 percent married daughters of craftsmen of unspecified status or servants. Direct comparison to Dijon is difficult because Mousnier's vague categorization lumps servants with craftsmen, but it does seem that male occupational endogamy in Paris was even higher than in Dijon.

**Table 3.2**
First marriage of artisan daughters, by groom's occupation, 1551–1650

| Occupation of groom | 1551–1600 | | 1601–1650 | |
|---|---|---|---|---|
| Artisan | 143 | 72.2% | 171 | 78.1% |
| Agriculture | 24 | 12.1% | 20 | 9.1% |
| Legal establishment | 7 | 3.5% | 7 | 3.2% |
| Merchant | 7 | 3.5% | 7 | 3.2% |
| Other | 17 | 8.6% | 14 | 6.4% |
| Totals | 198 | | 219 | |

Source: ADCO, *Notaires.*

to be the most promising route to mastership for aspiring journey-men, though this channel was never very wide. Of course, masters still needed journeymen to maintain production and some at least to reproduce themselves; masters' sons could not carry the whole load. But the exclusionary policy of the masters must have persuaded many other journeymen not to settle (and marry) in Dijon—hence the sharp decline in the numbers of daughters of journeymen eligible for marriage.

**Table 3.3**
Status of artisan brides and grooms, 1551–1650

| Status of groom | Number marrying a master's daughter | Percentage of master's daughters | Number marrying a journeyman's daughter | Percentage of journeymen's daughters |
|---|---|---|---|---|
| Master | | | | |
| 1551–1600 | 47 | 36.4 | 12 | 17.4 |
| 1601–1650 | 86 | 47.8 | 11 | 28.2 |
| Journeyman | | | | |
| 1551–1600 | 45[a] | 34.9 | 37 | 53.6 |
| 1601–1650 | 54[b] | 30.0 | 21 | 53.8 |
| Nonartisan | | | | |
| 1551–1600 | 37 | 28.7 | 20 | 29.0 |
| 1601–1650 | 40 | 22.2 | 7 | 17.9 |

Source: ADCO, *Notaires.*
[a]Fourteen of these jouneymen were the sons of masters and so might well be added to the number of masters, raising the total to 61 and the percentage to 47.3.
[b]Thirteen were masters' sons. Adding them to the number of masters marrying masters' daughters raises the total to 99 and the percentage to 55.0.

Marriages were not strictly financial affairs, nor did they tend to polarize the artisanat according to economic status. A wealthy widower, for instance, might find the beauty of a young bride a more compelling reason to marry than the amount of her apports. More generally, marital strategies aiming at securing networks of solidarity seem to have permitted a fair range of difference in wealth between bride and groom. Although great disparity was uncommon, noticeable differences were not, especially after 1600 (see Table 3.4). In 1638, for example, master clockmaker Jean Volant brought a respectable sum to his marriage—six hundred livres—but his bride, Marie Placart, daughter of a master pastrycook, brought twice that amount. On a more modest scale, in 1630 master buttonmaker Edme Nielle brought one hundred livres to his marriage with Philiberte Prudhon, daughter of a master tailor, but Philiberte marshaled four times his assets.[37]

In the first half of the seventeenth century only thirty-one of eighty-four (or 37 percent) of daughters of master artisans declared apports worth roughly the same as their artisan groom, while thirty-two (38 percent) of them brought more and twenty-one (25 percent) brought less. Table 3.4 demonstrates that masters had no particular aversion to marrying daughters to poorer *masters*, but it also shows that *journeymen* wishing to marry masters' daughters needed substantial resources, especially in the seventeenth century. There was probably a shortage of eligible males in Dijon.[38] Perhaps this scarcity of potential grooms partly accounts for the rather wide net masters with marriageable daughters were casting across Dijon's *master* artisanat; for other masters (but not journeymen) they deemphasized wealth as a criterion for marriage.

But if a master's daughter was likely to marry a master, the groom was unlikely to be a member of her father's guild. Between 1551 and 1600, of 198 first marriages of daughters of artisans, only 33 (16.7 percent) were endogamous by guild; this astonishingly low rate increased only slightly between 1601 and 1650 (to 49 of 219, or 22.4 percent). Of trades well represented in the sample, only butchers had an endogamy rate as high as 50 percent (four of eight) for the first

37. ADCO, *Notaires* #696, 28 Oct. 1638, #1938, 3 April 1630.
38. Jan de Vries, *European Urbanization, 1500–1800* (Cambridge, Mass., 1984), p. 178, notes that the excess of females appears to have been a European urban phenomenon.

**Table 3.4**

Marriages of artisans and masters' daughters, by apports of bride and groom, 1551–1650

Bride's apport, in livres tournois

| Grooms whose apport is valued (in livres tournois) at: | 1551–1600 | | | | 1601–1650 | | | | | | |
|---|---|---|---|---|---|---|---|---|---|---|---|
| | 50 or less | 51–100 | 101–250 | Totals | 50 or less | 51–100 | 101–250 | 251–500 | 501–1000 | 1001–5000 | Totals |
| **Masters** | | | | | | | | | | | |
| 50 to less | 3 | 0 | 0 | 3 | 0 | 1 | 1 | 0 | 0 | 0 | 2 |
| 51–100 | 0 | 2 | 1 | 3 | 0 | 5 | 2 | 2 | 1 | 0 | 10 |
| 101–250 | 0 | 1 | 3 | 4 | 1 | 0 | 4 | 4 | 2 | 0 | 11 |
| 251–500 | 0 | 1 | 2 | 3 | 0 | 0 | 1 | 8 | 7 | 3 | 19 |
| 501–1000 | 0 | 0 | 0 | 0 | 0 | 0 | 1 | 6 | 3 | 5 | 15 |
| 1001–5000 | 0 | 0 | 0 | 0 | 0 | 0 | 1 | 1 | 2 | 1 | 5 |
| Totals | 3 | 4 | 6 | 13 | 1 | 6 | 10 | 21 | 15 | 9 | 62 |
| **Journeymen** | | | | | | | | | | | |
| 50 or less | 2 | 2 | 0 | 4 | 0 | 0 | 1 | 1 | 0 | 0 | 2 |
| 51–100 | 0 | 2 | 0 | 2 | 0 | 1 | 0 | 1 | 0 | 0 | 2 |
| 101–250 | 0 | 1 | 0 | 1 | 0 | 3 | 4 | 0 | 0 | 0 | 7 |
| 251–500 | 0 | 0 | 0 | 0 | 0 | 1 | 1 | 3 | 1 | 0 | 6 |
| 501–1000 | 0 | 0 | 0 | 0 | 0 | 1 | 0 | 0 | 2 | 0 | 3 |
| 1001–5000 | 0 | 0 | 0 | 0 | 0 | 0 | 0 | 1 | 1 | 0 | 2 |
| Totals | 2 | 5 | 0 | 7 | 0 | 6 | 6 | 6 | 4 | 0 | 22 |

Source: ADCO, Notaires.

period, and only the tailors (eleven of twenty) in the second period. Several trades, most notably the cabinetmakers, seem to have had a positive aversion to corporate endogamy. The marriage between master cabinetmaker Pierre DuBois and Anne Yvert, daughter of a fellow guildsman, was the *only* endogamous match of thirteen involving cabinetmakers after 1600.[39] Journeymen fathers were as consistently exogamous by guild as masters, even though they probably had less choice of grooms because few journeymen had the means to marry. It is difficult to account for such low rates of endogamy unless artisans were deliberately avoiding intracorporate matches. They seem to have much preferred to establish marital bonds throughout the artisanat (including journeymen with bright prospects for mastership). In marriage as in the political battles over jurisdiction, solidarity among masters transcended the bounds of the guild.

If master artisan fathers sought sons-in-law across the spectrum of the artisanat, however, they increasingly preferred grooms born in Dijon; especially after 1600, geographic endogamy reinforced artisanal endogamy (see Table 3.5). The clockmaker Vollant and the buttonmaker Nielle were poorer than their brides, but they were native Dijonnais masters, like their fathers-in-law. Apparently, a master born in Dijon was worth some monetary sacrifice. Though the rate of geographic endogamy is lower for matches between masters and masters' daughters than for all artisan marriages, the trend is toward closing ranks. Of course, the community of master artisans could not survive if all outsiders were excluded. Since infusions of immigrant blood were essential, the question confronting the masters was which journeymen to let in. The evidence suggests that in Dijon there was a "core" of masters and chosen journeymen surrounded by an "envelope" of transient journeymen.[40]

A look at marriage patterns from the male perspective demon-

---

39. ADCO, *Notaires* #1707, 31 March 1609.

40. There has recently been much historiographical debate about the role of immigration in urban history. See de Vries, *European Urbanization*, esp. chaps. 9 and 10. Allan Sharlin, "Natural Decrease in Early Modern Cities: A Reconsideration," *Past and Present* 79 (1978): 126–38, divides early modern urban populations into a "core" of permanent residents and an "envelope" of temporary migrants. David Ringrose, *Madrid and the Spanish Economy, 1560–1850* (Berkeley, 1983), esp. chap. 3, supports Sharlin's view. For Dijon's artisan community between 1550 and 1650, however, though a core/envelope dichotomy is occupationally apposite, it does not work as well to distinguish natives and migrants.

**Table 3.5**
Geographic endogamy of daughters of artisans native to Dijon, 1551–1650

|  | Daughters of native artisans | | Daughters of native masters | |
| --- | --- | --- | --- | --- |
|  | Marrying native artisans | Marrying others | Marrying native masters | Marrying others |
| 1551–1600 | 70 (39.5%) | 107 | 31 (26.7%) | 85 |
| 1601–1650 | 98 (50.1%) | 97 | 66 (37.9%) | 108 |

Source: ADCO, *Notaires.*

strates the increasing tendency of masters to marry among themselves, bringing selected journeymen into their ranks by marriage to their daughters (see Table 3.6). The integration of non-native masters was declining (74.1 percent married native brides in the last half of the sixteenth century, 61.5 percent in the first half of the seventeenth), perhaps because the town council sometimes succeeded in admitting journeymen to mastership against the masters' wishes. These unwelcome newcomers may have found it most difficult to overcome the xenophobia of the masters when the time came to marry. Meanwhile, native masters continued to choose native brides at about the same rate, but the percentage marrying daughters of native masters rose sharply (from 43.8 percent to 64.2 percent), strong evidence of an emerging core of native masters bound by marriage ties.

Table 3.6 also shows the contours of an envelope of journeymen ineligible for mastership—or marriage to a master's daughter. Between 1551 and 1600, about half the journeymen marrying in Dijon were immigrants, and 40 percent of these non-natives found native brides among the artisanat. Between 1601 and 1650, fewer immigrant journeymen were able to start a family in Dijon, but the percentage who married the daughter of an artisan rose to 46.6 percent. These figures suggest that by the seventeenth century the immigrant journeymen marrying within the native artisanat in Dijon were the ones selected to enter the core of masters. The rest formed the envelope of journeymen generally marrying outside the artisanat.

The native journeymen, of course, had a better chance of attaining mastership. In the second half of the sixteenth century, 34.8 percent married the daughters of native artisans, and although fewer native

**Table 3.6**
Geographic endogamy of artisans, 1551–1650

| | Marrying native bride | | | | Marrying immigrant bride | Total |
|---|---|---|---|---|---|---|
| | Journeymen's daughters | Masters' daughters | Others | Total | | |
| **Immigrant Masters** | | | | | | |
| 1551–1600 | 4 | 12 | 4 | 20 | 7 | 27 |
| 1601–1650 | 0 | 13 | 11 | 24 | 15 | 39 |
| **Native Masters** | | | | | | |
| 1551–1600 | 6 | 25 | 26 | 57 | 24 | 81 |
| 1601–1650 | 3 | 61 | 30 | 95 | 41 | 136 |
| **Immigrant Journeymen** | | | | | | |
| 1551–1600 | 16 | 22 | 22 | 60 | 35 | 95 |
| 1601–1650 | 5 | 29 | 16 | 50 | 23 | 73 |
| **Native Journeymen** | | | | | | |
| 1551–1600[a] | 12 | 20 | 32 | 64 | 28 | 92 |
| 1601–1650[b] | 4 | 23 | 18 | 45 | 30 | 75 |

Source: ADCO, Notaires.
[a]Fourteen were sons of native masters.
[b]Thirteen were sons of native masters.

journeymen married in the first half of the seventeenth century, the percentage of those choosing daughters of artisans increased slightly, to 36 percent. Unlike the immigrants, who were choosing immigrant brides less often, 40 percent of native journeymen (up from 30.4 percent) were now marrying non-natives. And far fewer journeymen, native or non-native, were marrying the daughters of journeymen, largely because there were so few journeymen with families, and thus daughters to marry off.

Despite their policy of contraction, native master artisans were constrained to bring some journeymen into mastership by way of marriage. First choice, of course, went to sons of native masters, but other local boys were not the second choice. Native journeymen who were not sons of masters appear to have had no better chance to crack the master ranks than immigrant journeymen; what counted was money (see Table 3.7). The example of Claude Chalochet is telling. A journeyman tinsmith from Langres, in 1632 Chalochet commanded over 250 livres in assets, including, our status-conscious tinsmith was careful to point out, 50 livres' worth of clothing. This display was impressive enough to gain entrance into Dijon's master craft community by way of his new bride Catherine DesCombes, daughter of a native master tailor of moderate wealth (she brought three hundred livres to the match).[41] This pattern is clear in Table 3.7 for both bagues et joyeux and apports, though the small number of apports declared makes it impossible to generalize about them. Note, however, that if it was the poorer journeymen who were not declaring apports (and it probably was), the disparity between journeymen marrying masters' daughters and those marrying others was even wider than these figures indicate.

Yet for marriages *within* the master ranks, local birth *was* important, and wealth, as we have seen, only a secondary consideration. The masters were clearly closing ranks, while the envelope of poorer journeymen, both native and immigrant, grew. Few were able to penetrate the masters' circle, and unlike masters, most did not (in fact, could not) establish a web of marital alliances with other journeymen. They had to seek solidarity elsewhere—most notably, in compagnonnages. All but a few were consigned to play out their days as hired workers, or *alloués*.

41. ADCO, *Notaires* #1079, 5 Dec. 1632.

**Table 3.7**
Wealth brought to marriage by journeymen, 1551–1650

| | Bagues et joyeux | | Apports | |
| --- | --- | --- | --- | --- |
| Journeymen | N | Average amount (in livres) | N | Average amount (in livres) |
| Marrying native masters' daughters | | | | |
| 1551–1600 | 45 | 26.5 | 9 | 68.3 |
| 1601–1650 | 54 | 42.5 | 35 | 363.3 |
| Marrying others | | | | |
| 1551–1600 | 167 | 21.6 | 16 | 67.1 |
| 1601–1650 | 139 | 28.6 | 49 | 267.5 |

Source: ADCO, *Notaires.*

Widows of artisans show a somewhat different profile from that of first-time brides. Corporate endogamy was much higher when widows remarried.[42] Between 1551 and 1650 exactly half of all widows who remarried did so within their first husband's craft (55 of 110). It is surprising the figure was not even higher, for a widow would have the tools and shop to continue the trade of her deceased husband, and remarrying within the same craft was obviously economically convenient for both spouses. In some other respects, marital patterns for widows of artisans resemble those of first brides. For example, between 1551 and 1600 of sixty-four native widows marrying artisans, thirty-five (54.7 percent) took native grooms, and between 1601 and 1650, twenty-seven of thirty-seven (73 percent) did, as the artisanat closed ranks geographically.[43] Antoinette Villeminet, widow of a master cooper from Dijon is typical of these trends. In 1643 she married master cooper Jean Frochot, also a native, and merged her substantial resources with his. She brought fifteen hundred livres in cash plus half a house, and three *quartiers* and one *journal* of vineyard; he contributed two hundred livres cash and three *quartiers* and a half *journal* of vineyard.[44] In some cases, though, corporate endogamy

42. Couturier, p. 139, finds similar results and even more intense geographic endogamy among widows than among the rest of the population.

43. It is conceivable that the decline in the incidence of widow remarriage reflects a relative paucity of eligible males, which could drive dowries up. Widows may also have been marrying out of the artisanat altogether; my sample did not include this occurrence.

44. ADCO, *Notaires* #1166, 22 Jan. 1643.

was a secondary consideration. In 1637 Françoise Guillaumot, widow of a master weaver, married Nicolas Baugey, a master carpenter of substantial means (assets of six hundred livres). Both were already in the masters' circle, and both were native Dijonnais, and apparently these were more important factors than guild affiliation.[45] Table 3.8 suggests that this match, like that between Villeminet and Frochot, was not unusual: widows of native *masters* increasingly sought second husbands who were also masters and, more often than not, natives. There is a good deal of folklore about the ambitious journeyman who courts the master's widow; in Dijon he did so fairly successfully in the sixteenth century, even if he was an immigrant, but in the seventeenth he found the door closing.

As we saw in Chapter 2, artisan widows were rather secretive about declaring their assets in marriage contracts, but what figures we do have suggest, not surprisingly, that they commanded substantial resources compared to those of first brides and were rising with the general tide of increased prosperity in the artisanat. By itself greater wealth could account for the decline in marriages between journeymen and widows of masters, but there was also a juridical obstacle for journeymen. Guild statutes specified that a journeyman who married a master's widow must nevertheless go through the normal—ever narrowing—channels for mastership. The masters saw to it that widows were no shortcut for journeymen to acquire shops in Dijon.

Family solidarity, social standing, cultural experience (work), and geography—all supported the endogamy so strongly exhibited by Dijon's master artisans, but occupational endogamy was most significant. The overwhelming majority—around 75 to 80 percent—of artisan daughters married into other craft families, though guild endogamy was avoided. Widows pursued even this form of endogamy as well as others. Clearly, marriage helped to cement solidarity throughout the artisanat, especially among masters, but it was not a route to social advancement. It is, therefore, not surprising that female hypergamy outside artisan ranks was absent or that only one woman in ten married a rural man, either a farm laborer or a vigneron. The message is clear: endogamy reinforced the solidarity that economic and political forces also fostered. In marriage as in other aspects of life the artisans were increasingly solidary and parochial, defining them-

45. Ibid., #1951, 28 June 1637.

**Table 3.8**
Marriages of native widows of master artisans, 1551–1650

|  | Artisan grooms | |  |
|---|---|---|---|
|  | Journeymen | Masters | Other grooms |
| All grooms |  |  |  |
| 1551–1600 | 17 | 19 | 3 |
| 1601–1650 | 6 | 18 | 0 |
| Native grooms |  |  |  |
| 1551–1600 | 5 | 15 | — |
| 1601–1650 | 1 | 17 | — |

Source: ADCO, *Notaires.*

selves as distinct from other sectors of society. Indeed, the same tendency is discernible in patrimony and kinship.

In 1593 master butcher Pierre Griveau enjoined his three sons and one daughter to split his estate equally upon his death, thereby obeying the legal custom of Burgundy, which prescribed equal division of inheritances.[46] All children, not just males, divided their parental legacies equally, and marriage contracts as well as testaments like Griveau's imply that artisans followed this custom.[47] A clause in Dijon marriage contracts stipulated what happened to the estate in the event of the death of a spouse without issue. Increasingly in the seventeenth century the contracts specified how much of the inheritance went to the union, and so was retained by the surviving spouse, and how much reverted to the family bloodline of the deceased as *nature antien*. Such provisions show the degrees of kinship solidarity (property is seen as belonging literally to the lineage) and concern for protection of the patrimony.[48]

After 1600 a much greater percentage of marriage contracts involving artisans specified what became of the property brought to a marriage,

46. Ibid., #560, 12 Oct. 1593. See also Flandrin, *Families in Former Times*, p. 74; Gutton, *La sociabilité villageoise*, p. 44; and Emmanuel Le Roy Ladurie, "A System of Customary Law: Family Structures and Inheritance Customs in Sixteenth-Century France," in *Family and Society*, ed. Robert Forster and Orest Ranum, trans. Elborg Forster and Patricia Ranum (Baltimore, 1976).

47. See, for example, ADCO, *Notaires* #1941, 26 April 1628, where Jean Caillot, a master tailor, stipulated in his son's marriage contract that his other heirs would inherit equally with the one marrying, in order to keep the "peace" among his offspring.

48. For a discussion of this issue among the sixteenth-century Paris elite, see Barbara Diefendorf, *Paris City Councillors in the Sixteenth Century: The Politics of Patrimony* (Princeton, 1983), esp. chap. 7.

perhaps because as artisan patrimonies grew the stakes mounted. Only 16 of 429 craftsmen marrying between 1551 and 1600 bothered to stipulate what percentage of property brought to the marriage would return to the bloodline if the union were childless. In the first half of the seventeenth century 166 of 440 did. Daughters of artisans show the same pattern (see Table 3.9), but their percentage of participation is greater. In the last half of the sixteenth century contracts overwhelmingly specified equal division, but in the first half of the seventeenth century the balance shifted toward the lineage. By the 1640s nearly all the contracts favor the line. For example, whereas in 1609 Anne Yvert, the daughter of a master cabinetmaker, split her assets of three hundred livres equally between her new household and her lineage, in 1638 Marie Placart, daughter of a master pastrycook, marked only two hundred of her twelve hundred livres for the union. Her husband-to-be Jean Vollant was a bit more equitable, but even he allocated only two hundred of six hundred livres to his new household. Ten years later master chandler Pierre DesBauges and his future wife each reserved 70 percent of one thousand livres to their lineage.[49]

As apports were growing, artisans were increasingly reserving their inheritance to their blood relations. If a marriage produced no heirs, the intent was to keep the patrimony together for the lineage. Because master artisan patrimonies were getting larger through increased prosperity, masters had a greater financial stake in seeing them preserved. Nor would such a policy necessarily be contrary to solidarity, since usually many other males in an artisan's family were also craftsmen. Preserving the patrimony would still keep it within the artisanat.

In sum, my findings suggest that artisans of seventeenth-century Dijon emphasized family solidarity defined by blood more than their sixteenth-century forebears had.[50] This preference is corroborated by

---

49. ADCO, *Notaires* #1707, 31 March 1609, #696, 28 Oct. 1638, and #36, 13 Dec. 1648.

50. It seems, then, that Dijon's artisans reflect what Flandrin (*Families in Former Times*, p. 79) calls the "lineal spirit" more than the "household spirit." His observation (p. 9) that the concept of "*lignage* was more deeply rooted among the elites of society than the *peuple*" may have to be altered somewhat. Similarly, this apparent strengthening of lineal ties seems to suggest that the emergence of the nuclear family charted by Lawrence Stone, *The Family, Sex and Marriage in England, 1500–1800* (New York, 1977), may be more problematic for the lower classes in France than has previously been thought.

**Table 3.9**
Patterns of inheritance division in marriage contracts, daughters of artisans, 1551–1650

| | 1551–1600 | 1601–1610 | 1611–1620 | 1621–1630 | 1631–1640 | 1641–1650 | 1601–1650 |
|---|---|---|---|---|---|---|---|
| **Masters' daughters** | | | | | | | |
| Division favors union | 3 | 1 | 2 | 7 | 2 | 0 | 12 |
| Division favors lineage | 3 | 5 | 10 | 15 | 19 | 28 | 77 |
| Equal Division | 44 | 12 | 11 | 9 | 6 | 1 | 39 |
| Totals | 50 | | | | | | 128 |
| **Journeymen's daughters** | | | | | | | |
| Division favors union | 0 | 0 | 1 | 0 | 1 | 1 | 3 |
| Division favors lineage | 0 | 1 | 2 | 2 | 0 | 5 | 10 |
| Equal division | 8 | 1 | 0 | 1 | 1 | 0 | 3 |
| Totals | 8 | | | | | | 16 |
| **All artisans' daughters** | | | | | | | |
| Division favors union | 3 | 1 | 3 | 7 | 3 | 1 | 15 |
| Division favors lineage | 3 | 6 | 12 | 17 | 19 | 33 | 87 |
| Equal division | 52 | 13 | 11 | 10 | 7 | 1 | 42 |
| Totals | 58 | | | | | | 144 |

Source: ADCO, *Notaires*.
Note: Sample includes only contracts that give *apports* in monetary terms and in which the percentage of *nature antien* is calculable. This method minimizes the favoring of the line, for the real property—houses, vineyards, *rentes*, and the like—whose value is occasionally not stated, invariably reverted to the line.

the simultaneous increase in the number of family members called upon to give their *avis et consent* to the signing of a marriage contract. More and more uncles, brothers, and *cousins germains* appeared in the marriage contracts after 1600.[51] In legal depositions of the 1640s, the caveat that the witness be neither *paranté* nor *allié* to the accused was inserted in the protocol.[52] The implication is that kinship ties were so strong throughout society that the testimony of kinsmen of the accused was not to be trusted. The ties of blood and marriage extended even beyond the grave: one goldsmith's wife, for example, took great offense when the reputation of her deceased father-in-law was derided.[53] Furthermore, widows and widowers frequently received the *avis et consent* of the brothers, uncles, and fathers of the deceased spouse for their remarriage.[54]

Just as ritual or "spiritual" kinship knit the social hierarchy vertically, it also strengthened horizontal bonds within the artisanat, among masters and journeymen alike. Artisans not only asked social superiors to sanction their marriages but usually included fellow craftsmen as well, often in the same ceremony. At the signing of the marriage contract between the master glover Jacques Morelot and Anne Blondeau, the daughter of the master coppersmith Bernard, for example, an impressive cross section of society crowded into the room. Among those standing for the groom were a royal sergeant, a solicitor at the Parlement, a noble barrister, a merchant, and a master goldsmith. On the bride's side were two royal councillors at the Parlement, an *audiancier* at the Chambre des Comptes, a barrister and two solicitors at the Parlement, a greffier, a surgeon, two merchants, the concierge of the prisons, and a cluster of master artisans—a foundryman, a coppersmith, a cabinetmaker, a tapestry weaver, a chandler, and a tinsmith.[55]

Baptism was another occasion at which to seal ritual kinship horizontally as well as vertically. If an artisan could not find (or chose not

51. Gutton, *La sociabilité villageoise*, p. 57, notes that kinship bonds were very close in villages of early modern France. Since many of Dijon's artisans were immigrants from villages, they probably brought this mentality with them.

52. ADCO, BII 360/58, May–Sept. 1642.

53. Ibid., 360/53, 26 July 1594.

54. For example, ADCO, *Notaires* #1713, 13 May 1598, #368, 11 Oct. 1616, #1683, 20 April 1625.

55. Ibid., #1949, 29 Dec. 1642.

**Table 3.10**
Artisans choosing artisan godfathers, 1578–1595, 1642–1646

| | 1578–1595 | | 1642–1646 | | Totals | |
|---|---|---|---|---|---|---|
| | N | Percentage | N | Percentage | N | Percentage |
| **Masters** | | | | | | |
| Choosing a master of the same guild | 23 | 57.5 | 28 | 41.8 | 51 | 47.7 |
| Choosing another artisan | 17 | 42.5 | 39 | 58.2 | 56 | 52.3 |
| Totals | 40 | | 67 | | 107 | |
| **Journeymen** | | | | | | |
| Choosing a journeyman of the same guild | 19 | 46.3 | 23 | 41.8 | 42 | 43.7 |
| Choosing another artisan | 22 | 53.7 | 32 | 58.2 | 54 | 56.2 |
| Totals | 41 | | 55 | | 96 | |

Source: AMD, B Etat Civil.

to seek) a social superior to stand as godfather for his child, then he almost always chose another artisan. With a social superior trust thus fashioned served the interest of order, but with another artisan the rite emphasized solidarity. By diversifying their choices, artisans could overcome the contradiction of the institutionalization of trust in a hierarchical society (which served the interests of power) and fulfill their desire to construct other forms of trust, unaffected by such interests.[56] As Table 3.10 illustrates, in the seventeenth century masters increasingly cut across corporate boundaries and diversified their ritual ties with masters not of their guild. As we might imagine, only rarely did a master seek a journeyman godfather.

As a whole, journeymen show a similar profile, but the few who sought masters for godfathers increasingly selected them from guilds other than their own. Between 1578 and 1595, of the eleven journeymen who found master godfathers, five chose them from their own guild; yet between 1642 and 1646 of the twenty-two journeymen fathers seeking master godfathers, only six chose men from their own guild. Though the sample is small, given what we know about the formation of compagnonnages, it is not too surprising to find journeymen excluding masters of their own guild, who were becoming their enemies in the battle over control of the labor market. For masters, the point is not that corporate ties were unimportant—they certainly were—but that further interrelationships with artisans outside the guild but within their cultural milieu could only enhance the network of influence.

56. On the "moral" equality established in the baptismal rite, see Julian Pitt-Rivers, *People of the Sierra* (Chicago, 1961); Eisenstadt and Roniger, *Patrons, Clients, and Friends*, p. 2; Bossy, "Godparenthood," p. 196. On the contradiction inherent in the institutionalization of trust, see Eisenstadt and Roniger, p. 39.

# 4 Order, Conflict, and Honor

Thus far we have been exploring how a great many master artisans were establishing a solidarity that cut across guild boundaries. Yet however eager they were to form social bonds that would help to preserve order, the masters were unquestionably in competition with each other. Revealed in the records of the mayor's criminal court at the bailliage are the conflicts of the artisanat, which obliquely illustrate the norms of daily life through their violation.[1] One of the strongest norms among the artisans was honor, and their most notable conflicts related to the marriage strategies and growing patrimonies discussed previously. These battles can help to explain the contradictions embedded in artisan mentality.

Individuals are culturally constituted through a dialectical process in which they both make their world and are products of it. The cultural anthropologist Clifford Geertz, following Max Weber, has said that "man is an animal suspended in webs of significance he himself has spun" and that these webs constitute an "organized sys-

---

1. The commune of Dijon gained jurisdiction over criminal cases from the dukes of Burgundy, and retained the privilege from the kings of France when Burgundy returned to France. The abundant records of this mayor's court at the bailliage are in ADCO, BII 360.

tem of significant symbols."[2] This spinning is a dynamic process, where change creates contradictions, disjunctions, and conflicts; yet, paradoxically, the web also helps govern behavior. In other words, individuals act through a contradiction-ridden process to stabilize their lives.

Anthropologists and some historians have recently devoted much attention to the role of conflict and individualistic strategy in this process of cultural constitution, largely as a counterweight to the homeostatic emphasis of the structural-functionalists.[3] A demand for order and the related classificatory impulse may very well be universal human attributes, but the kind of order consciously sought and the forms the categorizing takes are culturally unique and fashioned through process.[4] Since community includes both sharing and conflict, social equilibrium is attained through constant struggle and rests in a fragile balance. As one social historian has recently put it, culture is a "medium in which conflicts are worked out . . . [and is] generated in the interplay of shared situations."[5] Through the inevitable forces of conflict, artisans—mostly masters but probably also journeymen with aspirations to mastership—struggled for order, for solidarity through consensus.[6]

If cultures are not viewed as fixed and mutually exclusive categories but rather as multidimensional repositories in motion, from which individuals appropriate significance and through which meaning is mediated, then artisan culture is likely to share characteristics of other cultures (like that of the vignerons) crowding the same social space and sharing much of the same discourse.[7] Until we understand

2. Clifford Geertz, *Interpretations of Cultures* (New York, 1973), pp. 4, 44.

3. Hans Medick and David Sabean discuss this approach and its implications for anthropological social history in their Introduction to *Interest and Emotion: Essays on the study of Family and Kinship*, ed. Medick and Sabean (Cambridge, 1984). Network analysis in anthropology has emphasized this also; see, for example, Jeremy Boissevain, *Friends of Friends: Networks, Manipulators, and Coalitions* (Oxford, 1974). On the relationship between agency and structure, I have found Anthony Giddens, *Central Problems in Social Theory* (Berkeley, 1979), very useful.

4. See Claude Lévi-Strauss, *La pensée sauvage* (Paris, 1963), pp. 17, 50; Ernst Cassirer, *The Philosophy of Symbolic Forms*, 3 vols. (New Haven, 1953), 1:46.

5. David Sabean, *Power in the Blood* (Cambridge, 1984), p. 95.

6. Sean Wilentz, *Chants Democratic* (New York, 1983), demonstrated this pattern in his masterful analysis of the making of the working class in nineteenth-century New York.

7. Roger Chartier, "Culture as Appropriation: Popular Cultural Uses in Early

other sectors of urban popular culture better we cannot always know
to what extent the assumptions and values, hopes and fears of artisans, their wives, and widows were culturally unique. Similarly,
though cultures are by definition consensual entities, their values are
not monolithically imposed. A more accurate image would be a spectrum of values; all members of a culture recognize the values, but
individuals vary in how much importance they attach to each.
Among masters and even more so between masters and journeymen,
there was a range of behavior. Unfortunately, the criminal records do
not always permit a distinction between master and journeyman to
be made, but some values—like honor, for example—are so univer-
sally accepted among masters that they become virtual hallmarks,
easily spotted by the historian. We must make distinctions among
cultures and within cultures whenever they are warranted, but since
we are often dealing with a shared discourse that includes masters,
journeymen with a hope of mastership, and at times, all of popular
culture, perhaps drawing the boundaries too sharply could be misleading and even anachronistic. As Daniel Roche points out, even
though "control of capital, . . . holding power over employees, the
possibility or at least the hope of a certain mobility all separate the
master craftsmen from those who are salaried in the strict sense of
the word . . . in the area of mores or mentality, a clear boundary is
difficult to establish."[8]

## The Structures of Artisan Mentality

Many years ago the historian Lucien Febvre coined the term *outillage
mental* to describe, as Robert Mandrou has paraphrased, "that appara-
tus . . . [used] for analyzing, describing and explaining the world, men
and God."[9] Geertz, in a similar vein, suggests that mind is "an organized system of dispositions which finds its manifestation in some
actions and some things."[10] Both definitions assume a collective

---

Modern France," in *Understanding Popular Culture*, ed. Steven L. Kaplan (Berlin,
1984), pp. 229–54.
    8. Roche, "Work, Fellowship, and Some Economic Realities," pp. 56–57.
    9. Robert Mandrou, *Introduction to Modern France, 1500 -1640*, trans. R. E. Hall-
mark (New York, 1975), p. 64; Lucien Febvre *Le problème de l'incroyance au 16e
siècle: La religion de Rabelais* (Paris, 1968), pt. 2.
    10. Geertz, p. 58.

view, a shared consciousness, and thus imply the importance of communication. Deciphering the meanings of gestures and speech—laden with symbolism—will be a major part of our concern, but first we must explore more deeply the mental structures of artisan culture.

Despite climbing literacy rates (see Chapter 6) artisan culture before 1650 was largely oral. In oral cultures thought and expression are more situational than abstract, and individuals define the self in terms of their life situation and the opinion others hold of them. Since externals command considerable attention in such cultures, there is a great emphasis on "reading" external signs.[11] For artisans, external manifestations, or style, almost literally "made the man" and placed him hierarchically. Dress and comportment displayed social rank,[12] and even trade. Craftsmen not known by name could be placed by their apparel, and so one was "dressed as a mason" or as a journeyman locksmith or another craftsman.[13] Similarly, the town council required that the various trades distinguish themselves from others by signs hung outside their workshops. Accordingly, in 1580 master pastrycook Blaise Aulpoys erected a sign outside his shop that indicated his *estat*; Aulpoys agreed that he could thereby be better recognized and so market his goods more effectively.[14]

Tools, too, symbolized occupation and status within a trade. In 1582 the town council forbade any but master carpenters "to carry about the town a carpenter's square (*rigloir*) which is the sign and mark that masters . . . wear in order to be recognized as received and passed into mastership."[15] No doubt it was a regulation masters willingly endorsed. How well visual images and self-definition were as-

11. Walter Ong, *Orality and Literacy* (London, 1982), p. 54. See also Paul Ricoeur, *Interpretation Theory* (Fort Worth, 1976), p. 35. "There is no identification which does not relate that about which we speak to a unique spatio-temporal network, and there is no network of places in time and space without a final reference to the situational here and now. In this ultimate sense, all references of oral language rely on monstrations, which depend on the situation perceived as common by the members of the dialogue. All references in the dialogical situation consequently are situational."

12. Jouanna, *Ordre social*, pp. 89–93. See Barthélemy de Chasseneux, *Catalogus gloriae mundi* (Lyons, 1546). This parlementaire from Dijon (until 1529) and Paris discussed the relationship between external attributes and social rank and condition. See also Stephen Greenblatt, *Renaissance Self-Fashioning from More to Shakespeare* (Chicago, 1980), esp. chap. 1.

13. ADCO, BII 360/60, Oct. 1643.

14. Hauser, "Les pouvoirs publics," p. 171; AMD, B215, fol. 292r, 12 July 1580.

15. AMD, B219, fol. 137r, 15 May 1582.

similated in artisan minds can also be seen by how artisans made their mark (sometimes in lieu of a signature). Often they drew tools or products of their trade—a baker's shovel, a tailor's shears, a locksmith's key, a basket maker's basket.[16] In the artisan culture of early modern Dijon image and essence were not clearly distinguished; an artisan's social position, his identity, and the visual representation of it were merged. A man's style, how he appeared, was his true self. Appearance was essence.

In some respects symbols and ritual are strategies for ordering experience and serve as instruments of social integration by making consensus possible.[17] Through symbols the chaos of sensual impressions is integrated into an ordered whole, invested with meaning, and thus made intelligible. The ordered whole, or shared common experience, is knit together by a communicative system of signs and common understandings.

Clearly, in one respect symbols are consensual and can foster solidarity, but their use can also be divisive. In the situational mind, meanings of words and symbols (gestures, inflections, physical expressions, and the like) depend upon the context of use. Indeed, in oral cultures words can be associated with power and force and can thus function in ways similar to tools or weapons.[18] The exchange of insulting words or gestures, on which I will say much more later, was a ritual laden with symbolism for a mentality that invested name calling and insults with utmost, sometimes lethal importance.[19] We must continually bear in mind that the use of symbols is never simply order giving.

The structures of a mentality are based upon systems of reference which measure and classify the chaotic impressions received from the environment by the senses. One of the coordinates of such a

16. For example, ADCO, BII 360/51, 10 April 1570, 24 Jan. 1571, 16 Sept. 1584, and *Notaires* #1724, 1 Oct. 1595.

17. Geertz, p. 127, Cassirer, 1:57, 78, 113; Pierre Bourdieu, "Sur le pouvoir symbolique," *Annales: ESC* 32.3 (1977): 408.

18. Walter Ong, *The Presence of the Word* (New Haven, 1968), esp. chap. 3; Sabean, p. 112, has found this view of the word in the mentality of the early modern German peasant. One need only think of the importance of exorcisms, catechisms, masses, and oaths to gauge the importance of the word to elite culture in early modern Europe, too, evidence perhaps of a residual orality.

19. Cassirer, 2:212, has called this mythical thinking. Jean Delumeau, *La peur en occident (XIVe–XVIIIe siècles): Une cité assiégée* (Paris, 1978) p. 86, calls it a *mentalité magique*. See also Mandrou, *Introduction*, p. 239.

system is time. For early modern artisans, tradition was the armature of time. The past provided a vector from which to project expectations and hopes for future stability. Custom was sufficient justification for the propriety of an action. Faced with innovations in production practices introduced by the town council, for example, master craftsmen would defend traditional practice. Things had been this way, they would claim, "since time immemorial" (*de toute anciennété*) and, ipso facto, should not be changed.

The passage of time was measured by sacred and profane demarcations. The distant past was often recalled not by specific years (though, of course, the legal and political world of the upper classes was exact in year and day) but by association with some memorable, often catastrophic, event—a famine, pillaging soldiers, "during the civil wars."[20] Occurrences within the past year were usually identified according to the nearest saint's day or religious holiday, for example, "the festival day of the birth of our Lord" or "the day of Saint Philibert's eve" or "one day [around the time of] Saint Jean's day." Weekdays generally were related to religious days: "the day after last Easter and the Tuesday following" or "the Saturday before the last festival of Saint Philibert."[21] The liturgical calendar appears firmly embedded in the artisan mind.

Hours of the day fell more readily into the secular realm, although references to "the hour of vespers" and the like are by no means uncommon, possibly because church bells sounded the hours and offices.[22] Artisans (unlike the legal elite) were imprecise in recollecting the time of day, never more specific than the hour or *et demy*. It is clear that time was not yet firmly associated in the artisan mind with function, for work was not performed at rigidly predetermined intervals. That time was not yet money suggests an attitude not yet capi-

20. In 1569, 1576, and 1589 the German Protestant mercenary troops called the *reîtres* devastated the Burgundian countryside. The memory of these events became embedded in popular mentality and served as reference points of time recollection. AMD, B279, fol. 240r, 20 May 1642. On the reîtres, see Drouot, *Mayenne*, 1:25, 103, 121, 126, 137.

21. Such locutions were used throughout the period. For examples of artisans or their wives employing such structures, see ADCO, BII 360/45, 29 Dec. 1563, 360/48, 20 Sept. 1568, 24 Sept. 1568, 360/53, 2 Dec. 1594, 360/58, 22 May 1642, 360/60, 24 March 1645.

22. For example, ADCO, BII 360/41, 24 April 1556, 360/47, 30 April 1567, 360/51, 2 March 1582.

talist, as does the masters' way of enhancing wealth by restricting their own numbers. Capitalists would rather expand production.

The other coordinate of a system of mental reference is space, and the most important spatial category for the resident artisan in his daily life was the neighborhood. An artisan's identity, both his self-image and the inseparable image others held of him, was closely tied to his neighborhood. Craftsmen spent much of their day within its confines and established strong relationships with their neighbors, both friendly and competitive. In this intensely public arena where interdependence and vulnerability were facts of life, individuals were extremely sensitive to neighborly judgment of their actions. Recent studies of Renaissance and early modern European cities have emphasized the physical and psychological importance of the neighborhood; the bonds between neighbors were as tight as (and often reinforced) kinship and friendship, but there was also great potential for enmity inherent in proximity.[23]

The neighborhood in early modern Dijon was defined by sight and sound. It extended as far as one could see or hear from the shop or house, including the street in front and the courtyard in back. Because most of Dijon's streets were short and crooked the extent of the visible and audible was rarely more than fifty yards in either direction.[24] But within those confines dozens of peering eyes filled the windows and multitudes of ears strained at walls to monitor the space. Neighbors were distinguished as *proche* if they lived next door or within the same building, and in the extremely dense living conditions one usually had several *proches voisins*.

The composition of a neighborhood was quite fluid by modern

23. Dale V. Kent and F. W. Kent, *Neighbors and Neighborhood in Renaissance Florence: The District of the Red Lion in the Fifteenth Century* (Locust Valley, 1982), esp. intro.; Diane Owen Hughes, "Kinsmen and Neighbors in Medieval Genoa," in *The Medieval City*, ed. Harry A. Miskimin, David Herlihy, and A. L. Udovitch (New Haven, 1977), pp. 95–111; Samuel K. Cohn, *The Laboring Classes in Renaissance Florence* (New York, 1980); David Garrioch, *Neighborhood and Community in Paris, 1740–1790* (Cambridge, 1986); and Roderick Phillips, *Family Breakdown in Late Eighteenth-Century France: Divorces in Rouen, 1792–1803* (Oxford, 1980), esp. chap. 4. (I am grateful to Sarah Maza for calling Phillips's book to my attention.) See also Arlette Farge, *Vivre dans la rue à Paris au XVIIIe siècle* (Paris, 1979), for many references to the importance of neighbors and neighborhood.

24. In the artisan mind street (*rue*) and neighborhood (*voisinage*) were clearly and closely associated. See, for example, ADCO, BII 360/58, Jan. 1631; AMD, G89, Nov. 1638.

standards. An analysis of four streets in St. Jean parish densely populated by master artisans, two between 1556 and 1579 and two others between 1630 and 1650, shows that neighborhoods must have carried a transpersonal quality.[25] Though resident artisans were more sedentary in the seventeenth century than in the sixteenth, still, few of them stayed in one place longer than three or four years; yet the neighborhood retained its cohesive, one might even say domineering force (see Tables 4.1, 4.2).

Neighborhood mobility differed from one street to another, but generally speaking, most artisans did not stay put for very many years. External factors such as war and high mortality took their toll, of course. Half the artisans living in the rue du Bourg and the small square Morimont in 1556 were gone by 1560, though their nonartisan neighbors were more stable. Disruptive religious conflict in the 1560s, when many Protestant artisans were expelled, increased their mobility. Though stability improved over the next decade, only on the rue du Bourg between 1566 and 1571 did more than half of the artisans remain on the street. After twenty-three years only 3 percent of the original artisan inhabitants of Morimont were still living there. Indeed, only one of eight stayed there from 1566 through 1579. Only one in seven of the Bourg's artisans resident in 1556 was still there in 1579, and only one-fourth of those of 1566 were.

In the two decades after 1630 artisans were relatively more sedentary—at least after 1636. Between 1630 and 1636 Dijon suffered from the effects of the Thirty Years' War, and mobility was relatively high. But after 1636, about 60 percent of the artisans of the rue de la Poulaillerie and the rue des Forges remained for at least four or five years, longer than their nonartisan neighbors. The craftsmen of Poulaillerie were especially stable. Over one-fifth of those living there in 1630 were still there in 1650, and 36 percent had been there over a decade by then. The artisans of the rue des Forges were a bit more mobile but still more sedentary than their sixteenth-century counterparts, at least after 1636.

---

25. The tax collectors over the course of the century of this study did not consistently note when they began certain streets, and it is quite likely that construction altered the configuration of the streets; so it is impossible to follow the same streets throughout the period. Nonetheless, I have taken care to choose a parish representative of the general population, particularly the artisanat, and then to focus on four streets that were also quite representative.

**Table 4.1**
Geographic mobility, by neighborhood, 1556–1579

| | Original population | Percentage of original inhabitants remaining | | | |
|---|---|---|---|---|---|
| | | *1560* | *1566* | *1571* | *1579* |
| **All inhabitants** | | | | | |
| Rue du Bourg | | | | | |
| 1556 | 75 | 60 | 36 | 27 | 12 |
| 1560 | 88 | | 39 | 28 | 15 |
| 1566 | 95 | | | 53 | 23 |
| 1571 | 85 | | | | 33 |
| Place du Morimont | | | | | |
| 1556 | 64 | 52 | 31 | 26 | 9 |
| 1560 | 69 | | 46 | 17 | 13 |
| 1566 | 100 | | | 44 | 18 |
| 1571 | 89 | | | | 37 |
| **Artisans** | | | | | |
| Bourg | | | | | |
| 1556 | 28 | 50 | 29 | 25 | 14 |
| 1560 | 34 | | 29 | 24 | 15 |
| 1566 | 40 | | | 55 | 25 |
| 1571 | 35 | | | | 37 |
| Morimont | | | | | |
| 1556 | 30 | 50 | 27 | 13 | 3 |
| 1560 | 33 | | 42 | 18 | 6 |
| 1566 | 40 | | | 38 | 13 |
| 1571 | 34 | | | | 38 |

Source: AMD, L168, L170, L195, L200, L205.

This evidence presents a picture of substantial turnover in artisan populations. Clearly, many new faces were continually appearing on Dijon's crowded streets, even in the seventeenth century (though we do not know if those who disappeared were dying or simply moving to another street). Meanwhile, the core of quasi-permanent resident artisans who anchored these neighborhoods slowly grew. Many were probably the home buyers we encountered previously. Thus, in the seventeenth century many artisans were becoming increasingly parochial in their local apprenticeship requirements, urban real estate acquisitions, marriage strategies, and in their more sedentary pattern of residence. (With this developing parochialism also came a bias against immigrants, which I will discuss shortly.) Moreover, despite unquestionable artisan mobility, neighborhoods remained cohesive. This unit of space must have carried a transpersonal quality. Those

**Table 4.2**
Geographic mobility, by neighborhood, 1630–1650

| | Original population | Percentage of original inhabitants remaining | | | |
|---|---|---|---|---|---|
| | | *1636* | *1639* | *1643* | *1650* |
| **All inhabitants** | | | | | |
| Rue des Forges | | | | | |
| 1630 | 103 | 47 | 30 | 22 | 14 |
| 1636 | 105 | | 53 | 35 | 23 |
| 1639 | 107 | | | 54 | 29 |
| 1643 | 114 | | | | 37 |
| Rue de la Poulaillerie | | | | | |
| 1630 | 122 | 53 | 34 | 20 | 13 |
| 1636 | 121 | | 60 | 39 | 23 |
| 1639 | 129 | | | 61 | 32 |
| 1643 | 136 | | | | 49 |
| **Artisans** | | | | | |
| Rue des Forges | | | | | |
| 1630 | 48 | 38 | 29 | 17 | 6 |
| 1636 | 47 | | 68 | 38 | 19 |
| 1639 | 51 | | | 57 | 26 |
| 1643 | 55 | | | | 35 |
| Rue de la Poulaillerie | | | | | |
| 1630 | 37 | 70 | 57 | 35 | 22 |
| 1636 | 62 | | 71 | 50 | 26 |
| 1639 | 67 | | | 66 | 36 |
| 1643 | 76 | | | | 57 |

Source: AMD, L230, L231, L232, L234, L238.

who moved into a neighborhood and stayed awhile shouldered the customary responsibilities and duties of neighbors. Yet, although core residents provided a modicum of continuity, most neighbors could not have known their fellows on the street for very long. Perhaps it is for this reason that in an emergency those in trouble did not shout any particular name but merely "Voisin!"

## Consensus and Conflict

The artisans' struggle for solidarity and consensus occurred in a conflict-ridden context of ambiguous relationships that were both competitive and interdependent. Craftsmen struggled for power and control over their peers but also tended to band together. Ambivalence pervaded their economic interrelationships, too. Artisans freely lent money to one another—in fact, were expected to—but when necessity demanded calling in a loan, debtors often reacted with violence. In densely packed neighborhoods artisans created networks of interdependency which fostered both solidarity and division. They used their networks to advance their own interests but also as bonds of trust that would promote social control and stability. Equilibrium, consciously sought in the form of solidarity and consensus, was a constant struggle for artisans in a world that by its very nature brought conflict.

It is an anthropological commonplace that oral cultures possess an agonistic tone, and the artisan culture of early modern Dijon was no exception. Communication and interaction occurred in a context of struggle. We have seen that master artisans were increasing their patrimonies after 1600 and devising marital strategies to attain their goals, competition for material and human resources affected much more in artisan life than just marriage. Artisans believed in the power of words, employed them as tools in their struggles, and left traces of their use in the judicial archives of Dijon. The criminal court records contain thousands of first-instance depositions (not encapsulations by scribes), which give us a rare look at the language of the street. Witnesses' own stories of what they saw and heard are recorded at length in these entertaining and informative bundles. Unfortunately, we do not know how complete the bundles are, and so any statistical results could be misleading, but close scrutiny of the use of language in lived situations described in over a thousand cases between 1550 and 1650 does yield the outline of a value system embraced by artisans (and partly shared with other cultures).[26]

26. Of course, one must be on guard against misleading elements. Leading questions by interrogators, neighbors with grudges, lying malefactors—all suggest that what appears in these records cannot necessarily be taken at face value. But by reading in context, with attention to the mundane and unextraordinary, it is possible to avoid some of these pitfalls. Arlette Farge, *La vie fragile* (Paris, 1986), demonstrates this method successfully, as does Gregory Hanlon, "Les rituels de l'agression en Aquitaine au XVIIe siècle," *Annales: ESC* 40.2 (1985): 244–68. Stereotype and repetition of elements interpreted in various changing contexts can help the historian penetrate the world of the street and the meanings behind the signs by which the people communicated. I have sampled over a thousand such records, the most useful of which have been depositions of witnesses, for, since most cases contain multiple depositions, varied perspectives on the *same* incident emerge. I have also spaced my sampling as evenly as possible from 1550 to 1650 to gauge changes in discourse.

These records are full of the formulaic name calling so typical of agonistic cultures; indeed, the repeated formulas and the equally predictable responses reflect a culture knit together by tacitly shared meanings but fractured by competition. The stakes in these verbal exchanges were high—often they ended in bloody combat—and they were highly polarized—participants were either good or evil, heroes or villains, friends or mortal enemies. Through them we can gain considerable insight into artisan values, assumptions, fears, and desires.[27]

In so many ways master artisans held strong notions of what was proper, but their assumptions did not obviate conflict. For example, they placed a high value upon personal property and condemned theft but were continually fearful that others were stealing from them. Similarly, with patrimonies growing, master craftsmen prized solvency and viewed indigence with disdain; yet the reactions of debtors whose loans were called in makes it clear that some artisans were sure that penury was never far away and afraid that they would succumb. In 1642 Henry Daumalle asked fellow carpenter Pierre Becquinot to repay a small loan of three blancs. He refused Becquinot's counteroffer of fourteen deniers, whereupon the borrower flew into a rage. Before flinging a three-blanc coin in his creditor's face and assaulting him with fists and feet, Becquinot rained verbal abuse on Daumalle, calling him, among other things, a thief (*voleur*). More than half a century before a master shoemaker, Odot Thomas, had demanded the repayment of a loan he had made to master painter Jean Ranquet, the brother of Thomas's deceased brother-in-law. Ranquet protested he could not pay because "he was not solvent," and when Thomas insisted, a fight ensued. Similarly, in 1617 a master blacksmith lent a royal sergeant with whom he served guard duty three and a half sous. When he tried to collect it, the sergeant flatly refused, showered his creditor with insults, resisted the arrest ordered by the captain of the guard, and fled for the remainder of the day.[28]

Many examples could be presented to demonstrate important aspects of artisan economic attitudes. Despite their moderately comfortable economic standing, few craftsmen in that harsh age ever felt completely sheltered from economic disaster, for war, harvest failure,

27. On polarity, see Lévi-Strauss, *La pensée sauvage*, esp. chaps. 1 and 2.
28. ADCO, BII 360/59, 1642, 360/51, 22 Oct. 1586, 360/57, Jan. 1617.

or plague could threaten all but the most affluent. As a result, access to credit was important within the artisan community. Its function, however, was ambiguous; it could be viewed as simply an impersonal business transaction, but credit also served as a system of mutual aid, and it created economic dependency.

Clearly, artisans often made small interest-free loans as a form of mutual aid; one master locksmith was most offended to be called a usurer. Such a grievous insult, he felt, was worthy of redress in a court of law.[29] Similarly, judging from the typical responses to loan collection, the time of repayment was not a decision to be made unilaterally by the creditor. In such a reciprocal system the free extension of credit was partly a moral obligation, a collective recognition of the necessity for mutual aid in a harsh world. It was a hedge against an uncertain future when the wheel of fortune might roll the creditor to the bottom.[30] The giving of credit, like any gift, could bind the receiver to return the favor in some form in the future. Indeed, calling in a loan may indicate that the wheel was already turning, forcing a creditor to violate traditionally sanctioned mutual aid agreements. Perhaps the fear of this reciprocal dependency helps explain why solvency was so valued by artisans. In their marriage contracts artisans or their parents generally agree to pay off the debts of the betrothed before the wedding. Likewise, in testaments the testator frequently instructs his heirs to pay his debts.[31] Artisans, it seems, did not wish to bring debts or their obligations into marriage or into eternity.

Credit was not only a form of sociability. It could also be used for economic coercion. Masters often advanced wages to journeymen, for example, and thereby legally bound the worker to their service until he could work off the advance, perhaps longer than the worker might have wished. Even master artisans could be brought into dependency by purchasing rentes from fellow masters. The debtors gained fluid capital in exchange for a financially mortgaged future; in the case of rentes, interest was levied "in perpetuity."

29. Ibid., 360/51, 2 March 1582.
30. Keith Wrightson and David Levine, *Poverty and Piety in an English Village* (New York, 1979), pp. 100–1, have found that in the village of Terling financial aid was readily found, most frequently from neighbors of similar social status, and the debts were usually small and interest free.
31. For examples of marriage contracts, see ADCO, *Notaires* #363, 2 Nov. 1584, #371, 30 April 1592, #1724, 24 Sept. 1595, #1715, 20 May 1601, #1701, 3 Sept. 1617, and for testaments, #384, 15 Sept. 1625; #1941, 1627.

Such relations were sanctioned not only in law but also in artisan morality, increasingly so in the seventeenth century. Calling someone a *banqueroutier* imputed fraud rather than innocent business failure, and such insults became more frequent in the seventeenth century, perhaps because of growing patrimonies.[32] This was a serious insult precisely because it undercut an artisan's commercial reputation. In 1638 master cooper Bénigne Derot shouted out in public that master dyer Gabriel LeGrand was a bankrupt and a thief. LeGrand complained that this was a great "impertinence," because it injuriously "fed rumor."[33]

Certainly artisans feared business failure and the indigence that would result; poverty was scorned. During the sixteenth century more and more beggars shuffled down Dijon's streets. If the Dijonnais masters were like their fellows in other parts of Europe, they were much concerned to mark themselves off from the "disorderly" poor.[34] The Dijonnais master embroiderer Berthelemy Vitrey certainly reflects this sentiment. In 1623 he considered it sufficient grounds to discredit a witness testifying against him by alleging that the deponent had sent his wife and children to beg in the streets—a sure sign to Vitrey of a disreputable character.[35]

Corresponding to this growing repugnance toward beggary was pride in the possession of property. As we have seen, many artisans eagerly acquired property, and they jealously protected it. In 1567 baker Jehan Roche heard that some shepherds were grazing their flock in his patch of rapeseed; he indignantly marched out to confront them and promptly got into a fight.[36] Similarly, artisans were constantly complaining to the authorities about vandalism—broken windows, defaced signs—inflicted by youths roaming the streets at night.

Perhaps the best index for judging how possessions were valued lies in attitudes toward theft, which imply sentiments about legitimacy and about the right of possession. Again, insults provide insight into

32. This certainly was the meaning in the eighteenth century. I wish to thank my colleague Judith Miller for this information.

33. ADCO, BII 360/58, Aug.–Sept. 1638, and see 360/63, 11 Nov. 1646.

34. In early modern England, according to J. A. Sharpe, *Defamation and Sexual Slander*, Borthwick Papers, no. 58 (York, 1980), p. 25, master craftsmen, the "middling" and "stable" sort, showed a "growing desire to mark their conduct off from that of the disorderly and ungodly poor."

35. ADCO, BII 360/57, Sept.–Oct. 1623.

36. Ibid., 360/47, 27 May 1567.

value judgments of artisans. Next to sexual slanders, the most common denunciations in acrimonious verbal exchanges related to thievery. *Larron* and *voleur* were the most frequent, but more colorful ones, such as "cutpurse," "merchant-robber," and "cow thief and highwayman," also appear in the records.[37] Constant repetition failed to mitigate the sting of an insult like *voleur*. In fact, the frequency of such accusations reveals just how unacceptable was this behavior and tended to reinforce the consensus about it.[38] The stigma attached to the word *thief* spanned the elite and popular cultures. During the 1590s a prisoner of war was executed wearing on his head a paper miter on which were the words "parricide, traitor, thief."[39] In the courts, too, to say that a witness was "a thief who had robbed a private home" was sufficient to discredit him or her.[40] Yet despite the evident abhorrence of theft, private property was not delineated very clearly in early modern France. In this area as in others, there was much ambiguity and outright contradiction.

Historians have recognized that a crisp demarcation of public and private space is anachronistic for early modern popular cultures. The records leave no doubt that artisans and their neighbors were packed cheek by jowl on crowded streets. It was typical that the workshop of master tailor Othelin Compagne lay only "four or five feet" from the entrance to the dwelling of fellow artisan Jehan DuChesne. Nor was it unusual that in the house of master shoemaker Pierre Chandelier, baker Claude Regnier, cabinetmaker Christophe Melesson and three others shared common walls, entrance, and stairway.[41] In these dense living conditions neighbors shared such communal resources as courtyards, latrines, wells, fountains, and streams, and rigorous distinctions between public and private space are inappropriate.[42] Ar-

37. For example, ibid., 360/41, 11 Sept. 1556, 360/44, 17 Dec. 1561, 360/48, 21 June 1571, 360/53, Aug. 1594, 360/57, 22 March 1616, 360/58, 8 Aug. 1638, 25 Nov. 1641, 360/59, 16 June 1642, 360/60, 31 Dec. 1643, 360/61, 2 Jan. 1645.

38. Anthropologists find frequent repetition of slanders common in oral cultures; repetition impresses upon the collective memory in the absence of written preservation. For a general discussion and overview, see Ong, *Orality and Literacy*, pp. 39–42.

39. Joachim Durandeau, ed., *Le journal de Claude Sullot, procureur au parlement de Dijon* (Dijon, 1911), p. 18.

40. ADCO, BII 360/57, Sept.–Nov. 1623.

41. Ibid., 360/44, 20 Aug. 1560, 360/51, 15 Nov. 1576.

42. In his study of the journal of the late seventeenth-century Lillois weaver Chavatte, Alain Lottin points out that Chavatte was overwhelmingly concerned with the public side of life and silent on the private (*Chavatte*, p. 373).

tisans spent much of their leisure time in the streets, playing games, dancing on holidays, or more commonly just passing the time chatting with neighbors. And at work, artisan shops were open to public scrutiny; indeed, many craftsmen deliberately extended their shops out into public space, plying their trade, as one cooper did, "devant sa maison en la rue du Bled."[43] In these conditions it was often difficult for the individual to know where "mine" left off and "yours" began.[44] Such ambiguity made for communalism and sociability but also for conflict springing from competition for resources, both material and human. Proximity and shared use of resources thus constituted a threat to peace.

Because neighbors were highly interdependent, they were continually vulnerable to one another. Any number of causes could kindle neighborly friction, but many disputes erupted from abuse of or competition for common resources. The wife of one master shoemaker, for example, continually quarreled with close neighbors with whom she shared a courtyard because the neighbors wanted her to dump her household wastes in the street, not the courtyard.[45] On another occasion a winegrower's wife fell into a public well and drowned. Without a shadow of sympathy, the neighbors of the street, fearing their water source had been polluted, tried to force the widower to dig another, at his expense. When he protested that he was too poor to undertake the project, he was showered with such abuse from the neighbors that he appealed to the magistrates for help.[46]

Credit, freely given between neighbors as between artisans, could, as we have seen, generate a fight when collection was attempted, as could the attempt to collect rent from a tenant sharing one's house.[47] Frequently neighbors were business partners, and disputes could erupt when one believed the other had violated some agreement about the use of a shared resource. Master mason Jehan Gon and his wife came to blows with their neighbor, cousin, fellow guildsman, and business partner Philippe Clammonet over the payment of a carter for transporting some stone they were using in a joint project.[48]

43. ADCO, BII 360/44, 2 Sept. 1561.
44. See Peter Schneider, "Honor and Conflict in a Sicilian Town," *Anthropological Quarterly* 42.3 (1969): 132.
45. ADCO, BII 360/58, May–Sept. 1642.
46. AMD, B283, fol. 43v, 27 June 1645.
47. ADCO, BII 360/53, Nov. 1594.
48. Ibid., 360/48, Sept.–Oct. 1571.

Contention could just as easily arise over the control of human resources, especially journeymen. When master goldsmith Almot Papillon and his wife Marguerite Rollet harbored a "servant" who had run away from fellow guildsman, neighbor, and kinsman Jean Cuisenier and his wife Elizabeth Carrelet, Carrelet was furious. She accused Rollet of "having no respect for the alliance between them or for the neighborhood" when she stole such an apparently scarce resource. More examples could be given—the insult of *recelleur des servants* is not uncommon throughout the period—but it is hardly surprising that master artisans would band together as neighbors to use some resource or that discord could erupt when such a union was ruptured.[49] Indeed, the "theft" of servants, since it included journeymen, struck at the very heart of the system of social control and worker subordination. The existence of masters willing to shelter runaway journeymen could easily encourage a worker to disobey his present master and leave his employment. Master artisans formed alliances and coalitions to advance their own interests in the labor market, but other forces—such as scarcity of skilled labor—were at work. Competition rendered them vulnerable to their fellows and neighbors.

Recognizing the extent of conflict between neighbors is important, but the neighborhood was also a mechanism of social control. Indeed, latent violence likely encouraged the formation of kinship and neighborhood alliances. Throughout the period, neighborhood solidarity is much in evidence. The density of living conditions promoted homogeneity of norms and values and led to a high degree of social control.[50] Though there is no way to quantify such an impression, neighbors seem to have grown less fractious among themselves. By the 1640s conflicts were less frequent between neighbors, perhaps because the neighbors were living together a little longer.

The penetration of vertical ties may have injected elite control to some extent. The "advice and consent" clauses of marriage contracts hint that socially vertical neighborly ties were being consolidated in the seventeenth century. Though still far from general, the mentions of "a friend and neighbor" noticeably increased in the marriage contracts involving artisans after around 1620. Between 1551 and 1617 only 5 of 645 contain such references to neighbors, whereas from

49. Ibid., 360/53, July–Aug. 1594, and see 360/60, 1643.
50. Boissevain, p. 37.

1618 to 1650, 22 of 338 do. And of those twenty-two, all but three mention neighbors of higher social status than the artisanat, and several include nobles of the robe.[51]

Such vertical ties may have helped to strengthen horizontal social bonds. In other societies anthropologists have observed that as rituals of personal relations become more formalized, other, less formalized relations seem to develop, often exhibited in an attempt to build "communitas."[52] Artisans may have informally solidified their horizontal links of neighborhood and craft as counterweights to the tightening of the vertical bonds of patronage in which they were increasingly entwined.

Horizontal solidarity assumes mutual obligations. One of these is the expected exchange of information—gossiping—which was considered an important duty in the oral culture of the artisans. The wife of master shoemaker Alexandre Massenot tried to discredit a hostile witness by alleging that every year in the twenty-five they had been neighbors—an extraordinary length of time in view of the relative mobility of resident artisans—the witness had withheld gossip from her. Clearly, Mme Massenot considered this a breach of neighborly expectations of the first magnitude.[53]

Such mutual obligations knit neighbors together and prompted them to act collectively in defense of common interests. When master armorer Henri Colinet built a forge in his house in 1554, his neighbors, dreading fire, quickly brought it to the attention of the authorities, who had the hazard demolished. Other neighborhoods complained about master butchers who slaughtered pigs in the streets or corralled their cattle there. The cows certainly did not distinguish between public and private space; they roamed freely into the houses located on the streets where the butchers had herded them. Other craftsmen felt the force of united neighborly action against them; the inhabitants of the rue de la Chapelle aux Riches

51. ADCO, *Notaires*. To cite all twenty-seven instances would avail little, but see, for example, #2047, 7 July 1647, in which two nobles of the robe sanction a marriage between the daughter of a master baker and another master baker, and are referred to as "voisins et amys." These neighborhood functions are remarkably similar to the patronage networks fashioned in medieval Genoa and Renaissance Florence. See Hughes, pp. 101–3; Kent and Kent, pp. 8–9.

52. Eisenstadt and Roniger, *Patrons, Clients and Friends*, p. 18.

53. ADCO, BII 360/60, May–Sept. 1643, and for another example of the importance of gossip, see 360/59, 9 April 1642.

complained to the authorities that the wastes from the dyers' trade polluted the neighborhood wells and the waters of the Suzon, the stream that flowed through the town.[54]

Immigration patterns may have contributed to this pattern of neighborhood solidarity. The peasants of northern and eastern France practiced the open-field system of cultivation, which required a strict collective discipline. Immigrants to Dijon in the late sixteenth and early seventeenth centuries, who usually came from the villages of eastern France, may have brought a communal mentality with them. Moreover, many immigrants, like their counterparts throughout early modern France, settled in neighborhoods where relatives already lived, creating overlapping bonds of kinship and proximity.[55] Even double ties, however, as the examples of the quarreling masons and goldsmiths attest, did not always ensure order.

Not only did neighborhoods act collectively, but the municipal authorities treated them as units. Frequently, the town council ordered entire neighborhoods (often specifying its members) to clear their streets of the *boue* that had accumulated there. Given the prodigious quantities of garbage that clogged the streets of old regime Dijon, it is not surprising to find instances of fines imposed on entire neighborhoods for shirking this responsibility.[56] Furthermore, if a parent died unexpectedly and named no guardian for minor children, the town council sometimes summoned the neighbors to elect a *curateur* from among themselves.[57]

The loyalty, solidarity, and cohesiveness of artisan relationships both with their neighbors and among themselves took other very

54. AMD, B191, fol. 136v, 9 Jan. 1554, B192, fol. 106r, 3 Aug. 1554, G305, 8 Oct. 1620, B217, fol. 69r, 26 Aug. 1559.

55. See Gutton, *La sociabilité villageoise*, pp. 13–14; Pierre de Saint Jacob, "Etude sur l'ancienne communauté rurale en Bourgogne," *Annales de Bourgogne* 13 (1941): 169–202, and "Les terres communales," *Annales de Bourgogne* 25 (1953): 225–40. For examples of artisan immigrant kin as neighbors, see ADCO, BII 360/44, 3 July 1561, 360/47, 16 Feb. 1566; and AMD, G89, March 1638. Flandrin, *Families in Former Times*, p. 34, suggests that in French villages kinship ties reinforced neighborhood solidarities, though he may overstate their importance. Heers, *Family Clans*, p. 137, leaves no doubt of the coincidence of ties of kin and neighbor in northern France, nor do Hughes and Kent and Kent for the patricians of medieval Genoa and Renaissance Florence, respectively.

56. AMD, B217, fol. 69r, 1 Feb. 1580; Cohn, p. 199, comments that entire parishes in Renaissance Florence were similarly treated as moral persons and collectively fined.

57. ADCO, BII 347/1, 1571.

visible shapes: keeping the peace, providing aid in time of crisis, and maintaining the customs of hospitality, visiting, and commensality.[58] The preservation of tranquility and order was a value of prime consideration. To supplement the ineffective municipal police, a sort of vigilantism emerged, often to protect a neighborhood against youth group violence. The rue de Porte Guillaume provides a case in point. One night a group of young males, including artisans and their sons, from the rue des Champs de Matz entered the rue de Porte Guillaume to beat up the son of an innkeeper living there. About ten o'clock, hearing cries of "Kill! Kill!" master shoemaker Louis DuBerne leaped from his bed, grabbed his halberd, and dashed down into the street, where he was joined by another neighbor, also clutching a halberd. Other neighbors had heard the noise and rushed outside too. As a witness recalled at the subsequent trial, "The neighbors of the street" wanted to "make them [the disruptive youths] cease their bad will." The next day, these same youths returned to the rue de Porte Guillaume—and found the neighborhood waiting for them. As soon as they entered the street the neighbors came after them with "swords and daggers" drawn and chased them off. A similar situation occurred in 1577. Young males roaming the walls of Dijon showered the rue des Crais with rocks "in such great quantity that several [inhabitants] of the . . . street were wounded and forced to withdraw into their houses." A bold winegrower, acting in defense of his neighborhood, climbed up on the wall to stop them and was beaten savagely by the youths. His life was saved only by the "neighbors of the street," including at least one artisan, who came to his rescue.[59]

Keeping the peace was a valued ideal, and consequently peaceableness with one's neighbors, sanctioned by traditional Christianity, was a valued characteristic of an individual's personality. The depositions of the *vie et moeurs* interrogations preliminary to granting mastership letters are full of accolades from neighbors declaring the candidate to be a "peaceable man." Of course, this was a stylized formula, but stereotypes and commonplaces reveal desiderata of society.[60] Clearly the Dijonnais, forced into daily close contact with neighbors,

---

58. Cohn has uncovered networks of mutual assistance among neighbors in quattrocento Florence's *popolo minuto*, as have Wrightson and Levine, pp. 99–109, in the English village of Terling.

59. ADCO, BII 360/48, 13 April 1572, 360/51, 25 Jan. 1577.

60. For example, AMD, G86, Aug., Nov. 1618, G89, Oct. 1638, July 1642.

wanted smooth relations. The ability to get along with others could justify much. In 1560, for example, one Marguerite, the wife of a mason, protested that she had lived twenty-two years in the same street (again, an extraordinary claim) without any "argument, contention, or quarrel with any of her neighbors."[61] This ideal of the peaceable neighbor may have helped prevent violence, or at least tempered its effects, by imbuing neighbors with a value system that emphasized nonaggression. In the course of a fight in 1643 two day laborers told Antoine Guillemin, a drill maker, that "if they were not his neighbors they would have killed him."[62]

When fights did occur, neighbors were expected to "make peace" (*mettre la paix*) as soon as possible, and they responded in bunches when fights erupted. Denise Fleurot, a winegrower's daughter, "was hailed by one of her neighbors to come into the street, having been informed that there were some people who were beating each other and who were crying 'Kill! Kill!' " The fight between the masons Gon and Clammonet and their wives discussed previously was ended by an intervening neighbor. A few years earlier, tailor Othelin Compagne was interrogated for knifing the *passementier* Jehan DuChesne. Asked "whether the said *passementier* . . . cried 'Murder!' and if the neighbors ran to help," Compagne admitted that he had heard the cry and knew that the neighbors had come running but that he had remained in his shop. It was decidedly odd for a neighbor to remain inside while there was a commotion in the street. The interrogator grew suspicious. "Why would the neighbors come running if it was not because of a wound?" he asked. "Is there a great distance between your shop and his [DuChesne's] entrance?" Sensing a trap, Compagne dodged self-incrimination by yielding no more information. "Je ne sçais rien."[63]

Neighbors responded promptly to noises and disturbances in the street. Fights were broken up, and men were expected to respond to screamed insults and threats of the combatants or a female neighbor's cry for help. So strong was this obligation that male neighbors felt justified in entering each other's houses to stop husbands from abusing their wives. In 1568 Claude Odot, a hosier, complained to a neigh-

61. ADCO, BII 360/44, 12 Sept. 1560: "débat, contention, ou noise à aulcungs de ses voisins."
62. Ibid., 360/60, 27 Oct. 1643.
63. Ibid., Sept. 1643, 360/44, 20 Aug. 1560.

bor, "Never again will I prevent the quarrels of my neighbors, because for having made peace between some I have been greatly insulted in return!" Odot was referring to his intervention in a domestic fight between the master plasterer Antoine Villot and his wife. Odot had heard her cry "Murder!" and so had dutifully run into Villot's house, where he found the plasterer beating her. Odot felt it his duty to upbraid Villot, who responded with insults. Children were quickly socialized into this network of neighborly expectation. In 1608 when the master locksmith Guillaume Obrest beat his wife and hurled her into the fireplace, his children, understandably horrified, ran to the nearest neighbor for help. The neighbor, who happened to be a craftsman himself, came instantly and saw Obrest slip out the back door.[64]

This obligation to intervene, springing from a desire for tranquility, was recognized in the artisan community as well as in the popular community as a whole, and the judgment of neighbors was respected, even feared. A mother quarreling with her daughter and artisan son-in-law in 1594 felt herself wronged and called for the neighbors' help. She ran into the street where her male neighbors had gathered in response to her cries. "Messieurs," she addressed them, "you will be witnesses to how these people have insulted me!" Pierre LeBlanc, a currier, then reprimanded the son-in-law: "It is not a good thing to beat your mother." This sort of judgment was appropriate, expected, and apparently carried some weight. Certainly the daughter had feared neighborly intervention. She told the authorities that she had tried to silence her distraught mother, pleading, "Be quiet, mother! The neighbors will think that someone is beating you!"[65] The expected role of neighbors in this domestic row is quite evident.

This willingness to aid neighbors in crisis and keep the peace is exhibited throughout the period. In the 1640s we still hear of neighbors intervening in fights. When Léonard Guillaumot, the son of a master plasterer, knocked down another master plasterer with a stone, he was prevented from inflicting any more harm "by all the neighbors running there." But such impromptu policing could be dangerous, even deadly. In 1643 a journeyman butcher was killed when he tried to break up a fight on the rue des Crais.[66]

---

64. Ibid., 360/47, 13 Sept. 1568, 360/57, 17 April 1608. Neighbors seem to have held similar sentiments in revolutionary Paris. See Roderick Phillips, pp. 182–83.
65. Ibid., 360/53, 10 Nov. 1594.
66. Ibid., 360/59, 12 Jan. 1643, 360/60, 13 July 1643.

If neighbors were always willing to intervene, they seem to appear on the scene much more quickly in the seventeenth century than they had in the sixteenth. By the 1640s the records contain many instances of violence thwarted by prompt action. Jeanne Robert, wife of a fowler, alleged in one petition to the authorities that "without the assistance and prompt *services*" of several neighbors who arrived in time to prevent the assault of one called the vigneron, she *would* have suffered more than just slanders. In another case, just as a journeyman tailor saw some young men attack a coppersmith's daughter, "*at the same instant* her neighbors ran there" to intervene. Two years later Pierre Noizot, wielding an unsheathed sword, "*would* have" struck the mason Nicolas Millot, witnesses tell us, had he not been prevented by neighbors who ran to the noise. One year earlier tailor Claude Lorrain, holding an ax in his hand, charged pastrycook François Jonas, but before he could land a blow, the weapon was ripped from his hand by another artisan neighbor.[67] Other examples of such prompt response could be offered from the 1640s, but not from the sixteenth century. True, peacekeeping was important throughout the period, but the evidence hints that neighbors were more ready to prevent aggression in the seventeenth century, perhaps because the bonds of neighborhood solidarity were tightening.

Networks were cemented by other forms of social exchange than provision of credit, aid, and peacekeeping. The unstructured sociability of drinking in a tavern creates a momentary link among participants, but more lasting and secure bonds were forged in forms of social exchange that entailed trust, reciprocity, and obligation. Perhaps the most prominent example of this behavior is visiting and sharing a drink or a meal in another's house under the laws of hospitality.[68] Like all forms of social exchange, drinking or eating in another's house requires trust, and partaking of the common substance establishes an informal bond of communitas based upon egalitarian

67. Ibid., 360/59, 22 Oct. 1642, 5 March 1642 (my emphasis), 360/60, 20 March 1644, 11 July 1643.

68. For a theoretical discussion of visiting, see Amal Vinogradov, Introduction to *Anthropological Quarterly* 47.1 (1974): 2–8. This entire volume is devoted to visitation patterns and their implications. On the "laws" of hospitality, see Julian Pitt-Rivers, *The Fate of Schechem; or, The Politics of Sex* (Cambridge, 1977), chap. 5. On sociability in general, see Maurice Agulhon, "La sociabilité, la sociologie, et l'histoire," *Arc* 65 (1976): 76–84.

assumptions.[69] Of course, it is a commonplace of social anthropology that commensality is a basis of community.

Bonds of sociability crisscrossed the popular cultures and intersected in Dijon's churches and taverns. Neighbors took communion together, and this ritual, at least in the mind of one journeyman painter in 1643, not only declared membership in the Catholic community but sealed friendships.[70] Taverns were gathering places for journeymen and other youths, as well as master artisans, vignerons, and neighbors. Imbibing can promote an easy familiarity and sense of equality (it was not uncommon for journeymen to address masters as *tu* in a tavern), but it can also lead to drunkenness and discord. Following a visit to a tavern, where the loser of a tennis game bought the drinks, vigneron Jacques Simeon and coopers Jean Gaulthier and Pierre LeBlanc, who had imbibed too much, fractured the conviviality by going after each other with stones and knives. Nearly a hundred years later the same sort of incident must still have been common. Beckoned from the window of a tavern, journeyman cabinetmaker François Sauvageot joined two youths, later identified as a roofer and a baker, whom he knew only by their last names. After drinking their fill, the three, "full of wine," said the witnesses, stumbled into the street, where, for reasons never established, they began to fight. One of the boys was severely wounded. Corporate bonds, too, could be confirmed and then broken by drink. Over half a dozen bakers, many of them masters, who had gathered to play a game of *quilles*, passed around and drained a jug of wine before starting. Then, when one contestant illegally crossed the line before throwing the ball, another challenged him on it and wound up having his skull cracked by one of the balls.[71]

That the sociability of the tavern could be easily dissolved is no surprise, for no great trust is established among the individuals. The sociability of visiting and commensality is another matter. The custom of dining with friends and neighbors was most important. Ar-

69. Victor Turner, *Dramas, Fields and Metaphors: Symbolic Action in Human Society* (Ithaca, 1974), pp. 49, 53, 272. Turner defines *communitas* as "an unstructured or rudimentarily structured and relatively undifferentiated . . . community, or even communion of equal individuals." On the solidarity established by sharing meals and drink, see Pitt-Rivers, *The Fate of Schechem*, pp. 109–10.

70. AMD, G89, Dec. 1643.

71. ADCO, BII 360/41, 24 April 1556, 360/60, 7 Sept. 1643, 360/59, 10 April 1642.

tisans and their wives often ate with other artisans, neighbors, and even winegrowers. So numerous are the archival references to sharing meals that it may have been unusual to dine alone. Marguerite, the widow of master artisan Felix Contremine remarked that "she and her late husband had oftentimes . . . drunk and eaten with . . . [the master sword polisher] Thibault DeRochefort and his wife as neighbors *ought to do.*" DeRochefort must seldom have dined alone, for another witness in the same trial stated that when he lived on the same street as Thibault he had eaten with him more than five hundred times! Even allowing for hyperbole, the message is clear: food and drink were frequently shared. Nor was Thibault's popularity unusual. Decades later we find the baker François Daultrey "supping with his family and one of his neighbors" or master furrier Bernard Fion "in his house with his neighbors, who were snacking together." Master pastrycook Jean Colombet told the authorities investigating master cooper Nicolas Marchant that the suspect was his friend, adding, significantly, that Marchant "hangs around with him, sometimes drinking and eating with him." Similarly, in an attempt to discredit a witness testifying against her, Claude Janeau, the wife of a master cobbler, claimed that Huguette Morel, wife of winegrower Michel Poignie, was "a friend of [the plaintiff] master cooper Denis Beleurgey . . . with whom she drinks and eats daily."[72]

The records do not say whether Colombet and Marchant or Morel and Beleurgey were neighbors as well as friends, but it is certain that craftsmen often ventured into other neighborhoods for meals, carrying their solidary networks with them. Master engraver Ancelme Bourberan was on his way home to another street after dining with the master sword polisher (and future fellow Calvinist) Jean Vignier when he witnessed a fight and left testimony incidentally describing his commensal activities of the evening. Similarly, master coffin maker Maurice Liet testified that he had gone into another parish to share a meal at the home of a certain master baker named Perot.[73]

Even masters and journeymen sometimes ate and drank together, evidence of conflicting vertical and horizontal tugs both sides must have felt in the nascent days of the war over the labor market. Master

---

72. Ibid., 360/48, March 1570 (my emphasis), 360/60, 23 Oct. 1643, 360/59, Aug. 1642, 360/44, 24 Aug. 1560, 360/59, June–Sept. 1642.
73. Ibid., 360/41, Sept. 1556, 360/60, Oct. 1643.

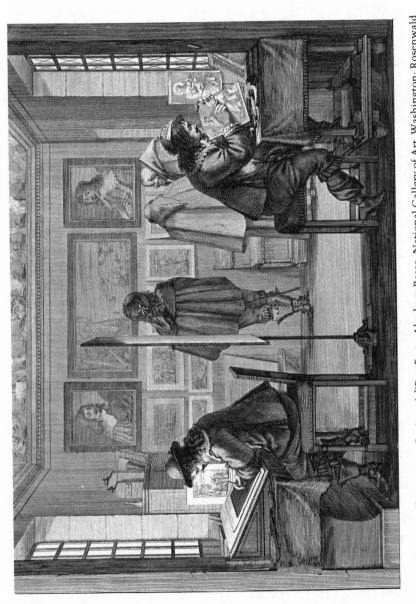

*Graveurs en Taille Douce au Burin et à l'Eau Forte*, Abraham Bosse; National Gallery of Art, Washington; Rosenwald Collection

dyer Gabriel LeGrand had supper with a master goldsmith and a journeyman one evening, and felt no condescension (though it may have been a paternalistic gesture) in escorting the journeyman back to the town gates after dinner to protect him from roving vagabonds.[74]

There is some evidence of commensality among journeymen, too. In 1561 Louis Gradard testified that a whole crowd of his fellow journeymen roofers had gathered to "sup together" at the Dauphin Tavern, "which is rented for the gathering of their company." This gathering sounds like a compagnonnage, as does a meeting of journeymen goldsmiths a year before. They had "supped together" at a tavern before returning to their masters' homes for the night.[75]

In many societies the laws of hospitality are stringent and specific. The taboo against showing hostility or rivalry to the host is one stricture apparently in force in Dijon artisan households.[76] Significantly, though this prohibition was sometimes violated in the sixteenth century, I could find no violations whatsoever in hundreds of criminal dossiers from the seventeenth century. Perhaps there was more concerted obedience to a more exacting norm of solidarity by artisans and neighbors. At any rate, in 1565 when the vigneron Claude Jona invited his "neighbors and friends" master oilmaker Claude Mynet, master carpenter Germain Chambrette, and master blacksmith Guillaume Jehannot to his house for dinner and a card game, Chambrette and Mynet broke the law of hospitality by getting into a fight over the game and wound up hurling pieces of Jona's furniture at one another. Jona's wife was most upset; it was wrong, she told them, to come to their house "to beat each other and create a scandal." In the same vein, when artisan Pierre LeMarquis came into the house of widow DuFour and thrashed another woman there, DuFour shouted, "It is a great wrong to commit such an act in [my] . . . house!" Similarly, the threat by Nicolas Chassin to kill fellow tapestry weaver Pierre Joly "at his table" was serious. Perhaps this was why he steadfastly refused to confess to saying it, even when pressed by the authorities and confronted with incriminating testimony.[77] The importance of commensality is thrown into relief by violations of the norms governing it.

74. Ibid., 360/58, Aug.–Sept. 1638.
75. Ibid., 360/44, 17 Dec. 1561, 25 July 1560.
76. Pitt-Rivers, *The Fate of Schechem*, p. 107.
77. ADCO, BII 360/47, Jan. 1565, 360/44, 5 Aug. 1561, 360/48, Sept. 1568.

## *Le Point d'Honneur*

It would be difficult to overemphasize the importance of honor in the daily life of the early modern Dijonnais. Honor operated at two inter-related levels, social status and personal virtue, or self-esteem. It served as society's measure of social standing in the hierarchy, and it measured worth within ranks.[78] At both levels, honor was a para-mount social value that enforced standards of accepted conduct and measured an individual's actions and worth against a norm recog-nized by peers, superiors, and inferiors. This conformity to a model of ideal conduct stiffened the strong traditionalism within artisan men-tality and was further reinforced for the upper classes by the rigidly hierarchical structure of society. Social anthropologist Julian Pitt-Rivers's comments are cogent:

> The ritual and ceremonial aspects of honour . . . demonstrate what is acceptable by reference to what is accepted. If the honour felt by the individual becomes honour paid by the society, it is equally the case that the honour which is paid by the society sets the standards for what the individual should feel. Transactions of honour there-fore serve these purposes: they not only provide . . . a nexus between the ideals of society and their re-production in the actions of indi-viduals—honour commits men to act as they should—but, on the social side, between the ideal order and the terrestrial order, validat-ing the realities of power and making the sanctified order of prece-dence correspond to them.[79]

In many respects master artisans, like their social superiors, aspired to the ideal of the honorable man. Duty and obligation, revenge and redress against insult and humiliation, even vindication by arms were all subsumed in a universal code of honor, which relied on the notion that the social hierarchy was established by God and mediated through signs and symbols by which the hierarchy could be "read." External manifestations made the man, and the notion of honor was closely tied to this emphasis on appearance; as Ronsard put it:

78. Hanlon, p. 244, points out that amour propre was at the base of an honorific system in seventeenth-century Aquitaine.

79. Julian Pitt-Rivers, "Honour and Social Status," in *Honour and Shame: The Values of Mediterranean Society*, ed. J. G. Peristiany (London, 1965), p. 38.

le velours trop commun
sous toi reprend ton vieil honneur,
tellement que ta remontrance
nous a fait voir la différence
du valet et de son seigneur.[80]

External gestures and symbols, such as carrying swords or having coats of arms, expressed honorable *qualité*. Despite repeated ordinances against carrying weapons, sword-bearing craftsmen continued to strut down Dijon's streets. One master artisan, Jean Blasme, a painter, even drew a coat of arms beneath his signature on a legal document.[81] Similarly, for artisans as well as for the upper classes, the word *devoir* was often used when social honor was in question, and could denote assumptions of obligation and hierarchy. Master baker Clement Menestrier complained to the municipal authorities that he had been slandered by his son-in-law, who had thereby violated the code by which he "owes [*doit*] honor and reverence" to his father-in-law.[82]

In society at large the ruling classes demanded that honor be paid them by their social inferiors, but this payment was sometimes withheld. Artisans had notions of their own about who possessed what degree of honor, and independent judgment from the bottom up tended to undermine a rigid hierarchy. Honor as personal virtue, then, was sometimes at odds with social honor and thus subversive of established order. Rampant violation of sumptuary legislation by artisans, to take one example, showed scant respect for a fixed hierarchy and is all the more significant in view of the importance of appearance to elites and artisans alike. Sometimes artisans defamed the character of their social superiors, especially public officials, with impunity. In 1578 master carpenter Germain Chambrette was working in St. Jean Square when Simon LeGourd, an alderman (and therefore at least a wealthy merchant or a lawyer), came up to him and told him he was doing a poor job. Chambrette retorted, "Go away! You have no right to command me!" to which LeGourd replied, "You do not know to whom you speak. You are a fool!" Chambrette countered with "You are nothing but an animal"; whereupon the alderman slapped him

80. Quoted in Jouanna, *Ordre social*, pp. 133–34.
81. ADCO, BII 360/51, 6 Sept. 1588.
82. Ibid., 360/53, 21 Aug. 1594.

across the face. Chambrette, when he was arrested, offered the implausible excuse that he did not know LeGourd was an alderman. Yet the alderman's clothing had undoubtedly told Chambrette that LeGourd was a social superior, to whom honor was theoretically due. It was not forthcoming.[83]

About two decades previously another artisan, master embroiderer Aubert Robelot, had denied honorific status to another alderman because he was a foreigner. Said Robelot to this illustrious immigrant, disdainfully addressing him as *tu*, "You are a Norman . . . and I am better than you!" Similarly, in 1581 Léonarde Micarde, a master baker's wife accused of selling underweight bread, insulted another alderman in *plaine rue*, calling him "thief, robber, and evil man who perpetually robs the town." She was arrested and forced to ask forgiveness on her knees in front of her shop, publicly withdrawing her slanders of the alderman's character in a ritual designed to reestablish hierarchical social honor.[84]

Artisans and vignerons knew they possessed honor, even if the upper classes failed to acknowledge it.[85] Artisan culture had a repertory of gestures and actions used to display honor, which are revealed through attempts to strip a peer of his honor, a form of theft. Honor was a possession and "worth" a great deal; hence, there was a close connection between honor and worthiness.[86] Slanderous exchanges demonstrate what qualities were defended as "honorable."

Artisans felt the duty to avenge or redress insults to their honor coming from their peers. In agonistic cultures like that of Dijon's artisans, affronts are read as attempts to gain superiority over social equals, and in Dijon there was an almost paranoid concern for reputation. Not surprisingly, craftsmen would not tolerate any defamation

83. AMD, B216, fol. 30r, 18 July 1578.
84. ADCO, BII 360/44, Aug.–Sept. 1561; AMD, B219, fol. 85v, 12 Dec. 1581.
85. Père Christoffe, a Jesuit preacher in Dijon in the early 1590s, castigated the vignerons for selling their votes in the mayoral election in exchange for food and cash, saying they give "their votes corrupted by gluttony and money." After the sermon, several vignerons demanded an explanation of why he had insulted them, insisting that they were *gens de bien*, a signpost phrase indicating possession of honor. Joseph Garnier, ed., *Journal de Gabriel Breunot, conseiller au parlement de Dijon, précédé du livre de souvenance de Pepin, chanoine de la Sainte-Chapelle en cette ville*, 3 vols. (Dijon, 1866), 3:128.
86. Similarly, John Demos, *Entertaining Satan* (New York, 1982), p. 79, finds seventeenth-century New Englanders considering one's good name a possession and slander thus a form of "theft."

of their character, which they interpreted as demeaning their worth as human beings and which sullied their reputation. As we have seen, growing patrimonies made marriage strategies increasingly important, and no one allied with "dishonorable" folk. One of the most frequent slanders was "You're worthless!" ("Tu ne vallois rien!"), which invariably elicited the ritual retort (bearing multiple meanings from social to economic, depending upon the context) "I am a worthy man!" ("Je suis un homme de bien!") or "I am a man of honor!" Insults to honor, usually strewn through conflicts that arose from other causes, often provoked outbursts of violence. The insulted frequently tried to exact immediate retribution through physical assault, to humiliate the antagonist by defeat "on the battlefield," in an apparent parallel to noble contests of honor.

Countless examples of such battles point up a crucial element in the concept of personal honor: its public character. Honor is rooted in a value system that measures individual behavior against some model approved by a collective conscience with common assumptions about what constitutes honorable behavior. Pitt-Rivers explains this notion concisely:

> Both words and actions are significant within the code of honour because they are expressions of attitude which claim, accord or deny honour. Honour, however, is only irrevocably committed by attitudes expressed in the presence of witnesses, the representatives of public opinion. The problem of public knowledge as an essential ingredient of an affront has been stressed by various authors. . . . There is no disagreement that the extent of the damage to reputation relates to the range of public opinion within which the damage is broadcast. . . . Public opinion forms therefore a tribunal before which the claims to honour are brought . . . 'the court of reputation' . . . and against this judgement there is no redress.[87]

There is no doubt that craftsmen were intensely concerned about their publicly defined reputations. In early modern Dijon, however, restitution of an artisan's honor could be attained in the courts of law as well as those of public opinion. In fact, the two were interrelated. The master locksmith/clockmaker Florent Febvre filed a complaint

---

87. Pitt-Rivers, "Honour and Social Status," p. 27. Arlette Jouanna, "Recherches sur la notion d'honneur au 16e siècle," *Revue d'Histoire Moderne et Contemporaine* 15 (1968): 607, also stresses the public element in codes of honor.

with the town council claiming that Michel Mallefert had slandered him publicly by calling him a usurer. Febvre declared himself to be "a worthy man, not a usurer," and demanded the enormous sum of five hundred ecus in damages. Hosier Claude Odot felt his honor impugned when Antoine Villot, a master plasterer, called him a cuckold. Odot warned him that he would seek redress *par justice,* meaning he would file suit and attempt to exact retribution by way of the municipal authorities. Similarly, in 1641 master shoemaker Jean Roux complained to the courts that the gardener Pierre Roussey had said to him that "he was worthless and harbored traitors to his majesty in his house." Roux added that in his absence "in different places and in the presence of different persons" Roussey had so slandered him that "his honor was engaged"; since such acts were "intolerable," he had filed suit at the mayor's court. François Dolin, a master weaver, complained to the town council that his "honor and reputation" had been impugned by other master weavers, who out of "ill will" had scratched out his mark at the *boutique au regard* (as the name implies a public place where the professional marks of all master weavers were etched). Dolin defended his symbol and his commercial reputation before the magistrates as he would his own person.[88]

Honor as a moral code had such force in the artisan's world because it was a familiar, public world. The neighborhood, densely populated, intensely intimate, formed the ideal setting for the development of a code of honor. As J. G. Peristiany notes, honor and shame "are the constant preoccupation of individuals in small-scale, exclusive societies where face-to-face personal, as opposed to anonymous, relations are of paramount importance."[89] The abundant eyewitness depositions in the criminal dossiers tell us that Dijon fulfilled the necessary criterion of such societies: it provided a public tribunal. Arguments may have erupted indoors, but the climax to the affair invariably occurred in the street. In 1643 a master tailor went to the home of master pastrycook François Jonas to collect payment for a piece of clothing; rebuffed, he called the pastrycook, among other things, a thief. Grossly insulted, Jonas ordered the tailor outside, fol-

88. ADCO, BII 360/51, 2 March 1582, 360/47, 13–24 Sept. 1568, 360/58, 22 Nov. 1641; AMD, B237, fol. 83r–v, 7 Jan. 1600. The *boutique au regard* was a control mechanism. All cloth had to be taken there to be stamped with the mark of the master before going to the next step in the textile production process, fulling.

89. J. G. Peristiany, Introduction to *Honor and Shame,* ed. Peristiany, p. 1.

lowed him, and loudly proclaimed that he was a worthy man; thereupon the two fought until a neighbor broke them up. Judging from the number of witnesses at the subsequent trial, the row attracted a big crowd.[90]

In the context of artisan social relations, a man's honor and a woman's shame were judged by others, so everything depended on how an action involving honor was interpreted. Here ritual becomes paramount. Everyone believed that words and gestures could strip away honor. References to *propos rigoreux* or *propos injurieux* are commonplace.[91] Though the lexicon of defamation was probably different, symbolic assaults on honor define a code shared by the elite and popular cultures. In fact, there is evidence that this was a pan-European moral code. The *Partidas*, a thirteenth-century Castillian legal code, lists some legal definitions of *injuria* which show striking parallels to the French word *injures* in the sixteenth and seventeenth centuries. There were *injurias* "of word, as when one man says something insulting to another in public. . . . Women are insulted or outraged by . . . making lewd proposals to them. . . . A man may be insulted by a deed, by a kick, by a blow of the hand, stick or stone, by pursuit with intent to wound, by tearing his clothes or by deliberate damage to his house or property."[92] These criteria were also at work in artisan culture, far from medieval Castille.

Though injurious words dominate our sources, gestures also played their part in affairs of honor. The best known in popular and elite cultures and for both genders was the *soufflet*, or slap across the face. The slap a master mason delivered to the cheek of the wife of a fellow guildsman triggered a brawl involving both artisans, their wives and the eighty-year-old mother of one of the combatants. On another occasion twenty years later, Bénigne LeBon, nursing a three-month-old insult to his wife's honor by master cabinetmaker Pierre Darboys, initiated his revenge with a *coup de soufflet*—a clear message to

90. ADCO, BII 360/60, July 1643.

91. Hanlon, p. 256, finds a similar situation in seventeenth-century Aquitaine, where rituals of aggression entail public confrontation, verbal exchange, and intervention by bystanders.

92. Julio Caro Baroja, "Honour and Shame: A Historical Account of Several Conflicts," in Peristiany, pp. 90–91. For a study of honor in eighteenth-century Languedoc, see Yves Castan, *Honnêteté et relations sociales en Languedoc, 1715–1780* (Paris, 1974); and for the nineteenth-century American South, Bertram Wyatt-Brown, *Southern Honor* (New York, 1982).

Darboys and bystanders what the conflict was about. The wives of a master blacksmith and a saddler were standing in front of their houses one Sunday when they witnessed what they called an "affront to honor"; they had seen a bailiff slap the face of a lawyer's wife.[93]

Gestures could be multiplied to reinforce an affront to honor. Vinegar maker Hugues DuTreul not only slapped the *praticien* Christophe Heron but snatched the hat off his head, thus compounding the insult.[94] Many social anthropologists have noted the connection of honor with the head; to expose it was an offense to the honor of both males and females.[95] In early modern France innumerable gestures of deference relating to the head (bowed, bared, touched, or cut off) also involved notions of honor, in artisan culture no less than others. Michel Guillemot, a carpenter, was dancing with a crowd of others in St. Michel Square when the vigneron Claude Portelot (who claimed Guillemot owed him some money) came up behind him, snatched his hat from his head, and refused to return it. The outraged carpenter wheeled and punched Portelot in the face.[96]

Women employed ritual violence associated with the head in affairs of honor, too. In 1642 Louise Regni, wife of a vigneron, witnessed a contest of honor in which the wife of a cooper was ritually humiliated by the wife of a master cobbler, who dragged her by the hair and smeared her face in the mud. Regni observed pointedly that the victim was "completely decoiffed and her face smeared with *boue*" ("toute décoifée et gastée du bouhe par le visage").[97] The sense of degradation is unmistakable. Decoiffed and thus stripped of her modesty, the victim had been further humbled by a symbolic "defacing," which carried scatological implications, given the noxiousness of Dijon's *boue*.[98]

Hurling *fange* and *ordures* was another ritualized gesture of denigration.[99] The very uselessness of garbage and household wastes

93. ADCO, BII 360/48, Sept.–Oct. 1571, 360/53, Aug.–Sept. 1594, 360/57, 1608. See also Pitt-Rivers, "Honour and Social Status," p. 25, on the ritual of face slapping and its relation to honor.
94. ADCO, BII 360/59, 24 Sept. 1642.
95. Pitt-Rivers, "Honour and Social Status," p. 25.
96. ADCO, BII 360/48, 5 Jan. 1568.
97. ADCO, BII 360/59, June–Aug. 1642.
98. Farge, *Vivre dans la rue*, p. 146, draws the same conclusion.
99. Mary Douglas, *Natural Symbols* (New York, 1982), p. 160. Similarly, Ong, *The Presence of the Word*, p. 117, suggests that taste (and thus smell) is the most discrimi-

may have symbolically reinforced the association of the valueless with the dishonorable. In any case, it is absolutely clear from the records that foul substances and scatological references were used deliberately in contests of honor. In 1560 a Catholic master goldsmith got his leg drenched when someone poured a chamber pot of urine out of a window; he was convinced this was no accident, since he was then walking down the rue des Forges—a stronghold of Protestants. Similarly, kicks to another's hindquarters were commonplace. Following a *coup de pied au cul* ("kick in the ass") to a master cooper's wife, innkeeper Charles Thiot rained dishonoring insults upon his victim. Another sort of scatological gesture was made by journeyman wheelwright Claude Boulangier, who came to the subterranean tavern of master cooper Claude Rebourg to drink some wine. The servingmaid accidentally knocked Boulangier's glass onto the floor, shattering it. The owner had not seen the incident, but he heard the noise. He blamed Boulangier and demanded he pay for the glass. The journeyman vociferously denied that he had broken the glass, refused to pay for it, and addressed Rebourg (a master and thus Boulangier's social superior) with dishonoring insults like cuckold, using the familiar *tu*. Then he headed for the stairs and scrambled up them rapidly. Close to the top he slowed down, hesitated, and then loudly farted, captioning his propitious gesture with the words "That's for you [*toy*] and yours!" The owner was greatly offended by this egregious insubordination. He complained to the authorities, who agreed that the journeyman had shown disrespect for him, his place, and the company and should be punished for it.[100]

In 1587 master baker Brice Bondard petitioned the civil authorities to make reparations to his honor ("faire reparation d'honneur"). A woman had "publicly" slandered him, calling him a bastard who did not know who his parents were, an evil and worthless man. Bondard countered these "atrocious insults" by proclaiming that he was a worthy man of good reputation ("bien famé et renommé"), born of a good father and mother "in loyal marriage."[101]

---

nating human sense and distinguishes what is agreeable to one's own organism. Therefore, "stink" expresses maximum rejection or repulsion. See also Alain Corbin, *The Foul and the Fragrant: Odor and the French Social Imagination* (New York, 1986).

100. ADCO, BII 360/44, July–Sept. 1560, 360/59, 9 April 1643, 19 Oct.–4 Nov. 1642.

101. Ibid., 360/51, 27 May 1587.

Bondard's stereotyped response to insult encapsulates many of the honorific concerns shared by artisans during the period. Honor mediated the most important social and economic relations in a craftsman's life. In a world where patron-client trust was important, the inability to command respect cast doubt upon one's dependability as either patron or client. Perhaps more important, honor mediated all business relations—recall the seriousness of the insult *banqueroutier* and the formulaic "Je suis un homme de bien," which proclaimed one's honorable integrity in the economic realm. Success and honor, thus, were closely related.[102] In marriage honor was dependent on a reputation for sexual propriety, which had to be defended at any cost.

Consequently, in artisan culture honor lost by one was honor gained by another.[103] Contests of honor became exchanges in an economy of respect. Though Bondard's complaint dates from the sixteenth century, it is during the seventeenth century that artisans become really touchy about their honor. More and more frequently they explicitly report that insults have forced their honor to be engaged.

In this economy of respect, reputation is paramount and certain qualities are valuable. Command of one's wits, a dominant theme in seventeenth-century peasant tales, was sure to garner respect, and insults often imputed the lack of sharp acumen.[104] In 1560 master mason Hugues Brouhée discredited a hostile witness, Jehan Capitaine, as "one of scant estimation and poor renown." Capitaine, "having lost his sense," was "a fool . . . [who] for a glass of wine" would do anything. Another mason corroborated that assessment, saying Capitaine was reputed to be a thief and a drunkard, "spoiled" by wine. Similar examples can be drawn from the seventeenth century. Louise Begin, a vigneron's wife, was also reputedly "spoiled by wine" and had lost her reason; no wonder, if her detractor's allegation that Begin drank four or five pints a day was true.[105] Perhaps the most convinc-

102. The close association between credit, integrity, and slander continues after the period, as the master cooper Toussaint Bourgeois illustrates. In 1689 he alleged in court that the insults of another "faire perdre son négoce et son crédit absolumment [*sic*]." ADCO, BII 360/121, 30 Dec. 1689.

103. Yves Castan, *Honnêteté*, p. 13, points out that honorific relations "exiger le maximum du reconaissance pour soi, tout en accordant la minimum possible à autrui."

104. Robert Darnton, "Peasants Tell Tales: The Meaning of Mother Goose," in *The Great Cat Massacre and Other Episodes in French Cultural History* (New York, 1985), pp. 49, 53.

105. ADCO, BII 360/44, 8 July 1560, 360/59, 23–24 Sept. 1642. For other examples

ing indicator of a heightened concern for acumen in the seventeenth century is the noticeable increase in the use of the insults *sot*, *fou*, and *ignorant*, frequently launched alongside *ivrogne*. The discourse of denigration and the association of drunkenness with stupidity suggest that the opposite of the insults—clearheadedness—was a much-valued attribute.

Judicial records can give the impression that artisans were an exceedingly rough-and-tumble lot, easily angered, and often at each other's throats. Yet, however paradoxical it seems, craftsmen did value peaceableness and order. Harsh times inevitably make life competitive and vexatious, and reality contradicts the ideal, but in artisan culture violent behavior was measured against a norm of order. True, exchanges of insults often led to bloodied faces and broken heads, but such things happened as a last resort, and prefatory insults may have functioned as substitutes for physical engagement. Effective threats could be better than blows, and indeed, the conditional tense was often used in insults. Master blacksmith Philibert DeRochefort assaulted the honor of mercer Estienne Billocard with allegations of sexual perversion, adding, "*If* I had my dagger, I *would* slash it across your body." Nearly a century later, master oil maker Antoine DuBois petitioned the authorities to make reparation to his honor by investigating a cloth cutter who had attacked him with insults "injurious to his honor" and who "*would* have . . . beaten him with his fists." The cloth cutter had shaken his fist in DuBois's face several times, calling him a worthless rogue—but never struck him.[106] Indeed, the public nature of most quarrels and the rapidity with which peacekeeping neighbors arrived at a scene of conflict may also reflect a general wish to prevent blows. Brandish a knife or a sword, shriek insults and threats, and one could expect that neighbors would quickly arrive to stop the action.

More insults related to sexuality than to anything else, and behind this defamatory discourse lurk ideas about order and security shared by society's lay and clerical elites, though perhaps not always for the

---

of insults alleging stupidity and drunkenness, see 360/51, 2 Nov. 1582, 22 Oct. 1586, 360/53, 9 Nov. 1594, 360/57, 20 Jan. 1617, 3 Sept. 1623, 360/58, 25 Nov. 1641, 360/59, 19 Oct. 1642, 360/60, 30 June 1643.

106. Ibid., 360/41, Sept. 1556, 360/59, 23 Oct. 1642, my emphasis. The slander *pandard* meant "worthy of being hanged," that is, absolutely worthless. A *coquin*, more simply, was a rogue.

same reasons. These ideas blended the moral and physical aspects of order.[107] In the mind of many a craftsman there was a connection between order and honor, a connection that becomes apparent in attitudes artisans shared about sexuality.

Bénigne and Bernarde, the daughters of master shoemaker Alexandre Massenot, were well known for their lascivious behavior; Dijon's syndic described them as having *passions désréglées*. Even in the face of overwhelming evidence to the contrary, the girls felt the need to defend their honor against "malicious gossip" about their "alleged" promiscuity.[108] Here, dishonor and natural disorder are associated in the magisterial mind. In an example from artisan culture, natural disorder and shamelessness were implied when the wife of a master goldsmith sneered to the wife of her husband's colleague that her daughter had "broken her legs while running after the boys." What is unsaid but implied is that men should pursue women, not the other way around.[109] Similarly, a man's honor was vulnerable to insults imputing violation of the natural sexual order. As the moral code apparently tightened in the seventeenth century, allegations of sodomy increased. To call someone a *bougre*, a *jean-foutre*, or a *jean-faire* (all slang for sodomite) imputed dishonorable nonmasculine behavior and invariably elicited the rehabilatory response "I am a worthy man!" or "I am a man of honor!" Again, the meaning of honor was connected to a natural sexual order. Calling someone a pimp [*maquereau*], especially for his wife, suggested both the sacrifice of honor for profit and the violation of the sanctity of marriage and the social order it supported.[110] This insult, thus, was more than sufficient to impugn honor, and it was hurled repeatedly in such contests.

Concern for the maintenance of order—both moral and physical—is in fact a key to deciphering some aspects of sexual attitudes of artisans. Prostitution, legally and morally tolerated in the Middle

---

107. My sampling method permitted a sensitivity to shifting emphasis in the discourse of slander, and there is no question that the incidence of sexual slanders increases noticeably in the first half of the seventeenth century compared to the second half of the sixteenth.

108. ADCO, BII 360/58, May–Sept. 1642.

109. Ibid., 360/53, July 1594.

110. On slanders alleging sodomy, see ibid., 360/47, 20 Sept. 1568, 360/51, 2 Nov. 1582, 46/1, 23 July 1584, 360/58, Aug.–Sept. 1638, 360/63, 11 Nov. 1646. On insults alleging *maquerellage*, see, for example, 360/48, 19 July 1569, 360/57, 3 Sept. 1623, 360/58, 8 Aug. 1638, 360/60, 6, 23 Oct. 1643.

Ages in Dijon, was outlawed in 1563.[111] But if there was a growing intolerance for prostitution in society's ruling classes, can we be sure artisans felt the same way for the same reasons? On the surface there appear to be similarities. Master blacksmith Claude Vachiet, for example, "detracted" from the honor of innkeeper Pierre Maistrise and his wife when he alleged that Maistrise's inn was a "public bordello," in a case that associated dishonor with prostitution.[112] Likewise, allegations of "procuring" and insults like *maquerelle* or *maquereau* reveal a public view of such activities as dishonorable. These epithets were hurled with ever greater frequency in the seventeenth century. Master embroiderer Berthelemy Vitrey was asked if he could refute the testimony that had been sworn against him by Claude Huissier, a soldier of the guard. Vitrey countered that Huissier was a "public pimp and a man of evil ways," and this reproach was taken seriously enough by the authorities to warrant investigating Huissier's alleged illicit activity. When seamstress Anne Boudot accused widow Franchot of being a "procuress who had sold girls . . . [and] had been flogged and branded" for it, she deliberately fired her insult in the street, and of course, Franchot had to reply that such insults were "against her honor."[113] In a tight marriage market, especially for widows, such allegations, if not countered effectively, would jeopardize widow Franchot's already slim chances for remarriage.

Always there was recourse to public opinion. Indeed, the belief in the efficacy of public reproach was not unique to artisan culture. In 1613 the Parlement of Dijon upheld a sentence of the town council convicting four women of "procuring and [leading] scandalous and shameless lives." Two were condemned to be led from the prison to the marketplace, wearing on their heads signs saying "public procuresses." They were then to be flogged *jusques au sang* and banished for life; the others were to be banished for five years.[114] Of course,

---

111. Jacques Rossiaud, "Prostitution, Youth, and Society in the Towns of Southeastern France in the Fifteenth Century," in *Deviants and the Abandoned in French Society*, ed. Robert Forster and Orest Ranum, trans. E. Forster and P. Ranum (Baltimore, 1978), p. 25. There are many examples of initiatives taken by the civil authorities to curb prostitution. For example, on 11 Feb. 1564 the town council ordered the expulsion of all concubines and prostitutes from Dijon within twenty-four hours on pain of hanging and prohibited journeymen and servants from concealing them. AMD, B200, fol. 152r–153r.

112. ADCO, BII 360/60, 30 Aug. 1643, and see 360/53, 26 July 1594, 360/60, 27 Oct. 1643, 360/63, 29 May 1647.

113. Ibid., 360/57, Sept.–Nov. 1623, 360/59, 21 Feb. 1643.

114. Ibid., 360/57, 11 Feb. 1613.

this was government action; we cannot be sure how many among the throng that attended such lurid spectacles morally condemned these women for the same reasons as the authorities. Nonetheless, these examples do seem to uncover an increasingly condemnatory attitude shared by many artisans and their social superiors. Society was evidently becoming less tolerant.

Many of the attitudes held by artisans and their families about honor and sexuality related to the institution of marriage. The Council of Trent had bolstered the authority of parents over the marriages of their children and had promoted the ethic that held sexual relations outside of marriage to be mortally sinful since they obviously were not aimed at procreation. At first glance, both the increased frequency of insults impugning the integrity of one's marriage and the more explicit and more frequent ripostes by the insulted parties seem be related to this new morality. Examination of these insults in their social context, however, offers another interpretation. For master craftsmen these slanders may have pertained just as much to their more mundane marriage strategies and growing patrimonies as to the more abstract Tridentine morality. It is also possible that the heightened sensitivity to sexual propriety reflects a growing desire among artisans to raise themselves above the vast underclass of the disorderly (both morally and physically) and transient poor.[115]

The demographic analysis of Chapter 2 sketched a marriage market where suitable males were in short supply. The masters' strategy to curtail their numbers in one sense boomeranged, for it became that much harder for masters to find suitable mates for their daughters. A daughter or widow with unstained reputation possessed an advantage in the search for a groom, an advantage that could be pushed further by smearing the good name of a competitor. During the seventeenth century, therefore, as patrimonies grew and the stakes of a good marriage mounted ever higher, masters became ever more sensitive to the honor of their own marriage as well as the reputation of their daughters, beginning with the legitimacy of their birth.

Likewise, since men were vulnerable through their women, the

---

115. Sharpe, *Defamation and Sexual Slander*, p. 25. The similarities between early modern Dijon and York appear striking in the context of defamation and honor. Around the middle of the sixteenth century Sharpe finds a great increase in the incidence of cases of defamation and further observes that the bulk of the litigants were the "rural middling sort" and that these artisans and yeomen and their wives showed "great concern for sexual good name and sexual honour" (p. 17).

selection of an honorable son-in-law was especially important. For this reason, in agonistic but relatively open societies female endogamy rates tell us more about community values than male rates. Marriage creates a fusion of honor, and it bears other weighty considerations, too. In Burgundy, the custom of partible inheritance tended to fragment the patrimony. Therefore, as patrimonies grew, more emphasis may well have been placed on good marriages and, hence, the bride's virtue.

Male control of female sexual activity—husbands and fathers controlling wives and daughters—lies at the heart of questions of marital honor, and so, forms of honorable behavior are gender specific. Males aggressively protect their women's honor, but women possess shame, a quality that becomes all the more important when reputation is crucial to marriage strategies and patrimonial holdings.[116] Because women necessarily led relatively public lives, artisans hardly felt confident about their control of their wives and daughters. This insecurity was enhanced by the penchant of craftsmen to dishonor one another by defaming each other's women and by deep-seated male ambivalence about female sexuality.

Historians are increasingly recognizing the ethnographic association of cats with unbridled female sexuality.[117] Indeed, it was far from uncommon for artisans to insult a woman by calling her a *chatte*, and the word also connoted the female sexual organ. In reply to the insult of the daughter of a master goldsmith, the wife of a fellow guildsman protested on her honor that she was neither a drunk nor a *chatte*, contrary to what her detractor had alleged. Just as tellingly, a well-known prostitute working the streets of Dijon was called simply *la chatte*. Likewise, the symbolism in the gesture of two journeymen tailors probably was not lost on their victim or the crowd. They pitched a live cat onto the head of a cleric leading a solemn procession past the house where they worked. Suspected of Protestantism, these youths may have been obliquely deriding the celibacy of Catholic clergy by flaunting female sexuality literally in the face of the priest.

116. See Jane Schneider, "Of Vigilance and Virgins: Honor, Shame and Access to Resources in Mediterranean Societies," *Ethnology* 10.1 (1971): 1–24; and Ramon A. Gutiérrez, "Honor Ideology, Marriage Negotiation, and Class-Gender Domination in New Mexico, 1690–1846," *Latin American Perspectives* 44.12, no. 1 (1985): 81–104.
117. See Darnton, "Workers Revolt: The Great Cat Massacre of the Rue Saint-Séverin," in *The Great Cat Massacre*, esp. p. 95.

Indeed, the association of the cat with uncontrollable female sexuality may help explain the intensity of embroiderer Richardot's anger against cobbler Odot Noble, whom he suspected of stealing his cat. Richardot became so infuriated when Noble denied culpability that he picked up one of the cobbler's shoes and threw it, striking (perhaps deliberately) Noble's wife.[118]

More direct evidence of the control males were expected to exert over the sexuality of their women once again comes from the lexicon of insult. Master blacksmith Philibert DeRochefort leveled a double hit at mercer Estienne Billocard, when he told him, sarcastically, "Buggerer! Go loosen your wife's cunt!"—that is, since Billocard allegedly preferred men, he had no cause to protect his wife's sexuality.[119] By far the most favored and presumably the most effective way to strip another male of honor, however, was to call him a cuckold (*coupaut*). Of course, such sexual insults were not new in the seventeenth century, but their increased incidence suggests a greater concern about sexual propriety. The Catholic reformers gave the subject greater prominence than it had had in traditional Christianity, and the Catholic clergy was preaching more on the sin of adultery.[120] But when we consider that such insults as calling someone's wife or daughter a whore (*putain*), slut (*garce*), or ribald (*ribaulde*), were invariably launched in contests of honor, a different perspective emerges. Countless scabrous salvos punctuate the dossiers, imputing the male's lack of control of his females and adding the stigma of illegitimacy to boot.

In 1642 master baker Pierre Regnault petitioned the authorities to redress "an atrocious insult against the honor of his marriage." Merchant Esme Maîtrise had called him a thief, a drunk, a devil, and a cuckold, but it was the last that stung Regnault most and prompted his petition. Fifty years before, craftsman Bénigne LeBon had brooded for three months after master cabinetmaker Pierre Darboys insulted LeBon's wife as a "ribald and a whore"; he finally avenged the stain on her reputation and his honor by slashing the cabinetmaker with a sword. The same mindset was operating when tanner Nicolas Benoist publicly made the rather free association that because Jacques Cha-

---

118. ADCO, BII 360/53, July 1594, 360/48, April 1571, 360/51, July 1584, 360/46, May–June 1565.
119. Ibid., 360/41, 11 Sept. 1556.
120. John Bossy, *Christianity in the West, 1400–1700* (Oxford, 1984), p. 38.

puis's wife had been married before, the merchant "had married a whore" (also suggesting ambivalence about remarriage in artisan culture). The merchant Chapuis defended her by claiming that she was "a worthy wife." In 1643 the son of toolmaker Pierre Bachotet recited a litany of insults against master baker Nicolas Rolliot and his wife, calling the baker a thief and a murderer and his wife a slut and a bastard, born of "a mother who had been *désaintée*" before her marriage. To further dishonor Rolliot before the court of public opinion, Bachotet had first slapped his wife's face, according to several witnesses, "in the middle of the street."[121]

As husbands had to protect the reputation of their wives, so fathers had to defend their daughters. To avoid disgrace (and remain competitive in the marriage market), master embroider Damien Gaudin filed a complaint with the authorities alleging that a draper named Noel had called his daughter a "whore" and a "ribald"; the draper had added, in the middle of a crowded street no less, that everyone knew she slept with "a monk from St. Bénigne named Monseigneur DeCharolle" and so was "worthless." Devastated by such "enormous slanders," she had burst into tears, and her father had promptly appealed to the authorities for redress and rehabilitation of his honor (and her reputation).[122]

Nor did a father's vulnerability cease with the acquisition of a son-in-law. Part of the masters' strategy to regulate their numbers was a code of honor that required close scrutiny of potential husbands for their daughters. A man could lose honor if he selected the wrong man. Small wonder, then, that familiarity with the future son-in-law would be prized or that greater honor would be attached to nativeness—recall the master embroiderer who denigrated the alderman because he came from Normandy. Those from out of town were suspect on that ground alone. Thus, in 1643 the wife of a master cooper sweepingly insulted the prince's coachman by calling his wife a whore and a slut, his daughter worthless, and himself equally worthless because he had been banished from his native country.[123]

---

121. ADCO, BII 360/59, 18 July 1642, 360/53, 1 Sept. 1594, 360/48, 23 Feb. 1569, 360/59, 25 Feb. 1643. For examples of the insult *coupaut* and variations, see 360/41, 24 April 1556, 17 Feb. 1561, 360/48, 30 July 1569, 360/59, 19 Oct. 1642, 17 March 1643, 360/60, 23 Oct. 1643. For examples of *putain, ribaulde, garce,* and the like, see 360/46, 15 June 1565, 360/48, 23 Sept. 1569, 360/51, 9 July 1584, 360/59, 11 June 1642, 21, 25 Feb., 9 April 1643, 360/63, 20 Nov. 1646, 30 July 1647.
122. Ibid., 360/51, July 1584.
123. Ibid., 360/44, 24 Aug. 1561, 360/59, 9 April 1643.

Indeed, the honor of an artisan was vulnerable through the whole range of his family connections, alive and dead. When some shepherds dealt him a blow, master baker Jehan Roche was outnumbered; so he went for his brother, who returned with him to seek revenge. Finding one of the shepherds alone, the brother said "I know it was you who wounded him. I assure you, I will show you, because you have caused me to lose face!" He then unsheathed his sword and twice slashed the shepherd's arm.[124]

The defense of family honor extended even to the grave. When the wife of a master goldsmith insulted a fellow guildsman's wife by telling her that her late father-in-law "had deserved the rope" (that is, to be hanged), the offended party retorted that the offender was "ill advised to . . . slander [her] as well as the deceased and their family, who have never been anything but worthy and honorable people." "It was unfitting," she continued, "to wish to violate the sepulcher of the dead by impugning the honor of the deceased, who when alive was a worthy and honorable man of complete integrity." In conclusion, she declared that she and her family "cannot and ought not suffer [to be] . . . so atrociously slandered." If, as it appears, honor was a collective possession, shared by all members of the family, living and dead, it is not surprising that insults were cast widely too. The wife of one master roofer invoked the curse of God on a colleague's wife, her deceased parents, and her kin up to the seventh degree.[125] Gestures as well as words insulted families, sometimes including future members. Analysis of the human topography of violence suggests that in honorific contests a kick to the stomach of a pregnant woman (disturbingly, a far from uncommon gesture) is a blow to the family line, as may be a kick deliberately delivered to a male's genitals.[126]

If the institutions of marriage and family are an important social context for the interpretation of artisan sexual morality, the neighborhood is an important spatial context. Indeed, the case of Alexandre Massenot, master shoemaker and father of the two bawdy daughters Bénigne and Bernarde, demonstrates the importance of all three. In 1642 he was offered three hundred livres, presumably as a dowry, to marry off one of his daughters; the offer was made by a group of neighbors, many of them master artisans, who were clearly hoping to

124. Ibid., 360/47, May 1567.
125. Ibid., 360/53, July 1594, 360/60, Oct. 1643.
126. For example, ibid., 360/57, 9 April 1608, 360/60, 6 Oct. 1643, 360/44, 26 Aug. 1561.

rid the neighborhood of at least one of the girls.[127] This example
intimates that in popular attitudes moral and physical order were
related. Promiscuity was condemned not just on moral grounds but
also because it attracted rowdy males to the neighborhood and thus
disrupted the peace and tranquility that, as we have seen in other
contexts, was keenly valued.

Part of the glue that held neighbors together was traditional Christian teachings on charity and fraternity; peaceful relations among
neighbors were a very important ideal.[128] For artisans, the physical
disruption to the neighborhood and the discord among neighbors that
came with unregulated sexual activity were the crux of the problem.
In the case of Massenot, long before a complaint was lodged with the
authorities, the shoemaker's neighbors had repeatedly asked him to
control his daughters. Several depositions show just cause for concern; they vividly recount scenes of disorder. Visitors (many were
*gens de qualité* and thus escaped punishment or even any investigation into their identity) gathered at all hours of the day and night,
drinking, gambling, and taking turns with Massenot's daughters. The
neighbors complained of the noise, and worse. Respectable women
were frequently chased if they wandered too near the cluster of lust-
ful males.

The Massenot girls were probably victims as much as offenders,
prisoners of their own reputation, which staked them out as common
property. When they resisted the overtures of the males, they and the
neighborhood suffered. Several neighbors (wives of artisans) recalled
in depositions that the night of carnival had been especially disruptive. The men came to Massenot's shouting "Sluts! *Maquerelles*!
Open your door!" One of the girls responded defiantly, "Thief! *Pandard*! Fuck you!" and then ran and hid. The men kicked in the door,
searched the house, and when they found the sisters, dragged them to
the workshop where, one witness related, "they remained for about
an hour without any noise." On other occasions neighbors' homes
were even entered with impunity by men searching for the girls.
Anne Barain, the wife of a master tailor, said several men had beaten
on their door one evening. When her husband opened it, one of the
men demanded, "Where are his girls, Bénigne and Bernarde?" Protest-

127. Ibid., 360/58, May–Sept. 1642.
128. See Bossy, *Christianity in the West*, chap. 4.

ing that the girls were neither there nor his, the tailor was rudely brushed aside by the men who searched the entire house for them.[129]

Many other lurid examples of the link between sexual promiscuity and neighborhood disorder—and neighborly action to remove the source of disorder—could be cited. In 1631 master cooper Antoine Villemereux and his wife were accused of prostituting their own daughter. Such behavior brought the usual cluster of clients (to whom the father allegedly sold wine while they awaited their turn) and the usual violence in the street and damage to the neighbors' property (mainly broken windows and bashed signs). Villemereux's neighbors, many of them craftsmen and presumably masters, had complained to him several times of this "scandalous life" and had asked him to curb it. A few years later, the DuTreul sisters (of a vinegar maker) were haled before the authorities to answer to frequent complaints by their neighbors of their "lewd and scandalous" behavior, which attracted "people of all conditions . . . day and night" and led to "quarrels and beatings" that disrupted the peace of the neighborhood.[130] It seems clear that artisans disapproved of prostitution and promiscuity largely because they wished to avoid the disorder and violence these activities brought to the neighborhood and the discord it engendered between neighbors. There was a strong connection between moral and physical order in artisan mentality.

129. ADCO, BII 360/58, May–Sept. 1642.
130. Ibid., 22 Jan. 1631, 1 Nov. 1640.

## 5 Royalists, Leaguers, Rebels, and Neighbors: Authority in Artisan Life

As we have seen, master artisans played a significant political role as the various public authorities contested for influence in the tangled thicket of overlapping jurisdictions. The king, wanting to assert control, was interested in reducing municipal autonomy, but to do so he was forced to rely on a bureaucracy with its own interests. As historians are learning, the bureaucracy was staffed with men anxious to exact concessions from the king, and the struggle over jurisdiction became as much a social as a political affair. Burgundy still awaits the kind of close scrutiny of its political life that Languedoc has recently received from William Beik, but it is certain that there, as elsewhere in France, the exercise of power was complicated and contradictory, dependent, at least in part, on social attitudes toward authority.

### The Holy League

Most artisan concerns were local concerns, but craftsmen were sometimes involved in affairs with national ramifications. They participated, for example, when the ultra-Catholic Holy League sought political ascendancy in France in the last quarter of the sixteenth century, and they also joined in the tax revolt of 1630 called Lanturelu. War and taxes were vivid reminders to the popular classes that they were enmeshed in a larger political net, but a more general artisan political awareness is also evident. For example, in a petition drafted in 1561 master furrier Jehan Chipporée cited clauses in the 1560 Edict of Orleans requiring that vagabonds be strongly punished for theft.[1] Nearly a century later, in 1639, during the worst phase of the Thirty Years' War in nearby Lorraine and the Franche-Comté, a fireside chat of a half dozen masters and journeymen cobblers and curriers ended in a fight over politics in the realm. Journeyman currier Charles Ligier from Lorraine declared that Louis XIII had no business "seizing Lorraine, knowing that it does not belong to him." He went on to impugn not just the king but his "ministers of state" as well (presumably the cardinal-minister Richelieu). Irked, the master cobbler Jean Cortot warned him that the "affairs of the realm" were not his concern. When the journeyman from Lorraine continued in a sarcastic tone that the emperor was greater than the king of France because there were many kings but only one emperor, the Burgundian Cortot slapped the impudent journeyman's face and rebuked him for not "extending obedience [*debvoir*] to his majesty . . . as a good subject ought to do."[2]

The authorities, of course, took any suspicion of lèse majesté seriously, and artisans seem to have considered it disreputable and even dishonorable. Accusations of harboring traitors to the king drove Jean Roux to seek redress from the authorities, for he considered "his honor engaged."[3]

No doubt the high mobility of artisans enhanced their political awareness. Lorrainers like the journeyman Ligier and other foreigners were not uncommon in Dijon. By far the greatest influx (judging from the places listed in the sample of marriage contracts) came from the imperial and later Spanish Franche-Comté, whose borders were less than a day's ride away. In times of open conflict between Habsburg and Valois or Bourbon the authorities worried about the threat of potentially hostile foreigners in their midst, but since borders could not be patrolled effectively, other measures were employed. Florentin Langloix, a weaver, was ordered out of town in 1639 when it was discovered that he had previously served in the garrison at Dôle in the

1. ADCO, BII 360/44, 6 Dec. 1561.
2. Ibid., 360/58, 28 Nov. 1639.
3. Ibid., Nov. 1641.

Spanish Franche-Comté, and two tailors who had lived in Dijon for over a decade were expelled with Langloix because they were natives of the Franche-Comté.[4]

Allegiance to the king of France had never been universal or un-mixed in Dijon's artisan community. In the rebellions that shook Dijon at the time of Burgundy's reunification with France in 1479, for example, artisans played a central role.[5] In the following century, many masters rallied to the Catholic Holy League, whether to resist increased royal taxation or from religious conviction or both. As early as the 1570s antitax sentiments were directed against King Henri III, and this opposition to royal authority laid the groundwork for the Holy League.[6] With the death of the Catholic duc d'Anjou, Henri III's brother and heir, in 1584, the Protestant Henri of Navarre became heir presumptive, and tension grew within the walls of Catholic Dijon. Throughout 1586 fear of a Huguenot coup rekindled persecution of suspected Protestants. By 1588 former Calvinists such as the famous master cabinetmaker Hugues Sambin, master mason Jean Clammonet, master painter Edouard Bredin, and master locksmith Florent Febvre were taking oaths to the Holy League.[7] As in Paris, anti-Navarrist sentiment reached its peak in the winter and spring of 1589, whipped up by histrionic popular preachers and by the assassination of the ultra-Catholic leader of the Holy League, the duc de Guise, who was celebrated as a martyr in Dijon.[8] In March 1589 all Dijonnais were required to take an oath of allegiance to the league and to its new leader the duc de Mayenne.[9] Because King Henri was not mentioned in the oath, rumors spread among *le peuple* that the town was no longer the king's, a sentiment shared by Henri himself,

4. AMD, B277, fol. 55r, 12 July 1639.
5. See André LeGuai, *Dijon et Louis XI* (Dijon, 1947).
6. Henri Drouot, *Notes sur la Bourgogne*, pp. 166–67, suggests that resistance by the Estates of Burgundy to royal authority in the area of taxation prepared the ground and made the league of 1585 more acceptable. The political conflict, in Paris as well as Dijon, also involved a protest against the new aristocracy of the robe which was closing off avenues of social access, the central theme of Drouot, *Mayenne*.
7. Giroux, "Essai sur la vie," p. 381.
8. Drouot, *Mayenne*, 1:259. As late as 1595 a young Jacobin assaulted the Navarrist pastrycook Girard Pastoreaulx with a large knife, saying, "Voilà ung beau coupt de Jacobins!" Pastoreaulx added that the Jacobins had hated him for years because he had denounced the regicide of Henri III. ADCO, BII 360/54, 8 July 1595.
9. Garnier, *Journal de Breunot . . . Pepin*, 1:47.

who on 31 March declared Dijon in rebellion and transferred its Parlement to Flavigny.[10]

The summer and fall were a terrifying time for royalists and Calvinists, as a royalist named Jean DePolinet found out. In September he was captured in Dijon and executed on the same day. As his body tumbled from the scaffold, several butchers and "other depraved inhabitants," in the words of a horrified royalist lawyer, fell upon it and tore off its "virile parts" and then hacked it up with their knives.[11] There are more grisly reports of leaguer conviction among the butchers. When the head of Mayor Jacques LaVerne (executed for attempting to betray the town to royalists) was severed from its body and rolled from the scaffold, a butcher scooped up the bloody trophy and led a throng of people in a parade through the streets of the city.[12] The butchers were diehard leaguers, but so were other artisans. When the captain of Dijon's fortress finally capitulated to Henri IV in 1595, thus ending the Wars of Religion, under his command were several butchers, joined, as a lawyer remembered years later, by some tanners, a draper, a mason, a parchment maker, a sword polisher, and a hosier.[13] Most were banished; not even such a lenient victor as Henri IV could forgive such sympathies.[14]

Some artisans blindly supported the league to the bitter end, but many more before 1595 had already begun to question whether rebellion was a good thing. As bad weather and harvest failure joined the adversities of war (notably, for townsfolk, in the form of quartered soldiers who voraciously consumed food and wood), popular sentiment veered away from the league. Other artisans, some definitely Protestants, had maintained their opposition to the league and had been jailed for it in 1589.[15] Even at the peak of league popularity in the late 1580s and early 1590s, there was widespread suspicion that Navarrists were within the gates.[16] In 1591 Dijon's magistrates could

10. Gras, *Histoire de Dijon*, p. 117.
11. Durandeau, *Journal de Sullot*, pp. 12–13.
12. Garnier, *Histoire du quartier du bourg*, p. 35.
13. Durandeau, *Journal de Sullot*, pp. 48–49.
14. Garnier, *Journal de Breunot . . . Pepin*, 3:23.
15. AMD, B226, fol. 181v, 3 Oct. 1589, a list of individuals jailed in the Cordeliers' monastery for refusing to swear the oath to the league. At least twelve of them were artisans, some verifiably Calvinist.
16. Suspicion of antileague activities was especially unbridled among the au-

count on sufficient volunteers from the artisanat to drive off enemy troops.[17] But during that same year an artisan's widow was arrested for toasting "the good graces of the king of Navarre." Her political loyalties appeared to concern the authorities more than her possession of a "heretical" pamphlet, perhaps because she claimed to be illiterate.[18] Indeed, during the ascendancy of the league in Dijon speaking against Mayenne, the mayor, or even Catholic preachers could land one in jail, as several unfortunate artisans found out. Master cobbler Denis Compain, for example, was imprisoned for speaking against the "prince [Mayenne] and against Father Chartée," a preacher. A similar fate befell the "poor roofer" Hugues Valée, overheard threatening the life of the mayor while on guard duty.[19]

By 1594 the tide of popular, and artisan, opinion was clearly shifting against the league. Dissent became more frequent and more visible. In the spring of that year the master chandler Jacques Gordan was apprehended with a bogus copy of an arret from the Parlement of Paris acknowledging Navarre as the legitimate king. Witnesses said Gordan had been bruiting this news about the streets of Dijon and waving his pamphlet; the authorities made it clear in his arrest and interrogation that they were extremely sensitive about popular opinion on such a matter.[20] A few months later a similarly bold sword polisher, arguing with a leaguer, thrust his ring in the other's face; engraved on the ring was the royalist mark of the fleur-de-lis, which, the sword polisher asserted, was the mark of "worthy men." The town council then discovered that some goldsmiths had made a great quantity of these rings.[21]

Pastrycooks also displayed their political allegiance. Many began sporting hats of black and white, Navarre's colors. The cobblers, during their celebration of their patron saint's day, chanted a royalist rhyme: "Craignons Dieu, aimons l'église, / Suivons le Roi, qui fort la prise." Neither display was missed by the mayor, but by 1594 he

---

thorities in 1590. Four cobblers, perhaps to deflect suspicion for their membership in a purportedly Navarrist guild, testified in court that they knew of "some *politiques*" still living in St. Pierre parish. ADCO, BII 360/52, 2 April 1590.

17. Durandeau, *Journal de Sullot*, p. 19.
18. ADCO, BII 360/53, 12 Feb. 1591.
19. AMD, C38, 13 July 1590; ADCO, BII 360/53, 24 May 1591.
20. AMD, B231, fol. 130r, 28 Jan. 1594.
21. Garnier, *Journal de Breunot . . . Pepin*, 3:86.

could do little. As the town council reflected in May, *le peuple* and even the worthy folk, Catholics all, were divided, and the people especially were getting restive, blaming the magistrates for the shortages of food and wood.[22] It was no resurgence of Protestantism that moved the people now; they simply wanted peace.[23] Prices were skyrocketing and war was fast approaching Dijon's gates. Conditions in 1595 were worse yet, and so was popular unrest. Artisans and others were gathering in houses and gardens, "under the pretext of passing the time," but in fact to discuss "affairs of state," especially the quartering of soldiers.[24] By May the people were near riot, insulting magistrates and league commanders openly in the streets.[25] The league parlement responded with an arret prohibiting any more quartering of soldiers.[26] This action may have forestalled popular insurrection, but it did nothing to stiffen the league's resistance to Henri IV; the royal victory came a month later at Fontaine-Française, scarcely twenty miles from the walls of Dijon. Three decades of peace and prosperity followed for Dijon's master artisans, and for a time they rewarded the king with their loyalty.

## Taxes and Lanturelu

Because artisan loyalty to the crown was to some extent fiscally motivated, so too was their opposition to royal and municipal authority. The populace in Dijon and throughout France resented royal taxes, which escalated sharply between 1576 and 1590 and again between 1625 and 1645.[27] In Dijon the winegrowers and master artisans shouldered most of the added burden. The artisan community proportionally paid almost five times more in 1643 than it had in 1556, and the winegrowers' burden was five and a half times greater, but the

---

22. AMD, B231, fol. 166v, 5 May 1594.
23. Henri Drouot, "Sur le froid en Bourgogne à la fin du XVIe siècle," *Revue de Bourgogne* 7 (1918–19): 115.
24. AMD, B232, fol. 233r, 1595.
25. Garnier, *Journal de Breunot . . . Pepin,* 3:511–12, 529.
26. AMD, I116, 22 May 1595.
27. See Benedict, *Rouen during the Wars of Religion,* p. 157; Emmanuel Le Roy Ladurie, *Carnival in Romans,* trans. Mary Feeney (New York, 1979), p. 41; Drouot, *Notes sur la Bourgogne,* p. 123; François Hincker, *Les français devant l'impôt sous l'ancien régime* (Paris, 1971), p. 65.

merchants' paid less than three times as much, and the legal establishment a scant one and a half times more.[28] Royal surcharges were added to municipal taxes on wine, grain, and flour, and of course, the royal salt tax was periodically increased.[29] Master craftsmen and winegrowers were bled by the indirect taxes, too, all the more onerous when they had workers, journeymen, and apprentices to feed. In 1574, a year of high prices on grain and wine, the Chambre des Comptes proposed an increase in the octroi on wine; the winegrowers were distressed enough to assemble and petition the chambre to withdraw it. Over a dozen of them were arrested, and one desperate winegrower wailed that if the increase went through all would be forced to forgo wine and drink only water again.[30] In 1578–1579 the Estates of Burgundy, joined by those of Normandy, Brittany, Picardy, and Champagne, resisted the increased fiscal impositions of the crown, and in 1588 the Estates of Burgundy protested not only the increase in the taillon, but also increases in the gabelle and a new tax on cloth.[31]

Artisans were relatively silent on taxes until 1595, but after that date sources repeatedly show them complaining about or dodging tax levies.[32] It is possible that the authorities, both royal and municipal, were becoming more efficient in collecting them and hence finding dodgers more often, but clearly, as taxes accelerated, artisans were also evading them more frequently. In 1597 a crowd of master craftsmen of many different guilds, led by master tailor Jacques Tardy and tinsmith Pierre Millot, gathered outside the Palais de Justice, the seat of Parlement. They demanded that Parlement refuse the royal request for an advance of twenty ecus per guild for the next mastership letter granted (honoring the birth of the dauphin). The masters' first concern was that such forced loans would become habitual. They were not satisfied by the stipulation that the new master would have to reimburse the guild, for under their own restrictive admission policy,

28. These figures reflect comparative ratios of percentage of total tax of household heads. AMD, L170, L234.

29. For example, AMD, G294, 13 Jan. 1617, B196, fol. 117r, 28 Jan. 1559, B267, fol. 127v–128r, 18 Dec. 1629.

30. AMD, B212, fol. 55r–v, 2 Aug. 1574.

31. Drouot, *Mayenne*, 1:125.

32. For example, see AMD, B235, fol. 182r–v, 30 Jan. 1598, G294, *Arrêt du Parlement*, 8 May 1600, B248, fol. 205r–v, 25 Feb. 1611, ADCO, BII 360/51, Nov.–Dec. 1612, AMD, B272, fol. 291r–v, 19 June 1635, B278, fol. 264v, 14 June 1641.

it would likely be their sons and sons-in-law who would have to pay. Tardy was voicing the collective sentiments of the masters when he went so far as to "cry out loud that it was necessary to take arms" over the matter, a threat that landed both leaders in jail for sedition.[33]

Master artisans of all guilds evaded the municipal tax on wine, and bakers and pastrycooks dodged those on flour.[34] Sometimes tax protests openly threatened sedition; in 1642 a placard nailed to a wall in the rue du Bourg, a thriving craft quarter, threatened the municipal magistrates with rebellion if they doubled the octroi on wine as planned.[35] Seditious words were also uttered by the *menu peuple* against the increase on the royal salt tax seven years before.[36] Threats like these were taken very seriously by the authorities, who were aware of the popular antifiscal rebellions sweeping across France during the 1630s. Indeed, Dijon itself had been shaken in 1630 by the great revolt of Lanturelu.

At 5:30 on the morning of 28 February 1630, the tocsin rang out from the bell towers of St. Michel and St. Philibert parish churches, but no magistrate had sounded the call to arms.[37] With four drummers beating the rhythm of rebellion, an organized band of about seventy common people, headed by the vigneron Anatoire Changenet, *le roy machas* of the recently concluded carnival festival, set off for the mansion of Nicolas Gagne, trésorier général de France in Burgundy. They forced open the door and poured inside. Every luxury item they could lay their hands on—tapestries, beds, dishes, linens, even gold and silver—they dragged out into the courtyard and heaped on a bonfire. Grain and salt they carried off with them, and Gagne's wine they drank on the spot. The rebels had drawn an approving

33. AMD, B235, fol. 68v–69v, 5 Aug. 1597. The increase must not have gone through, since there is no record that anyone paid what the crown had asked for.

34. Examples abound, but see AMD, B235, fol. 182r–v, 30 Jan. 1598 (wine), G294, 8 May 1600 (flour), B248, fol. 193v, 1 Feb. 1611, fol. 205r–v, 25 Feb. 1611 (flour), B272, fol. 291r–v, 19 June 1635 (wine), B278, fol. 264v, 14 June 1641, B281, fol. 173v–174r, 13 Oct. 1643 (flour). On these *tributs* elsewhere in France, see Le Roy Ladurie, *Carnival in Romans*, p. 154.

35. AMD, B280, fol. 128r, 19 Sept. 1642.

36. AMD, B272, fol. 188v–189r, 12 Jan. 1635.

37. The following account of the revolt is drawn mostly from four sources, a letter by M. Fleutelot, seigneur de Beneuvre and an official at the Cour des Aides, dated 7 March, which describes the riot of 28 Feb. in some detail (BMD, mf 911), the town council's deliberations (AMD, B267, fol. 157r–160v, 28 Feb.–1 March 1630), the municipal syndic's *procès verbal* (AMD, I117, 9 March 1630), and the *procès verbal* from the records of the Parlement (AMD, I117, 1 March 1630).

crowd, estimated at a thousand, who stood in the street and cheered the pillagers.[38]

The town council dispatched the syndic and municipal guard to deal with the disorder, but the syndic was overwhelmed by the number of rebels—he estimated five to six hundred—milling in Gagne's mansion or standing outside waiting for furniture to be thrown to them. The carpenter François Breton was even demolishing part of the house. The syndic's orders to cease were met with jeers, and he and his guard were driven into retreat.[39]

Having looted Gagne's mansion, the crowd surged through the streets, heading for their second target, the *hôtel* of Jean LeGrand, premier président in the Chambre des Comptes. It too was sacked, and its plush furnishings put to the torch. The authorities now tried a different tack to quell the riot. The mayor and six former parlementaires went to address the crowd at LeGrand's, hoping paternalistic respect would restore order. They succeeded with part of the crowd, but the rowdiest rioters refused to show "respect and deference" and drove these magistrates into headlong retreat, too.[40]

Their success elated the rebels. Led by the drummers and the strutting *roy machas*, singing the popular festival song "Lanturelu," the crowd marched to the home of Antoine Joly, greffier en chef au Parlement, and set it ablaze. Three thousand spectators, watching flames roar out of every window, laughed and told the rioters "they were doing well."[41] From there the rioters went off in different directions, to the mansions of Etienne DeLoisy, président de la Chambre des Comptes, Jean DeVillemereux, correcteur de la Chambre des Comptes, Chrétien Martin, avocat du roi à la Table de Marbre, and finally to the house of Premier Président au Parlement DeBerchere; each building was pillaged and its furnishings burned.

By this time it was late afternoon, and the magistrates had finally managed to assemble a dependable force to challenge the rebels. They met a group of lightly armed rioters in front of DeLoisy's house and left at least seven of them dead in the street, several wounded, and three taken prisoner. The rest withdrew to St. Philibert parish

---

38. BMD, mf 911, p. 49.
39. AMD, B267, fol. 158r–v.
40. AMD, I1117.
41. BMD, mf 911, p. 49.

and barricaded the streets. The town was now quiet, and the town council set about the difficult task of securing it.

The next day the marquis de Mirebeau, lieutenant gouverneur of Burgundy, arrived in town to begin the repression. The rebels issued a threat from behind their barricades that if an assault were made on their position, they would set the town afire and call for help from the vignerons in the countryside. Mirebeau tried an offensive anyway, but the rebels, rallied by a carpenter, met and repelled it, though they lost four men.[42] The authorities tried no more assaults on the rebel position. So unsure were they of internal security that nine days passed before they tried to arrest the ringleaders of the rebellion.

The town council spent the next week locating loyal *bourgeois et bons habitans* to fill the ranks of a militia. On 9 March the repression finally began.[43] Posting militia corps strategically throughout the town, the syndic marched into St. Philibert parish with 150 armed men and went directly to the house of *le roy machas*. He had escaped. The contingent searched the dwelling of every suspected ringleader, a hunt that took them to all parts of the town. Many of the wanted men were vignerons, but an unnamed paver and tapestry weaver were also sought, as were weaver Bonaventure Charlot (who had been killed at the barricades, leaving a widow and four children), furrier Jean DeLaNoix, journeyman locksmith François Motot (son of a deceased master of the trade and recently married to the daughter of a vigneron), and the carpenter François Breton, who had so exuberantly demolished the roofs of the sacked mansions. Some were arrested— four were found huddled in an attic—but most had slipped away. The carpenter Breton was spotted and arrested in a nearby village but escaped before he could be returned to Dijon.[44] The records mention only two executions: Jean DeLaNoix, the furrier, and Pierre Mutin, a vigneron, were hanged, drawn, and quartered, their remains impaled on pikes at Dijon's gates, a grisly reminder of what can happen to seditious men.[45]

---

42. Ibid., p. 51

43. For this account, see AMD, B267, fol. 169v–170v, 9 March 1630, and, more extensively, I117, 9 March 1630, which contains a fourteen-page *procès verbal* by the syndic.

44. AMD, B267, fol. 173r, 11 March 1630, I117, 13 March 1630. For François Motot's marriage contract, see ADCO, *Notaires* #685, 18 Oct. 1629.

45. AMD, I117, 20 March 1630.

Clearly, the rebels were drawn from the poorer ranks of society. It is unlikely that any were master artisans, and the locksmith Motot, though the son of one, had declared assets of only forty-five livres in his marriage contract a few months before the rebellion. Their targets in this insurrection were the homes (though not the persons) of rich officials. Was this a class war, or should we look for complicity from the local upper classes?[46]

Recent studies of absolutism in the seventeenth century should dissuade us from assuming the local elites were monolithic in their resistance to royal authority, but the salient line of political conflict in the revolt of Lanturelu does appear to pit Louis against Dijon's municipal magistrates. Just what role the local and regional royal bureaucracy played must await further study, but it is clear that Louis XIII believed that the town council had not done all it could to put down the rebellion promptly. Two months after the riot, the king came to Dijon to chastise the magistrates for their "nonchalance." He vented his wrath by revoking several of the municipality's traditional privileges, particularly those pertaining to the election of the mayor, a cause for great concern among the magistrates.[47] He also abolished Dijon's "abbey of misrule," the *mère-folle* and her *infanterie dijonnaise*, for presumed complicity in the rebellion. The "abbey" had traditionally been licensed to poke fun at the crown or its agents, but Louis had evidently ceased to see any humor in even feigned opposition to royal authority.[48] Finally, the king proclaimed that the town

---

46. The literature on popular uprisings in seventeenth-century France is extensive, but see especially Boris Porchnev, *Les soulèvements populaires en France au XVIIe siècle* (Paris, 1972); Roland Mousnier, *Fureurs paysannes* (Paris, 1967); Le Roy Ladurie, *Carnival in Romans*; Yves-Marie Bercé, *Histoire des croquants* (Geneva, 1974), and *Fête et révolte* (Paris, 1976); and Sharon Kettering, *Judicial Politics and Urban Revolt in Seventeenth-Century France* (Princeton, 1978).

47. AMD, B267, fol. 224r–227v. Henceforth, three mayoral candidates were to be elected (by a very restricted electorate) in Dijon, and Louis would then make a choice of which was to become mayor. On 10 June the town council implored the duc de Bellegarde, the governor of Burgundy, to intervene on the town's behalf to get the privileges restored. AMD, I117, 10 June 1630.

48. Unlike a remarkably similar tax revolt with class overtones in Romans in 1580, studied by Le Roy Ladurie, we know little about the role of carnival in Dijon's rebellion. One of the rebel leaders was the *roy machas* of carnival, and it seems likely that the theme of inversion, never as tidily separated from reality as the elite would have liked, erupted into a real rebellion. Changenet, however, could not have had any connection with mère-folle, which by 1630 had become an elite institution; Louis's action, therefore, was a gratuitous blow.

would be responsible for a huge indemnity to the victims of the riot (his royal officials); the ultimate total was a staggering sixty thousand livres.[49]

Was Louis right? Were the city magistrates intentionally lax in putting down the rebellion? The royal official Fleutelot gave a detailed account of the riot, in which he attests that some "bourgeois" spectators greeted the burning of royal portraits with "Long live the Emperor!"[50] Even if Louis was unaware of Fleutelot's account, however, he may have been justified in his suspicions. In 1629 Richelieu had begun an assault on the fiscal privileges of the various *pays d'états* of France (including Burgundy) to maximize royal revenues. The edict of 10 June 1629 abolished the Estates of Burgundy, the political body that had traditionally allocated the tax burden in Burgundy. The province was to become a *pays d'élection*. Of course, those whose interests were represented in the Estates considered this an attack upon their traditional privileges and hence upon their local power, and they met the edict with immediate resistance.

The edict could not take effect until it had been registered in the Chambre des Comptes of Burgundy.[51] So for the next eight months the mayor of Dijon, who, along with his syndic, was among the most influential members of the Estates, intensively lobbied the king to revoke the edict and the Chambre des Comptes to refuse to register it.[52] On 19 February 1630 the mayor, having returned from an interview with the king in Paris, announced that Louis—or, more precisely, Cardinal Richelieu—was adamant.[53] That same day a rumor spread among the common people of Dijon that the edict was going to be registered and that new taxes would then be inevitable.[54] The

49. AMD, I117, 7 Feb. 1631, which is a reiteration of a royal arret of 28 April 1630. A document dated 9 Dec. 1633 fixed the amount to be paid in indemnity, and one dated 30 Dec. reveals that Dijon tried to borrow the funds from the municipality of Paris. In 1646 the indemnity was still being paid.

50. BMD, mf 911, p. 51.

51. Paul Cunisset-Carnot, *Une mouvement séparatiste sous Louis XIII: L'émeute de Lanturelu à Dijon en 1630* (Dijon, 1897), pp. 14–15.

52. AMD, B267, fol. 145r, 29 Jan. 1630, concerns the deputation sent to Paris to remonstrate with the king; B267, fol. 152r, 12 Feb. 1630, concerns the remonstration with the Chambre des Comptes, specifically citing the edict as a violation of the privileges of the province.

53. AMD, B267, fol. 153v, 19 Feb. 1630.

54. Ibid., fol. 154r, 19 Feb. 1630. On the connection in the popular mind between the Edict of Elections and higher taxes, see AMD, I117, the *procès verbal* of the syndic

town council responded by stepping up the patrols of the night watch. On 26 February a portentous placard was nailed to the door of the palais of the Parlement which bore the threat: "You who are the *chef d'élection* [presumably Gagne], watch out for yourself and your house."[55] Next day, amid rumors that the edict would be registered the following day, discontent grew.[56] Insurrection reared its head on 27 February when a crowd formed and marched to city hall to demand the keys to the town from the mayor. When he refused, they went to the ramparts and called to their comrades in the *faubourgs* to gather at the sound of the tocsin the next day.

The city magistrates were in a delicate position. Certainly, they had no wish to be implicated in a rebellion or to appear to support popular resistance to an edict they did not want. The *threat* of popular insurrection could be an invaluable bargaining chip with Richelieu; yet popular resistance had to be contained or there would be anarchy in the town. The situation was ambiguous enough to make Louis suspicious of the magistrates' handling of the riot. The syndic was careful to report that he had encountered a force he could not deal with and that as soon as he had put together a larger and more dependable militia, he had returned to the attack, and this account was quickly sent off to the king. On 4 March, when the streets were quiet again and the town council was solidifying its grip on the town, the magistrates dispatched a "great deputation" to the king to affirm their obedience and fidelity and finger the rabble as the disloyal subjects. At the same time, they intimated that a "second and greater riot than the first" was a real possibility, and they continued to lobby for the revocation of the edict (the rumor that it was to be registered proved false).[57] Again, it was not in the town council's interest to begin a swift and decisive repression.

The magistrates correctly judged that Richelieu suspected their motives. On 16 April the council sent another deputation to Louis to denounce the "calumnious and vicious" rumor that the magistrates and *bons habitans* were in complicity with the rioters. They argued

---

concerning his patrol on the night of 27 Feb., when a group of disgruntled vignerons told him that they had heard the edict would bring more gabelles and that the added burden would be intolerable.

55. AMD, B267, fol. 156r, 26 Feb. 1630.
56. Cunisset-Carnot, pp. 19–20.
57. AMD, B267, fol. 164v, 4 March 1630.

that they had risked their lives and taken every possible precaution in dealing with the situation and pointed out that they had seized and punished some of the guilty.[58]

Nevertheless, the tardiness of municipal repression of the riot remains problematic. We should not assume that the authorities dragged their heels simply because it was in their interest to do so. Widespread passive sympathy for the cause of the rebels—the huge crowds of spectators cheering on the rioters—certainly could have impeded organized repression, and resistance by the militia could have paralyzed it. The official parlementary report on the disturbances of 28 February noted that the militia captains, responding to the mayor's call to arms, could not fill their ranks. Knowing, as we do, that Dijon's master artisans, the backbone of the militia, had a recent history of resisting increased taxes, we should not be surprised that they sympathized with the popular cause and ignored calls to repress the rebels militarily. The captains were forced to ask Parlement to demand that all citizens of whatever quality obey the mayor's call. The militia that finally acted was small (only 150 men) and comprised only "exemplary" citizens, clear hints that many artisans were absent.[59]

And yet, if many craftsmen considered the actions of the rioters a legitimate expression of resistance, they did not join the rebels behind the barricades. Like the magistrates, who may have hesitated but eventually repressed the riot, master artisans were becoming a prosperous group that prized order and stability. All-out rebellion was not in their interest, but sending an antitax signal to the crown was.

For two decades after 1625 taxes grew considerably, and not accidentally it was also a time of dearth and war.[60] In 1630 many vignerons and artisans alike feared a tax increase would squeeze them beyond endurance. In December 1629 a new salt tax had been levied in Dijon,[61] and we know that the threat of further new gabelles caused consternation among the rioters two months later. Another impost seemed too much to bear, and the poor feared that any increase would reduce them to starvation.[62] It is to be expected that

58. Ibid., B267, fol. 206r, 16 April 1630.
59. AMD, I117, 1 March 1630. Guard discipline continued to be a problem. See, for example, AMD, B267, fol. 169r, 8 March 1630.
60. Hincker, p. 65.
61. AMD, B267, fol. 127v–128r, 18 Dec. 1629.
62. AMD, I117, 27 Feb. 1630.

some of this fiscal anxiety might spill over into antagonism toward the rich. The first four targets of the rebels had been selected in advance: the word around town was that they wanted to "burn and tear down" the houses of those who promoted the edict of *élections*, primarily Trésorier Général Gagne, the two presidents of the Chambre des Comptes, DeLoisy and LeGrand, and the correcteur DeVille-mereux.[63] It is notable, moreover, that the rebels took great delight in *destroying*, not stealing, the objects of luxury, expressing animosity toward the visible signs of riches and thus against the rich them-selves. Nor was the crowd mindless in its violence. The rioters were careful not to burn buildings indiscriminately but put the torch only to those that were freestanding so the fire would not engulf the town. As for the furnishings, they were burned in the middle of the court-yards or the streets.

After their two victorious encounters with the syndic and the par-lementaires, the rioters seem to have divided their numbers and broadened their targets to include the homes of royal officials whose principal crime was excessive wealth—the greffier, the avocat du roi, and above all the senior royal official in Dijon, the premier président at the Parlement. It is impossible to say how far the pillaging would have gone had not the municipal counteroffensive halted it. Perhaps the sight of sedition exceeding the bounds of its original antitax moti-vation was the cue for the town council to begin repression in earnest and convinced master craftsmen to side with the forces of order.

Some have identified Lanturelu as exclusively a vigneron insurrec-tion.[64] Actually, it was a popular tax revolt, led by Dijon's poorer taxpayers, including many artisans, and it gained its initial successes from the complicity of master artisans, who for a time boycotted the militia, and even from the lethargy of municipal magistrates. Only when it evolved into a social war between haves and have-nots did the magistrates move in to repress it; only then did they co-opt enough master artisans on the side of order to secure the town.

## Attitudes toward Authority

Lanturelu reveals how ambivalent were artisan attitudes toward local

---

63. AMD, B267, fol. 158v, 28 Feb. 1630.
64. For example, Gras, pp. 125–26.

authority—the mayor, town council, and sergeants. In one sense law is a means of expressing power, never a simple matter in early modern France. To the complications of overlapping and competing jurisdictions must be added the sentiments of the governed. Many master artisans, as increasingly prosperous property holders, could find it in their interest to support certain forms of law and order, but they certainly did not concur in all the regulations involving their own interests, nor did the legal institutions of order fulfill all of their regulatory needs.

Throughout the period, the town council was much concerned about people who roamed the streets after curfew, since such activity all too often led to disorderly behavior. The proclamation of 11 March 1578 is entirely typical of its kind; it lumped night violence with idleness, carrying weapons, frequenting taverns, and wearing masks.[65] Repeated injunctions suggest repeated violations, and variations on the proclamation of 1578 flowed from the municipal pen. For instance, one in 1610 prohibited walking about armed and without a light after eight in the evening because of the assaults and vandalism that were common at night.[66] Destruction of property was a frequent occurrence, and victims ranged from the nobility of the robe to master artisans, who certainly had good reasons to endorse this kind of authority imposed from above. In 1628 the municipal syndic filed a suit in court protesting that many *malvivantz* were roaming through the town at night, armed, breaking many windows, especially in the houses of "persons of quality" such as "Messieurs du Parlement."[67] But the illustrious were not the only victims; Bénigne LeSeurre, a master hatter, requested apprehension and exemplary punishment by the authorities of "several young men . . . [who] had spent a part of the night *sur le pavé*, throwing stones . . . against his sign . . . [and] breaking it." Like his neighbors, he had been too terrified to go out and try to stop them; the ruffians, he said, would have murdered him.[68]

As many master artisans became comfortable property holders obedience to the authorities came to be in their own interest. There is no question that craftsmen, in some respects, acquiesced to authority, and there is some evidence that the acquiescence increased in the

65. AMD, I3, 11 March 1578.
66. AMD, B248, fol. 129v, 22 Oct. 1610, repeated on fol. 166r, 14 Dec.
67. ADCO, BII 360/58, 19 Feb. 1628.
68. Ibid., 360/60, 14 July 1643.

seventeenth century. For example, the insult *pandard* (one worthy of being hanged) was never used by the artisans in the sixteenth century. That it was one of their most common slanders in the seventeenth century suggests that the guildsmen and their wives and widows were accepting the legitimacy of punishment meted out by the authorities.[69]

Craftsmen also had some familiarity with the law and were willing to exploit it to their advantage. Like the rest of Europe during this time, Dijon saw a great increase in litigation, and the growing legal establishment found a ready clientele in the ranks of the artisans. Oftentimes they looked to the law as a last resort, but there were also many cases—disputes over honor, for example—in which artisans went immediately to court to redress grievances. Indeed, even the threat to go "to justice" found its way into the discourse of dispute, suggesting artisans were using the law to further their own interests in dealing with their fellows.[70]

This heightened acceptance of the established authority can also be seen in somewhat less tangible ways. Between 1550 and 1650, fewer and fewer craftsmen were hauled in for directly insulting high municipal officials (mayors and aldermen). Even the butchers and bakers muted their opposition to municipal authority in the seventeenth century.

But if there is an overall impression of growing conformity to law and order among the artisans, we must not assume total acquiescence. When the exercise of municipal authority was contrary to their interests, artisans continued to show disrespect for the authorities, even though they tended to avoid direct insults. Again the butchers and bakers are the best examples, but other artisans obliquely challenged the hierarchy for a variety of reasons. In 1572 the master hatter Pierre Cortoisie, still fuming over a large fine a former mayor had levied on him years before, mocked his persecutor's character in an argument with another hatter who had received his mastership letters from that mayor. The former mayor was not present, but the sarcastic insults took place in the anteroom of the town council chamber, and there were plenty of ears to hear. Two decades

69. For example, ibid., 360/58, 8 Aug. 1638, 25 Nov. 1641, 360/59, 18 Sept. 1642, 9 April, 7 May 1643, 360/60, 8 Aug., 23 Dec. 1643, 360/61, 2 Jan. 1645.
70. For example, ibid., 360/47, 13–24 Sept. 1568, 360/53, 10 Nov. 1594.

later, there was a case of more circumspect insult. Master shoemaker Jean Constantin, already suspected of Protestant sympathies, hung outside his shop a sign shaped like a large head and painted black and white (Navarre's colors). The sign was taken as a subtle insult to M. Grosseteste, an alderman who belonged to the Holy League. Brought in for questioning, Constantin protested innocence, arguing that his own nickname was *grosse tête* and that the sign was meant to display that, not to insult an alderman.[71]

If threats to take someone to justice are evidence of acceptance of authority, then disregard for such threats suggests indirect resistance. There are many such cases. For example, in 1594 the mother-in-law of weaver Philibert Bendelot countered his threat to take her to court to pay arrears in rent with "I don't fear *la justice!*"[72] Several decades later, a guard stopped master embroiderer Berthelemy Vitrey at one of the gates of Dijon. The guard informed Vitrey that he was subject to arrest, for Vitrey was carrying a sack full of grapes despite the mayor's proclamation that no one was allowed to go into the vineyards to pick grapes. Vitrey began "nodding and shaking his head" (*branlant et hochant*) as if he were feebleminded and told the guard that he did not care a whit about the prohibition, the mayor, or the aldermen. These words and the mocking gesture were reasons enough for the watchman to apprehend him. After his brush with the law, Vitrey showed yet another indirect rejection of magisterial authority. He sought revenge against the culprit who had "squealed" on him, assuming that the people do not betray one another to the authorities.[73]

The same sort of solidarity against the forces of the law was evident in 1572. A crowd of young artisans of the neighborhood were staging a charivari for some newlyweds in the rue du Bourg one night when the wife of a journeyman pastrycook shouted a warning that the syndic and the night watch were in the street and taking prisoners. The merrymakers scattered in all directions, and some of them found temporary refuge with a master cobbler.[74]

If the mayor and aldermen were largely spared direct insult by the seventeenth century (and the deliberations of the town council certainly seem to support that interpretation), the same cannot be said

71. Ibid., 360/48, April 1572, 360/53, 10 Dec. 1593.
72. Ibid., 360/53, 10 Nov. 1594.
73. Ibid., 360/57, Sept.–Nov. 1623.
74. Ibid., 360/48, April–May 1572.

for the officers of the guard. The master dyer Gabriel LeGrand got into trouble in 1638 for hurling abuse at master cooper Bénigne Derot when he was on duty as corporal of a guardhouse. The incident continued a private feud the two men had carried on for six months, but this time LeGrand was insulting someone fulfilling a public function. The town council sentenced him to perform a ritual of reversal and humiliation. LeGrand was ordered to return to the guardhouse "where will be the said corporal and in his presence and that of the guard, say that he had said the injurious words indiscreetly, and . . . ask their forgiveness."[75]

In their attitudes to law and order master artisans once again were ambivalent. They had good reason to prize peace in the neighborhood and protection of their growing property, and there is good evidence that masters did in some ways champion the law and order of the upper classes. But self-interest also moved them to oppose magisterial authority. Over time, many of Dijon's craftsmen shifted from direct rejection of authority to indirect ways of expressing opposition.

### Extralegal Control

The institution of the *mère-folle* and her *infanterie dijonnaise* provided a way to enforce the established order while criticizing it through "world-upside-down" parody.[76] In the fifteenth century mère-folle may still have been part of Ste. Chapelle's "feast of fools," its participants canons and chaplains.[77] Sometime during the sixteenth century, however, it became laicized, banished from the sanctuary to the street, perhaps because Dijon's clerical elite perceived sacrilegious abuses in it.[78] Whatever its origins, by the late sixteenth and early seventeenth centuries, the mère-folle had become a theatrical society financed by the municipal government with membership drawn from

75. Ibid., 360/58, Aug.–Sept. 1638.
76. Natalie Z. Davis, "The Reasons of Misrule," in *Society and Culture in Early Modern France* (Stanford, 1975), passim.
77. Joachim Durandeau, *La mère-folle de la Sainte-Chapelle de Dijon* (Dijon, 1910).
78. Luc Verhaeghe, *Vers composés pour les enfants de la mère-folle de Dijon vers la fin du 16e siècle* (Liège, 1968–69), p. 38. Verhaeghe sees this as part of a late medieval collective transformation of sacred feasts into lay ones (p. 32). See also Durandeau, *La mère-folle*, p. 66.

the economic elite of Dijon. The mère-folle and infanterie marched in parades and performed plays on many festive occasions, including not just carnival but also celebrations of royal births and marriages or visits of dignitaries.[79]

We know little about the transformation of membership, but by the early seventeenth century mère-folle, like the town council, was dominated by Dijon's legal establishment.[80] It is likely that only the wealthier artisans took an active part, and then only during the transitional period, the second half of the sixteenth century. Canon Pepin of the Ste. Chapelle, who kept a journal during this period, tells us that the wealthy tailor Pucard was a ringleader in mobilizing the infanterie to parody a royal commissioner in Dijon in 1576.[81] There is other evidence that popular and local elite cultures converged at that time in mère-folle. The society staged popular theater in public squares as part of its parodies, and its surviving verses display the talents of an unknown poet who was conversant with both French and the Burgundian *pâtois*—that is, the languages of the learned and the populace.[82]

By the seventeenth century, the artisans had been relegated to the "Swiss Guard" of the mère-folle and marched at the end of parades. Gaston Roupnel saw this demotion as a further symptom of the "dissociating" of Dijonnais society in the seventeenth century,[83] of which the clustering of the master artisanat into a middling social group appears to have been a part. The society itself, divorced from its popular element and perhaps challenged by itinerant professional acting troupes, declined and was ultimately abolished by the king in 1630.[84]

---

79. Joachim Durandeau, *Histoire de la mère-folle laique de Dijon* (Dijon, 1912), p. 38; AMD, B239, fol. 163v, 16 Sept. 1601.

80. Durandeau, *La mère-folle*, pp. 82–92. All the officers belong to society's elite. Durandeau, *Histoire de la mère-folle*, p. 66. See also Jean-Bénigne Lucotte DuTilliot, *Mémoires pour servir à l'histoire de la fête des foux* (Lausanne, 1741), pp. 67–68.

81. Garnier, *Journal de Breunot . . . Pepin*, 1:31. Pepin tells us that Pucard lived near the palais. On the tax rolls of 1579 I have located a quite wealthy tailor named Picard living in that area.

82. Verhaeghe, p. 47. He has done a linguistic analysis of these verses.

83. Roupnel, *La ville et la campagne*, p. 154.

84. Martine Grinberg, "Carnaval et société urbaine aux XIVe–XVIe siècles: Le royaume dans la ville," *Ethnologie Française* 4 (1974): 215–44, suggests that such societies became the plaything of the urban elites, became theatricalized, lost their age specificity, and ceased to function as social criticism. Having lost their traditional reason for being, they were supplanted by the emergence of professional acting troupes.

The culture of craftsmen, and indeed all of popular culture, maintained its own informal play institutions, which regulated behavior by measuring it against a norm of a perceived "natural" order. If they were elbowed out of the abbey of misrule, they continued to conduct *chevauchées* and charivaris, which were effective statements of popular morality.

Chevauchées, or *âneries*, as they were frequently called in Dijon, were popular rituals of humiliation, in which a transgressor was mounted backward on an ass and paraded through town, exposed to public ridicule. Chevauchées seem to have been the custom throughout France, at least since medieval times.[85] Though local variations existed, all were expressions of community censure in which imagery of reversal emphasized what was considered proper. In Dijon these rituals often involved husbands whose wives had beaten them, thus violating assumptions of paternalism and male dominance; such behavior was "a monster against nature."[86] Husbands who beat their wives during the month of May were other favorite victims. May, the month of fertility and therefore associated with fecundity and reproduction, was the woman's month. To beat a woman then was to go against nature and bring down public censure on the malefactor.

Chevauchées could be of two types: small neighborhood affairs or highly visible events that went beyond moral censure to include political criticism as well. Both types occurred in Dijon during the period (though the former must have been more frequent), and artisans were involved in both. Neighborhood âneries usually paraded miserable wretches accused of being beaten by their wives from one public square to the next, exposing them to ridicule and derision. Neighborhood ties made this institution effective. Masked neighbors were the chief protagonists, and if the culprit could not be apprehended, his nearest neighbor served in his place.[87]

85. Georges Guigue, ed., "L'ordre tenu en la chevauchée faicte en la ville de Lyon," *Archives Historiques et Statistiques du Département du Rhône* 9 (1828–29): 338. Joachim Durandeau, *La grande asnerie de Dijon: Etude sur la menée et chevauchée de l'âne au mois de mai* (Dijon, 1887), p. 31, finds medieval expressions in Venom-sur-Seine (1383), Comté de Dreux (1404), and Marempire-en-Saintonge (1417). On chevauchées in Langres in the sixteenth century, see Claude Noirot, *L'origine des masques . . . menez sur l'asne à rebours et charivary* (Langres, 1609), pp. 64–65.

86. Quoted by Guigue, p. 343, n. 1, from a verse dated 1578.

87. "Le charivari" (Exposition of Musée des Arts et Traditions Populaires, Paris, 1977). Though no date is given, the following popular verses are clearly traditional practices and ring true when corroborated by other sources: "Si l'on sait dans *le*

These ritual chastisements complemented the vigilantism that brought physical order to the neighborhood and are yet another aspect of contests of honor between neighbors. They evidence a ruthless censorship by neighbors, who are the watchdogs of a traditional moral order. In a culture based on honor, such public humiliation becomes a serious matter. Artisans, like everyone else in Dijon, were most concerned about maintaining a positive public image; they were terrified of being ridiculed by a chevauchée. The baker Bénigne Regnier responded to an allegation that "he wasn't worth anything" with the seeming non sequitur that "he had never been *chevalché* on the tombs of Notre Dame church." His words suggest that the judgment tribunal could include not just living neighbors but the dead as well.[88] That the neighbors were masked increased the censure. Abandoning personal identity, ordinary individuals became merely, and more powerfully, "neighbor." Transcending time and identity, the public tribunal, the neighborhood, was collective and transpersonal, a moral entity that commanded solidarity and unanimity from its members. Indeed, neighborhood ties were so strong that they sometimes transcended religion. In 1611 Dijon's Protestant Consistory admonished artisan Claude Phelizot and his wife for "participating in âneries with their papist neighbors."[89]

The nature of the imagery was also important, for as Natalie Davis and many others have shown, reversal was a way to emphasize proper order—a primary concern of artisans, as we have seen. In Dijon, as elsewhere, the victim was made to ride backward on an ass, but nowhere else, so far as I know, would final judgment sometimes be passed on the accused by the *wife* of the mayor.[90] In May of 1578 Dijon merchant Nicolas Briet petitioned the mayor to forbid his "ill-

---

*voisinage* / que ma Jeanne m'a souffletté / . . . sur l'âne je serai monté / . . . tenant la queue au lieu de bride," in Lucien Guillemaut, *La bresse louhannaise . . . traditions populaires* (Louhans, 1907), my italics. On Dijon, see Etienne Tabourot, seigneur des Accords, *Les bigarrures du seigneur des accords* (Geneva, 1969). Tabourot, a Dijonnais lawyer of the late sixteenth century writes, "A Dijon, au mois de May, chacun an, l'on a coustumé, par privilège exprès, de mener sur l'âne les maris qui battent leurs femmes, où il se fait très belle assemblée de plusieurs *voisins* et autres *masquez* en fort brave appareil" (quoted in Durandeau, *Asnerie*, p. 37, my italics). Guigue quotes Noirot of Langres (p. 339 n. 1). On the nearest neighbor serving in the culprit's place, see Durandeau, *Asnerie*, p. 31, and Garnier, *Histoire du quartier du bourg*, p. 46.

88. ADCO, BII 360/48, 30 July 1569.

89. P. Perrenet, "La communauté protestante de Dijon au début du dix-septième siècle," *Annales de Bourgogne* 2 (1930): 288.

90. Durandeau, *Asnerie*, p. 20.

wishing neighbors" (many of whom must have been artisans) from leading him around town on an ass "under the pretext" that they had received permission from the former mayor's wife. He contended that they had wrongly accused him of beating his wife. (The town council declined his request.)[91] Granting the mayor's wife the authority to judge in such cases is a role reversal suitable to the month of May.

The sixteenth-century town council tolerated neighborhood moral vigilantism of this sort, but by the eighteenth century elite culture had pulled away from such a value system. An arret from the Parlement of Dijon in 1746 proscribed the custom of "parading in the town, each year on Mardi Gras, a cow on which the neighbors had mounted those who were beaten by their wives."[92] The ass has given way to a cow, but the neighbors are still enforcing morality. Now, however, the elites no longer approve.

Aneries could express more than just moral censure. In 1576 Elie DuTillet, grand master of streams and forests in Burgundy, was parodied for wife beating in May.[93] This bold mockery, instigated by the aforementioned Pucard the tailor, voiced political criticism as well as moral censure. Such an illustrious target (a high royal official) warranted the involvement of mère-folle and her infanterie. Of course, DuTillet could not be forced to parade on an ass. Instead, he was parodied in four plays performed over four days.[94]

These four farces tell us that DuTillet's wife had danced during the festivals of May while her husband was absent; upon his return, hearing of her actions, he had given her a thrashing. But these plays also contain clear reference to DuTillet's controversial political activities. Earlier that year, he had presented an edict calling for the harvesting of vast amounts of woodland to be sold ostensibly for the crown. In the play this was interpreted as inimical to all Burgundians because of

91. AMD, I105, 16 May 1578.
92. Guigue, p. 341, n. 2. On the withdrawal of elites from popular culture, see Peter Burke, *Popular Culture in Early Modern Europe* (New York, 1978), esp. chap. 8.
93. The dating is ambiguous. Pepin says Pucard the tailor instigated the parody in 1583, but DuTillet was grand master only from 1573 until 1578, and his edict of reformation came in 1576. Verhaeghe dates the four plays at 1576, leaving Pepin's dating a mystery.
94. Durandeau, *Asnerie*, p. 39. When DuTillet returned from Beaune where he was during the parody, he was so enraged by this insult to his honor that he denounced the infanterie before the Parlement of Dijon and even before the king. Durandeau, *Asnerie*, p. 41.

the threat of deforestation (next to food, wood for heat was the most important commodity for the popular classes of Dijon). Worse yet, the "evil fox" was suspected of being motivated by the promise of lucrative gain.[95] It is plausible that it was this possibility that raised the competitive hackles of the local elites, for the planned harvest, and his profits, would permit this newcomer (the royal court at the Table de Marbre was not two decades old by 1576) to gather local power into his hands more effectively. Thus, popular and elite cultures united, each for their own reasons, to chastise DuTillet for both his moral failings and his political and economic ambitions. Two diarists, a canon at Ste. Chapelle and a lawyer, applauded the actions of Pucard the tailor and the infanterie.

Much has recently been written about the other popular method of moral enforcement, charivari, but some questions still linger—not so much about its function as about who participated in these institutions of "misrule" and how they may have changed over time. Charivaris were burlesques ridiculing those who transgressed traditional moral norms; by dramatizing the transgression on the public stage, the actors enforced the proper moral order. As Natalie Davis has pointed out, "The city charivari was used to mark . . . affronts to the sense of order or justice of the neighborhood."[96] Charivaris were performed on celebration of marriages in which there was a wide discrepancy in age between bride and groom (perceived as contrary to nature) or when a widow or widower remarried (thus reducing the pool of eligibles for the young).[97]

Indeed, the preservation of order is central to charivari. Jacques Rossiaud has suggested that beginning around 1450, as peace in the neighborhood began to take on higher priority, youth abbeys in Dijon (of which charivari was one) functioned as a way to reduce or temper youthful violence by ritualizing it. They did not suppress violence but channeled it into particular forms, which came to obey rules governing their expression.[98] Davis picks up the story in the six-

95. Verhaeghe, pp. 52–53. For text, see Durandeau, *Asneries, Jeu* 1.
96. Davis, "Reasons of Misrule," p. 117. More recently, see Natalie Z. Davis, "Charivari, Honor, and Community in 17th-Century Lyon and Geneva," in *Rite, Drama, Festival, Spectacle: Rehearsals toward a Theory of Cultural Performance,* ed. John J. MacAloon (Philadelphia, 1984), pp. 42–57.
97. Davis, "Reasons of Misrule," p. 106.
98. Jacques Rossiaud, "Fraternités de jeunesse et niveaux de culture dans les villes du sud-est à la fin du moyen âge," *Cahiers d'Histoire* 1 (1976): 85, 88.

teenth century, when the rule-giving function was apparently already in place. Youthful misrule had become the voice of the conscience of the community; it was granted license to ridicule transgressors of the traditional norms as a community service.[99] These rituals, in which craftsmen were leading players, complemented the artisans' concern for order, both moral and physical.

Davis suggests that until the late sixteenth century, the abbeys of misrule that staged the charivaris were youth groups that were being socialized to the conscience of the community by serving as its watchdogs. Late in the sixteenth century, in the larger cities of France, she says, these groups lost their age specificity and became neighborhood groups encompassing both young and old men.[100] In Dijon, however, charivari apparently continued to be a youthful activity throughout the period.[101] In 1572 a charivari was broken up by the night watch and the culprits were apprehended. Of the eleven men arrested and interrogated, the youngest was twenty, the oldest thirty, and the average age was nearly twenty-four. Clearly, these were "youths" according to sixteenth-century standards.[102] All were journeymen, but most were permanent residents of Dijon living on the rue du Bourg, and inasmuch as their last names were those of the master butcher families traditionally living on that street, they were probably masters' sons. In 1643 several young men engaged in a charivari were apprehended; again, most were journeymen and natives and so likely masters' sons. Of four suspects interrogated, the oldest was twenty-five and the youngest twenty. Furthermore, the consensus among the twenty-two witnesses was that the entire group (at least eight of whom escaped arrest) was composed of "young men" (*jeunes hommes*).[103] Conspicuously absent in either document is any mention of adolescents or anyone over thirty; that is, the merrymakers, in

99. Davis, "Reasons of Misrule," p. 107.

100. Ibid., pp. 111, 114.

101. Davis seems to associate mère-folle and charivari, but it should be pointed out that the former was a festive institution that encompassed the entire town, while charivari, as we will see, was predominantly a neighborhood expression. Rossiaud, "Fraternités," 80, has noted this distinction, too.

102. ADCO, BII 360/48, 9 May 1572. In three instances in the first half of the sixteenth century in the same archival series Rossiaud, "Fraternités," 83, n. 45, has found an age range of eighteen to thirty-six in neighborhood youth abbeys.

103. ADCO, BII 360/60, Oct. 1643.

these two examples anyway, were from the pool of eligible bride-grooms. These findings suggest that Dijon's institutions of "misrule" remained youth groups until 1650 or beyond.

But Davis's observations on the importance of neighborhood in these activities hold for Dijon. As we have seen, the neighborhood was a moral, transpersonal entity. Order in the neighborhood, as Rossiaud also has pointed out, was of overriding concern to its inhabitants. Since the youths involved were probably masters' sons, it seems likely that this extralegal institution served to socialize future masters into the value system of the urban neighborhood. We know that the youths were neighbors of the parties being ridiculed. The charivari was the vociferous conscience of the neighborhood and protector of the traditional values pertaining to marriage (so important to master artisans, as we have seen). The records present the image of the neighborhoods as cells within the city—or perhaps more accurately, since so many inhabitants were immigrants, villages within the walls—which exerted control over their members by force and moral censure.

The rituals in these two charivaris communicated symbolically. Like face-to-face contests of honor, the charivari of 1643 played on the theme of virility because a master shoemaker was remarrying a much younger woman. The young men sang songs outside the shoe-maker's house about *cornards*, and drew pictures on his door of a "virile member" and of a man's head with horns, by these signs asserting that the older husband will never be able to satisfy his young wife and so inevitably will wind up a cuckold. The merrymakers were obsessed with materialism. Sexuality and fertility merged in the popular mind, and fertility could be symbolized by excrement and even garbage. So the ritual of pelting the shoemaker's door with human excrement and street garbage constituted another dominant theme. All of this was a reproach to the older shoemaker's sexual capacity and conversely a youthful assertion that the bride, for natural reasons centering on procreation and continuation of the community, should have been left for a more youthful and virile husband.

Not surprisingly, the shoemaker felt his honor impugned, and when he complained to the magistrates he found a sympathetic ear, for the authorities had reservations about charivari. The clergy condemned it unequivocally; they saw the charivari as a deriding of the sacrament of marriage.[104] The civil magistrates, always concerned about the threat to public tranquility, were more ambivalent. The town council had repeatedly banned charivaris over the years, associating them with disorder, but a proclamation of 1611 tolerated certain traditional practices, while condemning others. Charivaris against widows who remarried were acceptable, but those against girls marrying widowers (like the shoemaker ridiculed in 1643) were prohibited, since they tended to be more violent, leading to "broken doors and windows" and to "impious words and seditions."[105] Certainly they did not see these raucous youths as neighborhood moral peace-keepers—further evidence that "order" can mean different things to different people.

104. Abbé Jean-Baptiste Thiers, *Traité des jeux* (Paris, 1686), p. 290.

105. AMD, B248, fol. 196r, 4 Feb. 1611. For examples of prohibitions, see AMD, B208, fol. 158r, 1 March 1577, B228, fol. 175r, 21 Feb. 1591, B231, fol. 136v, 15 Feb. 1594, B235, fol. 230v, 28 April 1598, B253, fol. 143v, 23 Oct. 1615.

# 6 Artisan Religion: Reformed and Traditional

When artisan religious expression is viewed culturally, the process of appropriation combines with domination and imposition.[1] For a time the Protestant Reformation splintered Dijonnais society and attracted many craftsmen to its banner, but force imposed by the authorities crushed the new religion in Dijon. After the Council of Trent, Catholic reformers and godly laymen attempted to purify traditional religious expression by imposing a new morality on the urban popular classes. To gauge the success of this venture, we must look at what religious belief came to mean to the artisan believer. If it appears that elements of reformed Catholicism were embraced by Dijon's craftsmen and their families, when we explore the social context of belief we will discover that much of the abstract Tridentine morality gained meaning in the context of continued traditional Christianity, as is consistent with a situational mentality.

---

1. On the issue of acculturation and implicit domination, see Robert Muchembled, "Lay Judges and the Acculturation of the Masses (France and the Southern Low Countries, Sixteenth to Eighteenth Centuries)," in *Religion and Society in Early Modern Europe*, ed. Kaspar von Greyerz (London, 1984), pp. 56–65, and Jean Wirth, "Against the Acculturation Thesis," ibid., pp. 66–78.

## The Rise and Fall of the Reformed Religion

In 1554 a terrified alderman reported a rumor to the town council that two-thirds of the Dijonnais were "Lutherans."[2] Though his estimate was a wild exaggeration and his denominational attribution incorrect, the Protestant community was growing in Dijon during the 1550s, and the civil authorities made concerted efforts to halt its spread. Every night innkeepers were ordered to report the names of all out-of-town guests to the mayor, and no peddler was permitted to remain in town for more than three days.[3]

Outbursts of iconoclasm became more frequent after 1555, though they never attained the proportions reached elsewhere in France or the Low Countries.[4] In 1557 three attacks on sacred images occurred in St. Nicolas and St. Philibert, parishes that soon became bastions of popular Catholicism.[5] In December of that year, some masons, reported the town council, "broke and impudently damaged the images of the saints . . . contemptuously leaving them in the public streets."[6] Scarcely a month later the town council met to discuss another incident, this time against the most revered image of the Catholic faith, "the effigy, image and remembrance of the Holy and Sacred Host."[7] Such iconoclasm may have been an expression of anticlericalism. In 1560 some images at the church of the Cordeliers (Franciscans) were broken.[8]

Certainly the civil authorities were concerned about such outbursts because of the threat to public order, but we must not overlook the overlapping of secular and religious authority; religious indignation was equally important. For Protestants, it has been pointed out, iconoclasm was a symbol of desacralization, a primary theme in the

2. AMD, B192, fol. 92v, 17 July 1554.

3. AMD, B194, fol. 125v, 27 Oct. 1556. The peddlers were suspected of selling heretical books.

4. Phyllis Mack Crew, *Calvinist Preaching and Iconoclasm in the Netherlands, 1544–1569* (London, 1973); Solange Deyon, *Casseurs de l'été 1566: L'iconoclasme dans le nord de la France* (Paris, 1981); and Carlos Eire, *War against the Idols* (Cambridge, 1986).

5. Jacques Fromental, *La réforme en Bourgogne aux 16e et 17e siècles* (Paris, 1968), p. 18.

6. Edmond Belle, *La réforme à Dijon des origines à la fin de la lieutenance générale de Gaspard de Saulx-Tavanes (1530–1570)* (Dijon, 1911), p. 24.

7. AMD, B195, fol. 139v, 17 Jan. 1558.

8. Fromental, p. 18.

Reformation.[9] For Catholics, however, iconoclasm was a desecration that threatened the entire community, since it was believed to provoke divine wrath. Hence candlelight processions, like the one ordered by the town council after the image smashing in St. Philibert in 1558, were rituals of purification that symbolically cleansed the community soiled by the "heretics." Since the "honor of God and Our Holy Mother Church" had been impugned, a procession to the place of desecration was deemed requisite.[10]

Whatever the actual size of the Protestant community in the early 1560s, it appears that the Calvinists felt strong enough to attempt to wrest control of the civil government from the Catholics. This Huguenot threat, to be felt in many towns in France, came to Dijon earlier than anywhere else. The populace had become increasingly polarized around religion in 1560 and 1561. In June 1561 the king authorized the Catholic Dijonnais to bear arms when they marched in the procession of Corpus Christi so they would be prepared for any disruptions contemplated by the Protestants.[11] Two weeks later the town council promised severe punishment to anyone giving asylum to Calvinist ministers.[12] One month later all suspected Huguenots were barred from holding public office. One such was the master goldsmith Guillaume Odinelle who was an essayeur de monnaie.[13]

The situation came to a head in the last week of October 1561. During that week Protestants had been assembling; on 26 October they gathered at the home of draper Jean Pourtault. Jean Caulot overheard some of the conversation and, alarmed, ran to the town council to warn that the Calvinists were "conspiring against the magistrates."[14] Three nights later several hundred Huguenots met at lawyer Jacques DePresle's and the next night at the home of master cabinetmaker Jacques DesVarennes (the magistrates had placed in-

9. Benedict, *Rouen during the Wars of Religion*, p. 64; Steven Ozment, *The Reformation in the Cities: The Appeal of Protestantism to Sixteenth-Century Germany and Switzerland* (New Haven, 1975).

10. AMD, B195, fol. 139v, 17 Jan. 1558. On this ritual, see Benedict, *Rouen during the Wars of Religion*, p. 64.

11. AMD, B198, fol. 133v–134r, 3 June 1561.

12. Belle, p. 40.

13. AMD, B199, fol. 36v, 15 July 1561.

14. AMD, D63, deposition of Jean Caulot, 29 Oct. 1561. For a fuller analysis of popular militant religiosity, see my "Popular Religious Solidarity in Sixteenth-Century Dijon," *French Historical Studies* 14 (Fall, 1985): 192–214.

formers in both gatherings).[15] The tense atmosphere broke outside of DesVarennes's when a Catholic crowd pelted the cabinetmaker's house with stones and garbage, though the besieged Calvinists were able to slip out after dark when the crowd had dissipated.[16]

The magistrates could contain the situation only until Toussaint, when, in an attempted coup de main, heavily armed Protestants from all parts of town gathered in the rue des Forges and sealed off both ends of the street with armed guards. The emergence of this fortified Huguenot stronghold in the heart of the town triggered a popular Catholic reaction. Hearing that the Protestants had called for help from the "gens des villes du pays," that afternoon some winegrowers rang the tocsin, while others on the rue des Champs sounded the *tabourin*.[17] Roused by these popular calls to arms, the Catholics paraded not immediately toward the nearby rue des Forges but rather into St. Nicolas parish, militantly Catholic as we will see, and there gathered more followers to their banner. The swelling crowd coursed through the streets, finally emerging at the fish market. Across the street were arrayed the Huguenots from the rue des Forges, led by master goldsmiths Bénigne DeVaulx and Jacques Largentier, master pastrycook Bénigne Placard, as well as several merchants and apothecaries, all called to arms by Edme the goldsmith who shouted, "To arms! The bailli and the king are for us!"[18] In the subsequent engagement insults and rocks were thrown, but only one arquebus found its mark, felling a Catholic dyer. This appears to have been the only serious casualty. Though neither the Protestants nor the Catholics were routed, a Protestant offensive, so greatly feared, was thwarted. Parlement quickly ordered the town council to arrest the armed inhabitants of the rue des Forges.[19] During the month of November the magistrates collected scores of depositions, assiduously noting the names of all Protestants involved. They then began the judicial suppression that continued intermittently for more than a dozen years.

The failed coup seems to have been the only serious effort of the Protestants to seize control of the town. Catholic repression in 1562, led by royal Lieutenant-Général Gaspard de Saulx-Tavanes and the

---

15. AMD, D63, *procès verbal*, 29 Oct. 1561.
16. Ibid., 30 Oct. 1561.
17. AMD, B199, fol. 81v, 2 Nov. 1561.
18. AMD, D63, 4 Nov. 1561, deposition of Pierre Caillin.
19. Ibid., 1 Nov. 1561.

militant Catholic mayor of Dijon Bénigne Martin, broke the political back of Calvinism. So strong was the opposition to Protestantism that the town council vigorously opposed the royal edict of pacification of 17 January 1562 and pressured Parlement to delay its registration. This edict, which authorized practice of the new religion outside the walled towns or within private homes, was in force in Dijon for only a month. Parlementary registration occurred on 2 February, and the massacre at Wassy, which began the civil war, occurred on 1 March.[20] Thereafter repression of Dijon's Huguenots began in earnest. In the spring of 1562 Tavanes authorized the expulsion of all Huguenot journeymen from Dijon, and in May the town council asked Tavanes to round up all the *chefs* of the new religion who were "causes of seditions."[21] In July the town council and Parlement demanded a "profession of faith" from the curés and their parishioners.[22]

No concerted Calvinist counteroffensive reached Dijon, but there were expressions of isolated resistance. Iconoclasm recurred; Protestant artisans continued to sing the Psalms, "in French" and "loudly and intelligibly" from their workshops, despite Tavanes's ordinances.[23] Huguenots suffered abuse from the Catholic populace, too. Catholics insulted them when the Protestants were returning to Dijon from the nearby village of Nuits where they heard weekly sermons (to Catholics, *dyableries*). The Catholics vituperated that "they must be beaten [*baptre*], killed and thrown in the moats" or "under the bridge" to purify the town through a "rite of violence," a forceful rebaptism.[24] The encounters could get physically violent. On 5 March 1563 a Protestant woman was kicked *par derrière* and the entire company she was with was pelted with stones and garbage [*fange*], the latter surely a symbolic gesture of desecration. The Protestants who reported this incident to the Parlement claimed that the

20. Belle, pp. 49, 172–75 (texts of opposition to edict); AMD, B199, fol. 149r, 3 Feb. 1562.
21. Belle, p. 71; Henri Hauser, Introduction to Belle, p. xxii; AMD, B199, fol. 234r, 15 May 1562. Hauser, p. xii, asserts that fifteen hundred to two thousand Protestants were expelled from Dijon in 1562. I find no archival evidence to support such figures.
22. Belle, p. 65.
23. On iconoclasm, see AMD, B199, fol. 268v, 3 June 1562. On singing, see ADCO, BII 360/45, 1 Jan. 1563, and 5 Jan. 1563.
24. AMD, D63. On purification by baptism, see Natalie Z. Davis "The Rites of Violence," in *Society and Culture*, pp. 152–187.

Catholic preachers were whipping up the populace against the Calvinists and were being paid for it by the town council.[25]

On 19 March the Peace of Amboise was issued, again granting the
Protestants the right to hold their services outside the town walls,
and again the Catholic municipal authorities fought it; nonetheless,
it was registered by the Parlement in June 1563.[26] For four years Dijon
was outwardly peaceful, but beneath the surface tension remained. In
spite of the new edict, the town council declined to readmit expelled
Protestants unless they were of "honorable quality, domiciled, habit-
uated and for a long time married in this town."[27] Because Dijon was
so close to Lutheran Germany, Calvinist Geneva, and the Huguenot
forces just to the south down the Saône Valley, security was of paramount concern to the magistrates.

Religious passion aside, the Catholic authorities had much to be
concerned about when the Huguenot artisans "scandalized" their
neighbors by singing the Psalms and working on holy days or when
they gathered in assemblies within the walls, for such activities could
easily generate violence and sedition.[28] Toussaint 1561 was still a
vivid memory, and the council used persecution and repression to
keep the Huguenots divided and weak. Artisans could be persecuted
in various ways. For instance, journeyman currier Jean Thomas submitted a masterpiece to the aldermen and jurés of his craft but was
denied mastership. He appealed to Parlement (much more moderate
in its dealings with the Huguenots), claiming that he was being dis-
criminated against because he belonged to the new religion, and Parlement ruled in his favor.[29]

The city magistrates were especially perturbed to find the Huguenots instructing children in the new faith. The schoolmaster Jean
DeGuy taught about forty children how to read and write in the
house of the master cabinetmaker Claude Motot, also a Huguenot,
using books by Calvin and Beza, as well as several Calvinist hymnals.

25. AMD, D63, 5 March, 1 Jan. 1563.

26. Belle, p. 83.

27. AMD, B200, fol. 5v, 22 June 1563, fol. 151, 26 June 1563.

28. For example, ibid., fol. 54v, 31 Aug. 1563, fol. 55v, 3 Sept. 1563, fol. 76r, 5 Oct.
1563, B201, fol. 50r–v, 14 Aug. 1564, fol. 141r, 1564; ADCO, BII 360/46, 3 Oct. 1564.
Imprisonment could result from Psalm singing, in spite of a royal edict of 9 May 1565,
which stated that Protestants could not be "molesté, recherché ny oultragé . . . en leurs
maisons" and that Psalm singing was permitted to them. AMD, I3, 22 May 1565.

29. ADCO, BII 360/46, 10 Oct. 1565.

He was arrested, and subsequent interrogations revealed that the house of the master cabinetmaker Hugues Sambin was also a place of Calvinist instruction. DeGuy was ordered to cease teaching (we have no record of any moves against Sambin), but he disregarded the order. Ultimately he was expelled from Dijon and his household goods impounded and inventoried.[30]

In September 1567 the events at Meaux triggered the second civil war, upsetting the fragile equilibrium that had existed in Dijon since 1563.[31] Tavanes sensed the changing climate and mobilized a radical Catholic organization, the Confrérie du Saint Esprit, to lead the struggle against Protestantism.[32] Its members took an oath pledging service to the king and the Catholic faith against the Huguenots.[33] Persecution ensued immediately. On 9 September 1567 Tavanes, responding to a request from the mayor, ordered all "qualifiés ou riches et opulans" Protestants in Dijon (including some master artisans) disarmed, placed under house arrest, and denied communication with Huguenots elsewhere in the country. All Huguenot "menu peuple, mécaniques et artisans" (here meaning lesser masters and journeymen) would be likewise disarmed but also expelled from town, though if they stayed at least two leagues away, Tavanes would provide an umbrella of protection for them in the name of the king.[34] Tavanes meant business. On 10 October he again ordered the town council to expel all Protestant journeymen, and ordered the parish captains to evict them if they failed to go peaceably.[35] We do not know how many actually left, but with the Treaty of Longjumeau in 1568, several hundred exiled Huguenots returned to Dijon.[36]

The Protestants who remained were forced to carry the tax burden

30. Ibid., 360/45, 5–10 April 1566, 356/6, 20 Jan. 1570. See also AMD, B203, fol. 104r, 3 Oct. 1566. On expulsion, see also Belle, pp. 212–13.

31. Drouot, *Notes sur la Bourgogne*, p. 31.

32. Ibid., p. 37. Drouot argues that this organization had a popular base, while Belle, pp. 110–11, suggests it drew from the clergy, nobility, and rich inhabitants. Unfortunately, no rolls survive, so the issue remains unresolved.

33. Belle, pp. 110–11; Gras, *Histoire de Dijon*, p. 115; Robert Harding, "The Mobilization of Confraternities against the Reformation in France," *Sixteenth Century Journal* 11 (1980): 87, 88. Harding, 98, has found that the Confraternity of the Holy Ghost appeared in several French towns (including Dijon) at this time, as did the brotherhood of the Rosary, another militantly Catholic confraternity.

34. AMD, D63, 9 Sept. 1567.

35. AMD, B204, fol. 94r, 10 Oct. 1567.

36. Belle, p. 124.

for royal soldiery, to work on fortification repair, and to clean moats. They were denied the right to vote in mayoral elections and to serve in public office.[37] In the face of such stiff repression, abjurations of Huguenots multiplied from the summer of 1568 on. On 15 October of that year, seventy-eight individuals returned to Holy Mother Church.[38] The records contain ninety-three certificates of abjuration dated 1570–1572; most came after St. Bartholomew's Day in 1572.[39] Such abjurations almost always included a statement that the repentant Huguenot accepted communion, transubstantiation being the most vehemently rejected Catholic doctrine, but these returnees were apparently not forced to undergo humiliating acts of penance.[40]

There was no massacre on St. Bartholomew's Day in 1572 in Dijon, but Léonor Chabot, count of Charny, Tavanes's replacement as lieutenant-général of the province, feared Huguenot sedition and ordered the arrest and incarceration of the Protestants; many promised to abjure if Charny would release them from prison.[41] We still hear of occasional secret assemblies of Huguenots afterward,[42] but the swift and determined repressions of 1562 and 1567–1568, followed by this equally decisive action, broke the back of Protestantism in Dijon. Huguenots never mounted a threat again.

The coup de main attempted in late October 1561 reveals the militancy of popular religiosity, both Calvinist and Catholic. It was, no doubt, the fervor of the Catholic majority that gave the authorities the confidence to begin suppression of Protestantism in 1562 and to accelerate it later in this troubled decade. Historians of Dijon have seen this confessional conflict as an expression of social conflict between Catholic vignerons and Huguenot artisans, indeed, of a civil war between two parts of the town.[43] We must guard against oversimplification, however. True, the geographic hub of the artisan-dom-

37. Ibid., pp. 126–27, 131; AMD, B206, fol. 178v, 14 June 1570, B207, fol. 225r, 17 June 1571.

38. Belle, pp. 207–8.

39. AMD, D66.

40. Compare, for example, the abjuration of the tailor François Brun of Dijon in Belle, pp. 221–22, and Benedict, *Rouen during the Wars of Religion*, p. 129.

41. AMD, B208, fol. 15v–16r, 31 Aug. 1572; Garnier, *Journal de Breunot . . . Pepin*, 1:9 (12 Sept. 1572), where Pepin applauds Charny's actions and corroborates that many prisoners abjured.

42. AMD, B212, fol. 128v, 20 Dec. 1574.

43. Hauser, Introduction to Belle, pp. xxi–xxii. See also Drouot, *Notes sur la Bourgogne*, p. 27.

inated Protestant community was St. Jean parish, and most militant winegrowers hailed from St. Nicolas and St. Michel, but many artisans did not live in St. Jean parish, and the great majority of them remained Catholic. Only a few months before the suspected coup in 1561, over 40 percent of the voting artisans had supported the militant Catholic mayoral candidate Bénigne Martin, evidence that the anti-Protestant popular base included winegrowers *and* artisans well before Dijon's Catholics mobilized in militant confraternities in the late 1560s.

Recent studies have found a greater attraction for Calvinism among artisans than in any other social group in France. Analyses of the social composition of Protestantism in several French cities and among French Protestant emigres to Geneva have found substantial artisan representation, led by textile workers, leather craftsmen, cabinetmakers, and goldsmiths.[44] For example, Emmanuel Le Roy Ladurie's figures for Montpellier in 1560 suggest overrepresentation of artisans, especially carders, hosiers, and tailors, and Philip Benedict concludes that Protestantism drew disproportionately from the artisanal elite in Rouen.[45] I have argued elsewhere that the sociology of religious affiliation on the popular level must take into account factors beyond occupation.[46] It has become commonplace to assume

44. The literature on the sociology of Protestantism in the sixteenth century is extensive, and growing. For studies on the social composition of Protestantism in Montpellier and Beziers, see Emmanuel Le Roy Ladurie, *The Peasants of Languedoc*, trans. John Day (Urbana, 1974), pp. 158–64. On Toulouse, see Raymond Mentzer, "Heresy Suspects in Languedoc prior to 1560: Observations on their Social and Occupational Status," *Bibliothèque d'Humanisme et Renaissance* 39 (1977): 561–68; and Joan Davies, "Persecution and Protestantism: Toulouse, 1562–1575," *Historical Journal* 22.1 (1979): 31–51. On Rouen, see Benedict, *Rouen during the Wars of Religion*, chap. 3. On Amiens, see David L. Rosenberg, "Social Experience and Religious Choice: A Case Study, The Protestant Weavers and Woolcombers of Amiens in the Sixteenth Century" (Ph.D. diss., Yale University, 1978). On Normandy, see David Nicholls, "Social Change and Early Protestantism in France: Normandy, 1520–1562," *European Studies Review* 10 (1980): 279–308. On Caen, see M. S. Lamet, "French Protestants in a Position of Strength: The Early Years of the Reformations in Caen, 1558–1568," *Sixteenth Century Journal* 9 (1978): 35–56. For the Midi, see Janine Garrisson-Estèbe, *Protestants du Midi* (Toulouse, 1980), pt. 1. On French expatriates, see Robert Mandrou, "Les français hors de France aux XVIe et XVIIe siècles," *Annales: ESC* 14.5 (1959): 662–75.

45. Le Roy Ladurie, *Peasants*, p. 160, finds from a tax census of Huguenots that 367 of 561 (69 percent) whose occupation is known were artisans. Benedict, *Rouen during the Wars of Religion*, pp. 80, 90.

46. Farr, "Popular Religious Solidarity."

that craftsmen were attracted to the new religion, but if we are to explain why so many artisans remained Catholic, even militantly, it is necessary to understand confessional association and religious belief in situational as much as abstract terms. Personal relations in Dijon operated in a matrix in which neighborhood solidarity as well as occupation was an important factor. Certainly, neighborhood solidarity was a desideratum of artisan culture, and individual neighborhoods tended to swing in one direction or the other, toward Calvinism or Catholicism. It seems likely that in this world of intensely personal relations, neighborhood loyalties and occupational familiarity (though not at the guild level—many guilds split over religion) combined to influence confessional affiliation.

From 1572 to 1585 little is recorded about Protestants in Dijon. Expressions of resistance to Catholic domination tended to be passive and nonpolitical acts, such as working on holy days or Psalm singing.[47] Most Protestants tried to operate within the law. About fifteen of them, including several artisans, were caught "assembling" in the house of a lawyer, but investigation revealed that they had met to determine how best to distribute among themselves the tax burden the king had imposed upon the Protestants. Immediately thereafter they went to the town council to ask permission to establish *presches* in the suburbs and nearby villages, though they met with refusal.[48]

Lawful comportment may have paid off in other ways, however. In the peaceful times between St. Bartholomew's Day and the militant Catholicism of the late 1580s, Protestants (or recent abjurers) do not seem to have been considered economic or even political pariahs. Of twenty-one known Protestant artisans who correlate with the tax rolls of 1556 and 1579, ten improved their condition over these twenty-three years, ten declined, and one, Bénigne DeVaulx, the master goldsmith, remained one of the wealthiest taxpayers in town. In 1579 eight of these twenty-one artisans still perched in the top fifth of taxpayers, and all but eight were in the upper half. Such figures hardly suggest that association with the reformed religion would lead to economic disaster.

Some Huguenot masters even seem to have held the trust of the

47. For example, AMD, B219, fol. 36v, 14 Aug. 1581, fol. 90v, 29 Dec. 1581.
48. AMD, D65, 19 Dec. 1581, also B208, fol. 94v, 15 Dec. 1581, B219, fol. 90v, 29 Dec. 1581.

civil authorities, for they served as jurés for their guilds. The renowned Sambin, the master painter Edouard Bredin, the master cabinetmaker Claude Motot, and the master goldsmiths Charles DeRoye and Guillaume Odinelle (chosen by their craft and accepted by the civil authorities)—all held this office *after* it was known that they were, or had been, Protestants.[49]

The respected Burgundian historian Henri Drouot argued that between 1579 and 1584 Burgundian Catholics were confident that they had extirpated heresy, and after that time the Wars of Religion became secular, centered on power struggles and social conflict.[50] The first Guisard League was organized by the militantly Catholic and politically influential Guise family as an antitax and thinly veiled antiroyal association in 1576. It was suppressed in September 1577 but reappeared in 1579 with, according to Drouot, a princely and popular base.[51] There are no existing lists of adherents to the league of 1579, but in its earlier incarnation of 1576–1577 many artisans, including several ex-Huguenots (four of them goldsmiths), took the oath and enrolled.[52]

When the Huguenot Henri of Navarre became heir presumptive in 1584, the league reappeared in a more militantly Catholic form, and by the fall of 1585, persecution of suspected Protestants had resumed in Dijon with a fervor not seen for over a decade. At the request of the duc de Mayenne—a Guise—homes of suspected Huguenots, many of them master craftsmen, were ransacked in search of caches of hidden weapons.[53] Rolls of suspects were drawn up so the searches could be

49. On Sambin as juré, see AMD, B198, fol. 15v. On Motot, see B199, fol. 17v, B203, fol. 20v, B205, fol. 17r, B216, fol. 15r, and B224, fol. 26r. On Odinelle, see B210, fol. 16v. On DeRoye, see B212, fol. 20r. On Bredin, see B216, fol. 15v, B227, fol. 25v, and B231, fol. 44r.

50. Drouot, *Mayenne*, 1:153. The central thesis of Drouot's magisterial work is that during the second half of the sixteenth century access to the sovereign courts, the central route of social advancement for society's elites, became increasingly blocked. At the same time the ranks of the lawyers were swelling, attracting away from trade the sons of merchants, whose aspirations for upward social mobility were thereby frustrated. These individuals turned to the Holy League to challenge the nobility of the robe and resurrect municipal authority. This thesis has been corroborated by Richet and Mousnier for Paris but recently found inappropriate for Rouen by Benedict.

51. Drouot, *Notes sur la Bourgogne*, pp. 117, 118, 170.

52. AMD, B208, 10 Jan. 1577. Unfortunately, this list does not contain occupational descriptions, but the goldsmiths Bénigne Richard, Guillaume Odinelle, Charles DeRoye, and Jean Cusenier and the tailor François Brun are all on the list.

53. For example, ADCO, BII 360/51, 16, 31 Oct. 1585.

comprehensive, and one from 29 October survives.[54] Sixty-nine
names appear on the list; among these are twenty-six artisans (38
percent). Suspected Protestants were still most densely concentrated
in St. Jean (twenty-five of them) and Notre Dame (seventeen), whereas St. Nicolas had only four and St. Philibert no suspects at all. These
patterns of occupational and geographic distribution are similar to
those of the 1560s, but the size of the Calvinist community has
shrunk tremendously. Furthermore, some individuals on the list may
not have been practicing Protestants. In the atmosphere of religious
passion and paranoia that existed in 1585, anyone associated with the
new religion in the past could easily be suspected. It appears that the
Catholic repression had very nearly extirpated the Huguenot heresy.
Rather than have their goods confiscated (recall that many of the
Huguenot artisans were quite well off), by the end of the year nine
artisans had formally abjured, four of them, including the painter
Bredin, for the second time.[55]

Still the persecution continued. In March 1589 all "suspects" (by
now not just Protestants but political opponents must have been
included) were either imprisoned, placed under house arrest, or expelled from town. Many of the same Protestant names from 1585 and
even before reappear. Jacques DesVarennes, the master cabinetmaker
and a ringleader of the original Calvinist community, was imprisoned, along with other cabinetmakers, tailors, and goldsmiths.[56] During the same month every citizen of Dijon was required to take an
oath to the Holy League. During the summer and fall the authorities
continued their concerted efforts to root out Protestantism inside the
walls. Aldermen went through their parishes administering oaths to
the league and reporting all suspects to the mayor. Some artisans
appear on these lists, including the forever suspect painter Bredin and

54. AMD, B223, fol. 82v–83r, 29 Oct. 1585.
55. AMD, D66. On those abjuring more than once, see AMD, B223, fol. 86r–v, 31
Oct. 1585, (François Brun, tailor), AMD, D65, 2 Oct. 1563 (Nicolas Hurtaut, tailor, who
was a Huguenot as early as 1563 and was still under suspicion in 1585. To prove that he
was a good Catholic in 1585, he demonstrated baptism records of his children, the
Catholic marriage of his daughter, and the attestation by neighbors who witnessed
Hurtaut receiving the sacraments. AMD, D65). Why weren't these individuals burnt as
relapsed heretics? They may have been "Nicodemites," but we may surmise no tangible proof was presented to warrant conviction (at least none surfaces in the archival
records).
56. AMD, B226, fol. 181v, March 1589, which refers to a roll of suspects drawn up 1
Jan. B226, fol. 140v–141v, 9 Jan. 1589.

the wife of Hugues Sambin.[57] The fate of the recalcitrant could be grim—a cobbler and a shoemaker were burned for heresy.[58] Most artisans, however, at least outwardly embraced Catholicism and took their place as solid citizens.

The records in Dijon mention Protestantism much less often in the seventeenth century, surely a sign that the Huguenots were few and their actions passive. Only sporadically do we hear of Psalm singing in public, iconoclasm, or disruption of processions.[59] It was an isolated incident when a Huguenot shoemaker could not resist pitching household wastes from his second-story window upon a Catholic procession passing underneath.[60] Despite their small numbers and passivity, however, the Huguenots were still harassed on occasion. Catholic preachers continued to vilify them, and they remained apprehensive and defensive, carrying weapons even during their burial ceremonies.[61]

Since documents from the Consistory of Dijon exist only for the years 1607–1613, 1619, and 1626, we know very little about the social composition of seventeenth-century Protestantism in Dijon. Few occupational descriptions accompany the names in these documents, but many family names are those of artisans known to have been Calvinists a generation earlier.[62] In the absence of a firm institutional or geographical base, it is likely that the family became the fundamental nucleus of the Huguenot community in Dijon.[63] At any rate, that community was minuscule. In 1619 the Dijon consistory counted only thirty-four adherents.[64] It was a far cry from the halcyon days

57. AMD, B227, fol. 65v–67r, 4 Aug. 1589.

58. AMD, B228, fol. 72v, 9 Aug. 1590, C38, 2 Jan. 1592.

59. For iconoclasm, see AMD, B253, fol. 123v, 2 Oct. 1615, B252, fol. 188r, 6 Feb. 1615, B258, fol. 169v, 18 Jan. 1621.

60. AMD, B252, fol. 188r, 6 Feb. 1615.

61. Durandeau, *Journal de Sullot*, p. 127 (on preaching against the Protestants); AMD, B252, fol. 188r–v, 6 Feb. 1615. Jean Berry, the cabinetmaker, complained to the authorities that his deceased coreligionist, whom the Huguenots were burying, had been blasphemed by three women who had been watching the ceremony. AMD, D66, 24 Feb. 1618.

62. Perrenet, "La communauté protestante," pp. 282, 283; Fromental, p. 121. The names Hut, Millot, Bergier, Sordot, and Lambert are examples of artisan family names associated with Protestantism throughout the period.

63. Katherine Faust, "A Beleaguered Society: Protestant Families in La Rochelle, 1628–1685" (Ph.D. diss., Northwestern University, 1980), has found family continuity in Protestant ranks.

64. Fromental, p. 121. The parish registers of the Protestant church of the nearby

of 1558–1561, when they numbered in the hundreds and had even tried to seize political control of the town.

## The Catholic Reform and the New Morality

Clearly Catholic domination was asserted in the rout of the Protestants, but did domination evolve into hegemony? That is, did the artisans absorb Tridentine doctrine and come to believe what the reformers of Catholicism intended? It is difficult to gauge belief, but there are indications that artisan religious practices responded to the new emphasis on traditional pious devotions (prayers, pilgrimages, confraternities), and the godly discipline that was at the heart of the new morality. Whether Dijon's master craftsmen and their families embraced the moral discipline pushed by the clerical and lay elites, however, is problematic. Historians have tended to agree that the Catholic reform penetrated the urban popular classes in the seventeenth century, but too often they have seen this process as imposition.[65] If it appears that craftsmen and their families embraced the reform, we must ask what the reform meant to them.

Even though the Tridentine decrees were resisted in France until the seventeenth century, as early as the 1550s lay authorities had begun to show steady concern with what they perceived as a lack of moral discipline and the propensity to public disorder exhibited by the popular classes. They associated disorder and immorality with mayhem in the streets because their conception of order carried cosmic and even apocalyptic overtones.[66] After the Council of Trent the clergy joined forces with the godly laymen, and in an important sense, the Holy League was an attempt to restore religion as the reference point of order, social control being part of the grand design

---

village of Is-sur-Tille survive at the *mairie*, and it appears that there, as in Dijon, the community withered away during the seventeenth century. Eight children were baptized there in 1641, but only one in 1675–76. I would like to thank Philip Benedict for this information.

65. Even recently, Philip Hoffman, *Church and Community in the Diocese of Lyon, 1500–1789* (New Haven, 1984), p. 35, assumes that "the Counter Reformation may well have been imposed upon . . . the common people in the cities."

66. J. A. Sharpe, *Crime in Early Modern England, 1550–1750* (London, 1984), p. 150, has found this attitude across the channel.

of the Catholic Reformation.[67] The movement brought together the urban ecclesiastical and lay elites, both of which became more and more sure that a rigorous separation of the sacred from the profane would achieve the desired goal of discipline and reform. One way to accomplish this division was to implant new sacred institutions. New churches of new religious orders cropped up all over the cityscape of Dijon, bringing with them newcomers of pious zeal. The points of contact between craftsmen and articulated dogma increased during the ascendancy of the Holy League, when the Jesuits, Capuchins, and Minims appeared in Dijon; then the trickle became a flood in the seventeenth century, when the rest of the new orders arrived. By 1700, in addition to the seven parish churches, there were twenty-seven religious establishments, more than double the number there in 1550.[68]

The sharper separation of the sacred from the profane was one of the major aims of Trent, and the partition applied to both space and time. We have seen that artisans assigned location by reference to religious monuments—"next to St. Pierre church" or "as far as the street leading from the Chapellotte aux Riches" or "near the [monastery of the] Minims," and so forth. It is possible, of course, that they did so simply because these monuments were the most notable landmarks. Artisans also reckoned time according to the sacred demarcations of the liturgical calendar, though again, the festivals associated with most religious holidays, rather than the sacredness of the time, may have been what made them memorable. Still, there can be no mistake that the reformers stepped up their efforts to purify popular culture, and proximity to the establishments of the new orders and the emphasis on popular preaching that emerged in the late sixteenth century did have some effect. That many craftsmen revered the clergy is suggested by frequent testamentary bequests. The Capuchins, one of the most important new preaching orders with popular connections, and the Jesuits received many such bequests from artisans and their wives and widows, as did the older orders, the more venerable Dominicans, Franciscans, and Carmelites.

The judicial records contain much impressionistic evidence of

---

67. Robert Descimon, "La ligue à Paris (1585–1594): Une révision," *Annales: ESC* 37.1 (1982): 94.
68. See Gras, p. 136; and Roupnel, *La ville et la campagne*, p. 130.

sincere religious belief, but how it reflects the Catholic reform is difficult to say. Artisans seem to have attended church, and some of them evidently considered charity, that great "theological virtue" of the Catholic Reform, a reverent duty.[69] In 1643 the wife of a master roofer associated dishonor with irreligious behavior when she publicly denounced an adversary for having a "black soul." A month earlier master tailor François Truche had believed his honor engaged by shoemaker Bénigne Rebourg's public accusation that Truche had "mocked the holy sacrament" and asserted that the officiating priest was "a fine glutton in taking the holy communion."[70]

To the impression of piety given by these isolated examples can be added a more methodical, though unfortunately small inventory of religious images and icons (paintings and crucifixes were the most common) owned by artisans. In the fourteen extant after-death inventories of artisans or their widows between 1554 and 1590, only one mentions religious articles; in 1605 one of four does; and in 1645 four of nine do. Though the sample is small, it seems that seventeenth-century artisans, that is, those exposed to the Catholic Reform, may have been more likely to own religious objects.[71] Of the twenty pieces of iconography that could be identified from the seventeenth-century households, Christ was represented in four paintings and five crucifixes, more often than any other figure. It is not surprising to find so many images of Christ in view of the emphasis on Christ in the Catholic Reformation. Mary appears alone in one painting as well as in a Nativity and an Adoration of the Magi, evidence of the cult of the Virgin, which continued to gather steam in seventeenth-century Dijon. Among sixty-three wills of artisans or their wives or widows between 1583 and 1650, which appeared in my sampling of the notary contracts, the first direct plea for intercession from the Virgin came only in 1648, but four of the five wills that year and both wills from 1650 specifically invoked her aid.[72] Other images in the postmortem inventories depicted St. Ursula, St. Francis, St. Jean of the Apoc-

69. For example, ADCO, BII 360/59, 9 Sept. 1642, 360/60, 24 June 1643, 10 March 1643; A. N. Galpern, *The Religions of the People in Sixteenth-Century Champagne* (Cambridge, Mass., 1976), pp. 63–65 (on charity).

70. ADCO, BII 360/60, 6 Oct. 1643, 5 Sept. 1643.

71. Ibid., 356/6, 7, 16, and 20.

72. ADCO, *Notaires* #1934, 10 Feb., 16 June 1648, #1223, 1 Sept., 22 Dec. 1648, #1944, 26 April, 25 May 1650.

alypse, St. Bernard, St. Jerome, St. Anne, the Good Samaritan, and Hanging Judas.[73]

The Catholic Reformation also included a dedication to educating the popular classes. No devotional literature or any other kind of printed material is listed in postmortem inventories of craftsmen, but we know that some artisans attended school.[74] An analysis of literacy rates among artisans and their wives, since they are quantifiable, might be a more suggestive index to the penetration of education in their ranks. Using a sizable sample of witness depositions in the criminal dossiers, it is possible to determine literacy rates among artisans, their wives, and widows, by rating the ability to sign one's name according to a three-point scale: (1) no signature or a mark only, indicating complete illiteracy; (2) a signature that is crabbed or awkward, suggesting some exposure to reading and writing but not facility with them; and (3) smooth, unforced signatures, indicating fluency.

According to these criteria between 1560 and 1594, nearly half (46.1 percent, or 179) of the 388 artisans sampled were totally illiterate and somewhat fewer (43 percent, or 167) could read well. Between 1608 and 1643 only a third (32.2 percent, or 172 of 534) were illiterate, and almost three of five (56.9 percent, or 304) were fully fluent.[75] The coopers in particular posted a truly remarkable turnaround. In the sixteenth century they were among the least literate of all crafts. Eleven of sixteen, or 68.8 percent, could not read at all. By the seventeenth century, however, nineteen of thirty, or 63.3 percent, could write fluently. Staunch Catholics in the 1560s, perhaps their faithfulness encouraged literacy in the seventeenth century as the Catholic Reform began to show its effects. By the seventeenth century, of crafts with at least twelve representatives in the sample, only the masons were predominantly illiterate, indeed, still massively so. Eleven of twelve could not sign their names.

73. Ibid., BII 356/16, 20.

74. AMD, G88, Oct. 1621 (a glover), Jan. 1621 (a weaver); ADCO, BII 360/51, 10 Jan. 1586 (a painter). Unfortunately, the sources provide no information about what artisans read, and though literacy certainly made elite culture more accessible, we can draw no conclusions about how literacy affected the craft population's general outlook.

75. These samples include only male artisans. Since they are drawn from a random selection of depositions in the criminal archives, they may be skewed toward violence-prone areas. Still, every craft is represented, many of them quite frequently. It appears that male testimony was preferred or perhaps that most violence occurred in male-dominated space. The incidence of journeymen witnesses declines, no doubt because the number of citizen journeymen in the population was shrinking.

Journeymen, not surprisingly, were not as likely to be literate as were masters in the sixteenth century, but they closed the gap considerably as their ranks contracted in the seventeenth. Literacy among the masters remained nearly constant; 59.2 percent (61 of 103) could read and write in the sixteenth century, and 58.8 percent (230 of 391) in the seventeenth. The percentage of literate journeymen grew, however, from 37.2 percent (106 of 285) to 51.7 percent (74 of 143). As we would expect, wives and widows of artisans were less literate than their husbands, but illiteracy among them declined in the seventeenth century. Seventy-two of eighty were completely illiterate in the earlier period, and only five (6.3 percent) could read fluently. By the later period, fifty-eight of eighty-five (68.2 percent) still could not read at all, but sixteen (18.8 percent) could read well.

These figures, especially for journeymen and women, reveal some new exposure to education, and the Catholic church was the likely place in seventeenth-century Dijon to get it. Perhaps the women benefited from the establishment of the Ursulines in 1608. In his testament, master shoemaker Pierre Grandsire enjoined his wife to see to it that their son was taught how "to read and write in the catholic and apostolic faith." Evidently Grandsire perceived a connection between literacy and religion.[76] Though the evidence is circumstantial, it seems likely that in the sixteenth century literacy was related to Calvinism, and in the seventeenth it was related to Catholicism.[77]

Scholars have also been investigating how Tridentine Catholicism affected attitudes toward death. In the Middle Ages, as Lionel Rothkrug remarks,

> The Europe-wide pilgrimage expansion, the multiplication of indulgences, the proliferation of saints, and the prodigious rise of confraternities must all be seen as different parts of a single penitential system. It was calculated to enroll the dead in a vast net-

---

76. ADCO, *Notaires* #560, 14 Jan. 1593.

77. These findings mirror those of other studies. For example, at Paris, 1550–1650, Pierre Chaunu, *La mort à Paris: XVIe, XVIIe, XVIIIe siècles* (Paris, 1978), pp. 330–31, saw a "massive" increase in literacy throughout the population, though he notes that his sample probably overly represents the elite. Male literacy rose from barely half (52.5 percent) in 1551–1600 to 86 percent for 1601–1650, because of the Catholic Reform. On the link between Calvinism, craftsmen, and literacy, see my "Popular Religious Solidarity."

work of reciprocal services, the totality of which constituted both the cult of purgatory and . . . the entire church conceived as "the unity under and in Christ of the faithful on earth, the souls in Purgatory, and the blessed in Heaven."[78]

This "penitential system" naturally affected the religious attitudes of Dijon's artisans well beyond the Middle Ages.

The cult of purgatory, which the Middle Ages bequeathed to the sixteenth and seventeenth centuries, as A. N. Galpern tells us, on a more general level reflects the importance of the late medieval inheritance of prayer.[79] Artisans and their wives and widows expressed their concern for the souls in purgatory in testamentary endowments for masses to be said to speed the soul's journey toward paradise. In Dijon during the Catholic Reformation, these endowments increased; in a sample of testaments from Dijon, between 1583 and 1598 only six of twenty-nine artisan testators or their wives or widows endowed masses for their souls, but between 1600 and 1650 thirteen of thirty-four did, suggesting a resurgence of late medieval piety.

The corporate element, embracing both the living and the dead, had become especially pronounced in traditional Christianity since the fourteenth century and had fostered a mentality of collective responsibility and collective redemption. Though Trent deemphasized corporate ritual, the collective nature of traditional Christianity remained important to seventeenth-century artisans, who appropriated elements of reformed Catholicism that could be assimilated into a culture of solidary-minded craftsmen. Thus, among artisans, collective, though not necessarily corporate forms of piety appear to have overshadowed the individualistic elements emphasized in the articulated dogma of the upper-class reformers.

Artisans certainly participated in pilgrimages, though never as members of any particular craft. They marched in parish pilgrimages like the one led by the priests of St. Michel to the distant shrine of St. Claude, many days' journey away in southern Franche-Comté.[80] Per-

---

78. Lionel Rothkrug, "Popular Religion and Holy Shrines," in *Religion and the People, 800–1700*, ed. James Obelkevitch (Chapel Hill, 1979), p. 33.

79. Galpern, chap. 2. See also Jacques LeGoff, *The Birth of Purgatory*, trans. Arthur Goldhammer (Chicago, 1985).

80. Claude Courtépée, *Description générale et particulière du duché de Bourgogne*, 2d ed. (Dijon, 1847–48), p. 110.

haps the favorite pilgrimage of the Dijonnais was to the image of Notre Dame d'Etang, located just a few miles beyond the walls. Since its "discovery" in 1435 curative powers had been attributed to the image, and veneration surged late in the sixteenth century and into the seventeenth, as more and more pilgrims begged the Virgin's intercession to alleviate plague and dearth.[81] Benefiting from the Marian cult encouraged by the Catholic reformers, the shrine became a popular goal for pilgrims from "all parts" of France and in 1640 Urban VIII recognized its sanctity and sent relics of several important saints to be housed there.[82]

Since the efficacy of such acts of faith depended upon collective participation, pilgrimages to the shrine frequently included "the clergy, the mayor, the aldermen, and all the people," certainly including many artisans. In 1645 journeyman Sébastien LaBrunet remarked in a deposition that he had been to the shrine "par dévotion."[83] About fifty years before, in July 1592, to end a drought the entire community of believers in Dijon had made a procession to the image.[84] The solidarity encompassed in such acts is evidenced by a vigneron, who, questioned about the moral rectitude of a weaver who was being considered for mastership, said that he could vouch for him because they had made a "trip to Notre Dame d'Estang" together.[85]

The primacy accorded charity and fraternity in traditional, pre-Tridentine Christianity was endorsed at Trent, with the proviso that they be kept firmly under episcopal control.[86] Historians have long recognized that the close association of craft corporations and confraternities blurred the distinction between the sacred and the profane.[87] Both institutions originated in the cultural matrix of medieval society and incorporated the sense of the communal and corporate. Salvation was the primary concern for members of confraternities,

---

81. Bernard Javelle, *Histoire de Notre Dame d'Etang* (Dijon, 1869), pp. 41, 45, 70–71.
82. Ibid. pp. 47, 52–53.
83. ADCO, BII 360/60, 25 March 1645.
84. Garnier, *Le journal de Breunot . . . Pepin,* 1:92.
85. AMD, G88, Jan. 1621.
86. On pre-Tridentine charity and fraternity, see Bossy, *Christianity in the West,* chap. 4.
87. Gabriel LeBras, "Confréries chrétiennes: Problèmes et propositions," in *Etudes de sociologie religieuse,* 2 vols. (Paris, 1955–56), 2:437; Coornaert, *Les corporations en France,* pp. 13, 232.

but the institution also fulfilled social functions. Prayers were offered for all members, living and dead, and provisions for the sick and the poor and for funerals were usually finely articulated in the statutes of confraternities.[88] Many crafts had their own confraternities to provide these spiritual services, and they reinforced the corporate solidarity evident in some other areas of the craftsman's life, helping to transcend the conflicts endemic to daily life.[89]

Stipulations of mutual aid for living members and their wives and prayers for the souls of dead colleagues inevitably appear in documents establishing craft confraternities or in contracts with the clergy for performance of such functions. In 1560 the artisans of the confraternity of St. Honoré paid the Jacobins for services "for the . . . salvation of the souls of the said master pastrycooks and bakers as well as for all the brothers and sisters of the confraternity of the said St. Honoré, living and dead."[90] In 1594 the new confraternity of the pastrycooks (under the patronage of St. Louis) established a contract with the Carmelites to celebrate two low masses weekly for all present and future masters of their trade.[91] The corporate element is just as clear in a similar document pertaining to the locksmiths, who contracted for masses "in order to pray to God for the whole *corps* of the said trade, and for the salvation of the souls of their deceased predecessors as well as for those and their wives who will die hereafter."[92] Such expressions of solidarity were taken quite seriously. The jurés of the pastrycooks complained to the town council that one of their masters had refused to go pray at the funeral of the wife of another master pastrycook, thus violating an ancient custom incumbent upon all masters of the craft.[93] This recourse to civil authorities, by the way, underscores the conflation of the sacred and profane.

The corporate nature of craft confraternities is apparent, but they also provided spiritual and social bonds that transcended guilds. The bakers and pastrycooks shared a confraternity until 1594; the drapers, fullers, and dyers all belonged to the confraternity of St. Trinité,

88. LeBras, "les confréries," 2:443.

89. Ronald Weissman, *Ritual Brotherhood in Renaissance Florence* (New York, 1981), pp. 78–79, suggests such a function in fifteenth-century Florence.

90. ADCO, E3527, 1560.

91. ADCO, *Notaires*, #726, 8 Aug. 1594.

92. ADCO, E3537, 1651, and see E3538, 22 July 1632, a contract for masses for the confraternity of the tailors.

93. AMD, G62, 2 Aug. 1619.

while the sword polishers and cutlers shared that of St. Jean Baptiste.[94] In 1616 the master masons, carpenters, roofers, and plasterers, contending that their crafts depended upon "une mesme société," requested civil approval to establish a confraternity and to "solemnize the holy days of St. Joseph and of the Four Crowns," patrons of their crafts "from time immemorial." These masters vowed to set aside half their dues "to the profit of the poor of their said trades."[95] This spiritual crossing of craft boundaries further suggests the solidarity among artisans that existed beyond guild corporatism.

Membership in craft brotherhoods, unlike other confraternities, was required of all artisans who became masters. Although the records are vague, it seems that journeymen and apprentices also joined and paid dues, but they had nothing to do with administration.[96] Some French journeymen apparently had their own confraternities in the sixteenth century.[97] In Dijon, however, there is no clear archival reference to such brotherhoods before 1677.[98]

These spiritual brotherhoods attained solvency not only by assessing membership dues but also, like the joint confraternity of several textile crafts (St. Trinité), by owning real estate and collecting rents.[99] All members of craft confraternities were required to pay dues to the communal treasury for the candle kept perpetually burning in the brotherhood's chapel, for funerals for deceased members, and especially for the celebration of masses for the members' salvation.[100] Guild statutes and confraternal account books list amounts of dues, frequency of payment, and delinquent members.[101]

At confraternal assemblies guildsmen elected officers called *pro-*

94. A. Chapuis, *Les saints patrons et les armoires des corporations dijonnaises* (Dijon, n.d.), pp. 16–17; Chapuis, *Les anciennes corporations*, pp. 361, 367.

95. AMD, B253, fol. 237v–238r, 5 Feb. 1616.

96. For example, cloth cutter apprentices paid six gros in dues for candle wax for the chapel. Chapuis, *Les anciennes corporations*, p. 196, and on hosier apprentices, see p. 228. In ADCO, BII 360/51, 11 June 1586, there is evidence that a journeyman hatter attended a service in the craft confraternity of St. Jacques.

97. Martin Saint-Léon, *Le compagnonnage*, p. 39.

98. AMD, D26.

99. ADCO, E3531. Also Paul Labal, "Artisans dijonnais d'autrefois: Notes sur la vie des gens de métiers de 1430 à 1560," *Annales de Bourgogne* 23 (1951): 101.

100. For examples of candles, see AMD, B193, fol. 106r, 8 Nov. 1555; for examples of masses, see ADCO, E3537, E3538.

101. For example, ADCO, E3537. Philibert de Rochefort, a sword polisher, was accused and prosecuted for not paying dues to his confraternity each Sunday. AMD, B199, fol. 267r–v, 3 June 1562.

*cureurs,* who legally represented the organization and kept the books.[102] It is not clear if guild and confraternal leadership was conflated, for little is known about the internal governance of guilds. In any case, the principle of hierarchy existed alongside the right of election. For example, the master weavers awarded the honorific confraternal baton, a staff with the image of the patron saint attached to the end, carried by the *bâtonnier* at the head of confraternal processions, according to seniority.[103] Similarly, in the honor-mediated processions of the confraternities, usually performed on the day of the patron saint, the masters marched in the order of their reception to mastership.[104]

It is very difficult, given the paucity of the surviving sources, to determine the relative vitality of these brotherhoods over time. Many had been established in the fifteenth century, several in the first half of the seventeenth, and some were reestablished after 1600 (for example, that of the locksmiths).[105] A. N. Galpern has found a decline in the popularity of confraternities in Champagne in the middle of the sixteenth century, but the post-Tridentine clergy encouraged them as a means of promoting the moral rectitude of their flock.[106] Indeed, the concern for discipline, both moral and social, not just in the Church, but also among the civil authorities, is perhaps the most fruitful perspective from which to study Dijon's confraternities.

After Trent the reformers made concerted efforts to use confraternities, especially such purely devotional ones as the Rosary or the Holy Ghost, as forces of stability and moral and social order by increasing the extent of clerical control.[107] In 1604 a papal bull made the confraternities exclusively "ecclesiastical bodies," subject to episcopal approval, without which they were declared to have no salvatory efficacy and hence no spiritual function.[108] If testamentary bequests

102. AMD, B256, fol. 313r–v, June 1619. On equality, see LeBras, "Les confréries," 2: 442, 445.
103. AMD, B281, fol. 81r, 10 July 1643. On the baton, see E. Fyot, "Les confréries de corporations et leurs bâtons," *Bulletin du Syndicat d'Initiative de Dijon et de la Côte-d'Or* (Dec. 1934): 56–58.
104. Fyot, 56.
105. ADCO, E3537.
106. Galpern, esp. chap. 6.
107. Coornaert, p. 235; Bercé, *Fête et révolte,* pp. 73–76. On the Rosary and the Holy Ghost, see Gutton, *La sociabilité villageoise,* p. 229.
108. LeBras, "Les confréries," 2:451, 457.

to confraternities are a sign of institutional piety, so too is growing membership in them. The seventeenth century saw advances on both counts. In my sample of wills only the poor received more bequests than the confraternities, and membership in these brotherhoods grew dramatically.[109] The Confrérie des Trespasses had 49 active members in 1590, 70 in 1603, 97 in 1617, 154 in 1624, and 251 by 1629.[110] The Confrérie des Rois grew comparably, from 99 members in 1583 to 208 in 1606 (the last year before women were admitted) to 327 in 1618 (including 59 women) and 492 in 1650.[111] Members of these confraternities were drawn from all sectors of Dijon society, and certainly many were craftsmen, though we have no way of knowing the exact number.[112] Like increased literacy and possession of religious objects, the growing membership in confraternities suggests that the Catholic Reform was reaching the artisanat in the seventeenth century.

The reforming clerical and lay authorities concerned with moral discipline and public order had good reason to be concerned about confraternal celebrations. The blurring of the boundaries between the sacred and profane, characteristic of the artisan, led, according to the reformers, to sacrilegious abuses. Artisans celebrated festive occasions as one big family, with banquets and libations that brought in their train "pleasures of the flesh and violence."[113] The proponents of the new morality, both clerical and lay, were deeply offended by the gambling, drinking, dancing, sex, and violence that these celebrations entailed on ostensibly holy days. Yet "abuses" of holy days were so deeply engrained in the popular mentality that the Church was preoccupied with correcting such behavior, says Gabriel LeBras, "from the Carolingian age to the French Revolution."[114] Trent simply brought about a more thorough and systematic campaign.

109. In a sample of sixty-three artisan wills (ADCO, *Notaires*), there were sixty nonfamily bequests—eleven to noncraft *fabriques* and confraternities, eleven to clerical orders, nine to godchildren, nine to craft confraternities, and twenty to the poor, including charity to beggars at the funeral and memorial masses and to the poor of the Hôpital du Saint-Esprit.

110. ADCO, E3495.

111. Ibid., J2582/46, 47, 48. See also Jean Rigault, "L'ancienne confrérie des rois de St. Michel de Dijon," *Mémoires de l'Académie de Dijon* 117 (1969): 81–85.

112. Many but not all names on the documents carry occupational description. Thus a statistical count is impossible.

113. J. Duhr, "La confrérie dans la vie de l'église," *Revue d'Histoire Ecclésiastique* 35 (1939): 472.

114. LeBras, "Les confréries," 2:456.

Such bacchanalian celebrations greatly perturbed the authorities, especially after the conclusion of the Wars of Religion. In 1600 the town council issued the following proclamation, which is typical in its content and telling in its sweep:

> On the remonstrances made by the syndic . . . the confraternities . . . of the *arts et mestiers* . . . [were] introduced to honor God and the patron saints . . . with the intention of good works. . . . [However,] for some years, instead of the honor and glory of God and the said saints only things to the contrary have been produced. . . . Derisions and insolences like games of dice, *blanques, quilles,* cards, and banquets . . . [lead to] such blasphemy . . . and excessive expenses that God is greatly offended and irritated.

The syndic went on to rail against the artisans who, on their festival days, dressed up in fools' costumes, with bells on their toes and tambourines in hand, and made all sorts of racket at the portals of the churches and even came into the churches with their bells and baubles "disturbing and interrupting the service of God" (and violating sacred space with such profanities). They also danced shamelessly in public and draped girls with colored ribbons (*livrées*). In the eyes of the godly, this intolerable behavior could only provoke the wrath of God and lead to disorder in the streets.[115]

Similar proclamations against such "willful disorder of the people" (in the words of the syndic) were issued in 1604, 1607, and twice in 1615, each time specifically implicating the artisans for scandalous behavior.[116] These sweeping condemnations directly associated such behavior with festivals, evidently the focal points of artisan celebrations. These were opportunities for craftsmen (many undoubtedly masters, though since we do not know the extent of journeyman participation in confraternities we likewise know little of their role in these festivals) to honor their patron saints and, as Galpern suggests, the intensity with which such festivals were celebrated indicates the importance of saints in traditional popular Catholicism.[117] What the authorities saw as abuses were simply the profane aspects

---

115. AMD, B238, fol. 103r–104r, 1 Sept. 1600.

116. AMD, B242, fol. 45v–46r, 2 July 1604, B253, fol. 92v, 11 Aug. 1615 (which also refers to the proclamation of 1607), I4, 18 Aug. 1615.

117. Galpern, p. 47. It is noteworthy that the baptized infant was invariably named after the godparent, and thus saints' names were passed on through a ritual merging of spiritual and secular patronage and intercession. See Galpern, p. 43.

of celebrations that were also occasions for craftsmen to affirm their solidarity with their fellows, all of whom shared the protection of the same saint; the feasting accompanying the festivals is but another aspect of the commensality so important in the daily life of master artisans.[118]

In the sixteenth century the reformers began to demand purification of the festivals. There were isolated assaults on aspects of popular culture, especially dancing, gambling, and masquerading, all of which offended secular concerns for order and the new clerical notions of moral personal conduct.

Dancing in the streets or in private homes had often been prohibited by municipal authorities in times of plague to reduce the possibility of contagion.[119] From the point of view of the new morality, dancing was seen as an expression of idleness, anathema to the reformers.[120] Worse still, such intermingling of the sexes was "immodest" and insulting to God, especially when performed during divine service and accompanied by "lascivious, dissolute, shameless and dishonorable songs."[121]

Compounding these "vices," dancers and singers were often disguised (*masqué*), much to the consternation of the reformers.[122] Artisans were fond of donning masks for many an occasion, despite the ordinances that flowed from royal and municipal pens. The authorities associated the wearing of masks with theft and murder.[123] More generally, masking violated "public honesty," since it denied the axiom that one is what one appears, and led to "disobedience."[124] Religious sanctions against masks were related to the secular and supported them. They were based on the assumption that to disguise

118. Jacques Heers, *Fêtes, jeux et joutes dans les sociétés d'occident à la fin du moyen âge* (Paris, 1971), p. 86; see also Heers, "Les métiers et les fêtes 'mediévales' en France du nord et en Angleterre," *Revue du Nord* 55 (1973): 193–206.
119. For example, AMD, B192, fol. 302r, 14 May 1555, B202, fol. 42r, 2 Aug. 1565, B234, fol. 137v, 10 Dec. 1596.
120. AMD, B238, fol. 124r, 22 Sept. 1600. See also Burke, *Popular Culture*, p. 209.
121. AMD, B229, fol. 124r, 10 Dec. 1591, I3, 24 May 1565, B227, fol. 46r–v, 11 July 1589.
122. AMD, B208, fol. 159r, 2 March 1577, B230, fol. 202v, 15 Jan. 1593.
123. Jean Savaron, sieur de Villars, *Traité contre les masques* (Paris, 1608), p. 13, mentions royal ordinances against masking by Francis I in 1539, Charles IX in 1561, and Henri III in 1579 and 1580. For municipal legislation, see, for example, AMD, I3, 11 March 1578, B272, fol. 196v, 23 Jan. 1635, B275, fol. 199r. Lottin, *Chavatte*, p. 322, finds the municipal authorities in seventeenth-century Lille deplored such activities no less.
124. Savaron, pp. 3, 33.

oneself, to appear other than as God had created one, was contrary to nature and an affront to God. Moreover, because the masker was stepping outside the natural order, diabolical *passions désréglées* could be the only outcome.[125]

The wearing of masks among the upper classes may well have served as a ritual reinforcement of order, since its upside-down imagery defamiliarized and, so, supported the established order. For artisans, however, masking may have been a liberating, liminal experience (thus, more prevalent during festivals and celebrations demarcating time), an expression of antihierarchical feelings, which was all the more powerful in a culture where appearance marked social identity. To step outside the natural, hierarchical order for a time proclaims equality.[126] Furthermore, masquerading and cavorting in fool's garb during festivals, though they offended the reformers' sense of propriety, depict notions of piety among artisans quite different from those of the authorities. In many cultures, masks and loud noises (bells on toes, rattles in fool's baubles) are believed to ward off evil spirits, and they may have functioned this way in early modern artisan culture as well.[127]

Gambling was another aspect of popular culture condemned under the new morality. Again, secular authorities reinforced the clerical, for gaming often led to public disorder in addition to violating religious sanctions. Many of the fights that made their way into the judicial records originated over games. Anger over losing, accusations of cheating, or any number of other reasons could trigger a brawl, as Dijon's magistrates were well aware. Most prohibitions against gaming focused on the artisans, who were apparently captivated by games of chance and skill. As Johan Huizinga suggested long ago, "Play . . . creates order, *is* order. Into an imperfect world and into the confusion of life it brings a temporary, a limited perfection. Play demands order, absolute and supreme. The least deviation from it 'spoils the game,' robs it of its character and makes it worthless."[128] There is no doubt that artisans were punctilious about the rules—recall the bakers who

125. Savaron, p. 3; Thiers, *Traité des jeux*, pp. 315–37. Noirot, *L'origine des masques*, p. 128, says masking is prohibited only to "people of low condition," but the proclamations in Dijon applied to all classes. See, for example, AMD, B275, fol. 199r.

126. Turner, *Dramas, Fields and Metaphors*, p. 243

127. For example, Heers, *Fêtes, jeux et joutes*, p. 131; Rossiaud, "Fraternités de jeunesse," 77–78.

128. Johan Huizinga, *Homo Ludens: A Study of the Play Element in Culture* (Boston, 1955), p. 10

fought because one had illegally crossed the line while playing *quilles* and had thus "spoiled the game." Artisans were attracted to games partly because of their order-seeking mentality. It was an incidental paradox, though no less bothersome to the authorities, that such an inherently orderly activity as game playing generated conditions that led to disorder.

Cursing, game-playing craftsmen flouted clerical teachings condemning blasphemy; ignored sacred time by playing cards, *quilles*, *boules*, and dice during divine services or during Lent; and violated sacred space by playing their games in the cloisters of monasteries and the portals of churches.[129]

A multitude of examples could be presented to support the view that popular culture enjoyed the "vices" of dancing, gaming, singing, and masquerading, especially during festivals. The avalanche of condemnations by the clerical and secular authorities, accelerating during the century after Trent reveals how remarkably resilient popular culture proved. Because all these vices converged on festival days, it was here, especially after the Wars of Religion, that the reformers concentrated their proclamations, and until 1615 they singled out the confraternal celebrations of parishes and guilds as the chief culprits. To succeed in "purifying" these popular expressions, however, it would be necessary to shatter an entire world view, for in traditional popular culture the sacred was manifest in and through the profane.[130]

In April 1646 the town council issued a proclamation in response to

> the great scandals that are committed . . . during the festivals of the parishes and the guilds, publicly, in the squares and streets, which had for good reasons been prohibited and had ceased for several years but that have insensibly and disobediently been reestablished. . . . The council . . . [again] prohibits . . . all persons from celebrating publicly in the squares and streets any guild or parish festivals . . . [nor are they to be] accompanied by beating drums or gambling

129. For instance, AMD, I105, 25 June 1572, B200, fol. 152ff., 11 Feb. 1564, B203, fol. 30v, 3 July 1566, B200, fol. 30r, 20 July 1563, B237, fol. 96v, 26 Jan. 1600, B227, fol. 239r–v, 7 March 1590, B197, fol. 95r, 10 Nov. 1559. And see E. Champeaux, "Les cimetières et les marchés du vieux Dijon," *Mémoires de l'Académie de Dijon* (1905–6): 146.

130. R. W. Scribner, "Cosmic Order and Daily Life: Sacred and Secular in Pre-industrial German Society," in von Greyerz, p. 26.

dens. . . . [The only festival permitted] is during the evening before
and the day of the birthday of St. John the Baptist, during which
time there will be a fireworks display on the square of St. Jean
Church.[131]

In the 1630s and 1640s the town council continued to rail against
gamblers who anger God by shooting dice during divine service,
young men who commit "insolences and derisions" by running
around in masks and banging on drums, and maskers who commit
"disorders and scandals" during carnival, suggesting that not all urban dwellers were brought around.[132] But, with the one significant
exception from 1646, between 1615 and 1646 the authorities were no
longer singling out the master artisans as the miscreants. There is, in
fact, a note of surprise in the proclamation of 1646; the authorities
were perplexed by the artisans' return to such "disorder" after so
many years of good behavior. This is not to suggest that artisans quit
playing games, donning masks, dancing, and singing—the judicial
records leave no doubt that they still enjoyed these pastimes—but
evidently they were confining their play to times and places the authorities found less objectionable. This limited "purification" of the
artisanat should caution us against sweeping generalizations about
the penetration of the new Tridentine morality. In fact, artisan religious expression continued to embrace elements of traditional and
popular Christianity.[133] The meaning of discipline and order was culturally mediated.

In artisan mentality belief in the continuity between the living and
the dead had much to do with the prevalent sanctity of tradition and
the absence of rupture between the present and the past. For early
modern artisans, as for all of popular culture, the dead were, as Jean
Delumeau puts it, "a particular genre of living," with which the liv-

131. AMD, B283, fol. 222v, 27 April 1646.
132. Joseph Garnier, *Inventaires-sommaires* (Paris, 1867), 1:141; AMD, B272, fol.
196v, 23 Jan. 1635, B282, fol. 231r, 17 Feb. 1645.
133. "Popular religion" is an ambiguous and problematic term. Here I use it in the
sense of a widely shared belief or practice that is not explicitly sanctioned by the
established religion, though it need not be antagonistic to it. In fact, popular religion
comprises a curious blend of orthodox and non-Christian elements. Of course, there
are multiple levels of cultural belief; here I speak only of those of the artisans. For a
recent treatment of the theme, see E. William Monter, *Ritual, Myth and Magic in
Early Modern Europe* (Athens, Ohio, 1985), chap. 1.

ing must deal; and they continued in this "amortal" state as long as they remained in the collective memory of the family, the craft, or some other social group.[134] In the commonplace formula, the deceased might be referred to as, for instance, the "late Jean Petit, while alive a furrier"; such a phrase does not imply the abrupt cessation of the individual with death. Furthermore, that the honor of a dead man's name and reputation could be impugned and redressed in the courts is another indicator that the boundary between life and death was blurred.

In popular mentality there was a direct association between everpresent death and the ritualistic celebration of life. In one fascinating example, Marie Gaspard, wife of master currier Nicolas Boulard, requested in her testament that a requiem mass be said for her at the time of next year's rogations, thus melding rituals of death with those of fertility and life.[135] "Rites of life" like this were connected with various festivals, most notably in May but also during the solstices and equinoxes. The festival of St. John the Baptist near the summer solstice and the festival of *brandons* near the spring equinox (the first Sunday of Lent) were marked by bonfires in the streets (later co-opted by the authorities, who set off fireworks), perhaps demonstrating a symbolic link with the life-giving forces of the sun.[136]

The diachronic unity of life and death can be seen in the uses to which the Dijonnais put those spaces where death was in closest possible proximity—the cemeteries. Cemeteries in Dijon were attached to churches. Some dated back to Roman days. St. Philibert, for example, had been a Roman cemetery in the second century and continued to be a burial place until the eighteenth.[137] During the Middle Ages they had served as marketplaces. In the early modern period, they were used for certain public functions (the mayors were elected in the cemetery of St. Philibert), and were called, as one contemporary put it, "the most beautiful public places of Dijon."[138]

---

134. Delumeau, *La peur en occident*, pp. 112–13.

135. ADCO, *Notaires* #730, 18 Aug. 1585.

136. Examples of such celebrations in Dijon are AMD, B258, 30 April 1621 (prohibitions against May celebrations), B284, fol. 239v–240r, 8 March 1647 (on prohibitions of *brandons* celebrations). References to the fires of St. Jean, celebrating the birth of St. John the Baptist, around the time of the summer solstice, can be found in AMD, B283, fol. 222v, 27 April 1646.

137. Gras, p. 21.

138. Champeaux, pp. 144, 152, 162.

Dancing and gambling were frequent in these holy places.[139] Apparently artisans shared the belief in the continuity of time beyond an individual life-span, which is a key component of the elemental materialistic world view that Mikhail Bakhtin and, more recently Le Roy Ladurie, Carlo Ginzburg, and R. W. Scribner have found active in popular mentalities.[140]

This materialism can be seen in the artisans' concern for the fate of the body after death; craftsmen and their families were, in Pierre Chaunu's words, "viscerally sensitive" to the fate of the body as well as the salvation of the soul.[141] Cemeteries became a focus of conflict when Protestantism gained adherents in Dijon, but something more than confessional rivalry determined the ritualistic actions of the combatants. In the Catholic view, burial of the "heretics" in Catholic cemeteries would pollute the sacred space. A Protestant mason was buried in St. Pierre cemetery in 1560, but the next day "some women of honor and good Catholics" opened the tomb, put a rope around the neck of the corpse, and dragged it out, shouting "this Lutheran, this Huguenot, this dog does not deserve to be buried with good Christians!"[142] Honor was just as operable in religious disputes as in social ones. Despite truces and edicts of pacification, the civil authorities of Dijon used their police power to deny Protestants burial in consecrated ground, basing their decisions on advice from clerics and theologians.[143]

139. For example, AMD, B192, fol. 302r, 14 May 1555, B238, fol. 124r, 22 Sept. 1600, I4, 18 Aug. 1615; ADCO, BII 360/48, 5 Jan. 1568, 360/60, Oct. 1643.

140. Carlo Ginzburg, *The Cheese and the Worms*, trans. John Tedeschi and Anne Tedeschi (Baltimore, 1980), p. 69; Mikhail Bakhtin, *Rabelais and His World*, trans. Hélène Iswolsky (Cambridge, Mass., 1968), esp. chap. 6; Emmanuel Le Roy Ladurie, *Montaillou: The Promised Land of Error*, trans. Barbara Bray (New York, 1978), p. 134. See also Cassirer, *Philosophy of Symbolic Forms*, 2:37. Ginzburg and Le Roy Ladurie are speaking of rural culture, but this materialism apparently permeated urban popular mentality, too. Scribner, p. 24, places what he calls a "crypto-materialism" squarely in the center of a sacramental view of the world in which the sacred is "manifest in and through" the profane; indeed, it provides the point of reference by which the profane, or secular, world is ordered. He suggests that this world view was typical of "pre-industrial popular belief." Thus, the Catholic Reformation, by seeking to distinguish the sacred from the profane, had to destroy an entire world view to be effective.

141. Chaunu, p. 319.

142. Fromental, p. 18.

143. AMD, B206, fol. 157r, 21 April 1570. See also Belle, pp. 130–31; and AMD, B208, fol. 172r, 29 March 1577, in which doctors from the Cordeliers, Carmelites, and Jacobins advised that the Church would be offended if Protestants were buried in sacred ground.

It may seem surprising that Protestants wished to be buried in Catholic consecrated ground, but consider the Protestant goldsmith Bénigne Fèvre's request: he asked the town council to allow him to be buried in St. Jean cemetery with his ancestors.[144] This desire was not defined by Catholic or Protestant theology but rather by tradition. Since the Middle Ages, the choice of the sepulcher had appeared as a clause in testaments.[145] During the sixteenth and seventeenth centuries, artisan testators still wished to be buried with, and frequently "on," their deceased relatives.[146] Such a predilection reflects a mentality, bound to tradition as much as doctrine, a feeling of unity between the living and the dead, especially among those who had been closely bound during life.

The unity of the living and the dead was, as we have seen, also encouraged by the Catholic cult of Purgatory, which revived during the Catholic Reform. Masses, paid for by testators and celebrated by clerics, were intended to speed the soul through Purgatory or, as the formula usual in the testaments says, for "the salvation and repose of one's soul." Almost one-third (nineteen of sixty-three) of the testaments from artisan families (nearly all masters) between 1583 and 1650 contained provisions for at least one mass to be said for the testator's soul. The frequency of such foundations reflects a solidarity between those still living and the departed, implying scrupulous execution of the testator's wishes by the living.[147] And on this point theological and popular attitudes converged, uniting the living and the dead in a community and mitigating the disruption of death through ritual.

Testamentary bequests to the poor were also rituals laden with both religious and social symbolism. In twenty different artisan testaments, the anonymous poor were given varying amounts of cash; for example, the widow of a master carpenter bequeathed one sou to each of the thirteen "poor women who will be present at her funeral," and a master cooper bequeathed three livres to the poor of the Hôpital du Saint-Esprit.[148] Such gifts reveal attitudes to the poor that, in Gal-

144. AMD, B208, fol. 911–v, 30 June 1579.
145. R. Folz, "L'esprit religieux du testament bourguignon au moyen âge," *MSHD* (1955): 14.
146. For example, ADCO, *Notaires* #1704, 1 Oct. 1605, #2700, 26 Sept. 1616, #1941, 1627, #1937, 1632, #1223, 22 Dec. 1648.
147. Chaunu, p. 317.
148. ADCO, *Notaires* #1937, 1632, #1694, 27 Aug. 1613.

pern's words, "touch the quick" of religiosity in early modern France, for they pertain to the good work of charity, the "supreme theological virtue" of a religion that resisted Luther's doctrine of justification.[149] Just as important, such displays of charity proclaim social status, since largesse to the poor elevates the benefactor above the inferior recipients.[150] As we have seen, master artisans increasingly sought to distinguish themselves from the poor. It is not surprising, then, that bequests to the poor increased as well. Of twenty-nine artisan testaments from 1583 to 1598, only six left anything to the poor, but among thirty-four wills dated from 1600 to 1650, fourteen included such bequests.

Endowments for masses for the soul of the deceased also increased after 1600 (from 20.7 percent to 38.2 percent of the respective samples), evidence that the testator expected a collective responsibility to carry out the request. Such legacies also illustrate the quickening pace of Catholic reform, as do the bequests to religious orders, which increased from three of twenty-nine (10 percent) in the sixteenth century to eight of thirty-four (almost 25 percent) in the seventeenth. Indeed, clerics received more than just cash: Geneviève Chasteau, widow of a master butcher, left a hundred livres to her godson, Father Antoine Meschine, "for his studies" and another forty livres to Father Bernard Marguerey for "a new religious habit."[151] An intriguing detail, which further confirms the importance of spiritual kinship among artisan families, is visible in Chasteau's will: the high incidence of legacies for godchildren.

The emphasis upon the eternal in sixteenth- and seventeenth-century testaments suggests a resistance to accepting death as final.[152] Perhaps comparing the number of testators who composed their wills on their sickbed or deathbed to those who made them while in good health can illustrate attitudes about the fear of death.[153] Although the small sample makes any results tentative, forty-nine of sixty-

---

149. Galpern, pp. 29, 30; Bossy, *Christianity in the West*, pp. 59–62, and 143–49.

150. Galpern, p. 34. Wrightson and Levine, *Poverty and Piety*, have found strikingly similar developments in Terling, Essex (a rural parish), between 1580 and 1640. There, new standards of religious behavior and personal conduct were introduced by Puritan reformers while the community was polarizing in material terms; these new moral standards separated the poor from the prosperous, the latter including the artisans.

151. ADCO, *Notaires* #1223, 22 Dec. 1648.

152. Chaunu, p. 314.

153. Ibid., p. 372.

three testaments explicitly stated that the testator was sick, and four more were made by journeymen going to war or on the Tour de France.[154] Artisans, it seems, preferred to think about the grim reaper only when he stared them in the face.

It seems paradoxical that a materialistic mentality viewing death as a regenerative part of a natural cycle should show itself so averse to recognizing the inevitability of death. Yet the identification of death as part of a vital natural cycle does not preclude fear of it. Indeed, if that cycle is viewed as life affirming, then death becomes a particularly disturbing anomaly.

Participants in popular religions, Michel Vovelle has suggested, expect to find the deity immediately present in their personal lives.[155] This demand for palpable, concrete manifestations of the divine explains the importance of concrete symbols, ritual, and external acts in such systems of belief. The emphasis on the tangible, which is central to artisan mentality, extends itself to the religious dimension. The importance of outward forms of piety has long been recognized by historians of the religion practiced in the sixteenth and seventeenth centuries. Mastership letters, for instance, emphasize the *acts* of Catholicism (going to mass, taking communion) as proof of orthodox belief.[156] This attitude helps explain elite indignation over blasphemy, a serious moral offense until the late seventeenth century. Offenders, including many craftsmen, could expect the most severe punishment for repeated cursing, especially in the later sixteenth century.[157] In 1577 a blaspheming tavern keeper was condemned to

154. For the testament of a journeyman tanner embarking on the Tour de France, see ADCO, *Notaires* #1223, 1 Sept. 1648; for one by the son of a sword polisher going off to war, who wanted to dispose of his goods if he were killed in action, #1225, 7 Jan. 1625.

155. Michel Vovelle, "Religion populaire: Problèmes et méthodes," *Le Monde Alpin et Rhodanien* 5 (1977): 23.

156. On the emphasis on external forms, see, for example, Lottin, p. 277; and Richard Trexler, *Public Life in Renaissance Florence* (New York, 1981). For Dijon, see mastership letters in AMD, G83–89.

157. Among craftsmen, for example, Philibert de Rochefort, blacksmith, was a notorious blasphemer. ADCO, BII 360/48, 20 Sept. 1568, and see 360/47, May 1567, in which witnesses state that the defendant Jehan Roch, a baker, blasphemed in the course of a fight. The interrogators were quite concerned about such manifestations of irreligion and repeatedly goaded Roch to confess to blasphemy. Roch must have been aware of the gravity of the charge, for in the face of depositions of witnesses, he repeatedly denied it.

kneel, with his head and feet bare, a rope around his neck, and a
burning taper in his hand, to ask pardon from the Virgin, the Apos-
tles, the king, and justice before meeting his end at the stake.[158] The
blasphemies themselves reveal a concern for the concrete and tangible. In a typical example, an excited shoemaker commenced a slanderous diatribe against another with the invocation "By the death of
God, the head of God, the stomach of God," detailing a conception of
palpable divinity.[159]

Artisans, of course, had no monopoly on this emphasis on the outward, concrete forms of religious expression. The elites also evidenced
this attitude in their ceremonies. Artisans, for example, participated
in the major processions of the liturgical year, as well as the special
processions called by the authorities to beg divine intervention for
poor weather, famine, plague, or other "scourges of God."[160] Such
processions were forms of collective piety rich in symbolism of unity
and concord, especially the Corpus Christi procession, with its devo-
tion to the Eucharist and its emphasis on the solidarity of the Christian community as a whole. But if processions are symbols of piety
and unity, then disruptions of processions signify a symbolic repudia-
tion of such a view. Recall the solemn procession of the clerics of the
Church of Mary Magdalene, winding its way through the streets of
Dijon in 1584 when a journeyman tailor leaned out of a second-story
window and pitched a "fat live cat" (*gros chat vifz*) onto the head of
the cleric leading the procession. The journeyman was arrested and
questioned extensively about his religious beliefs. Did he "make confession of the Catholic religion or of the so-called Reformed religion?"
How long since he went to mass? Had he ever attended a Calvinist
*presche?* The journeyman, apparently savvy to such interrogations,
insisted that he was a Catholic and gratuitously added that, in fact,
the last thing his father told him when he left his home in Lorraine

158. ADCO, BII 360/51, 8 Feb. 1577. See also Garnier, *Le journal de Breunot . . .
Pepin*, 1:23. By the late seventeenth century blasphemy was no longer prosecuted as a
primary offense, and those convicted faced a mere fine. Bernard Savonnet, "Fluctuations économiques et évolution de la criminalité: L'exemple de Dijon à la fin du XVIIe
siècle," *Economie du Centre-est* 79 (1978): 96.

159. ADCO, BII 360/60, 8 Aug. 1643.

160. On artisan participation, see AMD, B199, fol. 265r, 1 June 1562. The examples
of processions are legion, and specific references would be tedious. See Olivier-Martin,
*L'organisation corporative*, p. 147.

was "My child, be on your guard from becoming a Huguenot. If I find out that you have become one, I will disown you."[161] As far as the authorities were concerned, such disruptions threatened both the faith and public order, but the incident also shows popular symbolism at work. If this journeyman actually was a Huguenot, his action expressed much. In one symbolic act he fractured Catholic solidarity and perfectly imitated the Reformation.

The importance of palpability in popular religious mentality is nowhere more clearly displayed than in belief in witchcraft.[162] The mental baggage of magical world views includes a belief that natural forces merely express demonic or divine will[163] and that human activity can manipulate these wills. Those who hold such views come to believe that anything is possible, and this mentality stamps not just the popular but much of elite culture as well in sixteenth- and seventeenth-century France. The phenomenon of witchcraft is a superior example of this world view at work.

It is impossible to give any significant representation of witchcraft cases in Dijon or Burgundy during the period. Between 1574 and 1589 forty cases came before the Tournelle in Dijon, but the identity of the victims and their fates are not known.[164] The arrets of the Parlement from 1612 to 1626 include fifty-six individuals accused of witchcraft, but none came from Dijon.[165] Several decades before there had been accusations of witchcraft within the walls. In an inventory of prisoners from 1592 and 1594, four women (including the wife of a roofer and two widows) were languishing in jail as suspected witches.[166]

Arrets, trials, and prisoner inventories tell us of official concern about witchcraft, but what about popular attitudes? Slanders relating to witchcraft such as "witch," "baby eater," or "werewolf," existed in artisan defamatory discourse, both master and nonmaster, in the late sixteenth and seventeenth centuries.[167] Our best evidence, however,

161. ADCO, BII 360/51, 22 July 1584.
162. The bibliography on witchcraft is immense, but most of the major works are mentioned in the bibliography of Joseph Klaits, *Servants of Satan: The Age of the Witch Hunts* (Bloomington, Ind., 1985).
163. See Cassirer, 2:49
164. Drouot, *Mayenne*, 1:59, n. 1.
165. Louis Ligeron, "La jurisprudence du parlement de Dijon en matière de sorcellerie au début du 17e siècle," *MSHD* 33 (1975–76): 281–89.
166. AMD, C38, 2 Jan. 1592; ADCO, BII 360/53, 12 July 1594.
167. For example, ADCO, BII 360/53, 21 Aug. 1594, 360/60, 27 Oct. 1643.

comes from the trial in 1608–1609 of Perrenette Chappuis, alias *la menusière* [*sic*], a poor, seventy-five-year-old widow of a cabinetmaker.[168] Her trial, complete with numerous depositions, confrontations, and interrogations of the accused, gives us, in the words of the people themselves, invaluable material concerning popular religious beliefs as well as elite preoccupations with Satan's minions.

The unfortunate Perrenette had been imprisoned twenty years before as a suspected Huguenot for avoiding Easter mass.[169] She was now accused of raising hailstorms and destroying crops, using charms, prophesying deaths, killing children by witchcraft, attending Sabbats, having the devil's mark, having conference with the devil at night in her bed, and even making the candles in the churches of the Jacobins and St. Michel burn upside down. The most serious allegation (supported by popular testimony) was that she had caused a young girl named Anthoinette Colin to be possessed by the devil.[170]

Perrenette's responses under interrogation are especially informative. When asked if she had caused Anthoinette to become possessed, she answered no, that Anthoinette was already possessed when she met her. Did she not give *un morceau* to the said possessed, "which caused her to fall into frenzy"? Yes, it was true that she brought to Anthoinette a small *pain béni* from St. Servais near Cologne.[171] Perrenette had recently returned from a pilgrimage to the German Rome to "adore the three kings . . . and thousand virgins." She added that this bread had "great power (*beaucoup de force*) because of the benediction that was on it."[172] She had lent her bodice to cure the afflicted girl because all of Perrenette's clothing had been blessed at St. Servais

168. The trial appears in ibid., 360/57, 18 July 1608–March 1609.

169. AMD, C38, 16 Aug. 1590.

170. The resultant public exorcism became a local cause célèbre. In his journal, the lawyer Sullot comments that the "evil spirit" (*malin esprit*) left the "poor girl's" body thanks to the grace of God, the conjurations of the bishop of Damas, and the prayers to God made by the "ecclesiastical and lay persons who were there." Durandeau, *Journal de Sullot*, pp. 87–88.

171. A popular proverb had it that "pieces of blessed bread" (*morceaux de pain béni*) could be taken to remedy *diverses maladies*. Jean-Baptiste Thiers, *Traité des superstitions*, 4 vols. (Paris, 1697), 1:376.

172. Hoffman, p. 56, points out that it was the custom for parishioners to share in a church a piece of blessed bread called *pain bénit*, in an unofficial parallel to communion. As the sacrament united the believers in Christ, so the former united the believers in the parish. Chappuis must have felt that community solidarity would be an effective weapon against evil spirits.

by touching the relics there. After months of litigation, the trial proved inconclusive; there is no record of conviction or acquittal, but Perrenette certainly survived, since she appears on the tax roll of 1610.[173] Her trial could hardly be more explicit in portraying a belief in the effective force of *acts* and *things* in Dijon's artisan milieu.

173. In his closing judgment the syndic dismissed the charge of raising winds and hailstorms as *superstitions ordinaires*, but the charges of charming and *sortilège*, he felt, were "great and very important," so much so that "it is necessary that proofs be *entières trèsmanifestes et apparantes*" and clearer than any this trial had uncovered. Consequently, the syndic ruled that he did not have the authority to deny Perrenette's appeal of the day before. We have no record of this appeal or of her sentence.

# Epilogue

During the century after 1550 Dijon underwent remarkable changes that would mark its development to the end of the old regime. Its population increased by nearly half, it evolved from a textile-producing city into an increasingly prosperous administrative, judicial, and commercial center. These changes profoundly affected the artisans of Burgundy's capital. More and more craftsmen abandoned the moribund textile industry and moved into the service-oriented crafts, which were buoyed by an increased demand from population growth. The collapse of textiles precluded the proletarianization of many of Dijon's artisans, who avoided producing for nonlocal markets. They retained their economic independence because Dijon's merchants were preoccupied with the lucrative Burgundian wine and grain trade. These developments, of course, were beyond artisan control, but the artisan response to them displays cultural consensus. Motivated by economic gain but guided by a precapitalist psychology (they made no conscious effort to expand production), the master craftsmen of most guilds deliberately regulated their numbers by restricting admission to mastership. As a result, the artisan population in Dijon remained roughly constant, and demand for craft products outpaced their supply. So for most master artisans the pieces of the local pie got bigger. Dijon's master artisans prospered, making their greatest gains after the Wars of Religion.

Artisan prosperity mirrored that of the town. The median percentile of artisans among Dijon's taxpayers remained around 57, with more and more clustering in the middle range and escaping the poorest categories as the masters closed ranks. The cohesiveness among masters is displayed most dramatically in female endogamy rates, which hovered at over 75 percent, though, significantly, intraguild marriages were relatively infrequent.

The closing of ranks among master artisans was also revealed in a growing parochialism. Artisans increasingly identified themselves as propertied townsmen. Certainly the huge increase in urban investment and rural divestiture in the first half of the seventeenth century reflects such an attitude. Similarly, intramural geographic endogamy within the master ranks was important and increased in the first half of the seventeenth century, though the choice of journeymen permitted to enter the masters' circle through marriage was determined by sufficient funds rather than place of birth. More and more, accession to mastership was reserved for Dijonnais masters' sons and a few relatively well off outsiders. There thus developed a core of masters and selected journeymen surrounded by an envelope of journeymen who would toil perpetually as hired workers. The success of this exclusionary policy of the masters is evident in the decline in the number of artisan immigrants settling (or at least marrying) in Dijon.

Only occasionally has it been possible to distinguish the position of journeymen (and even less often women) in the craft world. As aspiring masters themselves (however illusory the hope), journeymen must have shared many of the values of the master craftsmen, and so in the realm of mentality perhaps it would be pointless to attempt to make fine distinctions between masters and journeymen. Concerning the relationships of master and journeyman to production and the labor market, the distinctions are much clearer. Journeymen did not own the means of production (except their tools), nor did they control the product of their labor; rather, they sold their skilled labor to guild masters in exchange for a wage and often room and board. Because masters blocked the accession to mastership for all but a few at a time when demand for skilled labor was increasing, many journeymen began to recognize the advantages in controlling the labor market. They defined their interests in opposition to those of the masters and began a struggle for control which would continue for centuries. Of course, worker solidarity did not spring up over night, but journeymen of several crafts did organize job placement institutions called compagnnonages to challenge the authority of the masters directly. True, journeymen certainly give no indication that they wished to abolish mastership altogether; so, even though they preceded the masters in attempting to control the labor supply, they were not as cohesive outside the craft as the masters were in other, noneconomic forms of solidarity. After all, journeyman and master relations were still framed in legal and customary traditions of paternalism and filial obedience. Aspiring but frustrated journeymen must have felt contrary ties to master and fellow journeyman.

Cultural solidarity among master artisans was a powerful force, but it would be misleading to ignore the discord that marred their relations. Competition for a labor supply limited largely by the masters' own exclusionary policy certainly created conflict within the guilds. Occasionally there was also strife between guilds when one craft encroached upon another's monopoly, but again, such competition was partly a consequence of policies that reduced supply at a time of increasing demand, creating a vacuum that sucked in illicit producers (most of whom, by the way, were not other masters).

The paradoxical coexistence of solidarity alongside conflict is evident in the craftsmen's mental as well as material world; indeed, the two are inseparable. On the one hand, master artisan mentality was marked by a desire for order and stability, which informed artisan social networks of loyalty and allegiance, binding together kin, craft, and neighborhood. The artisan's small-scale world was anchored in the neighborhood and intensely public. Solidarities were publicly and collectively defined and were enforced by a pervasive code of honor, which visited humiliation and ridicule upon the transgressor of established behavioral norms.

Craftsmen wrangled among themselves, frequently in contests of honor, which mediated so many of their relations, from commercial to marital. In fact, honorific disputes usually pertained in some way to female sexuality and male control of it. Again, the master artisans reaped the product of their strategy to control guild membership. The tightening of the marriage market in the absence of master grooms placed a premium on daughters' reputations and inflated dowries. No doubt, competition between artisan fathers encouraged acrimonious defamation of the competitor's daughter to elevate one's own.

Still, despite such competition, artisans played by the same rules, and so from an internal perspective, artisan culture appears cohesive because it was forged in the crucible of shared social experience and at times by perceptions of common interest. But what about the master craftsman's relations with the rest of society? What place did artisans occupy in the shifting constellation of power relations? We must avoid the trap of ascribing a naïve voluntarism to artisan actions. True, they followed their interests, but since artisans had no premeditated system guiding their actions, there was ample room for ambiguity of interest and outright contradiction. Dijon's master artisans were not as powerless as slaves in the American South, for example, but like them they existed in a complex situation of accommodation with and resistance to their social superiors.[1] Paradoxically, artisans fashioned a vital subordinate culture, which simultaneously served and subverted the dominant culture. When they identifed with the interests of the dominant classes, craftsmen did so for sound reasons. Their official voice was corporate, for the legal language of the day was written in the corportate idiom. Artisans addressed the authorities through the corporation because it was the only way legally sanctioned to defend their interests before the law and to ensure journeyman subordination. But corporatism does not preclude the parallel existence of a solidarity that transcended guild boundaries. It merely demonstrates that craftsmen borrowed from the elite ethos to serve their own interests and that they supported the established order when it suited them. Similarly, the new morality of discipline preached by the lay and clerical reformers increasingly struck a chord pleasing to master artisan ears, but the tune played was not always the same as the one heard. The meaning of the Tridentine message, no less than the corporate idiom or the discourse of the street, was culturally mediated and derived from the situations of lived experience.

Advancing their interests while dealing with inherited situations could bring artisans into conflict as much as ostensible compliance with the authorities. When the governing classes competed among themselves (notably over jurisdictions), the masters were not averse to trying to manipulate the situation to better their own position. They had no apparent interest in the extension of royal authority in the provinces, but because they opposed municipal regulation of their

---

1. See Eugene Genovese, *Roll, Jordan, Roll: The World the Slaves Made* (New York, 1976).

activities (especially admission to mastership), they played the various royal authorities off against the municipal, at one point even filing a "class-action" suit with the king to defend their collective interests.

In the constellation of power relations, then, master artisans were in the middle, standing between the competing public authorities and even between the rebels and the authorities during the revolt of Lanturelu. They were in the middle of the social hierarchy and of the economic scale of wealth distribution, as well, and they also found themselves lodged between the new morality of the godly, with its emphasis on discipline, and the older beliefs of traditional culture. Artisan culture was partly transformed, but the process involved appropriation as much as domination or resistance. Though the culture of the artisanat maintained recognizable characteristics, it shaded off into other popular cultures at one end and into elite cultures at the other.

Because master craftsmen clustered so close to the middle and possessed their own recognizable cultural characteristics, it is tempting to speak of a nascent class. So controversial is this term in the context of old regime France, however, that, if we are to be justified in using it, a definition as well as a brief look ahead at the eighteenth century is warranted. According to Anthony Giddens, Marx and Weber considered ownership of property "the most important basis of class division in a competitive market."[2] To be sure, competition and the distribution of property are important components, but more recent social theorists and historians have pushed for broader, more flexible definitions. Some have argued that classes are cultural constructions, products of lived experiences. E. P. Thompson suggests that "people find themselves in a society structured in determined ways (crucially, but not exclusively, in productive relations), they experience exploitation (or the need to maintain power over those whom they exploit), they identify points of antagonistic interest, they commence to struggle around these issues and in the process of struggling, they discover themselves as classes, they come to know this discovery as class-consciousness."[3] Thompson, of course, is addressing eighteenth-century England, but the ideas are perhaps more gen-

2. Anthony Giddens, *Capitalism and Modern Social Theory* (Cambridge, 1971), p. 164.
3. E. P. Thompson, "18th-Century English Society: Class Struggle without Class?" *Journal of Social History* 3 (1978): 149.

eral. They seem to apply to the master artisans of sixteenth- and seventeenth-century Dijon. Like Antonio Gramsci, Pierre Bourdieu, and many of a new generation of American social historians, Thompson considers the concept of class as the totality of cultural relations that subsume the material and the mental; he merges economic with social and power relations.[4] This concept of class bases the existence of classes in the experience of the agents. As Bourdieu recently put it, social classes emerge from the distribution of material property, on the one hand, and, on the other, from the classifications and representations produced by the agents from practical knowledge, the product of a structured system of schemas of perception (habitus) employed symbolically to make sense of the world, which classify society while providing people categories of identity. These two notions—the distribution of property within society and the schemas of perception— are inseparable, and mutually supportive. That is, the second is the product of but also reproduces the first. Classes, according to this interpretation, emerge in relational (between people and goods) and arbitrary systems and are demonstrated by symbols of distinction which classify the unequal distribution of goods and are expressed in sometimes shared, sometimes distinct cultural languages. Such systems are usually deemed "natural" by those who inherit dominant positions, but they may also be endorsed by those (like our master craftsmen) who find some of their interests satisfied by the existing system. Symbolic distinction, so important to Dijon's honor-conscious master artisans, reinforced the distribution of goods in the same way force and violence would, but provided a way for society to sidestep, to sublimate, the disorder it found abhorrent.[5] If this definition of *class* is acceptable, there is no reason it cannot be applied to old regime France or specifically to the master artisanat of sixteenth- and seventeenth-century Dijon.

To speak of nascent class—unless it is stillborn—implies develop-

---

4. See, for example, Sean Wilentz, *Chants Democratic* (New York, 1984). On the impact upon American historians of Gramsci's ideas on class, domination, and hegemony, see T. J. Jackson Lears, "The Concept of Cultural Hegemony: Problems and Possibilities," *American Historical Review* 90 (June 1985): 567–93. On Gramsci's political and cultural theory, see Walter Adamson, *Hegemony and Revolution* (Berkeley, 1980).

5. Pierre Bourdieu, "Capital symbolique et classes sociales," *Arc* 72 (1978): 13–19, and, more fully, *Outline of a Theory of Practice*, trans. Richard Nice (Cambridge, 1977).

ment. We might conclude by glancing ahead to the eighteenth century to see what happened to the master craftsmen of Dijon.[6] After 1643 Dijon's overall population continued to grow (according to the tax rolls of 1750, by 16 percent) but the growth of the elite, consuming classes—mercantile, legal, administrative, fiscal, judicial, ecclesiastic—was even more pronounced. Dijon continued to develop as an administrative, judicial, and commercial center along the lines laid out since the sixteenth century.[7] This development, of course, continued to bring wealth into the city, and spending by the affluent classes contributed to the transformation of the division of labor of the artisanat. As protoindustry in textiles took hold in the countryside, the city artisans continued to provide services and products oriented to local demand—especially in the luxury and building trades.

Between 1643 and 1750 the size of the artisanat represented on the tax rolls increased by 63 percent, a slightly misleading figure because by 1750 many more single females and journeymen were heading craft households. Male artisans (the tax rolls continued to conflate masters and journeymen) increased by 36 percent, and many, perhaps most, of those must have been journeymen. In a study of the Dijonnais guild community based on letters of mastership and the tax rolls during the eighteenth century, Edward Shepherd has found that from 1700 to 1790 the number of masters in each guild remained roughly constant.[8] In terms of wealth, since the guild continued to be the dominant mode of production, there was still no great accumulation and investment of capital, but it does appear that the masters continued to prosper. In fact, on the tax rolls of 1750, the top quartile of tax distribution comprises more artisans than ever before, and though there were also more artisans in the bottom quartile, they were disproportionately women and probably journeymen.

6. Elsewhere I have explored the occupational and economic transformation of Dijon's artisanat between 1450 and 1750. See my "Dijon, 1450–1750."

7. On Dijon as regional commercial hub, see Pierre de Saint Jacob, *Les paysans de la Bourgogne du nord au dernier siècle de l'ancien régime* (Paris, 1960), pp. 257, 305; Roupnel, *La ville et la campagne*, p. 112; Richard Gascon, "La France du mouvement," in *Histoire économique et sociale de la France*, ed. Fernand Braudel and Ernest Labrousse (Paris, 1977), 1:384–85.

8. Edward J. Shepherd, Jr., "Social and Geographic Mobility of the Eighteenth-Century Guild Artisan: An Analysis of Guild Receptions," in Kaplan and Koepp, p. 114.

On the face of it, it appears that trends begun centuries before continued into the eighteenth century. Shepherd, however, has discovered that by the eighteenth century guild mastership was much more open to immigrant journeymen than I found to be the case in the sixteenth and seventeenth centuries. Nevertheless, the low number of masters in the guilds may mean that masters were still restricting membership. At the present stage of research, it is impossible to put all of the pieces of this puzzle together. From the sources he has employed, Shepherd has not been able to study how long the journeymen permitted entry to mastership had been in town or how many were perpetually excluded or emigrated. In other parts of France at least, Cynthia Truant and Michael Sonenscher have found that a core/envelope situation continued into the eighteenth century.[9] In Dijon, too, this is likely to have been the case. Truant argues that most journeymen had no chance of reaching mastership, and Sonenscher finds a fiction of intimacy in the workshop disguising opposition between masters and journeymen. Until we know how many journeymen were *excluded* from the charmed circle in Dijon (the tax rolls certainly suggest there were many), it is difficult to assess how open Dijon's guilds were. Shepherd has found that relatively few sons of masters followed their father's occupation, and so it is highly plausible, as he speculates, that prosperity of artisan fathers permitted upward occupational mobility for their sons, thus creating an increased demand for immigrant journeymen in the craft ranks.[10]

These developments do not seriously undercut my argument for cultural cohesiveness and nascent class formation, and there are other developments that seem to support it. Shepherd has found that by the eighteenth century multiple guild membership was permitted in Dijon, something absolutely forbidden before 1650.[11] Apparently neither the civil magistrates nor the guildsmen made any effort to stop this development. He suggests that "where there was a significant overlapping of production and materials, the inevitable and interminable disputes that arose between guilds over monopoly and jurisdic-

---

9. Cynthia M. Truant, "Independent and Insolent: Journeymen and Their 'Rites' in the Old Regime Workplace," in Kaplan and Koepp, pp. 131–75; and Michael Sonenscher, "Journeymen's Migrations and Workshop Organization in Eighteenth-Century France," ibid., pp. 74–96.

10. Shepherd, pp. 118–19.

11. See AMD, B198, fol. 60v–61r, 15 Oct. 1560; ADCO, BII 360/51, 18 July 1577.

tion could be avoided or resolved by multiple guild memberships"
and adds, "Financial and economic interests seem to have been
stronger than corporate ideology in the realities of the guild community."[12] Of course, this has been a central argument of my book. It
appears that, though the corporate idiom remains the legal language
and the basis of the *public* persona of the master craftsman, interests
that transcended guild boundaries were powerfully at work within
the master artisan culture, interests that had begun to knit master
craftsmen into a class.

12. Shepherd, pp. 115–16.

# APPENDIX
# Estimation of Total Population of Dijon

It has been reliably argued that Dijon's ecclesiastical population, buoyed by the growth in religious orders stimulated by the Catholic Reformation, probably numbered about 850 in 1643, but only about 500 in 1556.[1] As for in-house servants, Dijon, the seat of four sovereign courts, had a wealthy and growing elite in its *noblesse de robe*. We know that 148 Dijonnais households were tax exempt in 1556, and this number grew steadily to 426 by 1643.[2] This increase translated into a growing demand for domestic service, which apparently was met.[3] Richard Gascon suggests that the mercantile elites of Lyons retained five to ten servants per household in the sixteenth

1. Roupnel, *La ville et la campagne*, p. 134. Roupnel tells us that only three of thirty-four religious establishments existing in Dijon in 1700 were founded after 1650: the Convent of the Refuge in 1653, the seminary in 1669, and the Lazarists in 1682. The Ursulines were established 1608, and the Jacobines 1610. The Oratorians were established in 1621, the nuns of the Visitation and the Bernardines 1623, and the Sisters of Ste. Marthe 1628.

2. In 1579 there were 186 tax-exempt inhabitants, and in 1610, 294. These figures, unlike those of 1556 and 1643, are based upon projections from a sampling of every other name on the tax rolls of 1579 and 1610.

3. Of 429 artisans or their sons marrying in Dijon between 1551 and 1600, 28 wedded servant girls. Between 1601 and 1650, 53 of 440 did, suggesting an increase in the number of servants in Dijon.

century.[4] Even if we estimate only two per household, however, the tax-exempt inhabitants of Dijon would have employed almost 300 domestics in 1556 and over 850 by 1643. No doubt they were not the only ones to retain servants. Because Dijon was a town of increasing wealth and a burgeoning legal establishment, it would not be unreasonable to assume that the wealthiest 25 percent of the tax-paying Dijonnais also retained a servant.[5] It would be realistic, then, to estimate almost a thousand servants in Dijon in 1556 and almost eighteen hundred by 1643.

To determine how many journeymen lived with their masters, it is necessary to know how many of the artisans appearing on the tax rolls were masters. Unfortunately, though the tax rolls generally tell us the occupations of the inhabitants, they do not specify whether craftsmen were masters or not. To overcome this difficulty, I have drawn names from sources sensitive to honorific epithets, such as marriage contracts, real estate transactions, town council deliberations, and court records, and cross-referenced them to the tax rolls. This procedure allows me to project that masters probably outnumbered journeymen on the tax rolls of 1556 by at least three to one and perhaps by as much as five to one. Of the 84 names of masters gathered from sources dated between 1550 and 1563, 62 (73.8 percent) matched on the tax rolls, while only 40 of 151 names of journeymen (26.5 percent) did. This rough ratio of three to one assumes that no epithets would change during this time span, but of course, some journeymen would have become masters between 1550 and 1556, and the tax rolls would not reveal this fact. Also, journeymen coming to Dijon after 1556 would further skew the results, since they would appear in the outside source but not at all on the rolls.

To clarify this situation and also to determine a maximum ratio of masters to journeymen on the tax rolls, I compared the cross-referenced percentage of journeymen drawn from outside sources dated 1557–1563 with masters from outside sources dated 1550–1556. We

4. Gascon, *Le grand commerce*, p. 344.

5. In 1556, 25 percent of the tax-paying populace would be 668; in 1643, 913. Le Roy Ladurie (*Carnival in Romans*, p. 4) has found that 13.6 percent of the households of Romans had live-in help in 1586. As the regional capital and seat of several sovereign courts, Dijon no doubt was a wealthier place. For a stimulating study on servants in eighteenth-century France, see Sarah C. Maza, *Servants and Masters in Eighteenth-Century France: The Uses of Loyalty* (Princeton, 1983).

know that thirteen of these seventy-nine journeymen (16.5 percent) were journeymen in 1556, since they appeared on the tax rolls. They represent a minimum percentage. Similarly, we know that forty-six of fifty-six masters from outside sources (82.1 percent) appeared as masters on the tax rolls. The ratio between these percentages is about five masters to one journeyman. Therefore, it seems that 75 to 83 percent of the artisans on the tax rolls were masters in 1556. In 1643 the ranges were much wider, from a ratio of roughly two to one (132 of 300 masters, or 44 percent, from outside sources dated 1638–1650 matched the tax rolls, while 27 of 111, or 24.3 percent of the journeymen did) to about six to one (99 of 172, or 57.6 percent, of masters from sources dated 1638–1643 matched the rolls, while only 3 of 34, or 8.8 percent, of the journeymen from documents dated 1644–1650 did). Thus, in 1643 at least two-thirds of the artisans on the tax rolls were masters, and perhaps as many as six of seven were.

My selection of names from outside sources was random. Since there was no control of the universe of the outside sources besides chronological constraints, absolute figures are not helpful in establishing ratios of masters to journeymen. But the percentage of cross-referenced matches of masters and of journeymen in outside source and tax rolls reflects the relative likelihood of master or journeyman to appear on the tax rolls. Therefore, a comparison of percentages of correlation of masters and journeymen yields a ratio that should reflect relative incidence of masters and journeymen on the tax rolls. In fact, I have assumed that the ratios of the relative percentages suggest a basis for projection. The outside sources were likely to gather substantial numbers of both masters and journeymen into the net, and indeed, the cross-referenced names mirror fairly closely the occupational and economic profile displayed for all artisans on the tax rolls. The leather, food, and construction trades lead the way in both periods, with the luxury trades bringing up the rear. Further, the average tax of the 102 cross-referenced masters and journeymen in 1556 was 12 sous (slightly higher than the average for all male artisans at 8.3 sous), and in 1643 the average for 156 masters and journeymen was 56.4 sous, again, only slightly higher than the male artisanat as a whole (50.5 sous). The similar profiles also justify assuming that the tax rolls as a whole are reasonably accurate in order of magnitude.

Thus, it is fair to assume that roughly three-fourths of the artisans on the tax rolls were masters. How many of these kept journeymen?

Hugues Sambin, an artisan of prodigious talent and wide fame, together with his father-in-law, retained eight journeymen in 1557.[6] It would probably be misleading to consider Sambin's crowded workshop typical, but it would not be an overestimate to assume that there were half as many live-in journeymen as masters in Dijon. Most artisans possessed moderate to substantial wealth, and so it was certainly within their means to retain at least one journeyman and frequently more. Since they would more than offset the poorer masters who could not afford another mouth to feed, a two-to-one ratio of masters to live-in journeymen would appear a bare minimum, and quite likely a low estimate.[7] Thus, in 1556 there would have been about 350 journeymen in Dijon who did not appear on the rolls (since there were 950 artisan households, three-fourths probably masters), and perhaps a similar number by 1643. The number of apprentices is insignificant for these global estimates, since apprentices were mostly local boys and would have been counted as children in another nuclear family.[8]

Finally, using 4.5 as the most probable coefficient of mouths per average early modern urban nuclear household, in 1556 12,700 people would have resided at 2,822 hearths, and in 1643, 18,400 at 4,081.[9] Adding all my estimates together, I have concluded that the total population of Dijon in 1556 likely approached at least 14,500. By 1643 it had burgeoned to perhaps more than 21,000.

6. Chapuis, *Les anciennes corporations*, p. 464.

7. The criminal records provide hints of corroboration. Whenever an incident that occurred in a shop is recounted by a witness, there is frequently a journeyman who lives on the premises on hand as witness. Similarly, the civil authorities often admonished masters to enforce their paternalistic control over their journeymen, implying that they lived under the masters' roof.

8. The register of the goldsmiths (ADCO, E3432) reveals that only fifty-one boys were apprenticed to master goldsmiths between 1568 and 1645. In Geneva, a larger town than Dijon during our period, between 1550 and 1603 only 250 apprentices were placed in trades that were also represented in Dijon. Maurice Garden, *Lyon et les lyonnais*, p. 191, observes that only a small number of apprentices were engaged each year in Lyonnais workshops in the eighteenth century. On English apprentices in seventeenth-century England, see Steven R. Smith, "The London Apprentices as Seventeenth-century Adolescents," *Past and Present* 61 (1973): 94–161.

9. Le Roy Ladurie, *Carnival in Romans*, p. 5, accepts this coefficient, as does Gascon, *Le grand commerce*, p. 345. Couturier, *Recherches sur les structures sociales*, p. 117, states that the coefficient varied from day laborers (3.56) to merchants (4.28) in Châteaudun in 1765; however, by that date, the age of widespread contraception had begun, and household sizes were likely to be smaller than in early modern Dijon. For a discussion of the historiographical controversy on coefficients, see Flandrin, *Families in Former Times*, pp. 53–65.

# Bibliography

Aclocque, Geneviève. *Les corporations, l'industrie et le commerce à Chartres du XIe siècle à la révolution.* Paris, 1917.

Adamson, Walter. *Hegemony and Revolution.* Berkeley, 1980.

Agulhon, Maurice. "La sociabilité, la sociologie, et l'histoire." *Arc* 65 (1976): 76–84.

Anglo, Sydney, ed. *The Damned Art.* London, 1977.

Ariès, Philippe. *The Hour of Our Death.* Trans. Helen Weaver. New York, 1982.

Bakhtin, Mikhail. *Rabelais and His World.* Trans. Hélène Iswolsky. Cambridge, Mass., 1968.

Baroja, Julio Caro. "Honor and Shame: A Historical Account of Several Conflicts." In *Honor and Shame: The Values of a Mediterranean Society.* Ed. J. G. Peristiany. London, 1965.

Bart, Jean. "L'égalité entre héritiers dans la région dijonnaise à la fin de l'ancien régime et sous la révolution." *MSHD* 29 (1968–69): 65–78.

———. *Recherches sur l'histoire des successions 'ab intestat' dans le droit du duché de Bourgogne du XIIIe à la fin du XVIe siècle.* Paris, 1966.

Baulant, Micheline. "Le salaire des ouvriers du bâtiment à Paris de 1400 à 1726." *Annales: ESC* 26.2 (1971): 463–83.

Baulant, Micheline, and Jean Meuvret. *Prix des céréales extraits de la mercuriale de Paris (1520–1698).* 2 vols. Paris, 1962.

Bayard, Jean-Pierre. *Le compagnonnage en France.* Paris, 1977.

Beik, William. *Absolutism and Society in Seventeenth-Century France: State Power and Provincial Aristocracy in Languedoc.* Cambridge, 1985.

———. "Magistrates and Popular Uprisings in France before the Fronde: The Case of Toulouse." *Journal of Modern History* 46 (1974): 585–608.

Bell, Rudolph M. *Fate and Honor, Family and Village: Demographic and Cultural Change in Rural Italy since 1800.* Chicago, 1980.

Belle, Edmond. *La réforme à Dijon des origines à la fin de la lieutenance générale de Gaspard de Saulx-Tavanes (1530–1570).* Dijon, 1911.

Benedict, Philip. "The Catholic Response to Protestantism: Church Activity and Popular Piety in Rouen, 1560–1600." In *Religion and the People, 800–1700.* Ed. James Obelkevitch. Chapel Hill, 1979.

——. "Catholics and Huguenots in 16th-Century Rouen: The Demographic Effects of the Religious Wars." *French Historical Studies* 9 (1975): 209–34.

——. *Rouen during the Wars of Religion.* Cambridge, 1981.

——. "The St. Batholomew's Massacres in the Provinces." *Historical Journal* 21.2 (1978): 205–25.

Benoist, Luc. *Le compagnonnage et les métiers.* 4th ed. Paris, 1980.

Bercé, Yves-Marie. *Fête et révolte.* Paris, 1976.

——. *Histoire des croquants.* Geneva, 1974.

——. *Révoltes et révolutions dans l'Europe moderne (XVI–XVIIIe siècles).* Paris, 1980.

Berg, Maxine, et al., eds. *Manufacture in Town and Country before the Factory.* Cambridge, 1983.

Bertucat, C. "La jurisdiction municipale de Dijon: Son étendue." *Revue Bourguignonne* 21 (1911): 89–235.

Billioud, Jacques. "La boucherie à Marseille au XVIIe et XVIIIe siècles: Monopoles, contrebande, franchise." *Provence Historique* 24 (1974): 68–85.

——. *Les corporations de métiers du bâtiment à Marseille aux 17e et 18e siècles.* Thèse compl. lettres, Université d'Aix-en-Provence, 1962.

Boissevain, Jeremy. *Friends of Friends: Networks, Manipulators, and Coalitions.* Oxford, 1974.

Boissonnade, Prosper. *Le socialisme d'état.* Paris, 1927.

Bon, Henri. *Essai historique sur les épidémies en Bourgogne.* Dijon, 1912.

Bossy, John. "Blood and Baptism: Kinship, Community and Christianity in Western Europe from the Fourteenth to the Seventeenth Centuries." In *Sanctity and Secularity: The Church and the World.* Ed. Derek Baker. New York, 1973.

——. *Christianity in the West, 1400–1700.* Oxford, 1984.

——. "The Counter-Reformation and the People of Catholic Europe." *Past and Present* 47 (1970): 51–70.

——, ed. *Disputes and Settlements: Law and Human Relations in the West.* Cambridge, 1983.

——. "Godparenthood: The Fortunes of a Social Institution in Early Modern Christianity." In *Religion and Society in Early Modern Europe, 1500–1800.* Ed. Kaspar von Greyerz. London, 1984.

Bouhier, P. *Les coûtumes du duché de Bourgogne . . .* Dijon, 1742–46.

Bourdieu, Pierre. "Capital symbolique et classes sociales." *Arc* 72 (1978): 13–19.

——. "Marriage Strategies as Strategies of Social Reproduction." In *Family and Society.* Ed. Robert Forster and Orest Ranum. Trans. Elborg Forster and Patricia Ranum. Baltimore, 1976.

——. *Outline of a Theory of Practice.* Trans. Richard Nice. Cambridge, 1977.

——. "Sur le pouvoir symbolique." *Annales: ESC* 32.3 (1977): 405–11.

Bouvier-Ajam, Maurice. *Histoire du travail en France des origines à la révolution.* Paris, 1957.

Braudel, Fernand, and Ernest Labrousse, eds. *Histoire économique et sociale de la France.* 3 vols. Paris, 1970–77.

Burke, Peter. *Popular Culture in Early Modern Europe.* New York, 1978.

Burkolter, Verena. *The Patronage System: Theoretical Remarks.* Basel, 1976.

Campbell, J. K. *Honor, Family and Patronage: A Study of Institutions and Moral Values in a Greek Mountain Community.* Oxford, 1964.

Carny, Lucien, R. Vergez, and G. de Crance. *Les compagnons en France et en Europe.* Eyrein, 1973.

Cassirer, Ernst. *The Philosophy of Symbolic Forms.* 3 vols. New Haven, 1953.

Castan, Nicole, and Yves Castan. *Vivre ensemble: Ordre et désordre en Languedoc (XVIIe–XVIIIe siècles).* Paris, 1981.

Castan, Yves. *Honnêteté et relations sociales en Languedoc, 1715–1780.* Paris, 1974.

Certeau, Michel de, Dominique Julia, and Jacques Revel. "La beauté du mort: Le concept de 'culture populaire.'" *Politique Aujourd'hui* (Dec. 1970): 3–23.

Champeaux, E. "Les cimetières et les marchés du vieux Dijon." *Mémoires de l'Académie de Dijon* (1905–6): 147–226.

Chapuis, A. *Les anciennes corporations dijonnaises: Règlements, statuts, et ordonnances.* Dijon, 1906.

———. *Les foires et marchés de Dijon.* Dijon, n.d.

———. *Les saints patrons et les armoires des corporations Dijonnaises.* Dijon, n.d.

"Le Charivari." Exposition of Musée des Arts et Traditions Populaires. Paris, 1977.

Chartier, Roger. "Culture as Appropriation: Popular Cultural Uses in Early Modern France." In *Understanding Popular Culture.* Ed. Steven L. Kaplan. Berlin, 1984.

Chartier, Roger, and Dominique Julia. "Le monde à l'invers." *Arc* 65 (1976): 43–53.

Chasseneux, Barthélemy de. *Catalogus gloriae mundi.* Lyons, 1546.

Chaunu, Pierre. *La mort à Paris: XVIe, XVIIe, XVIIIe siècles.* Paris, 1978.

Chauvet, Paul. *Les ouvriers du livre en France des origines à la révolution de 1789.* Paris, 1959.

Clark, Peter, ed. *The Early Modern Town: A Reader.* New York, 1976.

Clark, Peter, and Paul Slack. *English Towns in Transition, 1500–1700.* Oxford, 1976.

Clasen, Claus Peter. *Die Augsburger Weber: Leistungen und Krisen des Textilgewerbes um 1600.* Augsburg, 1981.

Clouatre, Dallas. "The Concept of Class in French Culture prior to the Revolution." *Journal of the History of Ideas* 45.2 (1984): 219–44.

Cohn, Samuel K. *The Laboring Classes in Renaissance Florence.* New York, 1980.

Collette, Emile. *Les foires et marchés à Dijon.* Dijon, 1905.

Colombet, Albert. *L'artisanat en Bourgogne.* Strasbourg, 1976.

Coornaert, Emile. *Les corporations en France avant 1789.* 2d ed. Paris, 1968.

Corbin, Alain. *The Foul and the Fragrant: Odor and the French Social Imagination.* New York, 1986.

Corfield, Penelope. "A Provincial Capital in the Late 17th Century: The Case of

Norwich." In *The Early Modern Town: A Reader*. Ed. Peter Clark. New York, 1976.

Courtépée, Claude. *Déscription générale et particulière du duché de Bourgogne*. 2d ed. Dijon, 1847–48.

Couturier, Marcel. *Recherches sur les structures sociales à Châteaudun, 1525–1789*. Paris, 1969.

Crew, Phyllis Mack. *Calvinist Preaching and Iconoclasm in the Netherlands, 1544-1569*. London, 1973.

Croix, Alain. *Nantes et le pays nantais au XVIe siècle: Etude d'histoire démographique*. Paris, 1974.

Cunisset-Carnot, Paul. *Une mouvement séparatiste sous Louis XIII: L'émeute de Lanturelu à Dijon en 1630*. Dijon, 1897.

Darnton, Robert. *The Great Cat Massacre and Other Episodes in French Cultural History*. New York, 1985.

——. "The Symbolic Element in History." *Journal of Modern History* 58 (March, 1986): 218–34.

David, H. *De Sluter à Sambin: Essai critique sur la sculpture et le décor monumental en Bourgogne au 15e et 16e siècle*. 2 vols. Paris, 1932.

Davies, Joan. "Persecution and Protestantism: Toulouse, 1562–1575." *Historical Journal* 22.1 (1979): 31–51.

Davis, Natalie Z. "Charivari, Honor, and Community in 17th-Century Lyon and Geneva." In *Rite, Drama, Festival, Spectacle: Rehearsals toward a Theory of Cultural Performance*. Ed. John J. MacAloon. Philadelphia, 1984.

——. "Ghosts, Kin, and Progeny: Some Features of Family Life in Early Modern France." *Daedalus* (Spring, 1977): 87–114.

——. "The Sacred and the Body Social in Sixteenth-Century Lyon." *Past and Present* 90 (1980): 40–70.

——. *Society and Culture in Early Modern France*. Stanford, 1975.

——. "A Trade Union in Sixteenth-Century France." *Economic History Review* 19 (1966): 48–69.

Delumeau, Jean. *Le catholicisme entre Luther et Voltaire*. 3d ed. Paris, 1985.

——. *Le péché et la peur: La culpabilisation en occident (XIIIe–XVIIIe siècles)*. Paris, 1983.

——. *La peur en occident (XIVe–XVIIIe siècles): Une cité assiégée*. Paris, 1978.

Demos, John P. *Entertaining Satan: Witchcraft and the Culture of Early New England*. New York, 1982.

Descimon, Robert. "La ligue à Paris (1585–1594): Une revision." *Annales: ESC* 37.1 (1982): 72–111.

——. *Qui étaient les seize?* Paris, 1984.

Descimon, Robert, and J. Nagle. "L'espace parisien: Les quartiers de Paris du moyen âge au XVIIIe siècle; évolution d'un espace plurifonctionnel." *Annales: ESC* 34.5 (1979): 956–83.

de Vries, Jan. *The Dutch Rural Economy in the Golden Age, 1500–1700*. New Haven, 1978.

——. *The Economy of Europe in an Age of Crisis, 1600–1750*. Cambridge, 1976.

——. *European Urbanization, 1500-1800*. Cambridge, Mass., 1984.

DeWald, Jonathan. *The Formation of a Provincial Nobility: The Magistrates of the Parlement of Rouen, 1499-1610.* Princeton, 1980.

Deyon, Pierre. *Amiens, capitale provinciale: Etude sur la société urbaine au 17e siècle.* Paris, 1967.

———. "Variations de la production textile aux 16e et 17e siècles." *Annales: ESC* 18.5 (1963): 939–54.

Deyon, Solange. *Casseurs de l'été 1566: L'iconoclasme dans le nord de la France.* Paris, 1981.

Didier, Philippe. "Les contrats de travail en Bourgogne aux 14e et 15e siècles après les archives notariales." *Revue Historique du Droit Français et Etranger* (1972): 14–69.

———. "Le critère de la distinction entre louage de services et entreprise." *MSHD* 29 (1968–69): 197–214.

———. "Les statuts de métier à Dijon au 14e et 15e siècles." *Zeitschrift der Savigny-stiftung für Rechtsgeschichte* 94 (1977): 68–88.

Diefendorf, Barbara. *Paris City Councillors in the Sixteenth Century: The Politics of Patrimony.* Princeton, 1983.

Dobson, C. R. *Masters and Journeymen: A Prehistory of Industrial Relations, 1717–1800.* Totowa, N.J., 1980.

Doucet, Roger. *Les institutions de la France au XVIe siècle.* 2 vols. Paris, 1948.

Douglas, Mary. *Implicit Meanings.* Boston, 1976.

———. *Natural Symbols.* New York, 1982.

Drouot, Henri. *Mayenne et la Bourgogne: Etude sur la ligue, 1587–1596.* 2 vols. Paris, 1937.

———. *Notes sur la Bourgogne et son esprit public au début du règne d'Henri III, 1574–1579.* Paris, 1937.

———. *La première ligue en Bourgogne: Les débuts de Mayenne (1574-79), notes.* Dijon, 1937.

———. "Sur le froid en Bourgogne à la fin du XVIe siècle." *Revue de Bourgogne* 7 (1918–19): 108–18.

———. "Vin, vignes, et vignerons de la côte dijonnaise pendant la ligue." *Revue de Bourgogne* 1 (1911): 343–61.

Duhr, J. "La confrérie dans la vie de l'église." *Revue d'Histoire Ecclésiastique* 35 (1939): 437–78.

Dupâquier, Jacques. *La population française au XVIIe et XVIIIe siècles.* Paris, 1979.

Durandeau, Joachim. *La grande asnerie de Dijon: Etude sur la menée et chevauchée de l'âne au mois de mai.* Dijon, 1887.

———. *Histoire de la mère-folle laique de Dijon.* Dijon, 1912.

———, ed. *L'infanterie dijonnaise.* Dijon, 1894.

———, ed. *Le journal de Claude Sullot, procureur au Parlement de Dijon sous les rois Henri III, Henri IV, et Louis XIII.* Dijon, 1911.

———. *La mère-folle de la Sainte Chapelle de Dijon.* Dijon, 1910.

DuTilliot, Jean-Bénigne Lucotte. *Mémoires pour servir à l'histoire de la fête des foux.* Lausanne, 1741.

Eire, Carlos. *War against the Idols: The Reformation of Worship from Erasmus to Calvin.* Cambridge, 1986.

Eisenstadt, S. N., and Louis Roniger. "Patron-Client Relations as a Model of Structuring Social Exchange." *Comparative Studies in Society and History* 22.1 (1980): 42–77.

——. *Patrons, Clients and Friends: Interpersonal Relations and the Structure of Trust in Society.* Cambridge, 1984.

Estèbe, Janine. "The Rites of Violence: Religious Riot in 16th-Century France, a Comment." *Past and Present* 67 (1975): 127–30.

Fagniez, Gustave. *Etudes sur l'industrie et la classe industrielle à Paris aux XIIIe et XIVe siècles.* Paris, 1877.

Fanfani, Amintore. *Storia del lavoro in Italia dalla fine del secolo XV agli inizi del XVIII.* Milan, 1943.

Farge, Arlette. *La vie fragile.* Paris, 1986.

——. *Vivre dans la rue à Paris au XVIIIe siècle.* Paris, 1979.

Farge, Arlette, and André Zysberg. "Les theâtres de la violence à Paris au XVIIIe siècle." *Annales: ESC* 34.5 (1979): 984–1015.

Farr, James R. "Crimine nel vicinato: Ingiurie, matrimonio e onore nella Digione del XVI e XVII secolo." *Quaderni Storici* n.s. 66, 22.3 (December 1987): 839–54.

——. "Dijon, 1450–1750: The Changing Social and Economic Structure of an Administrative Capital and Commercial Hub." In *Urban Society in Ancien Regime France.* Ed. Philip Benedict. London, forthcoming.

——. "Popular Religious Solidarity in Sixteenth-Century Dijon." *French Historical Studies* 14 (Fall, 1985): 192–214.

Faust, Katherine. "A Beleaguered Society: Protestant Families in La Rochelle, 1628–1685." Ph.d. dissertation, Northwestern University, 1980.

Febvre, Lucien. *Le problème de l'incroyance au 16e siècle: La religion de Rabelais.* Paris, 1968.

——. "Travail: Evolution d'un mot et d'une idée." *Journal de Psychologie* 41 (1948): 19–28.

Flandrin, Jean-Louis. *Les amours paysannes: Amour et sexualité dans les campagnes de l'ancienne France (XVIe-XIXe siècle).* Paris, 1975.

——. *Familes in Former Times: Kinship, Household and Sexuality.* Trans. Richard Southern. Cambridge, 1979.

——. *Le sexe et l'occident: Evolution des attitudes et des comportments.* Paris, 1981.

Folz, R. "L'esprit religieux du testament bourguignon au moyen âge." *MSHD* 17 (1955): 7–28.

Forestier, Henri. "Compagnons et compagnonnages dans les procédures criminelles des bailliages." *Annales de Bourgogne* 14 (1942): 265–66.

Forster, Robert. *The House of Saulx-Tavanes: Versailles and Burgundy, 1700–1830.* Baltimore, 1971.

Forster, Robert, and Orest Ranum, eds. *Ritual, Religion, and the Sacred.* Trans. Elborg Forster and Patricia Ranum. Baltimore, 1982.

Foucault, Michel. "The Discourse on Language." In *Archaeology of Knowledge.* New York, 1972.

Franklin, Alfred. *Dictionnaire historique des arts, métiers, et professions exercés dans Paris depuis la XIIIe siècle.* Paris, 1906.

Friedrichs, Christopher. "Capitalism, Mobility, and Class Formation in an Early Modern German City." *Past and Present* 69 (1975): 24–49.

———. *Urban Society in an Age of War: Nördlingen, 1579–1720.* Princeton, 1979.

Frijhoff, W. "Official and Popular Religion in Christianity: The Late Middle Ages and Early Modern Times." In *Official and Popular Religion: Analysis of a Theme for Religious Studies.* Ed. P. H. Vrijhof and J. Waardenburg. The Hague, 1979.

Fromental, Jacques. *La réforme en Bourgogne aux 16e et 17e siècles.* Paris, 1968.

Furet, François. "Pour une définition des classes inférieures à l'époque moderne." *Annales: ESC* 18.3 (1963): 459–74.

Fyot, E. "Les confréries des corporations et leurs bâtons." *Bulletin du Syndicat d'Initiative de Dijon et de la Côte-d'Or* (December 1934): 55–63.

Gaignebet, Claude. *Le carnaval: Essais de mythologie populaire.* Paris, 1979.

Galpern, A. N. *Religions of the People in Sixteenth-Century Champagne.* Cambridge, Mass., 1976.

Garden, Maurice. *Lyon et les lyonnais au XVIIIe siècle.* Paris, 1975.

———. "Ouvriers et artisans au 18e siècle: L'exemple lyonnais et les problèmes de classification." *Revue d'Histoire Economique et Sociale* 48 (1970): 28–54.

———. "The Urban Trades: Social Analysis and Representation." In *Work in France: Representations, Meaning, Organization, and Practice.* Ed. Steven L. Kaplan and Cynthia J. Koepp. Ithaca, 1986.

Garnier, Joseph. *Les anciens orfèvres de Dijon.* Dijon, 1889.

———, ed. *Correspondence de la maire de Dijon extraité des archives de cette ville.* Dijon, 1868–1870.

———. *Le feu de Saint Jean à Dijon.* Dijon, 1879.

———. *Histoire du quartier du bourg.* Dijon, 1853.

———. *Inventaires-sommaires des archives communales.* Vol. 1, Paris, 1867.

———, ed. *Le journal de Gabriel Breunot, conseiller au Parlement de Dijon, precédé du livre de souvenance de Pepin, chanoine de la Sainte-Chapelle en cette ville.* 3 vols. Dijon, 1866.

Garnier, Joseph, and E. Champeaux. *Chartes de communes et d'affranchisements en Bourgogne: Introduction.* Dijon, 1918.

Garreta, Jean-Claude. "Le St-Barthélemy à Dijon." *Bulletin de la Société d'Histoire du Protestantisme Français* 118 (1972): 736–37.

Garrioch, David. *Neighborhood and Community in Paris, 1740-1790.* Cambridge, 1986.

Garrisson-Estèbe, Janine. *Protestants du Midi.* Toulouse, 1980.

Gascon, Richard. *Le grand commerce et la vie urbaine au 16e siècle.* 2 vols. Paris, 1971.

———. "Immigration et croissance urbaine au XVIe siècle: L'exemple de Lyon." *Annales: ESC* 25.4 (1970): 988–1001.

Geertz, Clifford. *Interpretations of Cultures.* New York, 1973.

Genovese, Eugene. *Roll, Jordan, Roll: The World the Slaves Made.* New York, 1976.

Geremek, Bronislaw. *Inutiles au monde: Truands et misérables (1300–1600).* Paris, 1980.

——. "Les migrations des compagnons au bas moyen âge." *Studia Historiae Oeconomicae* 5 (1970): 61–79.

——. *Le salariat dans l'artisanat parisien aux 14e–15e siècles.* Paris, 1968.

Giddens, Anthony. *Capitalism and Modern Social Theory: An Analysis of the Writings of Marx, Durkheim and Max Weber.* Cambridge, 1971.

——. *Central Problems in Social Theory: Action, Structure and Contradiction in Social Analysis.* Berkeley, 1979.

Giesey, Ralph E. "Rules of Inheritance and Strategies of Mobility in Pre-revolutionary France." *American Historical Review* 82 (1977): 271–89.

Ginzburg, Carlo. *The Cheese and the Worms: The Cosmogony of a Sixteenth-Century Miller.* Trans. John Tedeschi and Anne Tedeschi. Baltimore, 1980.

Giroux, Henri. "Essai sur la vie et l'oeuvre dijonnais d'Hugues Sambin." *Mémoires de la Commission des Antiquités du département de la Côte-d'Or* 32 (1980–81): 361–413.

Goldthwaite, Richard. *The Building of Renaissance Florence: An Economic and Social History.* Baltimore, 1980.

Goody, Jack. *Bridewealth and Dowry.* Cambridge, 1973.

——. *Death, Property and the Ancestors.* Stanford, 1962.

——, ed. *Literacy in Traditional Societies.* Cambridge, 1968.

Gosselin, E. "Du prix des denrées comparé au salaire journalier des artisans de 1489 à 1789." *Revue de Normandie* 9 (1869): 114–27.

Gottman, Frank. *Handwerk und Bundespolitik: Die Handwerkerbunde am Mittelrhein vom 14. bis zum 17. Jahrhundert.* Wiesbaden, 1977.

Goubert, Pierre. *Beauvais et le beauvaisis de 1600 à 1730: Contribution à l'histoire sociale de la France du XVIIe siècle.* 2 vols. Paris, 1960.

Gras, Pierre, ed. *Histoire de Dijon.* Toulouse, 1980.

Greenblatt, Stephen. *Renaissance Self-Fashioning from More to Shakespeare.* Chicago, 1980.

Griessinger, Andreas. *Das symbolische Kapital der Ehre: Streikbewegungen und Kollectives bewusstein deutscher Handwerksgesellen im 18. Jahrhundert.* Frankfurt, 1981.

Grinberg, Martine. "Carnaval et société urbaine aux XIVe–XVIe siècles: Le royaume dans la ville." *Ethnologie Française* 4 (1974): 215–44.

Grosrenaud, Frédéric. *La corporation ouvrière à Besançon (16e–17e siècles).* Dijon, 1907.

Guigue, Georges, ed. "L'ordre tenu en la chevauchée faicte en la ville de Lyon." *Archives Historiques et Statistiques du Département du Rhône* 9 (1828–29): 305–431.

Guillemaut, Lucien. *La bresse louhannaise . . . traditions populaires.* Louhans, 1907.

Gutiérrez, Ramon A. "Honor, Ideology, Marriage Negotiation, and Class-Gender Domination in New Mexico, 1698–1846." *Latin American Perspectives* 44.12, no. 1 (1985): 81–104.

Gutman, Herbert. *Work, Culture and Society in Industrializing America.* New York, 1977.

Gutton, Jean-Pierre. *La sociabilité villageoise dans l'ancienne France.* Paris, 1979.

——. *La société et les pauvres: L'exemple de la généralité de Lyon, 1534–1789.* Paris, 1974.

Hanawalt, Barbara, ed. *Women and Work in Preindustrial Europe.* Bloomington, Ind., 1986.

Hanlon, Gregory. "Les rituels de l'agression en Aquitaine au XVIIe siècle." *Annales: ESC* 40.2 (1985): 244–68.

Harding, Robert. *Anatomy of a Power Elite: The Provincial Governors of Early Modern France.* New Haven, 1978.

——. "The Mobilization of Confraternities against the Reformation in France." *Sixteenth Century Journal* 11 (Summer 1980): 85–107.

Hauser, Henri. *Les compagnonnages d'arts et métiers à Dijon aux XVIIe et XVIIIe siècles.* Paris, 1907.

——. "Des divers modes d'organisation du travail dans l'ancienne France." *Revue d'Histoire Moderne et Contemporaine* 7 (1906): 357–87.

——. "L'organisation du travail à Dijon et en Bourgogne au XVIe et dans la première moitié du XVIIe siècle." In *Les débuts du capitalisme.* Ed. H. Hauser. Paris, 1927.

——. *Ouvriers du temps passé.* Paris, 1899.

——. "Les pouvoirs publics et l'organisation du travail dans l'ancienne France." In *Travailleurs et marchands dans l'ancienne France.* Ed. H. Hauser. Paris, 1920.

——. "La question des prix et des monnaies en Bourgogne dans la seconde moitié du XVIe siècle." *Annales de Bourgogne* 4 (1932): 7–21.

——. "La réforme et les classes populaires en France au XVIe siècle." *Revue d'Histoire Moderne et Contemporaine* 1 (1899): 24–37.

——. "Le site et la croissance de Dijon." In *Dijon et la Côte-d'Or en 1911.* Ed. Ch. Oursel. Dijon, 1911.

Hauser, Henri, and Henri See. "Sur le mot artisan." *Revue de Synthèse* 5 (1933): 256–60.

Heers, Jacques. *Family Clans in the Middle Ages: A Study of Political and Social Structures in Urban Areas.* Trans. Barry Herbert. Amsterdam, 1977.

——. *Fêtes, jeux et joutes dans les sociétés d'occident à la fin du moyen âge.* Paris, 1971.

——. "Les métiers et les fêtes 'mediévales' en France du nord et en Angleterre." *Revue du Nord* 55 (1973): 193–206.

——. *Le travail au moyen âge.* Paris, 1968.

Herrup, Cynthia B. "Law and Morality in Seventeenth-Century England." *Past and Present* 106 (1985): 102–23.

Hincker, François. *Les français devant l'impôt sous l'ancien régime.* Paris, 1971.

Hobsbawm Eric J. *Laboring Men: Studies in the History of Labor.* New York, 1964.

——. *Workers: Worlds of Labor.* New York, 1984.

Hoffman, Philip. *Church and Community in the Diocese of Lyon, 1500–1789.* New Haven, 1984.

Holt, Mack P. *The Duke of Anjou and the 'Politique' Struggle during the Wars of Religion.* Cambridge, 1986.

Horsley, Richard A. "Who Were the Witches? The Social Roles of the Accused in the European Witch Trials." *Journal of Interdisciplinary History* 9.4 (1979): 689–715.

Hsia, R. Po-chia. *Society and Religion in Munster, 1535–1618.* New Haven, 1984.

Hufton, Olwen. "Women and the Family Economy in Eighteenth-Century France." *French Historical Studies* 9:1 (1975): 1–22.

———. "Women without Men: Widows and Spinsters in Britain and France in the Eighteenth Century." *Journal of Family History* (Winter 1984): 355–76.

Hughes, Diane Owen. "Kinsmen and Neighbors in Medieval Genoa." In *The Medieval City.* Ed. Harry A. Miskimin, David Herlihy, and A. L. Udovitch. New Haven, 1977.

Huizinga, Johan. *Homo Ludens: A Study of the Play Element in Culture.* Boston, 1955.

Humbert, Françoise. *Les finances municipales de Dijon du milieu du XIVe siècle à 1477.* Paris, 1961.

Huppert, George. *Les Bourgeois Gentilhommes: An Essay on the Definition of Elites in Renaissance France.* Chicago, 1977.

Jaccard, P. *Histoire sociale du travail.* Paris, 1960.

Jacquot, Jean, and Elie Konigson, eds. *Les fêtes de la renaissance.* Paris, 1975.

Javelle, Bernard. *Histoire de Notre Dame d'Etang.* Dijon, 1869.

Jeannin, Pierre. *Merchants of the Sixteenth Century.* Trans. Paul Fittingoff. New York, 1972.

Jones, Gareth Steadman. *The Language of Class.* Cambridge, 1985.

———. "Working-Class Culture and Working-Class Politics in London, 1871–1900: Notes on the Remaking of a Working Class." *Journal of Social History* 7 (1974): 460–508.

Jouanna, Arlette. *Ordre social: Mythes et hiérarchies dans la France du XVIe siècle.* Paris, 1977.

———. "Recherches sur la notion d'honneur au 16e siècle." *Revue d'Histoire Moderne et Contemporaine* 15 (1968): 597–623.

Kaplan, Steven L. *Bread, Politics, and the Political Economy in the Reign of Louis XV.* 2 vols. The Hague, 1976.

———. "The Character and Implications of Strife among the Masters inside the Guilds of Eighteenth-Century Paris." *Journal of Social History* 19 (Summer 1986): 631–47.

———. "Réflexions sur la police du monde du travail, 1700–1815." *Revue Historique* 261 (1979): 17–77.

———, ed. *Understanding Popular Culture.* Berlin, 1984.

Kaplow, Jeffrey. *The Names of Kings: The Parisian Laboring Poor in the Eighteenth Century.* New York, 1972.

Kelley, Donald. *The Beginning of Ideology: Consciousness and Society in the French Reformation.* Cambridge, 1981.

Kent, Dale V., and F. W. Kent. *Neighbors and Neighborhood in Renaissance Florence: The District of the Red Lion in the Fifteenth Century.* Locust Valley, 1982.

Kettering, Sharon. *Judicial Politics and Urban Revolt in Seventeenth-Century France: The Parlement of Aix, 1629–1659.* Princeton, 1978.

——. *Patrons, Brokers and Clients in Seventeenth-Century France.* New York, 1986.

Klaits, Joseph. *Servants of Satan: The Age of the Witch Hunts.* Bloomington, Ind., 1985.

Knoop, D., and G. P. Jones. *The Medieval Mason: An Economic History of English Stone Building in the Later Middle Ages and Early Modern Times.* Manchester, 1949.

Labal, Paul. "Artisans dijonnais d'autrefois: Notes sur la vie des gens de métiers de 1430 à 1560." *Annales de Bourgogne* 23 (1951): 85–106.

——. "Le monde des métiers dans le cadre urbain: Aspects de la vie des métiers à Dijon de 1430 à 1560." Dijon: Faculté des lettres, Mémoire de diplôme d'études supérieures, 1950. Typescript copy in library of Université de Dijon.

Labarre, Albert. *Le livre dans la vie Amienoise au 16e siècle: L'enseignement des inventaires après decès, 1503–1576.* Paris, 1971.

Lamet, M. S. "French Protestants in a Position of Strength: The Early Years of the Reformation in Caen, 1558–1568." *Sixteenth Century Journal* 9 (1978): 35–56.

Lears, T. J. Jackson. "The Concept of Cultural Hegemony: Problems and Possibilities." *American Historical Review* 90 (June 1985): 567–93.

LeBras, Gabriel. "Les confréries chrétiennes: Problèmes et propositions." In *Etudes de sociologie religieuse.* 2 vols. Paris, 1955–56.

——. *Introduction à l'histoire de la pratique religieuse en France.* 2 vols. Paris, 1942–45.

LeBras, Gabriel, et al. "Pratique religieuse et religion populaire." *Archives des Sciences Sociales Religieuses* 43 (1977): 7–22.

Lebrun, François. *Les hommes et la mort en Anjou aux 17e et 18e siècles.* Paris, 1971.

——. *La vie conjugale sous l'ancien régime.* Paris, 1975.

Lecotté, Roger. "Les plus anciens imprimés sur le compagnonnage." *Bulletin Folklorique Ile-de-France* 30 series 4.4 (1968): 67–72.

LeFranc, Georges. *Histoire du travail et des travailleurs.* Paris, 1975.

LeGoff, Jacques. *The Birth of Purgatory.* Trans. Arthur Goldhammer. Chicago, 1985.

——. *Time, Work, and Culture in the Middle Ages.* Trans. Arthur Goldhammer. Chicago, 1980.

LeGuai, André. *Dijon et Louis XI.* Dijon, 1947.

Leroux, André. "Les industries textiles dans la Bourgogne d'ancien régime." *Annales de Bourgogne* 43 (1971): 5–33.

Le Roy Ladurie, Emmanuel. *Carnival in Romans.* Trans. Mary Feeney. New York, 1979.

——, ed. *Histoire de la France urbaine: La ville classique de la renaissance aux révolutions.* Paris, 1981.

——. *Montaillou: The Promised Land of Error.* Trans. Barbara Bray. New York, 1978.

——. *The Peasants of Languedoc.* Trans. John Day. Urbana, 1974.

——. "A System of Customary Law: Family Structures and Inheritance Customs in Sixteenth-Century France." In *Family and Society*. Ed. Robert Forster and Orest Ranum. Trans. Elborg Forster and Patricia Ranum. Baltimore, 1976.

Le Roy Ladurie, Emmanuel, and Pierre Couperie. "Le mouvement des loyers parisiens de la fin du moyen âge au XVIIIe siècle." *Annales: ESC* 25.4 (1970): 1002–23.

Lespinasse, René de, ed. *Les métiers et corporations de la ville de Paris*. Paris, 1879.

Levasseur, Emile de. *Histoire des classes ouvrières en France depuis la conquête de Jules César jusqu'à la révolution*. 2 vols. Paris, 1859.

——. *Histoire des classes ouvrières et de l'industrie en France avant 1789*. 2 vols. Paris, 1900–1901.

Lévi-Strauss, Claude. *La pensée sauvage*. Paris, 1963.

——. *La voie des masques*. Paris, 1979.

Ligeron, Louis. "La jurisprudence du Parlement de Dijon en matière de sorcellerie au début du 17e siècle." *MSHD* 33 (1975–76): 281–89.

Ligou, Daniel. *Le protestantisme en France de 1598 à 1715*. Paris, 1968.

Lottin, Alain. *Chavatte, ouvrier Lillois: Un contemporain de Louis XIV*. Paris, 1979.

MacFarlane, Alan. *Reconstructing Historical Communities*. Cambridge, 1977.

Malcolmson, Robert W. *Life and Labor in England, 1701–1780*. London, 1981.

Mandrou, Robert. "Les français hors de France aux XVIe et XVIIe siècles." *Annales: ESC* 14.5 (1959): 662–75

——. *Introduction to Modern France, 1500–1640*. Trans. R. E. Hallmark. New York, 1975.

Marcel, L.-E. *Le cardinal de Givry, évêque de Langres (1529–1561)*. 2 vols. Author, 1926.

Marion, Marcel. *Les impôts directs sous l'ancien régime*. Geneva, 1974.

Martin, John. "In God's Image: Artisans and Heretics in Counter-Reformation Venice." Ph.d. dissertation, Harvard University, 1982.

Martin Saint-Léon, E. *Le compagnonnage: Son histoire, ses coûtumes, ses règlements, et ses rites*. Paris, 1901.

——. *Histoire des corporations de métier*. Paris, 1897.

Mauss, Marcel. *Essai sur le don*. Paris, 1968.

Maza, Sarah C. *Servants and Masters in Eighteenth-Century France: The Uses of Loyalty*. Princeton, 1983.

Medick, Hans. "Plebeian Culture in the Transition to Capitalism." In *Culture, Ideology and Politics*. Ed. Raphael Samuel. London, 1982.

Medick, Hans, and David Sabean, eds. *Interest and Emotion: Essays on the Study of Family and Kinship*. Cambridge, 1984.

Mentzer, Raymond. "Heresy Suspects in Languedoc prior to 1560: Observations on their Social and Occupational Status." *Bibliothèque d'Humanisme et Renaissance* 39 (1977): 561–68.

Michaud, P. "Un maître ouvrier bourguignon: Euvrard Bredin." *Mémoires de la Société Bourguignonne de Géographie et d'Histoire* 26 (1910): 477–504.

Mintz, Sydney, and Eric Wolf. "An Analysis of Ritual Coparenthood." *Southwestern Journal of Anthropology* 6 (1950): 341–68.

Mols, Roger P. *Introduction à la démographie historique des villes d'Europe du 14e au 18e siècle.* 3 vols. Louvain, 1955.

Monget, Cyprien. *La Chartreuse de Dijon d'après les documents des archives de Bourgogne.* 3 vols. Montreuil-sur-mer et Tournai, 1898–1905.

Monter, E. William. "Historical Demography and Religious History in Sixteenth-Century Geneva." *Journal of Interdisciplinary History* 9.3 (1979): 399–428.

——. *Ritual, Myth and Magic in Early Modern Europe.* Athens, Ohio, 1985.

——. "Women in Calvinist Geneva, 1550–1800." *Signs* 6 (1980–81): 189–209.

Montias, John Michael. *Artists and Artisans in Delft: A Socioeconomic Study of the 17th Century.* Princeton, 1982.

Morineau, Michel. "Budgets populaires en France au XVIIIe siècle." *Revue d'Histoire Economique et Sociale* 50 (1972): 203–37, 449–81.

Mousnier, Roland. "Les concepts d'*ordres*, d'*états*, de *fidélité*, et de *monarchie absolue* en France de la fin du 15e siècle à la fin du 18e." *Revue Historique* 247 (1972): 289–312.

——. *Fureurs paysans.* Paris, 1967.

——. *The Institutions of France under the Absolute Monarchy, 1598–1789: The Organs of State and Society.* Trans. Arthur Goldhammer. Chicago, 1984.

——. *The Institutions of France under the Absolute Monarchy, 1598–1789: Society and the State.* Trans. Brian Pierce. Chicago, 1979.

——. *Social Hierarchies, 1450 to the Present.* Trans. Peter Evans. New York, 1973.

Muchembled, Robert. "Lay Judges and the Acculturation of the Masses (France and the Southern Low Countries, Sixteenth to Eighteenth Centuries)." In *Religion and Society in Early Modern Europe.* Ed. Kaspar von Greyerz. London, 1984.

Nicholls, David. "Social Change and Early Protestantism in France: Normandy, 1520–1562." *European Studies Review* 10 (1980): 279–308.

——. "The Social History of the French Reformation: Ideology, Confession and Culture." *Social History* 9 (1984): 25–43.

Noirot, Claude. *L'origine des masques . . . menez sur l'asne à rebours et charivary.* Langres, 1609.

Norberg, Kathryn. *Rich and Poor in Grenoble, 1600–1814.* Berkeley, 1985.

Olivier-Martin, François. *L'organisation corporative de la France d'ancien régime.* Paris, 1938.

Ong, Walter. *Orality and Literacy.* London, 1982.

——. *The Presence of the Word.* New Haven, 1968.

Oursel, C., ed. *Le livre de Dominique Cuny, chronique dijonnaise du temps de la ligue.* Dijon, 1908.

——, ed. *Livre de raison de la famille Robert.* Dijon, 1908.

Ozment, Steven. *The Reformation in the Cities: The Appeal of Protestantism to Sixteenth-Century Germany and Switzerland.* New Haven, 1975.

Ozouf, Mona. *La fête révolutionnaire, 1789–1799.* Paris, 1976.

Parent, Annie. *Les métiers du livre à Paris au 16e siècle (1530–60).* Geneva, 1974.

Perdiguier, Agricol. *Mémoires d'un compagnon.* Paris, 1964; orig. pub. 1854.

Peristiany, J. G. Introduction to *Honor and Shame: The Values of a Mediterranean Society.* Ed. Peristiany. London, 1965.

Perrenet, P. "La communauté protestante de Dijon au début du dix-septième siècle." *Annales de Bourgogne* 2 (1930): 280–94.

——. "Les protestants de la région dijonnaise durant la période de l'Edit de Nantes." *Mémoires de l'Académie de Dijon* (1933): 176–83.

Perron, Claude. "Les métiers à Verdun, 16e–18e siècles." Thèse de droit, Université de Nancy, 1963.

Perrot, Jean-Claude. *Genèse d'une ville moderne: Caen au XVIIIe siècle.* 2 vols. Paris, 1975.

Phelps-Brown, E. H., and S. Hopkins. "Seven Centuries of Building Wages." In *Essays in Economic History.* Ed. E. M. Carus-Wilson. New York, 1966.

Philips, Carla Rahn. *Ciudad Real, 1500–1750: Growth, Crisis, and Adjustment in the Spanish Economy.* Cambridge, Mass., 1979.

Phillips, Roderick. *Family Breakdown in Late Eighteenth-Century France: Divorces in Rouen, 1792–1803.* Oxford, 1980.

Phythian-Adams, Charles. *Desolation of a City: Coventry and the Urban Crisis of the Late Middle Ages.* London, 1979.

Pieri, Georges. "Les particularités de la puissance paternelle." *MSHD* 26 (1965): 51–90.

Pingaud, Léonce, ed. *Correspondence des Saulx-Tavanes au XVIe siècle.* Paris, 1877.

Pitt-Rivers, Julian. *The Fate of Schechem; or, The Politics of Sex.* Cambridge, 1977.

——. "Honor and Social Status." In *Honor and Shame: The Values of Mediterranean Society.* Ed. J. G. Peristiany. London, 1965.

——. *The People of the Sierra.* Chicago, 1961.

Porchnev, Boris. *Les soulèvements populaires en France au XVIIe siècle.* Paris, 1972.

Poulantzas, Nicos. *Pouvoir politique et classes sociales.* Paris, 1972.

Prudhon, Jean. "La réception de l'Edit de Nantes en Bourgogne (1594–1600)." *Annales de Bourgogne* 31 (1939): 225–49.

Pullan, Brian. "Wage-earners and the Venetian Economy, 1550–1630." *Economic History Review* 2d ser. 16 (1964): 407–26.

Quenedey, Raymond. "Le prix des matériaux et de la main-d'oeuvre à Rouen du XIVe au XVIIIe siècle." *Bulletin de la Société d'Emulation . . . de la Seine-Inférieure* (1925): 331–56.

Rapp, Francis. "Les confréries d'artisans dans le diocèse de Strasbourg à la fin du moyen âge." *Bulletin de la Société de l'académie du Bas-Rhin* 93–94, n.s. 73–74 (1971–72): 10–28.

——. "Les croyances et les pratiques à la fin du moyen âge en occident." *Le Christianisme Populaire* (1976): 105–21.

——. "Réflexions sur la religion populaire au moyen âge." *La Religion Populaire* (1976): 51–98.

Reddy, William. "Skeins, Scales, Discounts, Steam and Other Objects of Crowd Justice in Early French Textile Mills." *Comparative Studies in Society and History* 21 (April 1979): 204–13.

*Règlement politique.* Dijon, 1580.

Richard, Jean, ed. *Histoire de la Bourgogne.* Toulouse, 1978.

Richet, Denis. "Aspects socioculturels des conflits religieux à Paris dans la seconde moitié du 16e siècle." *Annales: ESC* 32.4 (1977): 764–89.

Ricoeur, Paul. *Interpretation Theory: Discourse and the Surplus of Meaning.* Fort Worth, 1976.

———. *Time and Narrative.* Trans. Kathleen McLaughlin and David Pellauer. 2 vols. Chicago, 1984, 1985.

Ridard, Abel. *Essai sur le douaire en Bourgogne.* Dijon, 1906.

Rigault, Jean. "L'ancienne confrérie des rois de St. Michel de Dijon." *Mémoires de l'Académie de Dijon* 117 (1969): 81–85.

Ringrose, David. *Madrid and the Spanish Economy, 1560–1850.* Berkeley, 1983.

Roche, Daniel. "Work, Fellowship, and Some Economic Realities of Eighteenth-Century France." In *Work in France: Representations, Meaning, Organization, and Practice.* Ed. Steven L. Kaplan and Cynthia J. Koepp. Ithaca, 1986.

Rock, Howard B. *Artisans of the New Republic: Tradesmen of New York City in the Age of Jefferson.* New York, 1979.

Rosenberg, David L. "Social Experience and Religious Choice: A Case Study, The Protestant Weavers and Woolcombers of Amiens in the Sixteenth Century." Ph.d. dissertation, Yale University, 1978.

Rossiaud, Jacques. "Fraternités de jeunesse et niveaux de culture dans les villes du sud-est à la fin du moyen âge." *Cahiers d'Histoire* 1 (1976): 67–102.

———. "Prostitution, Youth, and Society in the Towns of Southeastern France in the Fifteenth Century." In *Deviants and the Abandoned in French Society.* Ed. Robert Forster and Orest Ranum. Trans. Elborg Forster and Patricia Ranum. Baltimore, 1978.

Rothkrug, Lionel. "Popular Religion and Holy Shrines." In *Religion and the People, 800–1700.* Ed. James Obelkevitch. Chapel Hill, 1979.

Roupnel, Gaston. *La ville et la campagne au XVIIe siècle: Etude sur les populations du pays dijonnais.* Paris, 1955.

Ruggiero, Guido. *The Boundaries of Eros: Sex Crime and Sexuality in Renaissance Venice.* New York, 1985.

Rule, John. *The Experience of Labour in Eighteenth-Century English Industry.* New York, 1981.

Sabean, David. *Power in the Blood: Popular Culture and Village Discourse in Early Modern Germany.* Cambridge, 1984.

Saint Jacob, Pierre de. "Etude sur l'ancienne communauté rurale en Bourgogne." *Annales de Bourgogne* 13 (1941): 169–202.

———. "Mutations économiques et sociales dans les campagnes bourguignonnes à la fin du XVIe siècle." *Etudes Rurales* 1 (1961): 34–49.

———. *Les paysans de la Bourgogne du nord au dernier siècle de l'ancien régime.* Paris, 1960.

———. "Les terres communales." *Annales de Bourgogne* 25 (1953): 225–40.

Salmon, J. H. M. *Society in Crisis: France in the Sixteenth Century.* London, 1975.

Savaron, Jean, sieur de Villars. *Traité contre les masques.* Paris, 1608.

Savonnet, Bernard. "Fluctuations économiques et évolution de la criminalité: L'exemple de Dijon à la fin du XVIIe siècle." *Economie du Centre-est* 79 (1978): 87–107.

Schanz, G. *Zur Geschichte der deutschen Gesellenverbande.* Leipzig, 1877.

Schmitt, Jean-Claude. "Les traditions folkloriques dans la culture mediévale: Quelques réflexions de méthode." *Archives de Sciences Sociales des Religions* 52 (1981): 5–20.

Schnapper, Bernard. *Les rentes au XVIe siècle: Histoire d'un instrument de crédit.* Paris, 1957.

Schneider, Jane. "Of Vigilance and Virgins: Honor, Shame and Access to Resources in Mediterranean Societies." *Ethnology* 10.1 (1971): 1–24.

Schneider, Peter. "Honor and Conflict in a Sicilian Town." *Anthropological Quarterly* 42.3 (1969): 130–54.

Scott, Joan W. *The Glassworkers of Carmaux: French Craftsmen and Political Action in a Nineteenth-Century City.* Cambridge, Mass., 1974.

Scoville, Warren. *Capitalism and French Glassmaking, 1640–1789.* Berkeley, 1950.

Scribner, R. W. "Cosmic Order and Daily Life: Sacred and Secular in Pre-industrial German Society." In *Religion and Society in Early Modern Europe, 1500–1800.* Ed. Kaspar von Greyerz. London, 1984.

Sébillot, Paul. *Le folklore de France.* 4 vols. Paris, 1904–7.

Sewell, William. "*Etats, Corps*, and *Ordre*: Some Notes on the Social Vocabulary of the French Old Regime." In *Sozialgeschicte Heute: Festschrift für Hans Rosenberg.* Ed. Hans-Ulrich Wehler. Göttingen, 1974.

——. "Visions of Labor: Illustrations of the Mechanical Arts before, in and after Diderot's *Encyclopédie*." In *Work in France: Representations, Meaning, Organization, and Practice.* Ed. Steven L. Kaplan and Cynthia J. Koepp. Ithaca, 1986.

——. *Work and Revolution in France: The Language of Labor from the Old Regime to 1848.* Cambridge, 1980.

Sharlin, Allan. "Natural Decrease in Early Modern Cities: A Reconsideration." *Past and Present* 79 (1978): 126–38.

Sharp, Buchanan. *In Contempt of All Authority: Rural Artisans and Riot in the West of England, 1586–1660.* Berkeley, 1980.

Sharpe, J. A. *Crime in Early Modern England, 1550–1750.* London, 1984.

——. *Defamation and Sexual Slander in Early Modern England: The Church Courts at York.* Borthwick Papers, no. 58. York, 1980.

Shepherd, Edward J., Jr. "Social and Geographic Mobility of the Eighteenth-Century Guild Artisan." In *Work in France: Representations, Meaning, Organization, and Practice.* Ed. Steven L. Kaplan and Cynthia J. Koepp. Ithaca, 1986.

Shorter, Edward, ed. *Work and Community in the West.* New York, 1979.

Smith, Steven R. "The London Apprentices as Seventeenth-Century Adolescents." *Past and Present* 61 (1973): 94–161.

Sonenscher, Michael. *The Hatters of Eighteenth-Century France.* Berkeley, 1987.

——. "Journeymen's Migrations and Workshop Organization in Eighteenth-Century France." In *Work in France: Representations, Meaning, Organization and Practice.* Ed. Steven L. Kaplan and Cynthia J. Koepp. Ithaca, 1986.

——. "Journeymen, the Courts and the French Trades, 1781–1791." *Past and Present* 114 (1987): 77–109.

——. "The *Sans Culottes* of the Year II: Rethinking the Language of Labor in Revolutionary France." *Social History* 9 (October, 1984): 301–28.

——. "Work and Wages in Paris in the Eighteenth Century." In *Manufacture in Town and Country before the Factory*. Ed. Maxine Berg, et al. Cambridge, 1983.

Stone, Lawrence. *Family, Sex and Marriage in England, 1500–1800*. New York, 1977.

Tabourot, Etienne, seigneur des Accords. *Les bigarrures du seigneur des accords*. Geneva, 1969.

Thiers, Jean-Baptiste, abbé. *Traité des jeux . . .* Paris, 1686.

——. *Traité des superstitions . . .* 4 vols. Paris, 1697.

Thomas, Keith. *Religion and the Decline of Magic*. New York, 1971.

——. "Work and Leisure in Pre-industrial Society." *Past and Present* 29 (1964): 50–62.

Thompson, E. P. "18th-Century English Society: Class Struggle without Class?" *Journal of Social History* 3 (1978): 133–65.

——. *The Making of the English Working Class*. New York, 1966.

——. "The Moral Economy of the English Crowd in the Eighteenth Century." *Past and Present* 50 (1971): 76–136.

——. "Patrician Society, Plebeian Culture." *Journal of Social History* 7 (1974): 382–405.

——. "'Rough music': Le charivari anglais." *Annales: ESC* 27.2 (1972): 285–312.

——. "Time, Work Discipline and Industrial Capitalism." *Past and Present* 38 (1967): 56–97.

Tilly, Charles. *The Contentious French: Four Centuries of Popular Struggle*. Cambridge, Mass., 1986.

Tilly, Louise A., and Joan W. Scott. *Women, Work and Family*. New York, 1978.

Tilly, Louise, and Charles Tilly, eds. *Class Conflict and Collective Action*. Beverly Hills, 1981.

Tocqueville, Alexis de. *The Old Régime and the French Revolution*. Trans. Stuart Gilbert. Garden City, 1955.

Trenard, Louis. "Dévotions populaires à Lille au temps de la contre-réforme." In *99e congrès de la société savante, section d'histoire moderne*. Besançon, 1976.

Trexler, Richard. "Florentine Religious Experience: The Sacred Image." *Studies in the Renaissance* 19 (1972): 7–41.

——. *Public Life in Renaissance Florence*. New York, 1981.

Truant, Cynthia M. "Compagnonnage: Symbolic Action and the Defense of Workers' Rights in France, 1700–1848." Ph.d. dissertation, University of Chicago, 1978.

——. "Independent and Insolent: Journeymen and their 'Rites' in the Old Regime Workplace." In *Work in France: Representations, Meaning, Organization, and Practice*. Ed. Steven L. Kaplan and Cynthia J. Koepp. Ithaca, 1986.

——. "Solidarity and Symbolism among Journeyman Artisans: The Case of 'Compagnonnage.'" *Comparative Studies in Society and History* 21 (April 1979): 214–26.

Turnau, Irena. "La bonneterie en Europe du 16e au 18e siècle." *Annales: ESC* 26:5 (1971): 1118–32.

Turner, Victor. *Dramas, Fields and Metaphors: Symbolic Action in Human Society*. Ithaca, 1974.

———. *The Ritual Process: Structure and Anti-Structure.* Chicago, 1968.

Tyler, William R. *Dijon and the Valois Dukes of Burgundy.* Norman, 1971.

Unwin, George. *Industrial Organization in the 16th and 17th Centuries.* Oxford, 1904.

Verhaeghe, Luc. *Vers composés pour les enfants de la mère-folle de Dijon vers la fin du 16e siècle.* Liège, 1968–69.

Vinogradov, Amal. Introduction to *Anthropological Quarterly* 47.1 (1974): 2–8.

Vovelle, Michel. "Les attitudes devant la mort: Problèmes de méthode, approches, et lectures differentes." *Annales: ESC* 31.1 (1976): 120–32.

———. *Idéologies et mentalités.* Paris, 1982.

———. *Metamorphose de la fête en Provence.* Paris, 1976.

———. *Piété baroque et déchristianisation en Provence au XVIIIe siècle.* Paris, 1978.

———. "La religion populaire: Problèmes et méthodes." *Le Monde Alpin et Rhodanien* 5 (1977): 7–32.

Walker, Mack. *German Home Towns: Community, State, and General Estate, 1648–1871.* Ithaca, 1971.

Walter, John, and Keith Wrightson. "Dearth and the Social Order in Early Modern England." *Past and Present* 71 (1976): 22–42.

Weissman, Ronald. *Ritual Brotherhood in Renaissance Florence.* New York, 1980.

Wiesner, Merry E. *Working Women in Renaissance Germany.* New Brunswick, 1986.

Wilentz, Sean. *Chants Democratic.* New York, 1983.

Williams, Dale E. "Were 'Hunger' Rioters Really Hungry? Some Demographic Evidence." *Past and Present* 71 (1976): 70–75.

Wirth, Jean. "Against the Acculturation Thesis." In *Religion and Society in Early Modern Europe.* Ed. Kaspar von Greyerz. London, 1984.

Wolfe, Martin. *The Fiscal System of Renaissance France.* New Haven, 1972.

Wolff, Philippe, and Frédéric Mauro. *Histoire générale du travail.* 4 vols. Paris, 1960.

Wood, Merry Wiesner. "Paltry Peddlers or Essential Merchants? Women in the Distributive Trades in Early Modern Nuremberg." *Sixteenth Century Journal* 12.2 (1981): 3–14.

Wrightson, Keith. *English Society, 1580–1680.* New Brunswick, 1982.

Wrightson, Keith, and David Levine. *Poverty and Piety in an English Village.* New York, 1979.

Wyatt-Brown, Bertram. *Southern Honor.* New York, 1982.

Yardeni, Myriam. *La conscience nationale en France pendant les guerres de religion, 1559–1598.* Louvain, 1971.

Yeo, Eileen, and Stephen Yeo, eds. *Popular Culture and Class Conflict, 1590–1914: Explorations in the History of Labor and Leisure.* Brighton, 1981.

Zimmermann, Jean-Robert. *Les compagnons de métiers à Strasbourg, du début du 14e siècle à la veille de la réforme.* Strasbourg, 1971.

Zmyslony, M. *Die Bruderschaften in Lubeck bis zur Reformation.* Kiel, 1977.

# Index

*Library of Congress Cataloging-in-Publication Data*

Farr, James Richard, 1950–
    Hands of honor.

    Bibliography: p.
    Includes index.
        1. Artisans—France—Dijon—History—16th century.
    2. Artisans—France—Dijon—History—17th century.
    3. Dijon (France)—Social conditions.   I. Title.
    HD2346.F82D554   1988      331.7'94      88-47724
    ISBN 0-8014-2172-1 (alk. paper)